CRAFT TODAY

CRAFT

TODAY
POETRY OF THE PHYSICAL

Paul J. Smith
Edward Lucie-Smith

AMERICAN CRAFT MUSEUM

WEIDENFELD & NICOLSON

EXHIBITION SCHEDULE

American Craft Museum, New York, NY
October 26, 1986–March 22, 1987

The Denver Art Museum, Denver, CO
May 16–July 5,1987

Laguna Art Museum, Laguna Beach, CA
August 7–October 4, 1987

Milwaukee Art Museum, Milwaukee, WI
February 12–April 10, 1988

J.B. Speed Art Museum, Louisville, KY
May 16–July 10, 1988

Virginia Museum of Fine Arts, Richmond, VA
August 9–October 2, 1988

Library of Congress Cataloging-in-Publication Data

Smith, Paul J.
  American craft today.
  Bibliography: p. 316
  1. Decorative arts–United States–History–20th
century. 2. Handicraft–United States–History–20th
century. I. Lucie-Smith, Edward. II. American
Craft Museum (New York, N.Y.) III. Title.
NK808.S634 1986   745'.0973   86-11063
ISBN 1-55584-014-0
ISBN 1-55584-023-X (pbk.)

Published by Weidenfeld & Nicolson, New York,
A Division of Wheatland Corporation,
10 East 53rd Street, New York, NY 10022

Manufactured in Japan by Dai Nippon Printing Co.
Designed by Dana Levy, Perpetua Press
First Edition 1986
10 9 8 7 6 5 4 3 2 1

34
86

CONTENTS

This publication
was paid for by
The J.M. Kaplan Fund

Exhibition sponsored by
Philip Morris Companies Inc.

Additional funding from the
National Endowment for the Arts
and the
New York State Council on the Arts

ACKNOWLEDGMENTS

An exhibition of this scope requires the involvement and dedication of numerous individuals. For their invaluable input and support throughout the project, I wish to thank the members of the advisory committee: Thomas S. Buechner, President, Corning Museum of Glass; Barbara Haskell, Curator, Whitney Museum of American Art; David R. McFadden, Curator of Decorative Arts, Cooper-Hewitt Museum; and Edward Lucie-Smith, author and critic. An additional note of thanks is due to Edward Lucie-Smith for contributing the major catalogue essay, thus giving a perspective to the craft movement in America.

The members of the American Craft Council and American Craft Museum staff have been unsparing in their efforts throughout this undertaking and deserve special mention. Lois Moran, Editor of *American Craft*; Josanne LaValley, Director of Development; and Joanne Polster all gave generously of their time and expertise. I wish to thank Kathleen Nugent Mangan, former ACM Curator, who continued as a consultant for this exhibition. For their dedication and extensive effort in researching and collecting the works for the exhibition, I am grateful to Frances Kelly, Coordinator of Circulating Exhibitions; Anthea Zonars, Museum Intern; Doris Stowens, Registrar; and Warren Wesley, Superintendent of Shipping. I also wish to thank the past and current trustees of the ACC, who were important resources for many aspects of this project.

The production of the exhibition catalogue itself presented several challenges. For the unfailing professionalism with which they met these challenges, I am thankful to Dana Levy, catalogue designer; George Erml, photographer; and Tish O'Connor and Mitch Tuchman, editors. Thanks are also due to Mitch Bader and Ann Adelman for editing portions of the text. I am grateful to Terri Lonier for conducting the preliminary study for the exhibition and compiling the artists' biographies; to Pat Malarcher for editorial assistance; to Derek Ostergaard for contributions to the text; and to Sybille Millard, picture researcher for the historical images. I wish to express appreciation to Sharon Emanuelli, who compiled the chronology. This could not have been accomplished without the extensive support of the ACC Fellows, archivists, librarians, public information officers, professors and staff of schools, universities, museums, art centers, and organizations around the country who provided vital assistance in collecting and confirming data.

Many other people throughout the United States provided assistance by facilitating the viewing of work in their respective regions. I am grateful to Jamie Bennett and Jonathan Bonner for assistance in Boston and Providence; to Tommy Simpson in Connecticut; Steve Madsen in Albuquerque; Ed Carpenter in Portland; LaMar Harrington, and Larry Metcalf in Seattle; William Alexander, Louise Allrich, and Marvin Lipofsky in San Francisco; and Arnold Ashkenazy in Los Angeles.

Numerous galleries and organizations shared their resources enthusiastically and loaned works to the exhibition. I am especially thankful for their efforts.
Private collectors also provided important support and loaned works from their collections. In some cases, although artists duplicated works already existing in private collections for the exhibition, the collectors generously allowed their pieces to be photographed for the catalogue. I wish to thank Jan Clee, Doyle Hartman, and Maurice and Charmaine Kaplan for making these special arrangements and facilitating the photography of works by Jon Brooks, Tom Joyce, and Greg Litsios. An exhibition of this scope is made possible only with the cooperation of the artists. The willingness of these 286 artists to provide information and lend works of art has been an invaluable contribution, for which I extend gratitude and thanks.

This exhibition would not have been possible without the generous support of Philip Morris Companies Inc., who sponsored both the New York showing and the national tour. Additional support was received from the National Endowment for the Arts, a federal agency, and from the New York State Council on the Arts. We are also grateful to The J.M. Kaplan Fund for a generous grant to produce the publication documenting this exhibition.

It is impossible to mention everyone whose efforts have contributed to the realization of this exhibition. However, to all those who gave so liberally of their time and knowledge, I am sincerely grateful.

Paul J. Smith
Director

SPONSOR'S STATEMENT

The art critic Barbara Rose once observed that Americans prefer "the literal and the actual" over "the allusive or the metaphoric." This may be one reason why so many of us enjoy the art of craft, and why we tend to be impatient with the distinction between applied and "high" art.

The craft movement is in the midst of a renaissance in the United States. According to a recent Louis Harris survey on the arts sponsored by our company, more Americans participate in craft-making than in any other art form. In our automated world, the handmade object offers a rare sense of timelessness and intimacy.

Philip Morris's sponsorship of this exhibition is an expression of our abiding commitment to the arts. It gives large numbers of people an opportunity to explore fields new to them, just as they did with our earlier sponsorship of exhibitions on Op and Pop Art, the art and culture of American Indians, blacks and the frontier West, to name only a few.

On the occasion of its thirtieth anniversary, we salute the American Craft Museum for inaugurating its new building with the most comprehensive exhibition of American craft since 1969.

In bringing together the works of some of our most sophisticated craft artists, the American Craft Museum has created a new standard of quality and professionalism.

Hamish Maxwell
Chairman and Chief Executive Officer,
Philip Morris Companies Inc.

Dedicated to

Aileen Osborn Webb (1892–1979),
founder and patron of the American Craft Council,

and

David R. Campbell (1910–1963),
president of the American Craft Council,

pioneers in fostering the craft movement in this century.

CRAFT TODAY

POETRY OF THE PHYSICAL

Paul J. Smith

CRAFT TODAY: Poetry of the Physical is a celebration of the handmade in the 1980s. In the exhibition works by 286 artists illustrate the skill, imagination, and vitality characteristic of contemporary craft. The collection represents many of America's outstanding artists specializing in clay, fiber, glass, wood, and metal. These professionals range in experience from people who have been working for more than fifty years to emerging younger artists. Many are internationally known, and all are residents of the United States. Together these artists and their works comprise an overview of the dynamic creativity of craft today.

In its broadest sense *craft* refers to the creation of original objects through an artist's disciplined manipulation of material. Historically craft was identified with producing objects that were necessary for life. Today the word *craft* in America has new connotations. Modern industrialized society eliminates the need to make by hand essentials for living. As a result craft has transcended its traditional role and meaning. The term *craft* now must be defined in the context of a society that focuses on greater efficiency by technological achievement. In one sense this concentration simplifies complicated times. But in giving us more automation and leisure, it challenges our lifestyles. As our world becomes more dependent on technology, we are required to do specialized tasks that often disassociate us from a sense of total accomplishment. Craft, which by its very nature represents a unity of hand and spirit, counteracts this alienation, reaffirming the human element in daily life. Amid mass production the craft experience can impart greater meaning to individual expression.

The craft movement in America, which has rapidly expanded since the end of World War II, is part of the specialization that now characterizes society from medicine to engineering to the arts. Certainly the arts have never included such a diversity of disciplines as in the 1980s, with greater recognition given to architects, graphic artists, photographers, fashion and furniture designers, as well as to craftsmen. Curiously, although more distinct activities are developing, specific limitations on individual creative pursuit are lessening. When specialization increases, the categories blur; today's artist has access to a broader range of creative possibilities than ever before.

Contemporary craftsmen come from a variety of educational backgrounds. Most in this exhibition attended art programs at a university or private art school. Excellent opportunities outside the formal university structure—including evening schools, short-term courses, and specialized summer programs—are also common, giving many young artists their aesthetic and technical grounding. Others receive their training by the time-honored tradition of serving as apprentices at the side of a master. Still others learn craft through avocational activities, transforming sideline interests into full-time commitments. A vast amount of technical information is available from conferences, films, books, and periodicals.

The motivation to pursue a career in craft stems from many sources, one of which frequently is the wish for a more self-directed occupation. It is indicative of the 1980s, however, that craftsmen not only value their independence, the love of work and material, and the pride of making something well that they can share; they also want their work to provide a livelihood. An increasing number of professionals are supporting themselves without recourse to teaching or other supplemental employment. The expanding marketplace has superseded university patronage, which had provided the dominant support system in previous decades. Today, while many people function individually or with assistants, the trend for groups to work in small production studios is growing. Their output ranges from items to be sold directly in the marketplace to commissioned pieces for specific sites. As a complement to their work craftsmen have developed marketing skills to an unprecedented degree and have thus come to a better understanding of their work as a viable small business.

The remarkable growth in the field over the last two decades has resulted in a proliferation of resources. For the professional the opportunity to show work is provided by more and more museums, galleries, and other exhibition sites. Opportunities are increasing for artists to create commissioned works for clients and to collaborate with architects. Patronage and support have increased among both private and corporate collectors. This desire to collect crafts, even on a modest scale, has affected average American consumers, who in recent years have become more aware of quality and good design.

The American Craft Museum organized *Craft Today: Poetry of the Physical* to provide a curatorial perspective on craft in the 1980s as the museum inaugurates its new home and celebrates its thirtieth anniversary. The exhibition is an outgrowth of research and reporting on trends over the past three decades. Concentrated research for the project for the last two years has included a review of more than five thousand slides and extensive staff travel to private studios around the nation. A panel of professionals served as advisors with assistance from other individuals throughout the country. This assembly of more than three hundred works shows the astounding breadth of object-making—from unique personal statements to pieces made for a special function.

Looking at this rich landscape of works, one can see the plurality of purpose that has been and continues to be a characteristic of the object-making movement. The 1980s represent a period of refinement rather than of experimentation for its own sake. While tied to its rich historical roots of function, craft today is distinguished by the sophisticated level of its aesthetic. This aesthetic, which evolves from the process of making and the artist's spiritual involvement with the material, enables the contemporary craftsman to transcend traditional forms and techniques, creating works of genuinely new significance.

This collection of works reflects the rich variety of visual creativity found in every form of art in the United States today. We do not have a national style: diversity is the American image. The philosophy of freedom throughout our educational system (for the arts as well as other fields) is one of the major causes of this diversity. Unlike many foreign training institutions where technical tradition is taught formally before students are permitted to experiment, American schools encourage students to develop creativity and skills simultaneously. Coupled with this open attitude toward experimentation is a spirit of cooperation among craftsmen and a willingness to share freely information and techniques.

The handcrafted forms now being developed relate to technical evolution and also to a wide range of international cultural influences, both historical and contemporary. Many artists are creating new interpretations of ancient techniques and styles, giving fresh expression to long standing craft traditions. The insatiable desire to develop new skills through constant experimentation has brought an enormous new technical vocabulary to each medium. With technique resolved, the central concern is to make an object as beautifully and as well as possible but also to develop its expressive possibilities. Any vocabulary can be drawn upon for that result. Still it should be noted that in craft one seldom finds work that is crude or unpleasant. Beauty is not always associated with contemporary art, yet it continues to be honored in the crafts.

The new interest in design has also influenced craft. Design and decorative elements from both modern and historical eras are inspiring many artists, as can be seen in the stylized graphic forms and surfaces of their works. The forms and clean lines of some current pieces reflect a growing interest in modern design; in others there is a strong connection with historical styles in decorative arts, such as Art Nouveau, Art Deco, and Modernism. The recent enthusiasm for collecting historical decorative arts has lent credibility to contemporary object-making, strengthening appreciation of current work.

These observations on craft today prompted the decision to group together works on the basis of "intent." Four areas emerged as the structure for the exhibition: the object as statement; the object made for use; the object as vessel; and the object for personal adornment. Inevitably, when some three hundred works are sorted into categories, gray areas result. The four categories of *Craft Today: Poetry of the Physical* are not meant to separate the works in a definitive way and are not hierarchical distinctions. They were conceived primarily to clarify a confusing variety of activities and to aid the viewer in understanding the vast range of contemporary craft. Within the four categories the exhibition has been organized into groups of work that emphasize the stylistic characteristics of individual pieces. Viewers will discover that similar conceptual themes have been given startlingly individualized interpretations.

The object as statement, which includes both two-dimensional and sculptural pieces, presents works created primarily for their aesthetic value. This section focuses on works that make a unique personal statement, an approach that continues to be an important direction in object-making. The broad iconography of the work is characteristic of the many styles of art today, ranging from some that are purely decorative to others that provide social commentary.

The object made for use concentrates on the growing interest in making unique items designed for specific functions. From pieces intended to be integrated into architecture to items for the tabletop, these works point to the resurgence of interest in the useful object. Such activity has led a growing number of craftsmen to set up limited production studios or to design prototypes for manufacture. Renewed enthusiasm for the functional has been particularly evident in the field of handmade furniture. Previously most furniture makers limited themselves to natural woods and classical designs. Many furniture makers today are pushing the boundaries of material, technique, and concept. They are experimenting with innovative laminates, incorporating color and graphics, working with contrasting surfaces, and developing new concepts to help them achieve expressive as well as functional forms.

The object as vessel features a form that retains a dominant influence on object-making and is one of the richest areas of craft expression. Encompassing all media, this section surveys those qualities that are typical of the vessel today. Some of these works relate to classical shapes of the past while in others the exaggeration of elements suggests a search for totally new forms. The objects range from a functional ceramic bowl to a metal vase to a woven container. In each the physical properties of the material lend stylistic impact.

The object for personal adornment includes clothing as well as jewelry. American jewelry makers have continued to search for new applications of traditional materials while participating in the international trend toward exploring the jewel-like qualities inherent in vernacular materials. In clothing a sophisticated understanding of construction has evolved, allowing the uniqueness of form that is possible when a garment's design, structure, and fabric are developed together from the outset. Wearability is a dominant concern in making handmade garments and jewelry, since the completion of a piece is a function of how the wearer presents it. At the same time garments and jewelry are also designed to serve as objects on display when they are not being worn.

These four areas of *Craft Today: Poetry of the Physical* honor the vitality found in current American craft. The exhibition should be viewed, however, as a selection, not representing all the talented artists who are presently at work. Ultimately a curatorial viewpoint must be justified by its ability to reveal: The object is the message. The viewer's challenge is to discover the poetry of the physical.

CRAFT TODAY
HISTORICAL ROOTS AND CONTEMPORARY PERSPECTIVES

Edward Lucie-Smith

This catalogue celebrates the first comprehensive survey of current American craft to be held since *Objects USA* in 1969. In its richness, depth, and complexity the exhibition is unrivaled by any previous effort. My essay, outlining the development of American craft and design, suggests a context for the objects and the tradition in which the contemporary craftsman works. The chronicler of the history of American craft faces a substantial challenge and many practical problems, even if he confines himself to the events of the past one hundred years. The subject has been much less thoroughly researched than the history of American art during the same period. Much craft history, especially the most recent, is oral rather than written and has been affected by some of the distortions to which oral history is notoriously subject. What craftsmen are often does not coincide with what they feel themselves to be, nor do the directly traceable roots of their activity always coincide with the myths that they have created for themselves.

The earliest period of American craft covered in this essay—from the late 1870s until America's entry into World War I in 1917—is now reasonably well documented in print, thanks to recent survey exhibitions and the enthusiastic labors of devoted scholars in this comparatively new field. The main error in these efforts has been a failure to distinguish between what is strictly craft, a form of making in which the artisan is involved both in the whole process of design and in the use of hand skills, and the decorative arts, in which the craftsman may produce unique objects but works under the strict control of an outside designer, even if no industrial processes are involved.

Chronicling the history of American craft from 1918 onward is more difficult. Craft continued to flourish, perhaps more than has been recognized, during

American Windsor side chair, c. 1820–1840.

the interwar period, but historians have usually focused their attention on the rise of industrial design. Important subjects, such as the involvement of the Works Progress Administration (WPA) crafts, remain largely unchronicled.

Since World War II, recording craft activity has often and understandably been sacrificed to making craft. The years since 1945 have been ones of intense growth. Craftsmen have usually been more interested in things that pointed toward the future, in the "how" of craft, and in new techniques and ways of approaching materials, than they have been in recording the events of the immediate past. Historical material does exist in print, but it is found more often in the back issues of magazines, especially *Craft Horizons*, than in readily accessible books. Furthermore the recent history of craft as it is reflected in print is subject to some unexpected distortions. For example, although ceramics is not the largest field of activity—that honor almost certainly belongs to fiber—in the recent history of American craft ceramics is more fully recorded than work in any other medium. My comments here and the chronology compiled by others, which forms another section of this catalogue, are first attempts to address a massive subject, which should in due course attract wider efforts from researchers. If a major narrative history of the past century of American craft appears within the next few years, it will perhaps derive some impetus from the present enterprise.

The evolution of American craft and design

The contemporary American sensibility shows a more obvious and direct influence from folk roots than do its European counterparts. The reasons for this are complex. The first settlements, English and Dutch, did undoubtedly transfer most elements of their countries' existing class systems to the other side of the Atlantic. This was modified by the conditions the settlers found, by the kinds of people they were, and by their increasing sense of a separate, non-European identity. Although some elements in pre-Revolution society remained aristocratic (or with stricter accuracy, oligarchic), the idea of individual liberty was intensely important. Many had, after all, left Europe to escape

New England Shaker side chair, c. 1880.

both civil and religious persecution. This instinct came into conflict with a broader political and economic system that assumed that the colonies, as they then were, would be content to exchange the raw materials of the New World for European manufactured products. Instead the settlers evolved their own forms, often the work of sturdy pragmatists who relied on basic skills rather than on specialized training. They looked at things afresh and changed them as a result. There was, for example, a continuous reevaluation of the hand tools familiar in Europe, as these were tested against American conditions. Benjamin Franklin seems to have been one of the first to realize the significance of this process; he defined man as "a tool-making animal." In 1848 a German publication, *Handbook for Settlers in the United States,* informed prospective emigrants that the American Kentucky ax was different from and distinctly superior to the hand axes familiar to Europeans: "Its curved cutting edge, its heavier head, counter-balanced by the handle, gives the axe greater power in its swing, facilitates its penetration, reduces the expenditure of human energy, speeds up the work." By this time the trickle of newcomers from Europe had become a flood. The majority of these immigrants were not from the top of the social heap, and the traditions they brought with them were largely folk traditions.

The American atmosphere also added a stringency of its own. The reshaping of familiar forms, purely practical in the case of the Kentucky ax, became a matter of declared aesthetic preference in that of the American Windsor chair. This is usually both more elegantly and more boldly drawn than its typical British counterpart, often taller in proportion with thinner spokes set farther apart. With Shaker furniture, which is even simpler and more stringent in design than the American Windsor, an unconscious aesthetic preference has been supplemented by something that expresses a complete way of life. The Shaker sect, which from about 1815 produced furniture of instantly recognizable type, consisted of people who found tolerance in America for religious beliefs that made them unwelcome elsewhere. In due course their designs found a responsive public, which did not necessarily share the convictions held by the designers, and sale of furniture to outsiders provided the Shakers with economic support that made their way of life more viable. It is a curious irony that most surviving Shaker furniture, though it bespeaks a unique, introverted way of life, was made from the mid-nineteenth century onward for non-Shaker use, and the majority probably postdates the runaway success of the Shaker exhibit at the *Philadelphia Centennial Exposition* of 1876.

The harshness of pioneer conditions led logically to a certain simplicity of taste bred from a respect for the serviceable. It also led to an apparent and equally logical opposing impulse: a hunger for domestic adornment. What was decorative was usually homemade and characteristically involved a thrifty recycling of materials. Making adornments for the home was generally regarded as the work of women. The supreme expression of the American folk spirit is the patchwork quilt, and making these was always women's work, although men might help by cutting the wooden patterns for the basic shapes. It is more important to note that these quilts were genuine vehicles for deeply felt emotion that could be expressed in no other way. As one quiltmaker described her feelings: "It took me more than twenty years, nearly twenty-five, I reckon, in the evening after supper when the children were put to bed. My whole life is in that quilt. It scares me sometimes when I look at it. All my joys and all my sorrows are stitched into those little pieces." Quilting, however, was often a collective activity, and these collectively made quilts are direct expressions, not of the individual psyche, but of the whole community that produced them. Many were made at family and neighborhood gatherings and were intended to commemorate special occasions. They are a record of sharing (which appears equally strongly, though in a different form, in the current American craft scene) and a testament to feelings of community.

The Colonial Revival in America began simultaneously with a revival of interest in the crafts, but the two are not the same thing (though there are a few evident links). The same *Philadelphia Centennial Exposition* that promoted the Shaker workshops also directed attention to colonial artifacts, which were admired for their historical associations. Manufacturers started to produce both copies and adaptations of colonial furniture. But late nineteenth-century ideas of colonial style covered a wide range from the primitive oak of the Pilgrim fathers to the sophisticated creations of the early nineteenth-century cabinetmaker Duncan Phyfe. In the first two decades of the twentieth century, as exemplified by the career of the collector turned manufacturer Wallace Nutting, taste became more strictly antiquarian. Nutting began to amass a large collection of Americana after leaving the ministry in 1905. During the next five years he restored a number of historic houses, and in 1917 he began to manufacture reproductions of items in his own collection for sale to the general public. He had a number of rivals in the American furniture trade. Enthusiasm for colonial furniture increased during the twenties, and copies of increasingly fine quality were made. These are now, thanks to age and use, even more difficult to distinguish from originals. The close copies did not, however, usually have a craft accent, because the models chosen were predominantly sophisticated ones. In 1930 the Danersk Furniture Company announced that it had paid $8,500 for an eighteenth-century Chippendale-style chair by the Philadelphia craftsman Donald Gillingham and boasted that it was producing an exact replica.

Some copies of colonial artifacts were made by people who were identifiably part of the Arts and Crafts movement. Members of the Deerfield Society of Blue and White Needlework, for example, adapted patterns from objects that

Star of Bethlehem quilt, c. 1840–1850.

they saw in the Memorial Hill Museum in Deerfield, Massachusetts. Their products were shown in the *Buffalo Pan-American Exposition* of 1901 and led to a revival not merely of colonial styles but of colonial skills in other craft fields as well. Carpenters and other woodworkers began to discover the techniques used by their ancestors, just as the needleworkers had done.

Scholarly investigation of the surviving traditions of American folk craft had to wait until much later, the thirties. In 1937 Allen H. Eaton's pioneering book, *Handicrafts of the Southern Highlands*, described the survival of familiar crafts, such as weaving, chair and basket making, and leatherwork. Eaton also wrote about more esoteric activities, such as feather fan making and the construction of mountain dulcimers. His book and the activity of later students and collectors called attention to the role played by craft in the lives of the American pioneers and to the stubborn survival of these traditions, especially in rural and isolated communities, such as those in the Appalachian mountains. His study was particularly attuned to the mood of its time; the economic plight of the Depression era focused attention on issues of survival, self-support, and independence, and the political isolationism of the period prompted a search for native roots. This impulse is also reflected in the literature of the epoch and in the work of American landscape painters, especially that of Thomas Hart Benton. Unintentionally and unconsciously Eaton's text also called attention to something else: the class division and stemming from it, a difference of attitude and purpose between the traditional rural craftsmen he described and the educated craftsmen who could now trace a fifty-year lineage to the Arts and Crafts Revival of the last two decades of the nineteenth century.

Native Americans

It seems natural to look for sources of contemporary craft among the original inhabitants of the American continent, but here the issues are more complex. Sympathetic interest in the arts of the American Indian manifested itself

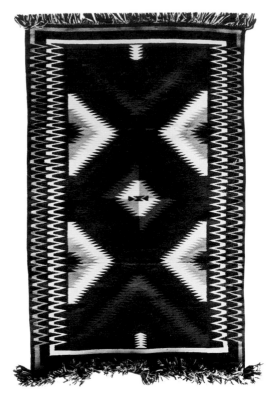

Navajo blanket, c. 1880–1890.

early. It certainly predates the general rise in popularity of primitive and tribal art that took place only after 1900. Early admirers of Indian craft included those who came to the arid Southwest because its dry climate was beneficial to sufferers from tuberculosis and other pulmonary diseases. By the 1890s such admiration caused various members of the Denver Art Association to propose that a museum planned for the city include a representation of Southwestern native art.

Those who wished to save the Indian way of life from extinction began at the same time to recognize that Indian arts and crafts could become an economic lifeline for their communities. The Indian Industries League was founded in 1889 with this intent. By 1900 the government-supported Indian program at the Normal and Agricultural Institute at Hampton, Virginia offered training in the Indian arts of beadwork, basketry, and pottery. Though the dangers of commercializing Indian products were recognized very early, inevitably the reviving Indian crafts responded to the patronage that was now predominantly non-Indian. At the urging of traders, craftsmen produced nontraditional items for new markets, like the rugs using sacred sand painting designs made by the Navajo from 1900 onward. Equally nontraditional was much of the jewelry made in Southwestern workshops; in the thirties, for instance, the Hopi began to transfer pottery and textile patterns to silverwork, where they had never previously been used. A less visible change affected pottery making, where designs did not change so drastically, but social relationships were irrevocably altered. Outside patrons encouraged leading potters to sign their products, and this change, which began in the twenties, marked an acceptance by these craftsmen of their role as individual creators, a concept alien to tribal society. Indian crafts, however, have remained recognizably Indian and apart from the American mainstream. The patrons preferred them that way, while for the actual makers their products became a proud assertion of a separate identity.

Artifacts made by non-Indians deliberately imitating Indian styles also became popular for a time, but the differences between the two categories are significant. A famous Tiffany vase of about 1900, for example, is made of copper inlaid with silver in a pattern that imitates those on Indian baskets. The handles are thickly studded with the rough turquoise associated with Indian jewelry. This luxurious fantasy bears the same relationship to Native American culture as the chinoiserie figures produced in various European porcelain factories do to Qing dynasty culture in China. The object owes much of its effect to a deliberately paradoxical aesthetic: it borrows Indian motifs but clearly belongs to a different culture.

From 1900 onward American designers exploited other pre-Columbian styles for decorative effect. This tendency showed itself more clearly in architecture and the popular decorative arts than it did in craft. What has been called the Mayan Revival style was first used in some details of the Pan American Union Building, built in 1910 in Washington, D.C. This aesthetic was developed further in a series of masterpieces by Frank Lloyd Wright, including the now-demolished Midway Gardens (1913–14) in Chicago and the celebrated Hollyhock House (1917–20) in Los Angeles. A more flamboyant version of the style can be seen in some of the great movie theaters built in the boom years of the twenties. Later still Mayan Revival was blended with standard Art Deco elements and lingered in attenuated form during the Depression. In the crafts of the tens and twenties Mayan motifs had a limited impact on certain items subordinate to the architect's vision, chief among them ironwork and tiles.

A direct influence from pre-Columbian art upon the American craft scene only came much later, and then it was mainly confined to fiber art. After World War II, American weavers discovered the complexity and inventiveness of Inca textiles and were profoundly affected by what they learned. The Inca influence in the fiber arts was part of the responsiveness to primitive and exotic cultures that became general at that time.

The craft revival in America

The nineteenth-century craft revival in America, whatever it absorbed from the American background, was originally inspired by the concepts of the English Arts and Crafts movement. Its philosophy was most concisely stated by John Ruskin in the chapter "On the Nature of Gothic" in the second volume of *The Stones of Venice*, published in 1853 and then issued as a separate pamphlet the following year. Ruskin enunciated three rules for craft:

1. Never encourage the manufacture of any article not absolutely necessary, in the production of which 'invention' has no share.
2. Never demand an exact finish for its own sake but only for some practical or noble end.
3. Never encourage imitation or copying of any kind, except for the sake of preserving records of great works.

It was left to Ruskin's disciple William Morris to put these rules to practical effect. Described by his first biographer John W. Mackail as "an aristocrat and a High Churchman," Morris nevertheless saw no dishonor in manual labor and heeded Ruskin's dictum: "It would be well if all of us were good handicraftsmen of some kind, and the dishonour of manual labour done away with altogether.... In each of several professions, no master should be too proud to do the hardest work."

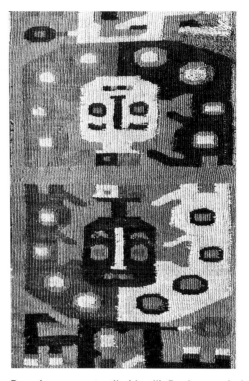

Peruvian woven textile (detail), Pre-Inca period.

The American Arts and Crafts movement did not, however, depend on British influences alone. It responded to European Art Nouveau, the impact of which is clear in many products from the Tiffany Studios and can also be seen in the furniture of Christian Rohlfs and the ceramics of Artus van Briggle. It absorbed ideas from the Werkbund in Germany and the Vienna Secession. A screen made in 1905 at the Craftsman workshops in Syracuse, New York, has German Jugendstil motifs decorating its linen panels. Influence from the designers of the Wiener Werkstätte, notably Josef Hoffmann, is evident in the furniture manufactured by the Charles P. Limbert Company of Grand Rapids, Michigan from 1902 onward. A prominent member of the Roycroft Community, Dard Hunter, went to Vienna in 1908, and came into direct contact with what was being done there. He left Roycroft and returned to Austria in 1910 but seems to have remained in communication with his former associates.

The American Arts and Crafts movement spanned a wider gamut sociologically as well as stylistically than its English counterpart. Participants included individuals working alone, sometimes with little thought or even need for financial profit; idealistic communities using craft not only as a means of financial support but as a channel for the expression of unconventional social beliefs; and purely commercial manufacturers who seized on the popular Arts and Crafts look for profit. There remains a fundamental confusion in recent writing as to whether the Arts and Crafts movement is simply a stylistic category in the development of American decorative arts or whether any general conclusions about the evolution of American society can be drawn from it.

Nineteenth-century textile (detail),
designed by William Morris.

The Arts and Crafts movement in England dates from the beginning of the 1860s, when the newly married Morris moved into the Red House, built for him by his friend, the architect Philip Webb, and began decorating it according to his own taste. In 1862 the firm of Morris, Marshall, Faulkner & Company achieved its first major public recognition at the *International Exhibition* held at South Kensington. The beginning of the movement in America is tardy by comparison, nor did it achieve celebrity so rapidly. No single date clearly marks its inception, but the foundation of the Women's Pottery Club in Cincinnati in 1879 is significant. The club grew out of a women's china painting class—decorating ready-made blanks had long been a popular hobby for American women—and its moving spirit was a socially prominent young woman, Marie Louise McLaughlin, daughter of the city's leading architect. She and her colleagues were inspired by a visit to the *Philadelphia Centennial Exposition,* where they saw and admired a group of French barbotine ware decorated with colored slips under the glaze. The women attempted this new and more ambitious technique, but more important, as members of the middle and upper-middle class, they became obsessed with the idea of working with their own hands at what had been considered a laborious and dirty occupation. The Women's Pottery Club was within a year faced with a local rival, the Rookwood Pottery, founded by Maria Longworth Nichols. Rookwood became one of the standard-bearers of the new craft movement.

The evolution of Rookwood reflects the mixed and uncertain aims of the whole American Arts and Crafts movement. The first period of Rookwood's production, from 1880 to 1884, is dominated by the work of the wealthy amateurs whose enthusiasm had led to its foundation. A great variety of techniques were employed, not all of them suited to the nature of the material. The establishment then began to concentrate on a narrower range of techniques, more skillfully used. The underglaze slip was evenly applied by means of an atomizer, and a standard range of background colors was devel-

Earthenware pitcher, 1889–1890, Rookwood Pottery Company.

oped, duly designated Standard Rookwood. By 1889 Rookwood had progressed sufficiently to be awarded a gold medal at the *Paris Exposition,* and the pottery had become financially profitable. In 1890 its founder retired, and the Rookwood Pottery Company was incorporated much like any other business. While Rookwood's wares remained of high quality, its early idealism more or less vanished.

The main stylistic influence at Rookwood was French, especially the new *Japonisme,* which had been made popular by the Impressionists and their followers. There was also a more direct Japanese influence: Between 1887 and 1915 Kataro Shirayamadani, a Japanese pottery decorator who specialized in painting misty landscapes, worked at Rookwood. Such a direct influence, however, was exceptional in this period. Another obvious example of Japanese taste comes from California, but it is obvious only from the objects themselves, since supporting documentation seems to be lacking. The luxurious furniture designed by the architects Charles and Henry Greene for a group of houses built soon after 1900 shows the influence of both Chinese and Japanese furniture. It can be seen in the forms themselves, in a few details of ornamentation, and also in the actual construction. The models must have been provided by examples imported by San Francisco dealers in oriental art.

The *Japonisme* practiced at Rookwood blended into the general enthusiasm for Art Nouveau, which manifested itself most conspicuously in the items produced by the Tiffany Studios in New York. Louis Comfort Tiffany himself was more active in the decorative arts before 1902 (after which he devoted himself largely to jewelry), but he continued to direct the firm he had founded until the late twenties. During the earlier period Tiffany was famous for superb stained glass, iridescent glassware, and intricate metalwork, as well as for ceramics. His products were appreciated in France as well as in America. One of his chief admirers was Samuel Bing, the German entrepreneur whose shop, L'Art Nouveau, which opened in Paris in 1895, gave its name to

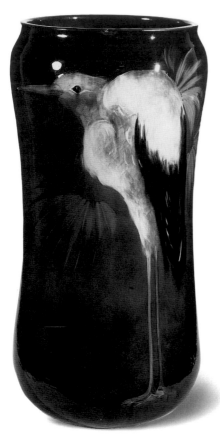

Earthenware umbrella stand, c. 1890,
J.B. Owens Pottery Company.

the whole movement. Bing recognized that American Art Nouveau differed from its French counterpart, most of all in its eclecticism. He was probably thinking specifically of Tiffany when he wrote:

> In more or less conscious fashion, America took something from every civilization, but this was done very judiciously, by taking earlier creations apart piece by piece, changing them, then adding something of her own by returning to the study of nature, and using the contributions of ultramodern forms of science. As these strange combinations assumed a profound unity of character, they became the point of departure for a new aesthetic, one attuned to local conditions, determined in time, and attuned to the spirit of the people.

As Bing implies, late nineteenth-century America was both a stylistic and an ethnic melting pot, and the Arts and Crafts designers took ideas from every source open to them. Harvey Ellis, a gifted architect briefly employed by Gustav Stickley from 1903 to 1904, transformed Stickley's rather heavy line of furniture by introducing ideas borrowed from the Scottish architect Charles Rennie Mackintosh, whose austere taste was in accordance with Stickley's own principles. The intricate web of influences prevalent at the time ensured that Mackintosh's ideas were also absorbed second hand by American designers, thanks to the Scotsman's impact on the Wiener Werkstätte.

These disparate influences were bound together by an impulse to strip things down to first principles, both in terms of manufacture and in terms of use. This was perhaps a protest against the complexity that seemed to be overtaking American life. It accounts for the appearance of much of the furniture produced in Stickley's workshops, by the Limbert Company, and by the Roycroft Community in East Aurora, New York. Ironically this urge toward simplification made Arts and Crafts furniture easier to produce by industrial or semi-industrial methods. These heavy pieces, without inlay, veneer, or any sort of carving, did not call for refined skills in woodworking. In America the Arts and Crafts movement was often negative rather than positive, a rejection of a society that seemed dominated by the needs of industry rather than by a genuine revival of hand skills.

Even among the individual craftsmen who were connected with the movement (and it is they who most closely resemble their counterparts of the present day), levels of skill varied widely. Frances M. Glessner, a leader of Chicago society, turned the conservatory of her house into a silversmith's shop, but to judge from exhibited examples, her products were fairly unambitious. Silversmithing was only one part of a busy life, which included her Monday morning reading classes and beekeeping at her summer home in New Hampshire. Craft was a more central and vital means of expression for George Ohr, the self-styled "mad genius" who ran the Biloxi Art Pottery from the early 1890s until he closed it in 1909 to become a Cadillac dealer. Ohr thought that his work should be judged by the same standards as the fine arts, and it is not altogether surprising that he has become a cult figure in certain sections of the present-day American art community; one of his pots is depicted in a recent canvas by Jasper Johns. His work demonstrates incredible technical skill: the bizarre, asymmetrical vessel-forms with their incredibly thin walls are squeezed and folded to create new and surprising images. Ohr became celebrated for his exhibitions of throwing skills and used to demonstrate at industrial fairs under large banners that read: "I am the greatest potter in the world. Let any man prove otherwise."

Before World War I another segment of the American craft world was community-based. It is symptomatic that the best known of these, the Roycroft Community, with the closest links to the English Arts and Craft

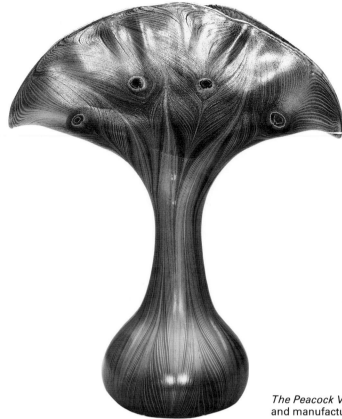

The Peacock Vase (Favrile glass vase), c. 1896, designed and manufactured by Tiffany and Company.

movement, was created by a man who was a brilliant publicist for craft rather than a craftsman or designer himself. Elbert Hubbard, born in 1856, began his career peddling soap door to door, then built up a mail-order soap business, which prospered thanks to clever advertising. Tiring of this, he sold his manufacturing interests and in 1893 published a novel under the pseudonym Aspasia Hobbs. It seems to have been his literary inclinations that led him to visit William Morris at the Kelmscott Press in 1894. There he became fired with Arts and Crafts ideals. He returned home to East Aurora to set up his own press. This in turn spawned a bindery, which led to the creation of a craft leather shop. By 1901 the Roycroft book catalogue mentioned a line of furniture, and this was followed by the manufacture of copperware. The Roycroft Copper Shop was organized in 1908 by Karl Kipp, a former banker.

Much of what was produced, not merely the books, was sold from catalogues, similar to the way that Hubbard had sold soap. In March 1903 he wrote to a friend, "The Roycroft began as a joke, but did not stay one; it soon resolved itself into a Commercial institution." Here he did himself less than justice, since the Roycrofters, as they came to be called, evolved a real community spirit under his leadership. This survived the tragic deaths of Hubbard and his second wife, who were drowned when the *Lusitania* was sunk in 1915, but the organization never completely recovered. Hubbard's son managed to keep it going until 1938.

Other communities, more typical of American utopianism, did not center their existence on craft but used craft skills as a way of maintaining a communal style of living. Essentially they were the beneficiaries of the vogue for craft rather than the initiators of it. The Shakers have already been mentioned. Another even more remarkable community was founded at Oneida, New York by John Humphrey Noyes. At Oneida all property was held in common, and "complex marriage" was practiced, exclusivity among sexual partners being discouraged. The Oneidans at first attempted to support themselves through farming, but from 1854 onward they concentrated on products that could be manufactured and sold. They took pride in the inven-

George Ohr, *Bowls* (clay), c. 1900.

tiveness of what they made; this technical inventiveness supported their belief that they were superior to the rest of the world. One abundant source of income was an ingenious animal trap; later the community launched into silk thread manufacture, and in 1877 they began producing silver-plated flatware.

The heyday of utopian communities like Oneida was nearly over by the time the American Arts and Crafts movement hit its stride. In 1879, the year in which the Women's Pottery Club and the Rookwood Pottery were founded in Cincinnati, Noyes was forced to flee to Canada under threat that a morals charge would be brought against him. He lived seven more years, continuing to exercise his influence over the community from exile, but the strict rules he had imposed were relaxed gradually by his followers, a pattern recurrent among American utopian communities; those that did not collapse altogether were absorbed in most cases into the American mainstream. The Oneidans gave up complex marriage and turned themselves into a joint-stock company in 1881. The Oneida brand name still survives today.

After 1900 craft gradually gained a foothold in communities of a very different type, American universities. An important pioneer in this respect was Charles Fergus Binns, who had been superintendent of the Royal Worcester Porcelain Works in England and who first came to America in connection with the *World's Columbian Exposition* held in Chicago in 1893. In 1900 he established the New York School for Clayworking and Ceramics at Alfred University (the second college-level ceramic school in the United States and more significantly, the first with a ceramic art program). Binns was immensely energetic. He wrote extensively and lectured frequently; he carried on a widespread correspondence with the faculty of other universities, while the students he trained went on to teach in educational institutions throughout America. The stylistic range at Worcester had been wide. Perhaps in reaction against this Binns promoted a particular aesthetic. The pots he liked were reinterpretations of Tang and Sung works from China and similar, highly refined work from ancient Egypt and Persia. During his directorship and for many years afterward craftsmen tended to speak summarily of the Alfred pot. He encouraged ceramists to look for roots within the clayworking tradition itself rather than to accept other stylistic influences, declaring that a pot could only be measured against another pot. He thus promoted the view, which became prevalent between the wars, that craft was a closed and separate field of activity that defined its own aesthetic.

The most significant craft enterprises of the period, like Rookwood, had a strongly commercial tinge. The most influential and in some ways the most ambitious figure in the prewar American Arts and Crafts movement was Stickley. Born in 1857 in Osceola, Wisconsin, Stickley's early career as a furniture maker took place strictly within the commercial furniture trade, and the simplicity of his earliest designs was the product of necessity. They were also, by his own account, dependent on the machine. As he recalled later: "We had no money to buy machinery. I went to a maker of broom handles who had a very good turning lathe...and with it blocked out the plainest parts of some very simple chairs made after the 'Shaker' model.... The very primitiveness of the equipment, made necessary by lack of means, was really a golden opportunity to break away from the monotony of commercial forms."

At first Stickley turned out eclectic copies and adaptations of colonial furniture, but he was already influenced by what he knew of Ruskin and in 1898 traveled to Europe, where he met leaders of the Arts and Crafts movement, as well as Samuel Bing and other Parisian promoters of Art Nouveau. In 1900 at the annual furniture show in Grand Rapids he exhibited a new line of simple, massive furniture. The trade name he chose for this was Craftsman, and the style immediately caught on. Through his magazine, *The Craftsman,* founded in 1901, he became America's greatest propagandist for the Arts and Crafts ethos. He frequently contributed articles and in one issue made at least an implicit claim that craft was the new national art of the United States:

> But like all art, it must spring in the first place from the common needs of the common people.... Merely to make things by hand implies not advance in the development of an art that shall make its own place in world history as a true record of thought and life of this age, any more than the making of them after "original designs" implies that these designs are the outgrowth of thought based upon that need which is the root of inspiration to the true craftsman, as well as upon his personal desire for self-expression.

Stickley did make attempts, at least to begin with, to live up to the prevailing idea that craft ought to involve some kind of community ideal. In his workshops at Syracuse, he introduced a semicooperative scheme, but it was unsuccessful and was dropped after only three years. An attempt to build a model farm and establish a small family community in New Jersey also failed. The kind of craft he purveyed did not really affect the way people lived; it did not change the lives of his workers nor of the purchasers who acquired his products through ordinary commercial outlets. (At one time he had franchises as far apart as Boston and Los Angeles.) He did, however, provide members of a society that was inexorably mechanizing itself with a fantasy of rural life. His success was based on an agreed fiction, and it vanished with the superficial fashion for Arts and Crafts design; in 1915 Stickley's empire collapsed in bankruptcy.

One striking aspect of the Arts and Crafts movement in the United States in the years before World War I is the involvement of women, its closest links with the folk craft of the pioneer epoch. Following the Women's Pottery Club of Cincinnati and Rookwood, many women involved themselves in craft, often choosing specialties that were not regarded as traditional to their sex. In Chicago there were women woodcarvers, some working under the aegis of the Chicago Society of Decorative Art, founded in 1877. Although much of this work was unambitious in scale, *American Cabinet Maker* reported in 1879 on the work of Mrs. Christian Olenson, who had learned cabinetmaking and carpentry from her father and had designed and constructed nearly all the furniture in her own house, "all handsomely carved and deftly put together." Later female furniture makers in Chicago included Louise C. Anderson, who made pieces in the simple, massive style favored by Stickley, and Madeleine Yale Wynne, the widowed daughter of the inventor of the Yale lock, who was well known for her bridal chests. Both were skilled metalsmiths as well.

Women's efforts in the crafts were acknowledged at the *World's Columbian Exposition,* where they were allotted a special building housing both American and foreign exhibits. Among the American exhibits were examples of pottery, bookbinding, silversmithing, leatherwork, and stained glass. In the Process Room, Elizabeth Abel of the New Century Guild of Philadelphia demonstrated how stained glass was made, cutting the glass, polishing, and leading it. The *New York Times* reacted to the stained glass, designed and made by women, installed within the building by remarking loftily that "women are dangerously near man's work." If women's involvement in the late nineteenth-century craft revival leads our thoughts back to the days of the pioneers, it also takes them forward to the craft situation today. It is probable that, among the leading craftspeople working in the United States today, women form a slight majority.

Mission rocking chair, c. 1910, Stickley Brothers Quaint Furniture Company.

Craft in America between the wars

Some elements of the prewar Arts and Crafts movement were carried forward into the postwar period. For instance, the Stickley idiom was not abandoned during the twenties but modulated into the Mission style, a new version with greater pretensions to historical accuracy. This adaptation was popular in the Southwest and in California. A revival of colonial styles was popular in the East. The influence of the Wiener Werkstätte also continued to be felt as a pervasive influence on design.

One important channel for this influence was the film and theater designer Josef Urban, who had studied at the academy in Vienna before World War I and returned to visit his mother in Austria in the summer of 1921. On this occasion he came into direct contact with the Werkstätte and helped the organization establish a salesroom of its own in New York. The venture was well-received by the American press and was originally a financial success. But turnover soon fell below expectations and the workshops did not always deliver the goods required. In addition there were difficulties and misunderstandings between the craftsmen and their backers in New York, and the venture was closed down at the beginning of 1924. A second attempt, made in 1929, also ended in failure. Strong Wiener Werkstätte influence is evident in furnishings designed by Urban, which use massive classical forms, derived ultimately from Empire designers such as Charles Percier and P.F.L. Fontaine. The Empire style was transmitted through midcentury Austrian Biedermeier and finally passed on to the Werkstätte's own designers. These influences can also be seen in twenties American design in general.

The specific mark made by the Wiener Werkstätte on American craft of this period was on ceramics. Small ceramic groups and figurines from this source had a considerable effect in 1928, when the American Federation of Arts organized the *International Exhibition of Ceramic Art,* which opened at the Metropolitan Museum of Art in New York and traveled to seven other cities. The liveliness and wit of these small-scale sculptures and the freedom and tactility with which the material was used impressed visitors to the show. Two of the leading exponents of this fanciful Austrian style, Vally Wieselthier and Susi Singer, subsequently settled in America, and their work influenced American-born colleagues. Some Americans, such as Russell Barnett Aitken and Viktor Schrekengost, went to Vienna to study at the Wiener Kunstgewerbeschule. The whimsical statuettes and small groups produced by the Americans who responded to this tendency were eclipsed by subsequent work in ceramics that seemed more committed, serious, and true to the nature of the material. They have only recently been rediscovered and now seem charmingly evocative of their epoch.

By the mid-twenties the general influence of the Wiener Werkstätte was already being overtaken by the new Art Deco style from France, popularized by the great 1925 *Exposition Internationale des Arts Décoratifs* in Paris. At first American efforts in this manner aped the high style sophistication of French originals by designers like Emile-Jacques Ruhlmann, but once established in the United States, Deco design became more popular in its appeal and was adapted to its new environment by the addition of industrial and mechanistic motifs, which celebrated America's prowess as the world's greatest industrial power. This aspect of popular Deco, however, also seemed to make it inherently unsuitable for craft use. It was characteristically applied to things that were mass produced: clocks, radios, and inexpensive dressing table sets, as well as compacts and cigarette cases in base metal.

The Bauhaus model for design and education

The new profession of industrial design was established at the beginning of the thirties and tended to switch attention away from the craftsman. American industrial design springs from an indigenous tradition, more pragmatic than that of the Bauhaus. Its original impulse came from the Depression. Designers were called in to give a new look to goods that had suddenly ceased to sell, and their solution was often to design new and more glamorous packaging around existing mechanical components. Raymond Loewy's redesign of the Gestetner duplicating machine, which dates from 1929 and was the foundation of his success, is a perfect example of this process. Many of Loewy's commissions, both during the thirties and later, came from automobile manufacturers and makers of heavy industrial equipment. During the decade he scored a big success with his designs for Hupmobile and for the Pennsylvania Railroad. His domestic designs are often for refrigerators and other kitchen appliances. His rival, Norman Bel Geddes, was less successful in gaining acceptance for his schemes, but his book *Horizons*, published in 1932, made him one of the leading prophets of his time and led to an invitation to create a Futurama depicting the world of 1960, which was the main feature of the General Motors Pavilion at the New York World's Fair of 1939. This, needless to say, was extremely technological in its emphasis; it was a huge hit with visitors. Industrial design became a catchword of the period, as craft had been before World War I, and the industrial and technological world, spurned by the founders of the Arts and Crafts movement, regained much of its glamour with the public.

Craft, nevertheless, continued to be sheltered by educational institutions. One of the most prestigious was the Cranbrook Academy of Art in Michigan, the fruit of a collaboration between George C. Booth, the newspaper proprietor and philanthropist, and the Finnish-born architect Eliel Saarinen. Founded in 1927, Cranbrook, like the Bauhaus established eight years earlier, aimed to provide an environment where fine artists, craftsmen, and design-

Lady's desk and chair in Art Deco
style, twentieth century, designed
by Jacques-Emile Ruhlmann.

ers could work together on equal terms. The Bauhaus, which began with a
strong commitment to the crafts, had by the mid-twenties begun to emphasize design for industry. But this attitude did not develop so quickly at
Cranbrook and did so less completely. The school produced a distinguished
group of industrial designers, among them Harry Bertoia and Charles Eames,
but typical Cranbrook products of the twenties and thirties show a strong
commitment to handwork as the expression of a nonindustrial ethos.

The WPA's involvement in craft during the thirties was probably more important than that of any single educational institution, but the printed record of
its activities in the field is extremely scanty, unlike the ample documentation
of the mural projects carried out under the same sponsorship. It is known
that about three thousand different handicraft projects were established. The
aim was as much idealistic as practical: to foster self-respect as well as self-
sufficiency during harsh financial times. As Allen H. Eaton writes: "Of all government efforts, state or federal, to promote handicrafts, it may be said that,
valuable as many of them proved to be in concrete terms, they were even
more powerful as symbols of a great and new conviction in American life, the
conviction that an economic depression need not rob our people of their skills
of eye and hand." Most of the WPA craft projects seem to have involved objects for use, but there was also a ceramic sculpture division, which encouraged fine artists to work with humble clay. One of the sculptors employed
was Isamu Noguchi.

Craft after World War II

The Bauhaus profoundly influenced American craft but in a special sense and
only after its own demise. There had, of course, been architects in America
between the wars who were aware of the Bauhaus; cases in point were Ru-
dolph Schindler and Richard Neutra, at work in California from the twenties
onwards. Neutra's Lovell house of 1929 has been directly compared to Mies
van der Rohe's Barcelona Pavilion of the same year. But both Schindler and
Neutra were Austrian, not German, and neither trained at the Bauhaus.

Cranbrook Academy of Art Museum,
1938–1942, Eliel Saarinen (architect).

The leading Bauhaus architects, such as Walter Gropius, Marcel Breuer, and Mies van der Rohe, began to have an impact in America only when they arrived in person, as refugees from Nazi persecution. At the end of the thirties they began to establish themselves in their new country, and in the forties the clean spare lines of the International Style, which they espoused, became the dominant architectural idiom. The interiors of these new buildings, as well as their exteriors, were stripped of all architectural ornament. Familiar details, such as doorcases, cornices, and moldings, were impatiently swept away. The new interiors needed to be warmed and humanized, and by the late forties this new situation provided obvious opportunities for craftsmen, particularly for weavers.

The strange thing was that Bauhaus craftsmen, as opposed to architects, never really rooted themselves in the United States despite frequent assertions to the contrary. The many brief biographies of Bauhaus professors and alumni included in the comprehensive catalogue of the exhibition *50 Years Bauhaus* (London: Royal Academy, 1968) indicate that, of the craftsmen chosen for this comprehensive show, only the weaver Anni Albers and the potter Marguerite Wildenhain-Friedlander taught and made craft in the United States. The practitioners of craft remained in Germany; it was the architects, planners, and industrial and advertising designers who found a new opportunity in America.

What the Bauhaus did affect profoundly—at an especially crucial moment— was the pattern of American art education. An immense expansion of university involvement with the crafts followed World War II. During the war the United States armed services ran vocational arts and crafts programs, which provided a taste of, and perhaps for, craft activity. The crafts had also formed part of the rehabilitation programs set up for wounded servicemen. The GI Bill of Rights, which offered veterans opportunities for higher education, laid no restriction on subjects, and some of those who took advantage of its provisions opted for craft training within a university framework. This demand led to more specialized art courses being offered as well as an

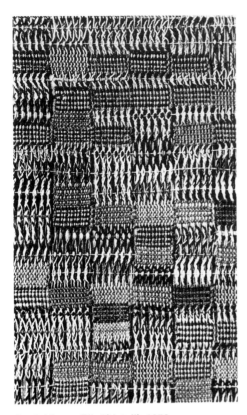

Anni Albers, *Tikal* (detail), 1958.

expansion of their scope and quality. Growth triggered in this way continued until the end of the sixties; for a long time newly trained craftsmen did not have to look farther than the university for their careers. Without professional pressure the craftsman emphasized the acquisition of skills, building a technical tradition, and recovering techniques from the past that could be made the subject of research in a university context. The production of work to be sold in the marketplace was not the primary goal.

Meanwhile the Bauhaus had become a major influence on the general structure of art education in America. The basis of the Bauhaus method was the all-important preliminary course, in which students learned from experience about forms and materials, without vocational specialization. Robert Rauschenberg was a student of Josef Albers (previously director of the Bauhaus preliminary course) at Black Mountain College during the late forties, and has given a succinct account of the nature of his teaching: "He did not teach you how to 'do art.' The focus was on your own personal sense of looking. When he taught you watercolor, for example, it was about the specific properties of watercolor, not about making a good picture." Attachment to Bauhaus principles became so fanatically dogmatic at certain American institutions that nonbelievers could find themselves in trouble. Mark Rothko was refused tenure at Brooklyn College in 1954 specifically because he was opposed to the Bauhaus teaching methods espoused by his colleagues.

This new teaching changed the attitude that craft is a closed field of activity, responsive only to its own aesthetic. Craftsmen became keenly aware in their formative years of new movements in contemporary art. Ironically, in adapting Bauhaus methods of education, the American schools in the long run seem to have led craftsmen away from the objectives that the Bauhaus itself pursued during its period of greatest prominence in Germany, from the mid-twenties, when Lázló Moholy-Nagy took over the preliminary course, until its dissolution in 1933. Nevertheless, the assumption that the role of the craftsman is to produce prototypes for industry, central to Moholy-Nagy's teaching, did initially root itself in America and is to some extent confirmed by the careers of successful weavers such as Dorothy Liebes and Marianne Strengell.

The flamboyant Liebes in particular attracted a great deal of acclaim. In a recent article the contemporary fiber artist Ed Rossbach recalled the impact she made:

> In what was then interpreted as an exciting breakthrough for women and the crafts, Liebes was a successful woman designer working for industry. In photographs she appeared paradoxically at a beautifully hand-carved loom, with yarns that would be called high tech today. The image that she created—a woman pursuing womanly activities (textiles were regarded then, as they are now, as a woman's area), yet living a glamorous life in a world of architects, designers, industrialists and wealthy clients—helped transform concepts about the nature of handweaving.

Liebes represents a high point in the intermittent and never fully sustained alliance between American industry and the crafts, because she regarded it as part of her function to produce "experimental material for reproduction in the weaving factories." But the impulse she represented was overtaken by another.

What changed the course of craft development is that the switch to the Bauhaus pattern of teaching coincided with the rise of Abstract Expressionism, the most powerful and original new art movement ever to appear in America. The new generation of craft students were as close to its origins as their contemporaries, students of painting and sculpture, and it was inevitable that they would be affected by it. Abstract Expressionism was a movement that stressed individualism above all else; its point of focus was the mysterious nature of the individual psyche. Those affected by it inevitably had little interest in or sympathy for the collectivism of modern industry.

The change that took place in craftsmen's attitudes toward their own activities during the late fifties and the sixties still has to be assessed fully by American criticism, and the view I give here is a personal one. Since World War II, New York always has been regarded as the focus for new developments in American painting. The crafts too maintained an important official presence in the city after the foundation of the American Craft Museum in 1956. But the crafts tended to attract more attention in areas where painting and sculpture were not dominant. If one looks specifically at the history of Abstract Expressionism, only one artist closely associated with the movement, Clyfford Still, spent a large part of his career on the West Coast. In contrast, California has possessed an important craft scene since 1900 or earlier, and the history of California craft has a continuity not visibly paralleled in California painting and sculpture. In the years since World War II, California society has consistently been characterized by a taste for innovation and a lack of respect for established categories. The arrival of the potter Peter Voulkos to teach at Otis Art Institute in Los Angeles in 1954 provided the catalyst that transformed an already volatile local situation.

Voulkos was already recognized as a potter of dazzling technical skills. He regularly won major prizes in important national exhibitions; his first award, in the *Ceramics National Exhibition* in Syracuse, had come in 1949. In 1953 he taught a summer session at Black Mountain College where he met Albers, Merce Cunningham, and John Cage. This experience put him in closer touch with some of the developments in American art of the previous decade. At Otis he began to make ambitiously large ceramic pieces that more and more openly abandoned vase forms and aspired toward the condition of sculpture. The freely improvisational nature of Voulkos's technique and the freedom of his attitudes toward the evolution of his own work soon prompted comparisons with Abstract Expressionism, which had then reached its zenith in the East.

Voulkos, however, differed in important respects from the major Abstract Expressionist masters. They too were often gregarious, but Voulkos was far more willing to share not merely general ideas but actual information about technical processes that they often kept as closely guarded secrets. He was willing to work in an almost collaborative fashion that was alien to the Abstract Expressionist ethos. His undoubted competitiveness was fueled not by a desire for recognition and worldly success but by the desire to surpass his contemporaries in pure skill, a quality more measurable in the handling of clay than it was in the handling of paint and canvas. Voulkos's innate playfulness encompassed a well-developed sense of irony and a feeling for the grotesque.

Voulkos very soon found associates and sympathizers in Los Angeles, among them John Mason, Kenneth Price, and Billy Al Bengston. When he moved up the coast to Berkeley in 1959, the innovative California ceramics movement took root in northern California as well, flourishing there even more vigorously. In adopting an Abstract Expressionist stance more than ten years after the appearance of Abstract Expressionism itself, Voulkos had been acting in a manner long customary with craft, following in the footsteps of an established fine art movement. A new group of ceramic sculptors in Los Angeles,

Dorothy Liebes in her New York studio (right). Her design for automotive upholstery fabric (detail), 1957 for Chrysler Corporation (above).

prominent among them Robert Arneson, found equivalents for the statements being made by Pop artists in New York at a time when Pop was still evolving. A direct comparison can be made between Arneson's wobbly typewriter in ceramic and the soft eggbeaters in vinyl stuffed with kapok which Claes Oldenburg was making at the same moment. A number of these Pop-oriented West Coast ceramists were represented in the *Funk Art* exhibition organized by Peter Selz in Berkeley in 1967.

The *Funk Art* show received uneven press, both at the time and later. Many critics were inclined to dismiss it as being trivial as well as vulgar. Funk humor they found juvenile, especially when compared with the impassive irony of New York Pop. Nevertheless, the exhibition had an importance that generally has been overlooked: It marked the moment when the barrier between art and craft was for the first time completely swept aside. Arneson, who was included in the show, has remained an important figure in the American craft scene and is represented in the present exhibition. William T. Wiley, another of Selz's choices for the show and now equally eminent, has never been by any stretch of the imagination connected with craft. Yet at the time of the *Funk Art* show both of these men's work had something genuinely in common and could be presented within the same framework without any distinction being made.

The date of the exhibition was significant as the sixties were in all respects a turning point for American craft. Although the universities had strengthened the crafts in the years since the war, they had also restricted and to some extent imprisoned them. This situation changed when university growth slowed in the late sixties. Teaching posts still existed, but with graduation a student could no longer assume the automatic right to be given one. There were also major changes in American society, which became less conformist and experienced a strong revival of the desire to get back to nature. A revulsion against industry once again began to manifest itself. For those who wished to drop out of urban industrial society, the practice of craft seemed an alternative way of life.

A throwing demonstration by Peter Voulkos at Teachers College, Columbia University, 1956 (left) and his slab ceramic construction, 1956 (right).

At the same time American society became increasingly mobile. Means of communication improved, and economically it became easier to travel. Craft students, like many other American students, acquired the habit of *wanderjahre*, a period of restless wandering and investigation before they finally settled into some kind of professional life. In many cases these travels took them outside the United States, to societies such as India, Java, Peru, and Mexico, where the practice of crafts still formed an important part of daily life. They were duly impressed by what they found.

As the crafts emerged from the universities, a new and broader market for them slowly began to form. This market, which had not been so strong since the high tide of enthusiasm for craft in the years immediately before World War I, owed much to the craftsmen themselves, who undertook their own marketing. Fine artists, then enjoying the first benefits of an enormous sales boom (which has continued to the present day), were able to rely on the services of astute dealers, who were often in a position to offer contracts to successful artists, guaranteeing that the dealer would take the artist's entire output. Even today only a handful of craftsmen enjoy such privileged situations. A few galleries, always in big cities, sell the work of top-line craftsmen on precisely the same basis that painting or sculpture are sold, but their appearance is very recent. Other galleries, again usually in large cities, have regular exhibition programs but also carry a varied stock of crafts and thus operate partly as craft shops. Finally there are numerous sales outlets for crafts, usually in small shops located in areas where there is a high concentration of craftsmen. Most craftsmen begin their careers by doing business with outlets from this third category, and quite a few are content to remain in that position.

If this part of the craft market to some extent parallels the market in fine art, the other part is based on the craft fair. Art fairs do of course exist; they are generally international, and their main purpose is to bring together a large number of dealers, otherwise widely separated geographically, for the convenience of the connoisseur. Within this framework artists as indepen-

Robert Arneson, *Typewriter,* 1966.

dent exhibitors play only a marginal role. Craft fairs, even the more ambitious ones, are different: the craftsman is generally also the salesperson. The purchaser thus makes direct contact with the man or woman who created the work. Though today's craft market exhibits features inherited from the very earliest epoch of the craft revival, it is fair to say that in its present form it stands on foundations laid two decades ago.

Contemporary craft perspectives

The tone of the contemporary craft world was set during the sixties. Contemporary craftsmen remain a society within a society, distinguished from the world surrounding them by their perception of craft and their choice of it as their primary occupation. This perception incorporates important attitudes: first, that craft provides the individual with the satisfaction of imposing himself on the material world, a feeling that has deep roots in the American pioneer spirit; and second, that the practice of craft is an effective means of self-realization. The craftsman learns about the world and about society through commitment to craft; through manipulating materials—experiencing their cooperation or resistance—he explores his own nature as a human being. The level of personal satisfaction increases with the degree of craft skill attained. Despite the materialism of American society, more and more people think that total mastery of a craft offers greater satisfaction than the pursuit of purely material goals. This feeling has even spread to people who do not practice a craft but nevertheless regard professional craftsmen as role models.

Within the American craft community there is an intricate web of relationships. The exact linkages are often influenced by chance: particular craftsmen studied or taught together at a particular school; they inhabit the same region; they have social and aesthetic ideas in common. Yet Americans do not cease to be competitive when they dedicate themselves to the crafts, and one of the chief links between craftsmen is an intense rivalry in the realm of technical inventiveness and refinement. Any process, new or old, is pressed to its limits. But unlike the European workshops of the Middle Ages and the Renaissance, contemporary American craftsmen are not disposed to keep their discoveries secret. Rivalry goes hand in hand with typically American sharing. This combination has recently produced an explosion of skills; the technical means available to the craftsman have never been so refined or so diverse.

Despite the breakdown of the barrier between art and craft in the sixties, craft continues to play a variety of roles. It is still the modest rival of industry: A large proportion of craftsmen continue to produce objects intended for everyday use. These items, produced in late twentieth-century America, do not compete in price with their industrial equivalents, nor are they expected to. The people who buy them are in search of something that retains the intimacy of the human touch and makes ideas of quality concrete. Craft objects are considered to be of lasting value because they remain superior to fashion.

Such objects are both decorative in themselves and serve the desire felt by most of us to embellish and decorate our surroundings. The client shares the pleasure the craftsman takes in displaying his virtuosity and may feel an almost physical response to seeing materials treated in virtuoso fashion, akin to the identification felt by spectators watching a sport played at the highest level. Craft also nourishes the still irrepressible taste for luxury, the delight in fine materials whose intrinsic qualities are enhanced by skill.

Craft has ceased, however, to be mere decoration, and the craftsman has become the rival of the fine artist. Craft objects increasingly tend to be used in precisely the same way as paintings and sculptures in domestic and other interiors—as space modulators and as activators of particular environments, lending their own emotional coloring. We respect and value them as totems and touchstones as we do fine art.

This last function of craft is an interesting one and deserves more analysis than it has received hitherto. The realignment of our hierarchy of artistic values owes much to the growth of what Andre Malraux called the "Imaginary Museum" (1952). Malraux's thesis is that the proliferation of illustrated art books has made objects of all cultures widely available and broadened our definition of art. In particular, ancient and non-Western cultures have become accessible to people who are not professional archaeologists and anthropologists; products from these societies are now thought of not as scientific specimens but as art on a level with the more familiar products of Western civilization. This new accessibility has struck a heavy blow at the traditional distinction between the fine and applied arts established by Renaissance art theory since in these non-Western cultures such categories have never been established. At first only old or exotic objects—such as an ancient Egyptian headrest or an African heddle pulley—were recategorized as art, but increasingly it seems illogical not to consider modern craft in the same way. Malraux's theory has been instrumental in producing a shift in perception. It is now possible to see a chair, old or new, in several ways simultaneously: as an object to sit on, as a decorative item that may be part of a larger scheme, and as sculpture.

Contemporary craft has, in any case, been considerably influenced by non-Western cultures. The influence exercised by Inca textiles on postwar American weaving, for instance, has already been noted. A more general influence has come from Japan, whose culture is now approached more directly and seen more profoundly than it was at the time of the original craft revival. The influence comprises not only a wide range of typically Japanese techniques

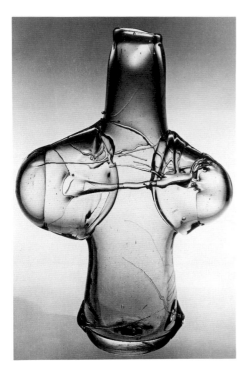

Harvey K. Littleton, founder of the studio glass movement, at work in his studio. (right) and his *Cross Vase,* 1964 (above).

that have been taken up and adapted by craftsmen in the United States but also the Zen philosophy underlying much Japanese craft activity.

Contemporary craft and contemporary art

In one sense the world of contemporary American craft seems to have developed as an entity in itself. If one looks at the careers of some of its senior figures, especially those who have taught extensively, such as Voulkos or the glassmaker Harvey K. Littleton, it is even possible to construct a family tree that demonstrates the influence of a particular craftsman on successive generations of students, many of whom, in turn, have become teachers. But to read the achievement of American craft in this narrow way is deeply misleading.

It is evident that the barriers between art and craft, which were first thrown down in the sixties, have not been reerected. But defining the relationship between contemporary art and contemporary craft is not easy, although it is clear that both have sprung from similar roots. In America craftsmen and artists share an educational background and many other influences. They also share many fundamental assumptions about their work. The recent work of Wendell Castle, one of the best-known furniture makers in America, demands to be judged by criteria that have little to do with either function or decoration. He has created a series of thirteen clocks, *Masterpieces of Time,* which proceeds from objects that tell the time to others that are interpretations of time. One *trompe l'oeil* piece, called the *Ghost Clock,* has no face and is carved to resemble a traditional grandfather clock swathed in a concealing cloth. Castle, who began his career as a sculptor, is here returning to his roots. His clocks are symbolic and narrative objects much like the chairs of Scott Burton, which, whether practicable as seating or not, are universally accepted as fine art by commentators.

One of the factors that has helped to bring the idea of craft and the idea of art close enough together for confusion to arise between them is the way in which art theory has developed during the last two decades. Critics long ago accepted that the notion of abstraction, when applied to painting or sculpture, covered two things that were essentially different from one another. The work could make use of imagery that was a simplified, generalized, and thus abstracted version of something observed in the real world, or it could use shapes that were entirely nonreferential. Constantin Brancusi's *Bird in Space* is an example of the first; Piet Mondrian's gridlike compositions are examples of the second.

The next step, connected with the birth of post-Painterly Abstraction followed by that of Minimal art, was to see the object as something created *ab initio*. It was something entirely new that the artist added to a preexisting world of objects. It did not acknowledge its predecessors, shouldering them aside in order to make room for itself. Not merely did it make no reference to things observed in the real world, it deliberately shunned all reference to previous art. Though never admitted by its promulgators, this theory of "objectness," which pertains, for example, to the early black paintings of Frank Stella or the sculptures of Tony Smith, was also a quasi-theological one: the creative artist is perceived as someone who mimes and tries to rival the activity of the prime Creator.

The theory did not account for the position of makers who thought of themselves as craftsmen rather than artists. The working craftsman had from the very beginning without self-consciousness created objects and duly added them to a preexisting world of objects. The potter's activity with clay is one of the most traditional metaphors for the workings of prime cause; under strict application of the theory of objectness outlined above, it is difficult to make any valid distinction between a simple pot and one of the galvanized steel cubes of Tony Smith.

What is truly different is the maker's view of himself. The potter says, "I am a craftsman," often rejecting the notion that he is also making art. Similarly the modern fiber artist and the modern abstract painter may differ chiefly in the maker's acceptance or rejection of the label *artist*, used without qualification. Since the development of the so-called soak-stain technique, in which extremely dilute acrylic paints are used on unprimed canvas, many painters have made it their chief aim to achieve complete integration of surface and ground. Craftsmen who work with colored paper pulp do the same thing— arguably with greater completeness. But they still think of their activity as being essentially different from that of the painter.

The differences between art and craft, when they do not depend chiefly on the maker's own categorization of his or her work, often seem to boil down to standards of skill. It is one of the shibboleths of late modernism that the artist is allowed to use any technique he wishes, whether he has been trained in it or not. The modernist emphasis on total originality gives a special value to autodidacticism in these matters. Late modernist artists are often admired for technical clumsiness, as if the signs of struggle were proof of their originality. Craft accommodates the spontaneous and apparently unfinished (a Japanese legacy) and the self-consciously plain and rustic, but it does not deny the true natures of the materials used. Judged by their command of craft, contemporary fine artists often look crude and sloppy.

Craft places little value on autodidacticism. Instead, it holds to the idea that most technical skills are objective knowledge which can be passed from one craftsman to another. This has played a major role in creating separate histories for each of the main media, each of which now has its own tradition.

Wendell Castle, *Ghost Clock,* 1985.

Scott Burton, *Pair of Rock Chairs,* 1980–1981.

Closely related to this is the idea of sharing, already discussed, which is so crucially important to the contemporary American craftsman.

The fact that craft technique has become a language through which craftsmen communicate with one another, as well as with the general public, has also had other consequences. Craft is more socialized than the fine arts; it perceives the maker not only as an individual asserting individuality through his or her work but as a member of both a larger and smaller community. The larger is the lay public, his audience and source of patronage. The smaller is composed of his fellow craftsmen with whom he communicates in friendly rivalry and through a shared obsession with the possibilities offered by a particular set of processes. In either of these roles the craftsman is not separate, as the contemporary artist often seems to be, but is completed both personally and professionally by what surrounds him.

Still he is not absolved from the demands for originality and self-transcendence, which are also imposed on the painter or the sculptor. In some ways these demands are more severe. The total mastery of his materials—the craftsman's aim—inevitably raises the question of what is to be done with these skills once they have been acquired. It is striking that contemporary crafts have freed themselves from expectations about the end result. In dimensional weaving neither shape nor form nor even the actual material is specified in advance. All three depend on what the weaver's imagination can encompass: on his or her skill in handling materials, on pressing skills that have never been tried in this context into service, or on revealing new characteristics in those that are thoroughly familiar. A work of this kind may delight the senses, but more importantly it also reveals to us by direct demonstration a little more about the nature of the world.

PLATES

STATEMENT

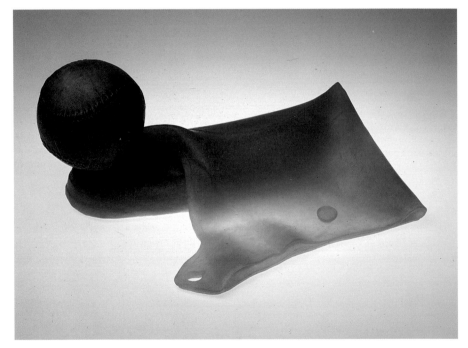

Preceding Page
1 Fumio Yoshimura *Three Bicycles*

Above
2 Marilyn Levine *H.R.H. Briefcase*

Below
3 Douglas Anderson *Boot Lace*

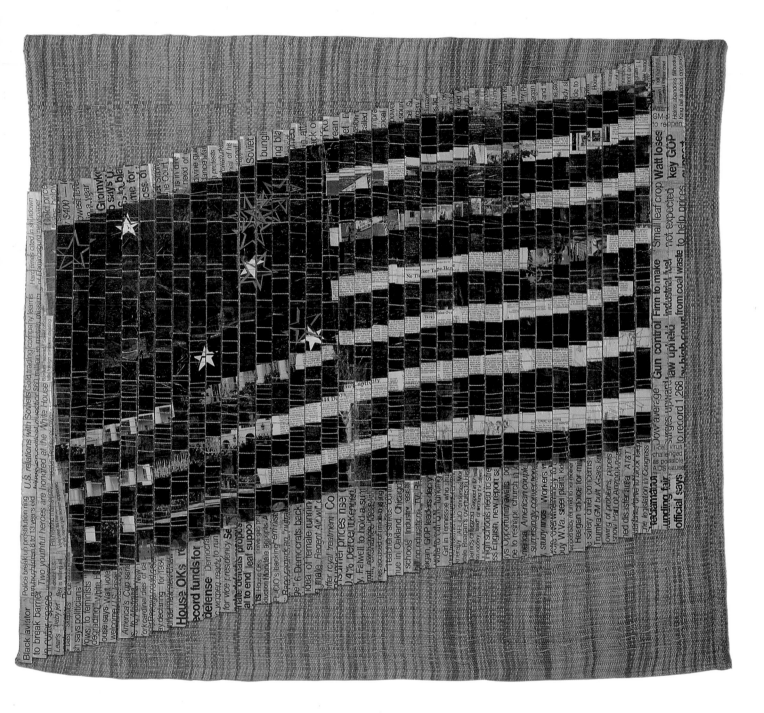

4   Arturo Alonzo Sandoval   *State of the Union No. 4 (Return of the Hostages)*

5 Richard Shaw *V. Partch, D. Shaw*

6   Louis B. Marak   *Green Rag Box*

48

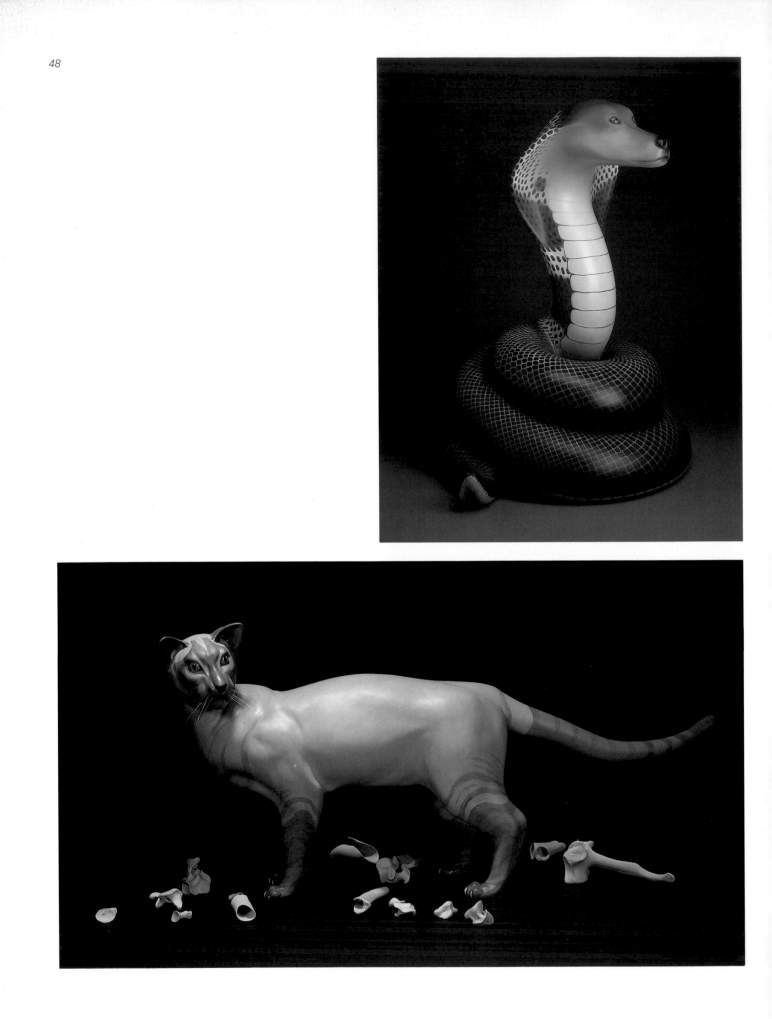

Above
7 Jack Thompson (a.k.a. Jugo de Vegetales)   *Snake Doggess*

Below
8 Lizbeth Stewart   *Predator*

Opposite
9 Frank Fleming. *Screamer*

10 Jack Earl *For thou hast been a strength to the poor, a strength to the needy in his distress, a refuge from the storm, a shadow from the heat, when the blast of the terrible ones is as a storm against the wall*

Opposite
11 Michael Lucero *Dream De*

12 Robert Arneson *Persistence*

13   Patti Warashina   *Dinnerware Fiesta*

hen De Staebler   *Seated Figure with Cleft*

15   Robert Brady   *Golfus*

16   Nancy Carman   *Muerte Contra Mis Enemigos*

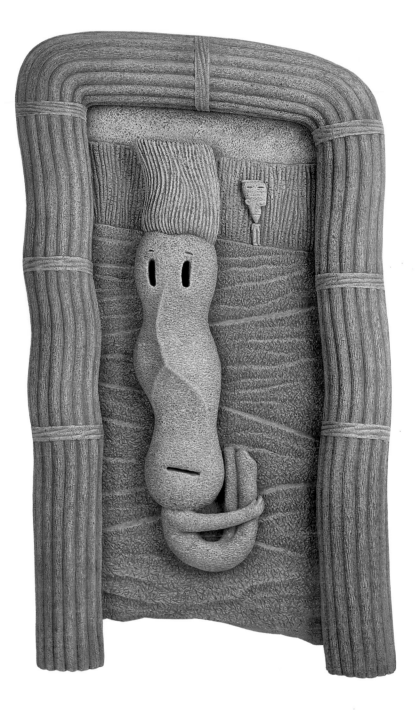

17   Jan Holcomb   *Freefall*

18 Peter VandenBerge *Zwartman*

Opposite
19 Viola Frey *Leaning*

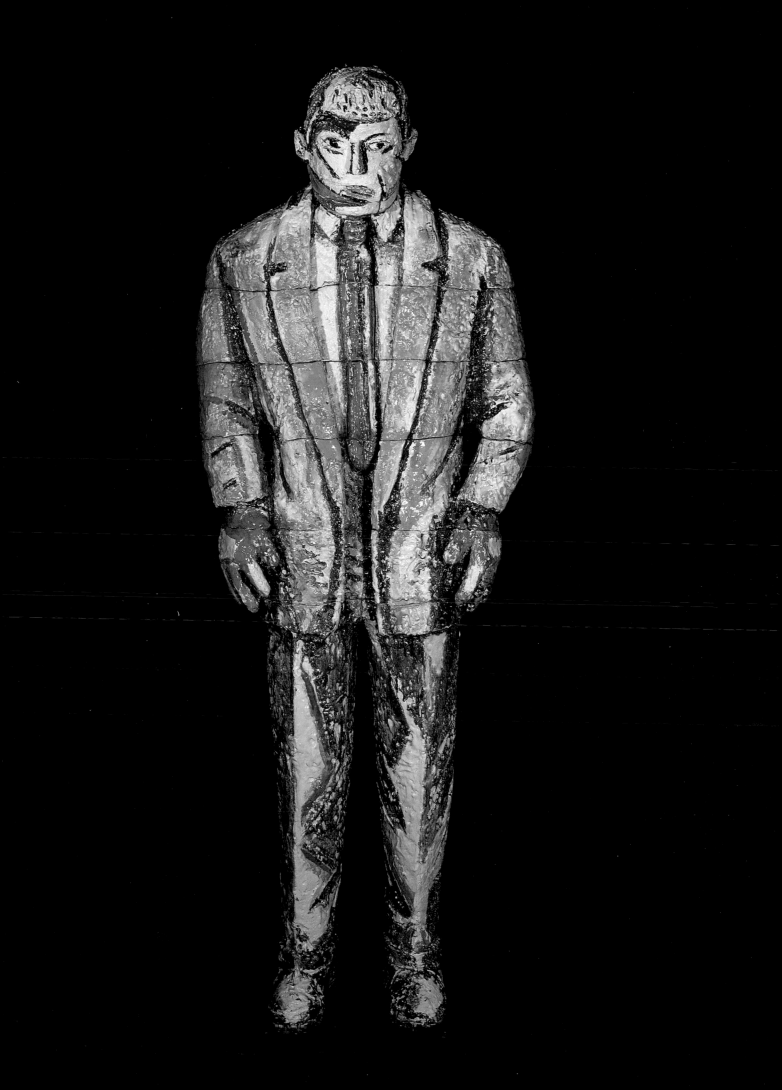

20 Judy Moonolis *Couple*

Opposite
21 Patrick Siler *Bourgeois Cer*

24   Kenneth Price   *Mungor*

Opposite
25   Scott Chamberlin

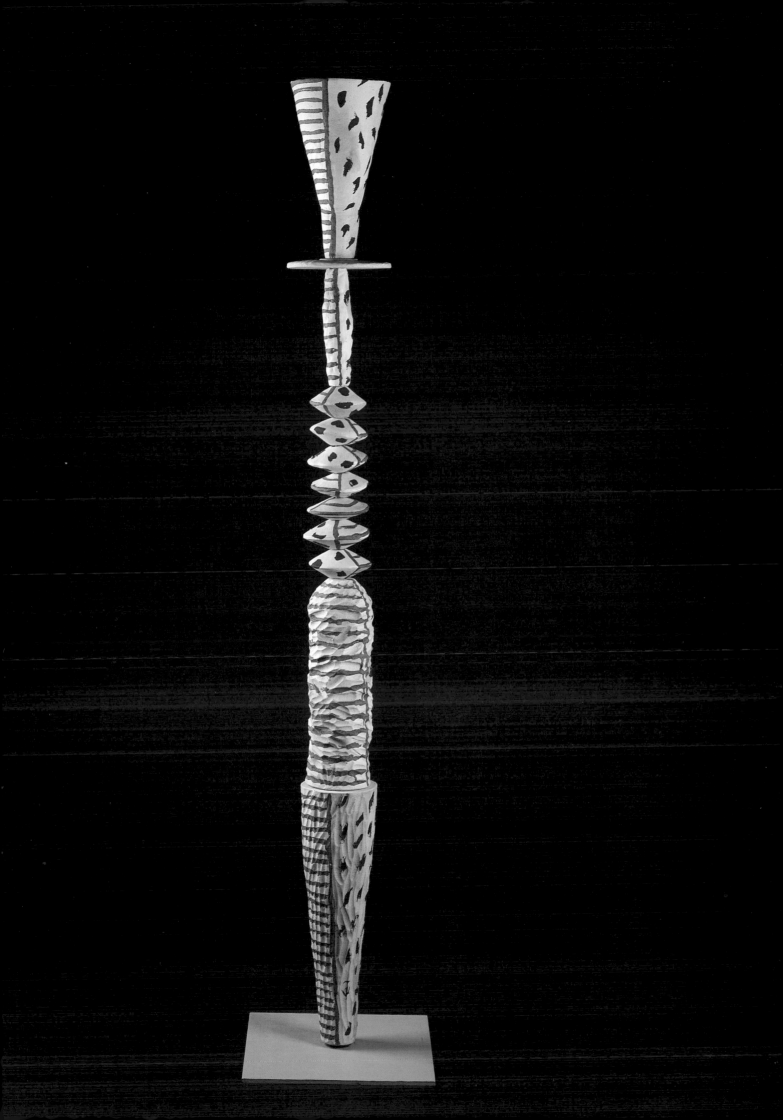

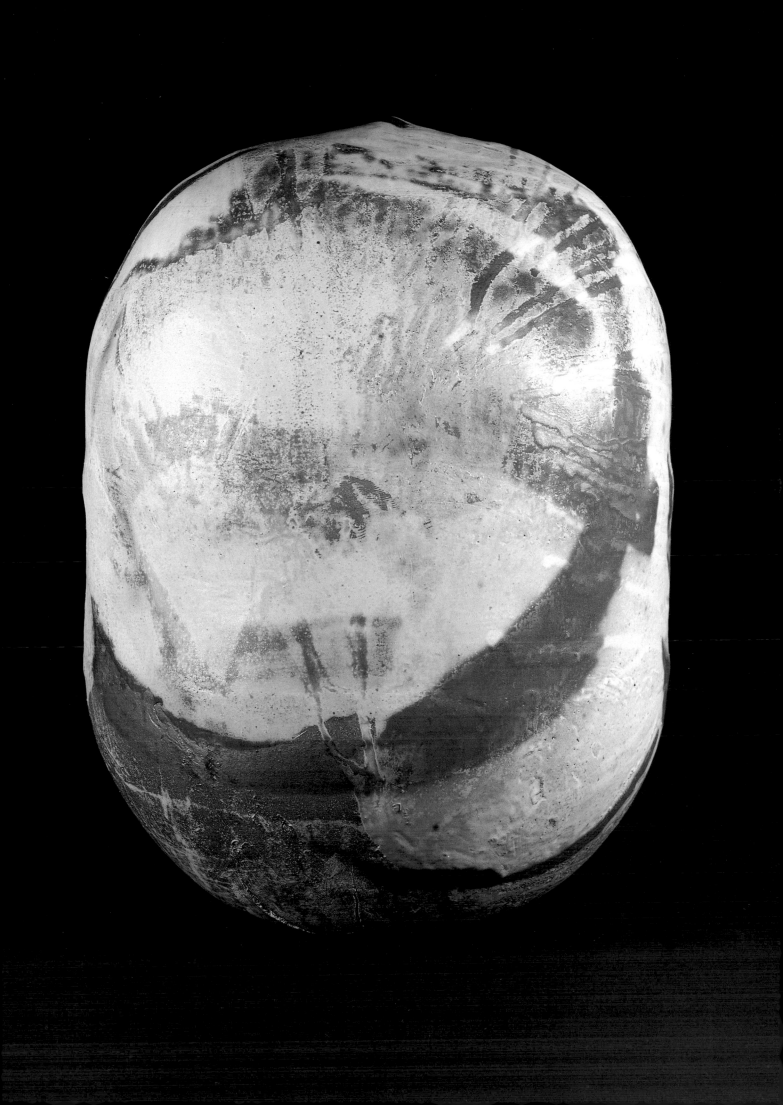

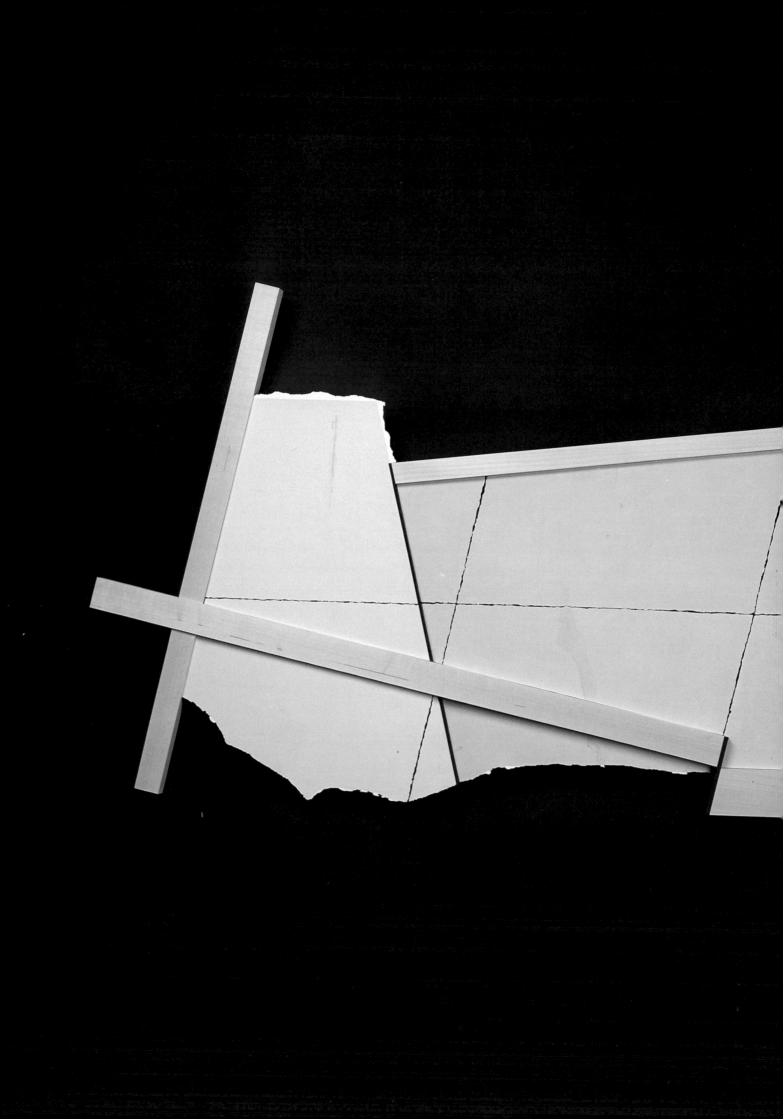

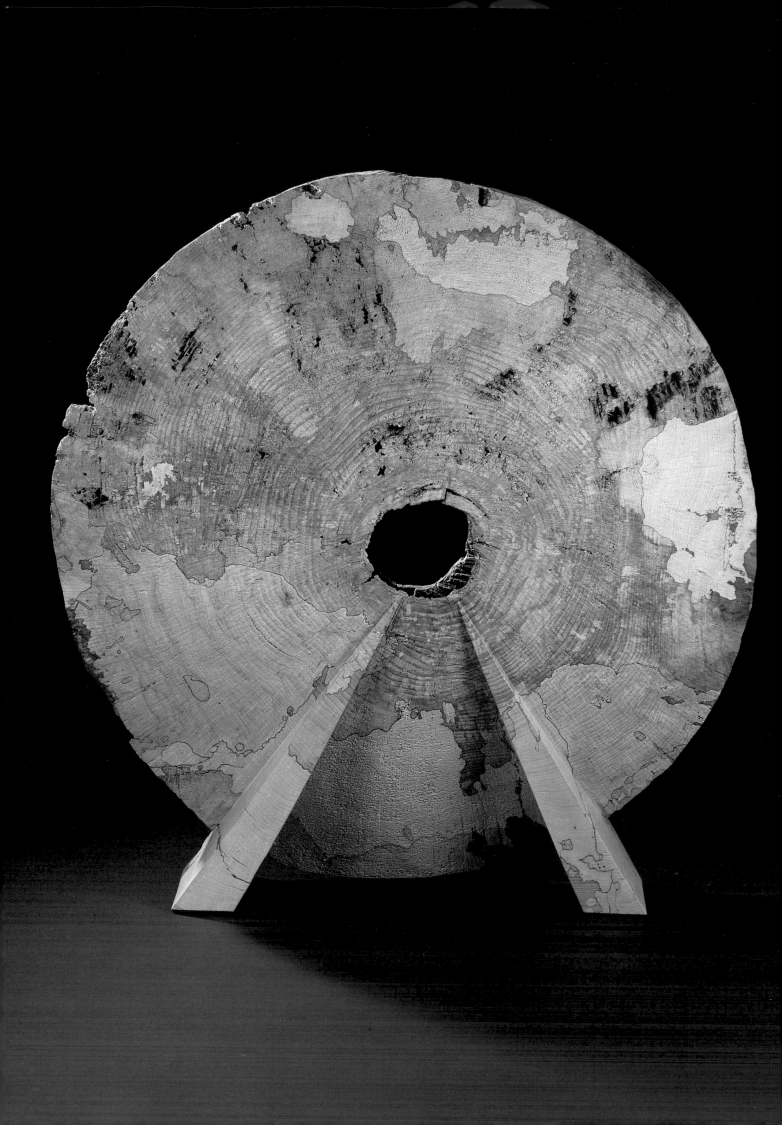

33 Sam Hernandez *St. Elmo's Fire*

hardt Knodel   Panel from *The Pontiac Curtain*   35   Michael Olszewski   *The Sin of Omission*

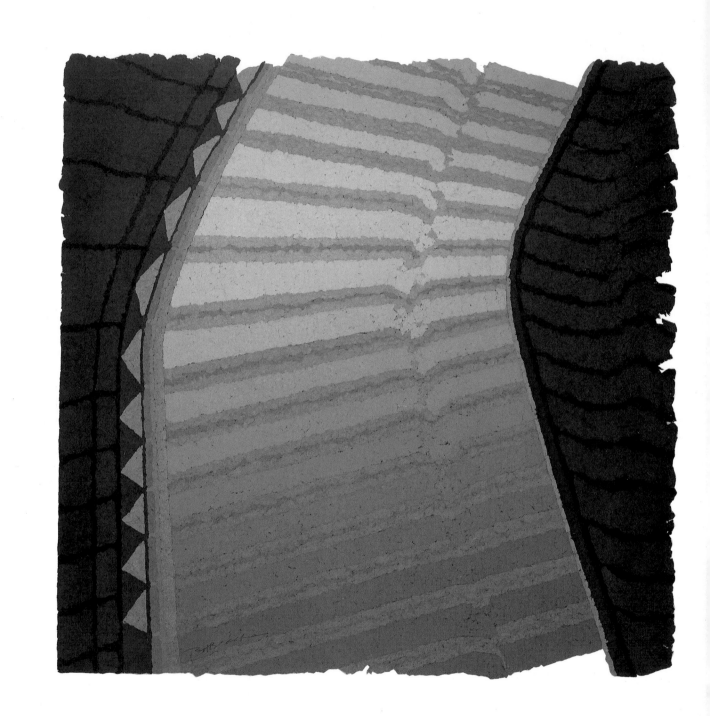

36   John Babcock   *Descending Angel*

Opposite
37   Glenn Brill   *Now You*

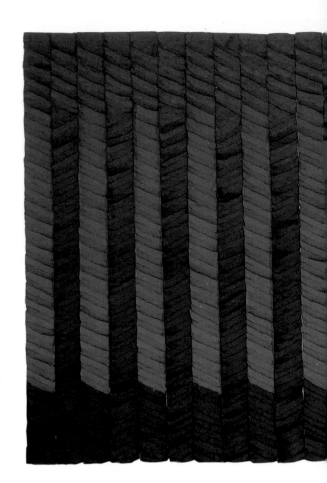

Above
39   Joan Sterrenburg   *Binary Barrier*   Below
40   Adela Akers   *Compostela*

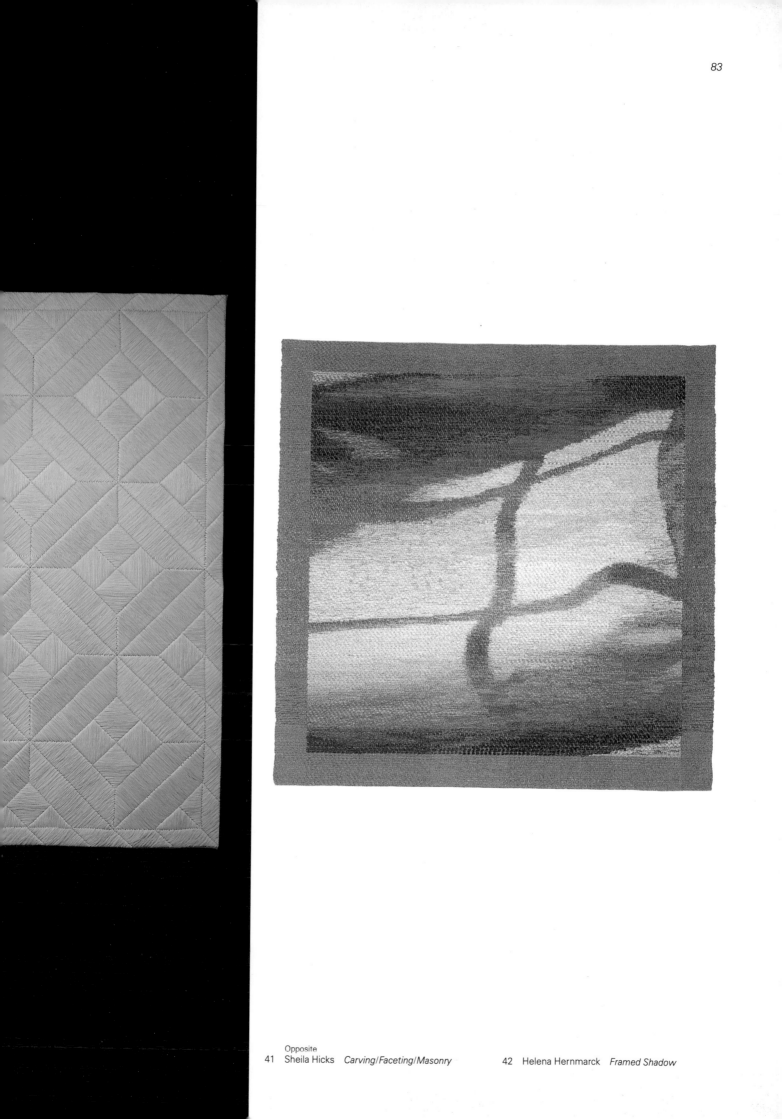

Opposite
41 Sheila Hicks *Carving/Faceting/Masonry*   42 Helena Hernmarck *Framed Shadow*

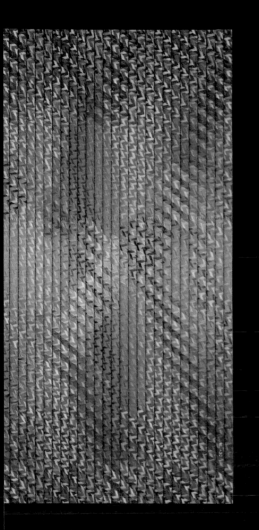

Opposite
43 Kris Dey *Backwater*   44 Tom Lundberg *Lucky Steps*

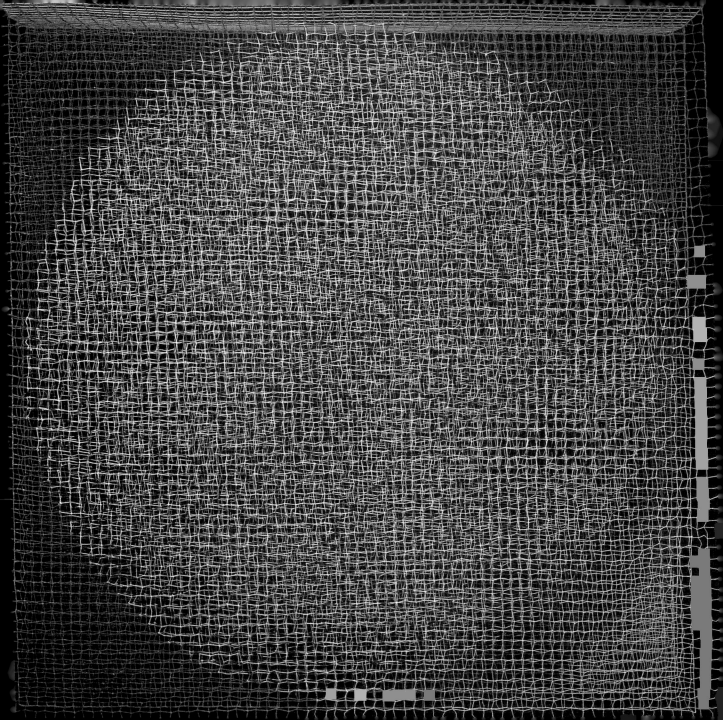

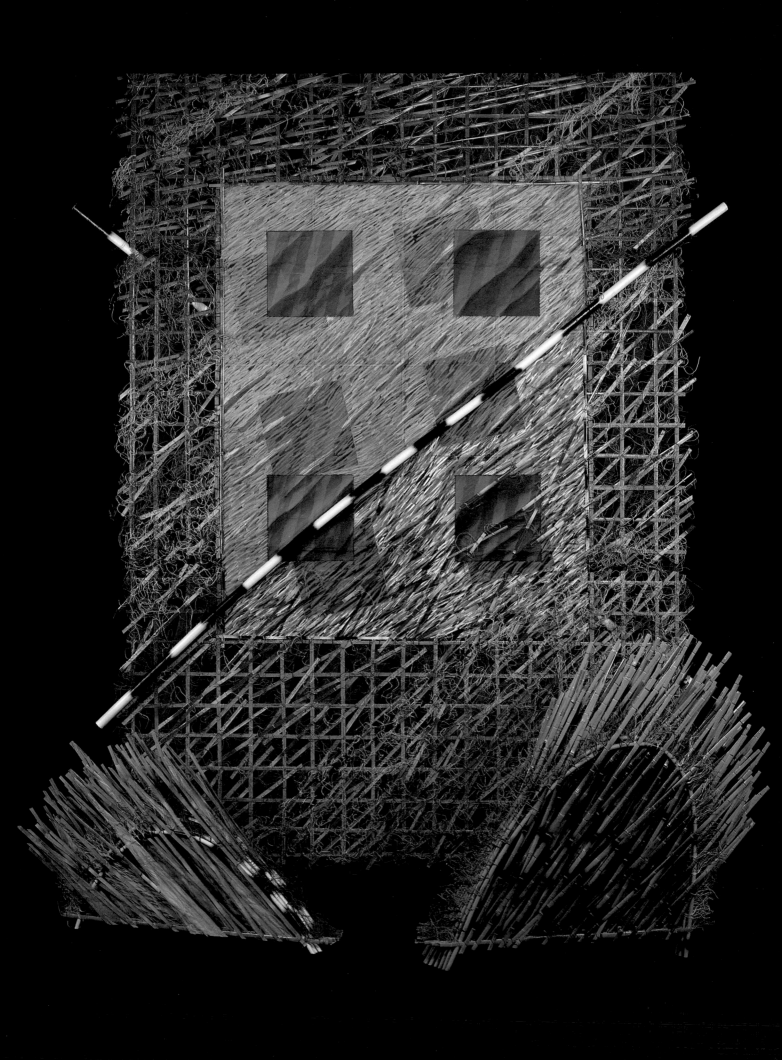

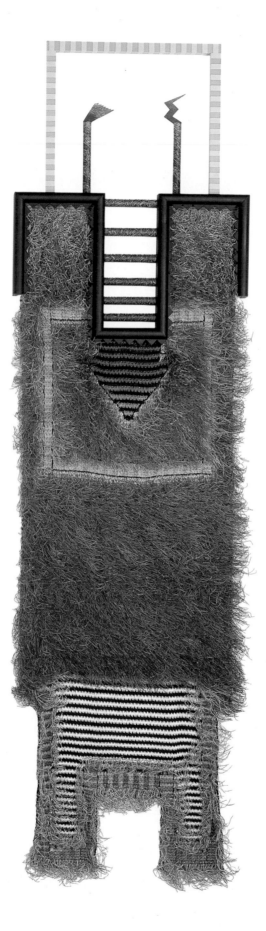

52   Janice Lessman-Moss   *Passing Dreams II*

53   Neda Alhilali   *The Serpent's Laughing Skin*

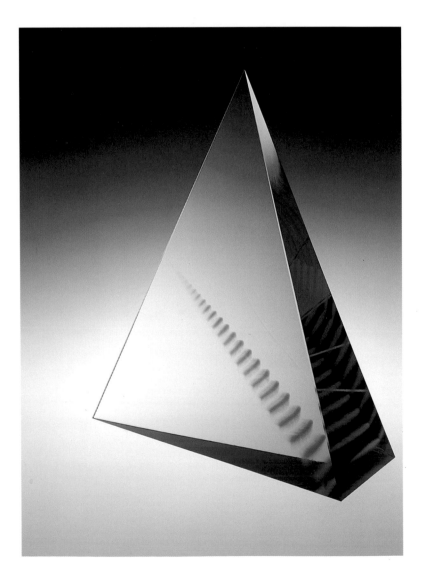

Above
54　Harvey K. Littleton　*Opalescent Yellow Squared Pair*

Below
55　Mark Peiser　*Pyramid, IS288*

56 Robert Kehlmann *Cloak*

57 Marvin Lipofsky *Pilchuck Series: Pacific Sunset*

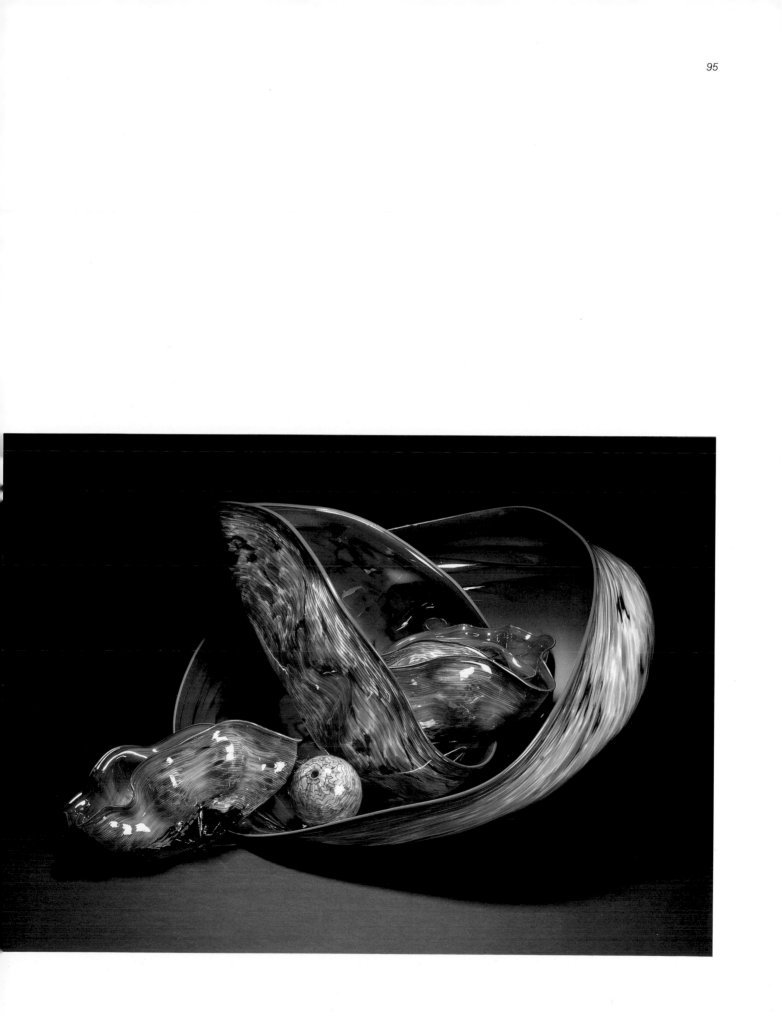

58　Dale Chihuly　*Purple Violetta Macchia Set with Green Lip Wraps*

59   Paul Seide   *Frosted Radio Light*

Opposite
60   Richard Marquis   *Shard*

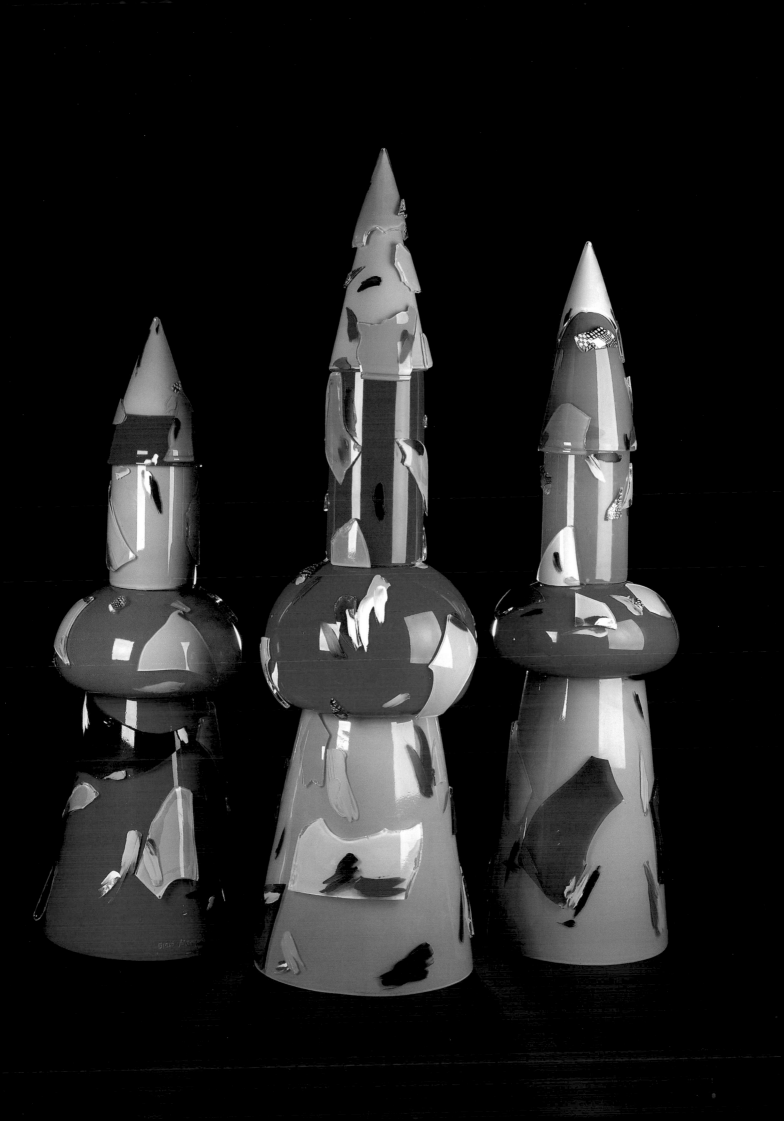

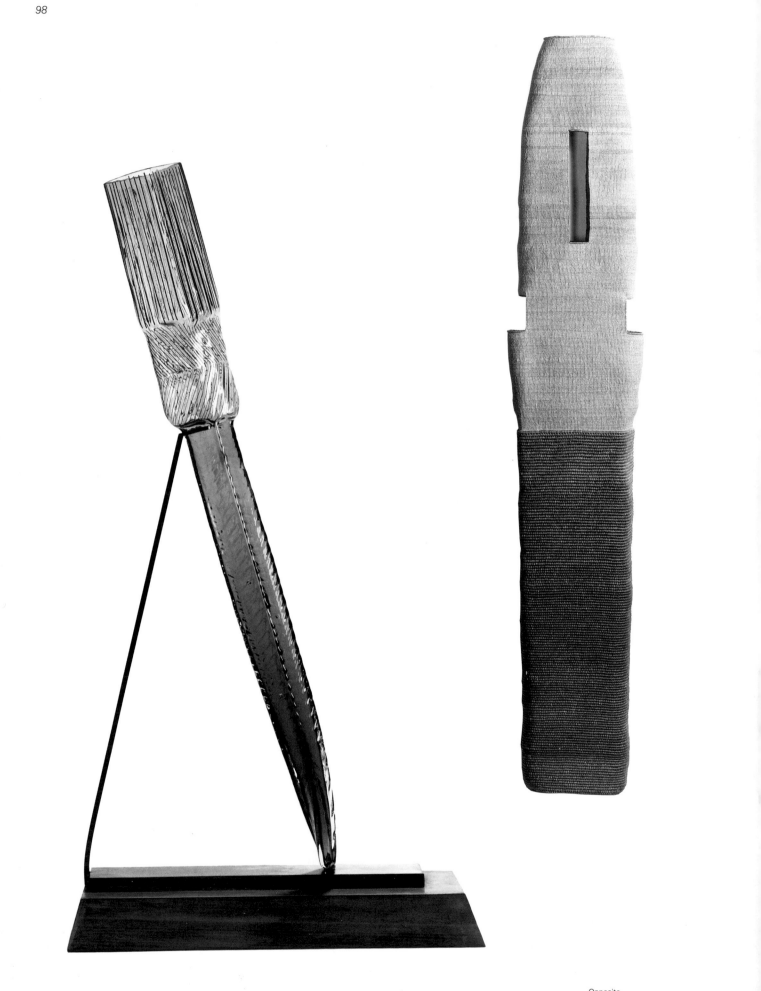

61   Jon F. Clark   *Leaning Tri-Form*   62   Ferne Jacobs   *Soft Paddle*   Opposite
63   Joey Kirkpatrick / Flora Mace   *Figure with*

64   Stephen Dale Edwards   *Man*

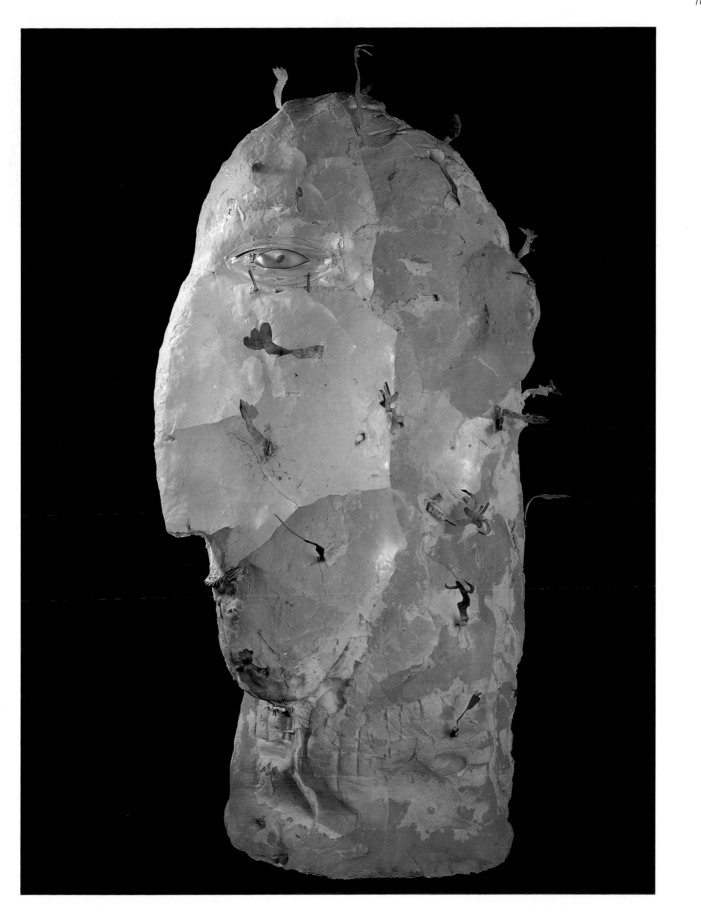

65 Hank Murta Adams *Head with Flowers*

Overleaf
66 Paul Marioni *The Warriors, Shapers of Our Destiny*

67 Steven I. Weinberg Untitled

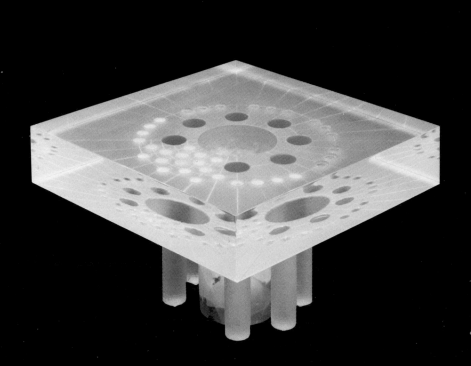

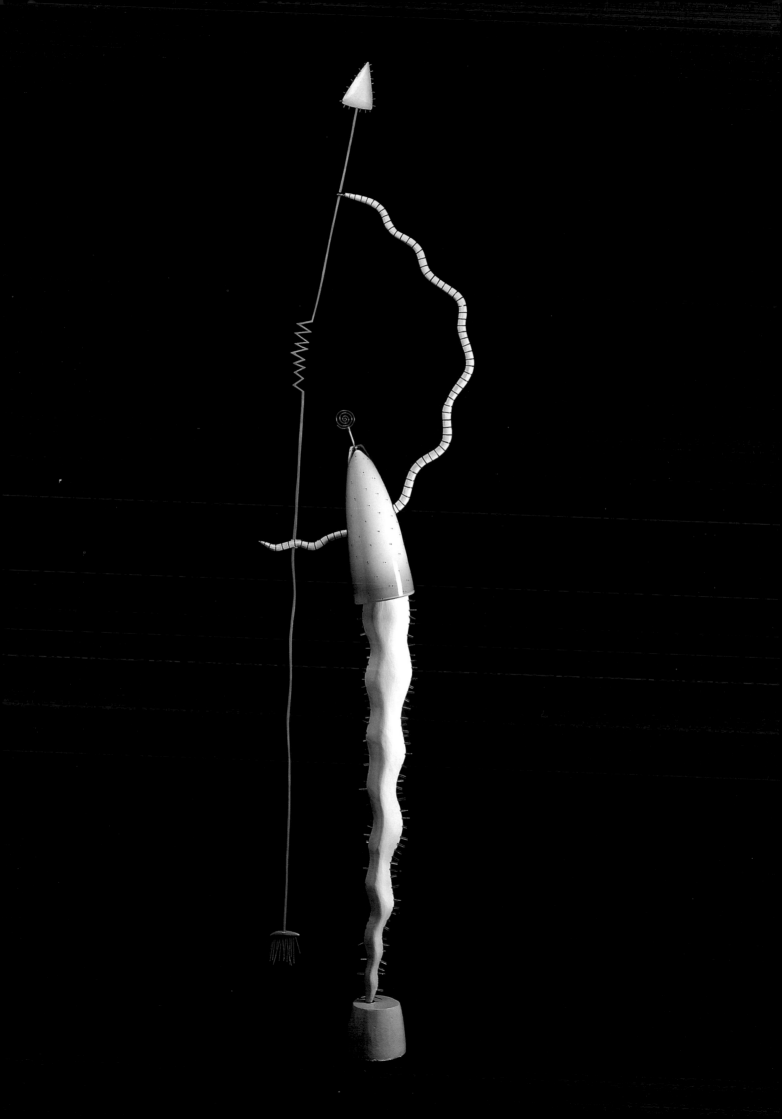

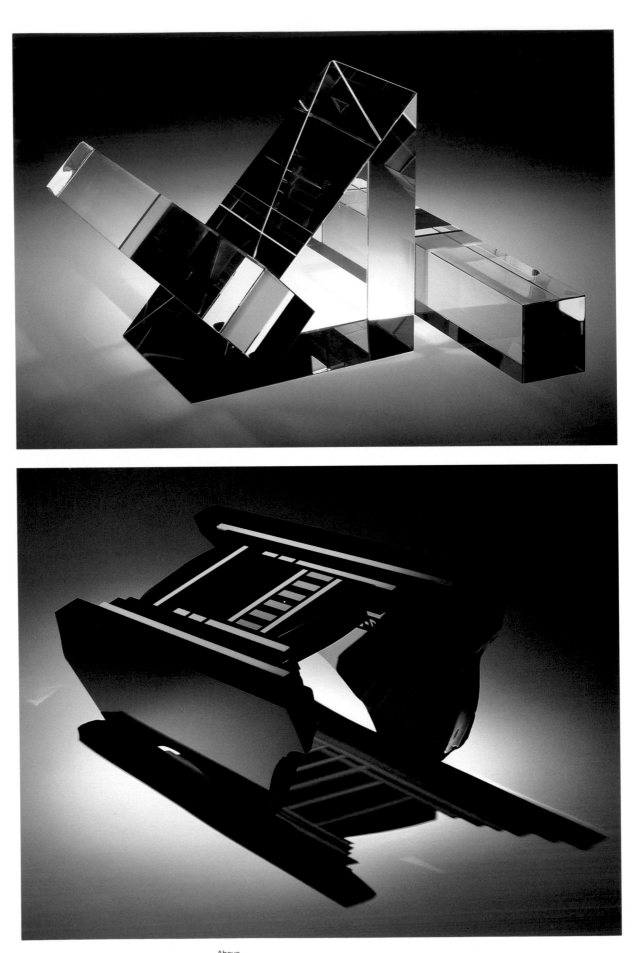

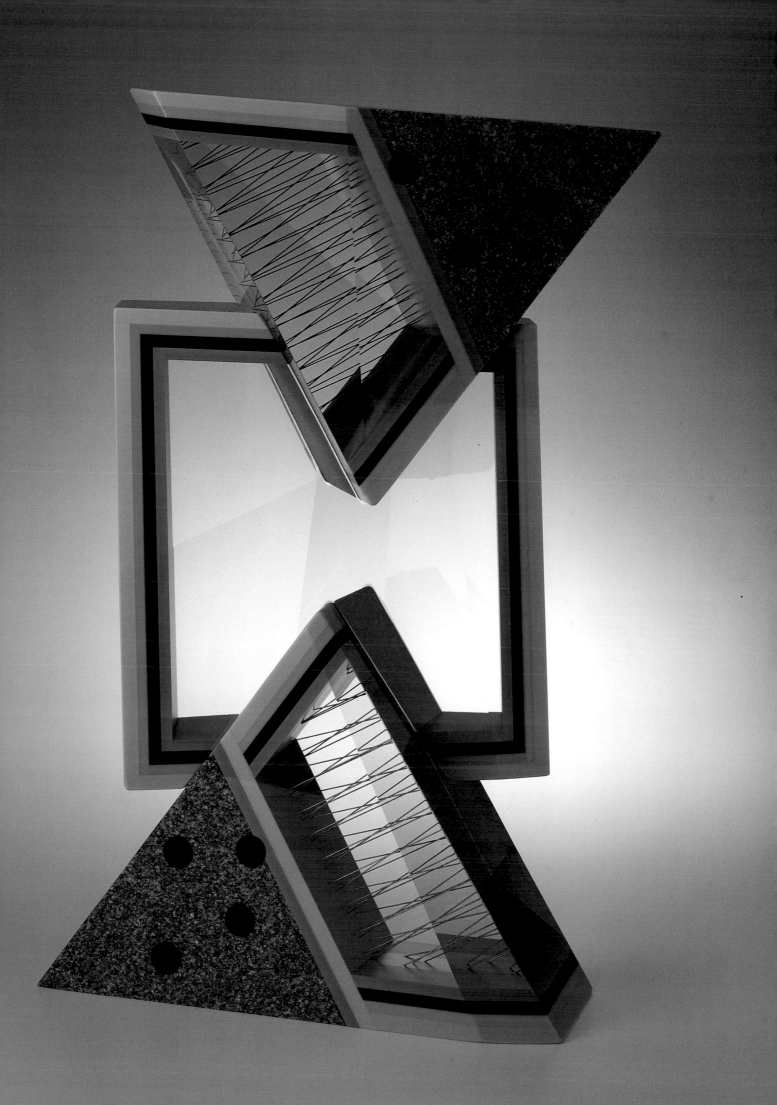

72   Michael Cohn   *Roll Over Mondrian and Tell Brancusi the News #17*

Opposite

73   Howard Ben Tré   *Co*

74 Susan Stinsmuehlen *A Fancy Monitor*

Opposite
75 Henry Halem *Bl*

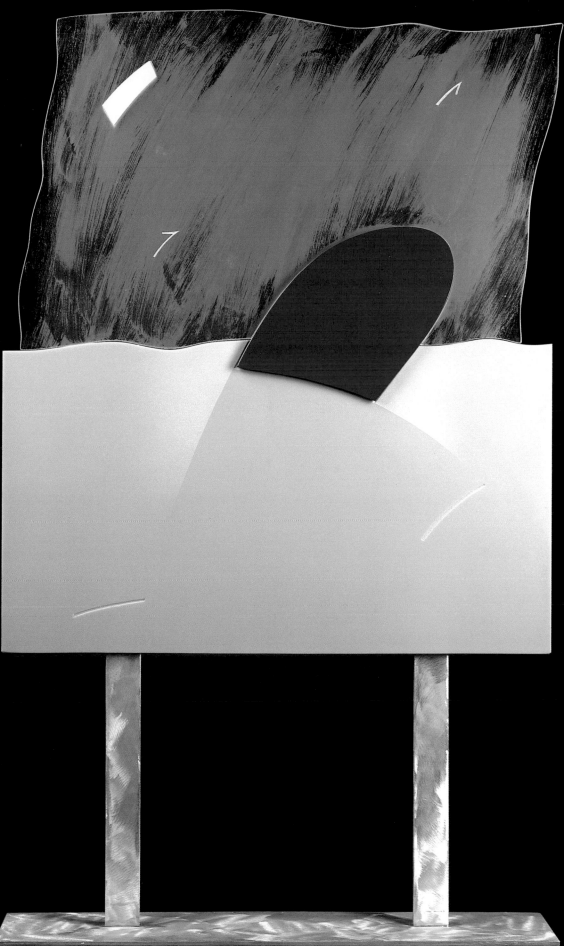

Above
76 Jay Musler   *Voyage to Vogue*

Below
77 Albinas Elskus   *Four Columns*

Opposite
78 Carol Shaw-Sutton   *Su*

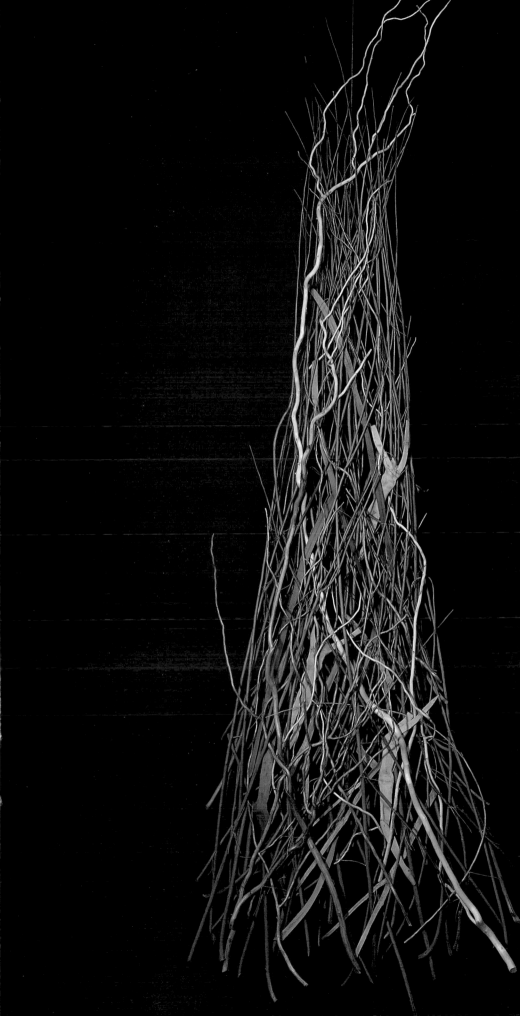

79   Faith Ringgold   *No More War Story Quilt Part II*

Opposite
80   Donald Reitz   *Giver*

81 Dina Barzel *Green Egg*

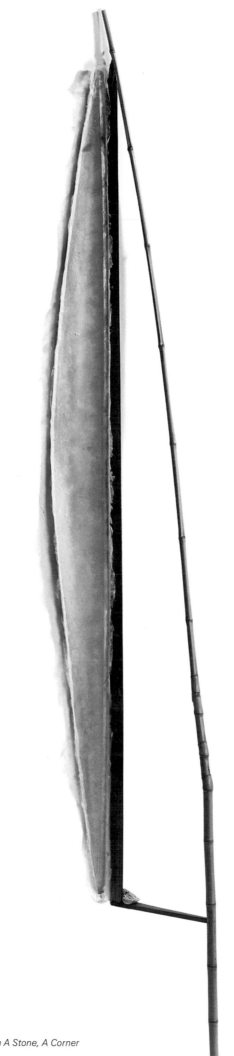

82   Winifred Lutz   *Leaf Covered Sun, Time In A Stone, A Corner*

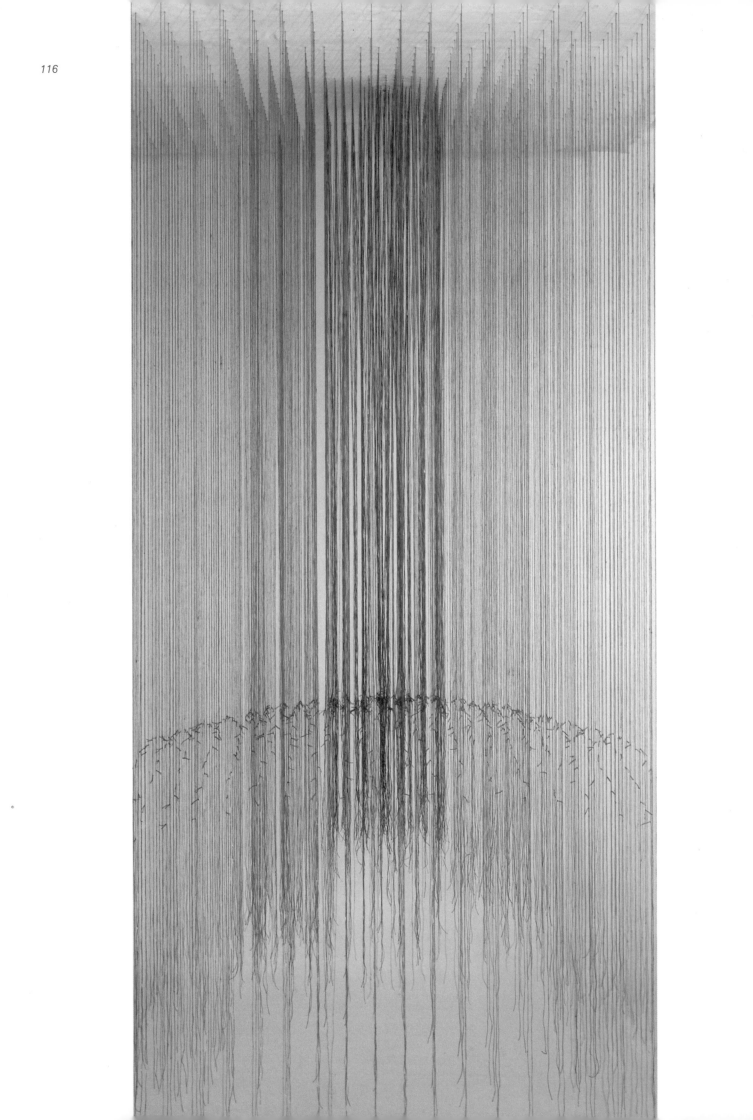

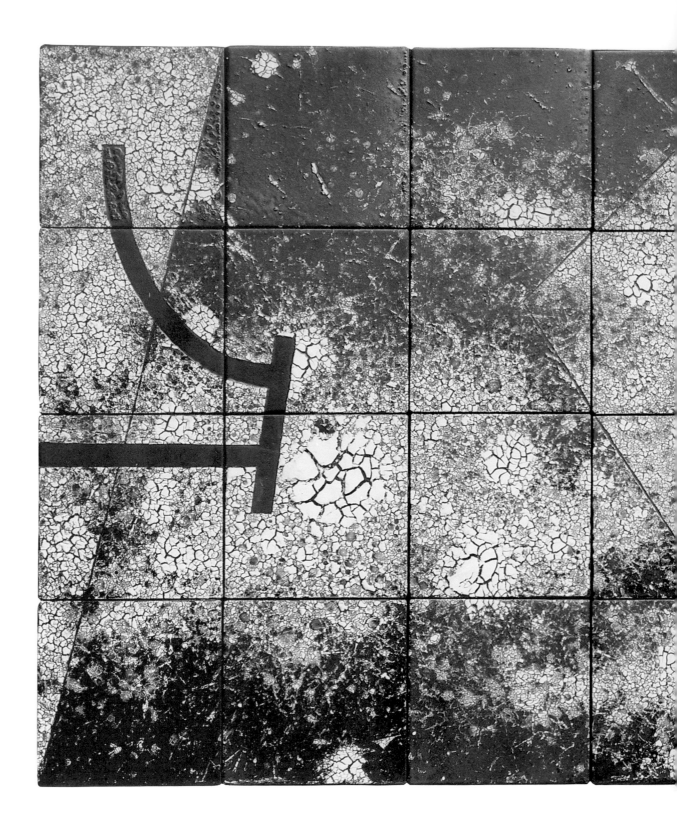

85   Robert Sperry   #565

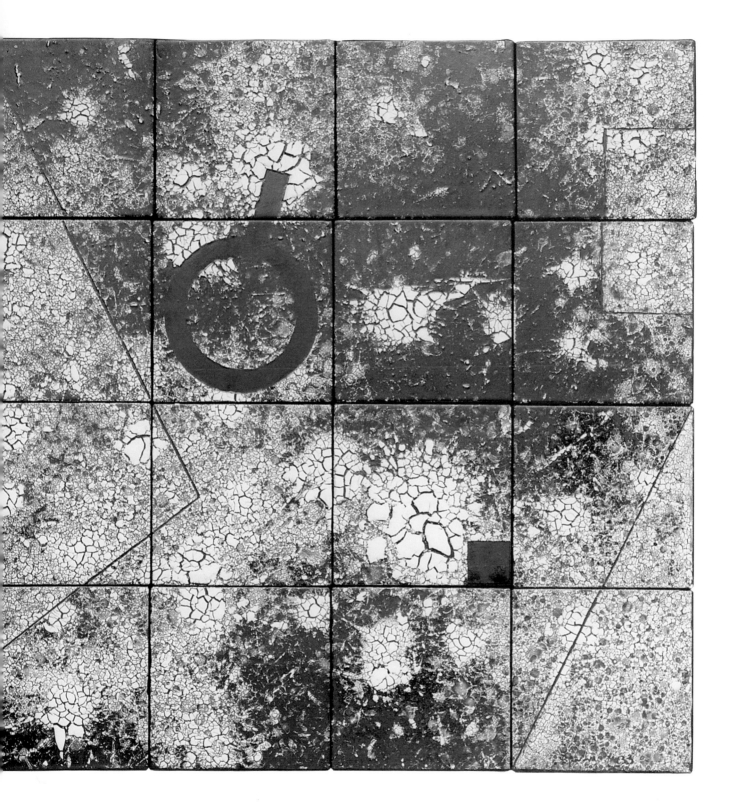

86 Walter Nottingham *Shrine*

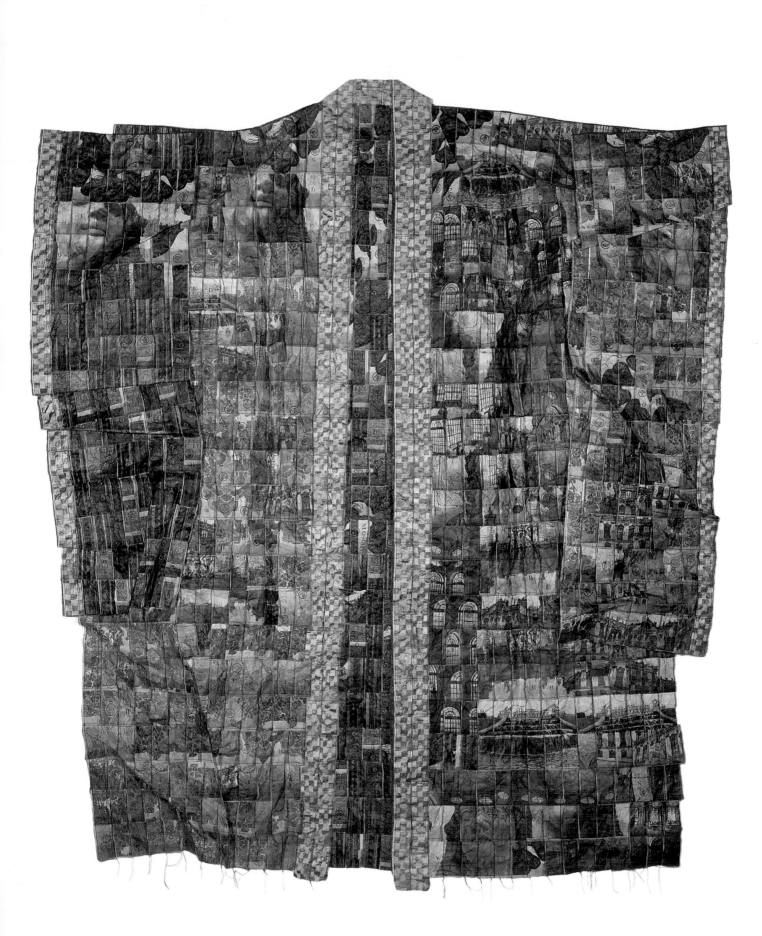

87   Katherine Westphal   *Past Splendor*

88   Dominic Di Mare   *Domus Series #7, Darkest River*

89   Karyl Sisson   *Skins*

90 Cynthia Schira *Dark Light*

aire Zeister   *Tri-Color Arch*

92   Anne Wilson   *China Spotted Fur I*

93 Patricia Campbell   Model for *Column III*

94   L. Brent Kington   *Europa*

Overleaf
95   Warren Seelig   *Brighton*

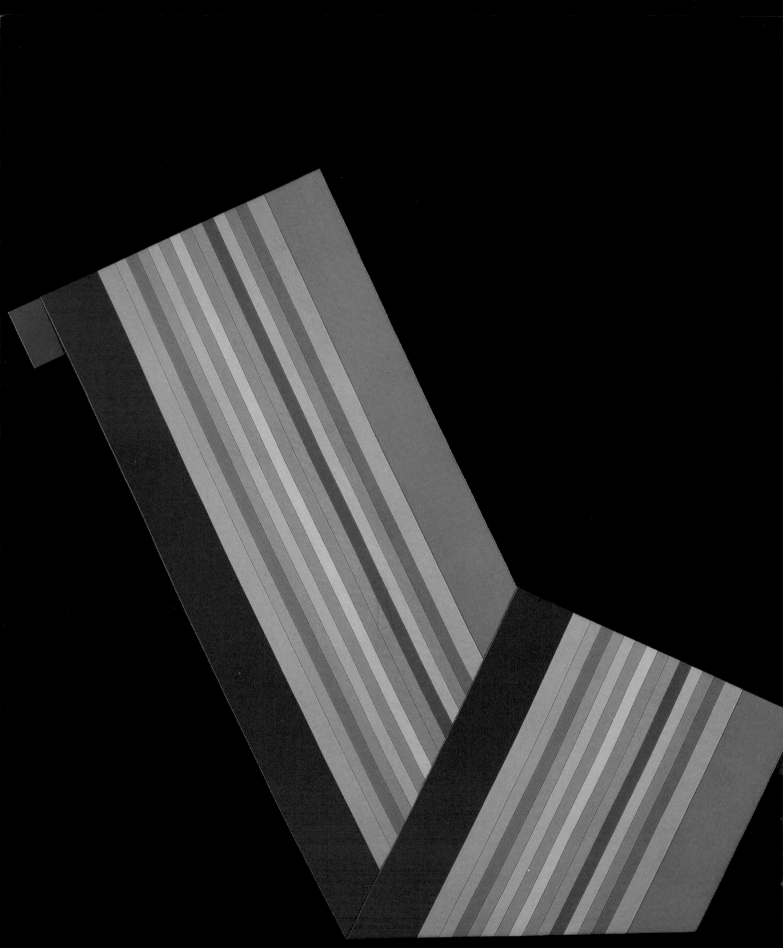

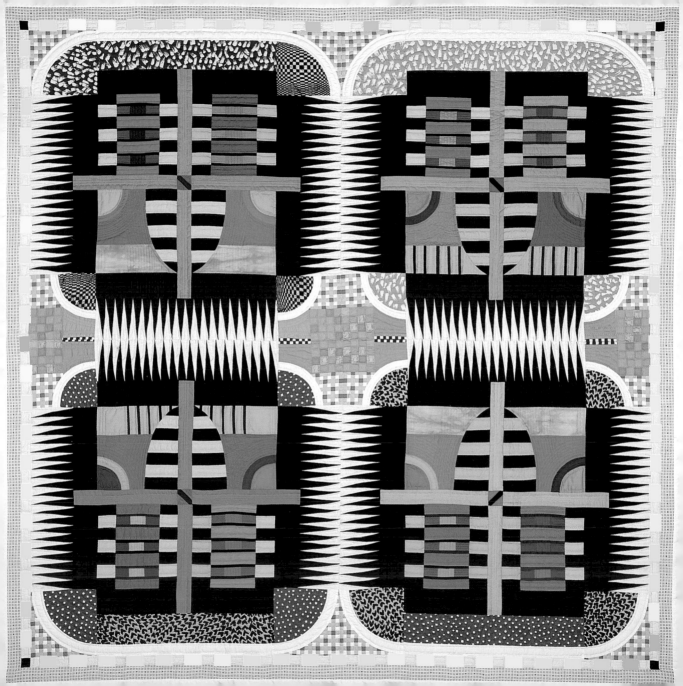

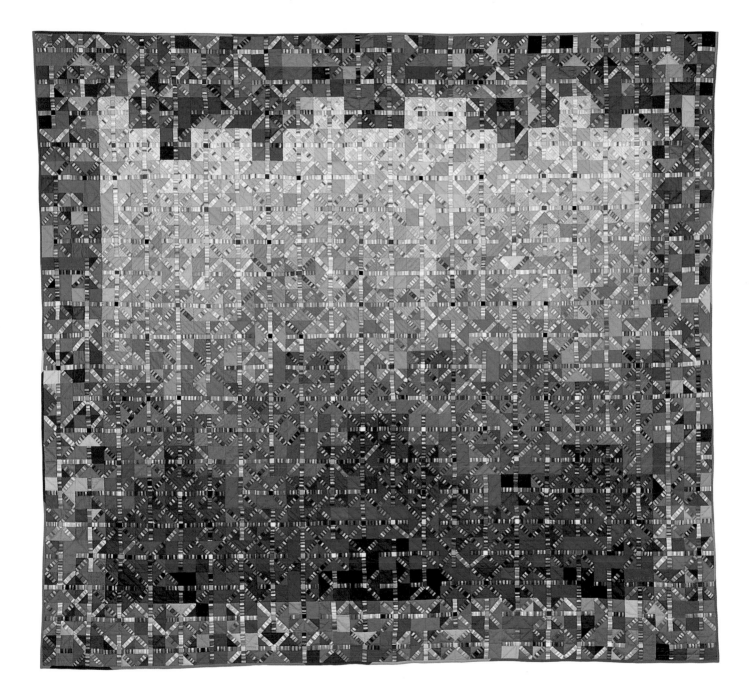

98   Pamela Studstill   *Quilt #53*

Overleaf
99   Sherri Smith   *Galaxy*

100   Jarmila Machova   *Nofret II*

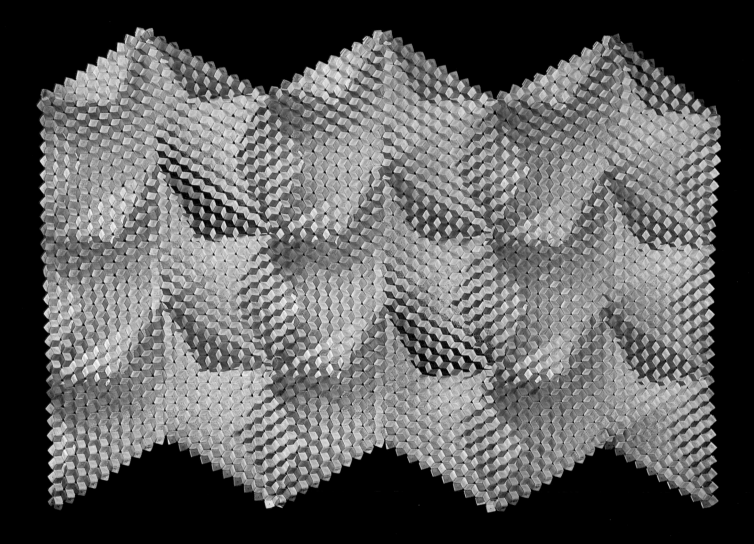

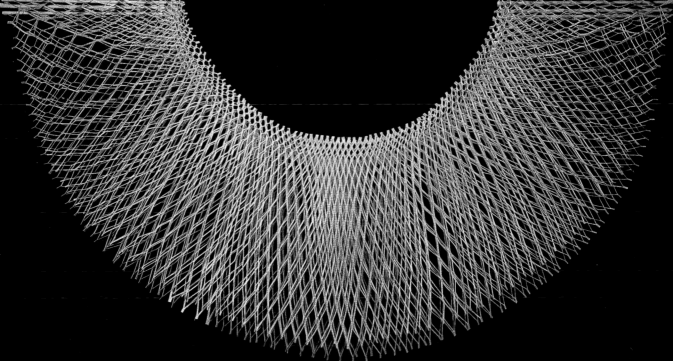

101 John McNaughton *It's Not Easy Keeping It Together*

Opposite
102 Alphonse Mattia *Primates, Geome*

103 Alan Siegel *Aegean*

104 Tommy Simpson *Home Sweet Home*

Overleaf
105 John Cederquist *2-D Thonet*

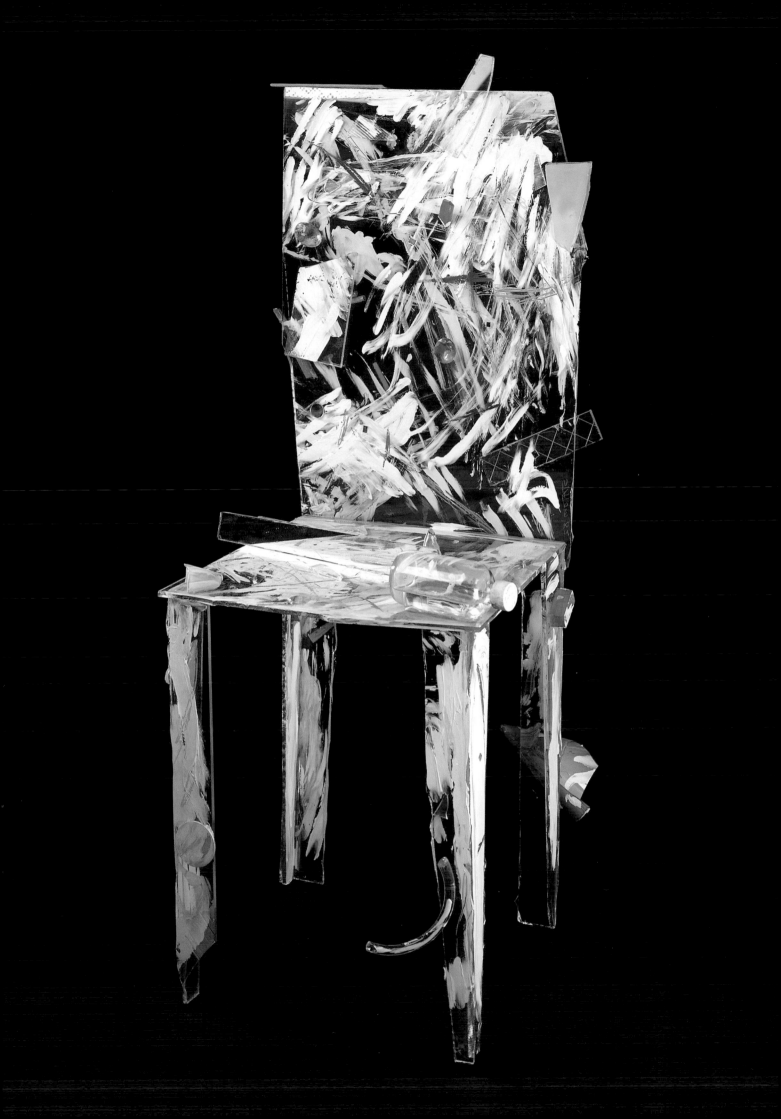

THE OBJECT

MADE FOR USE

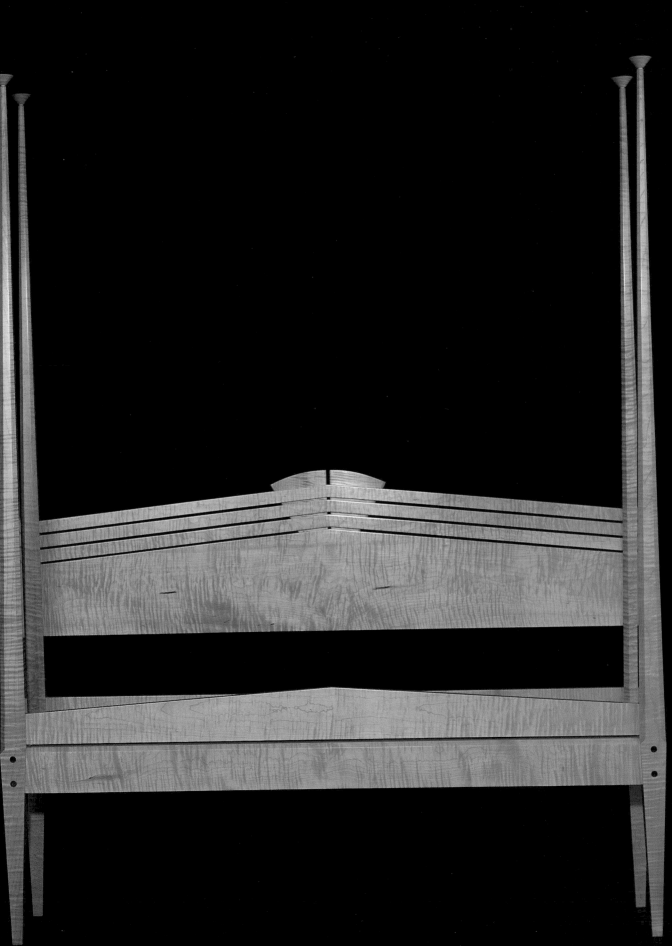

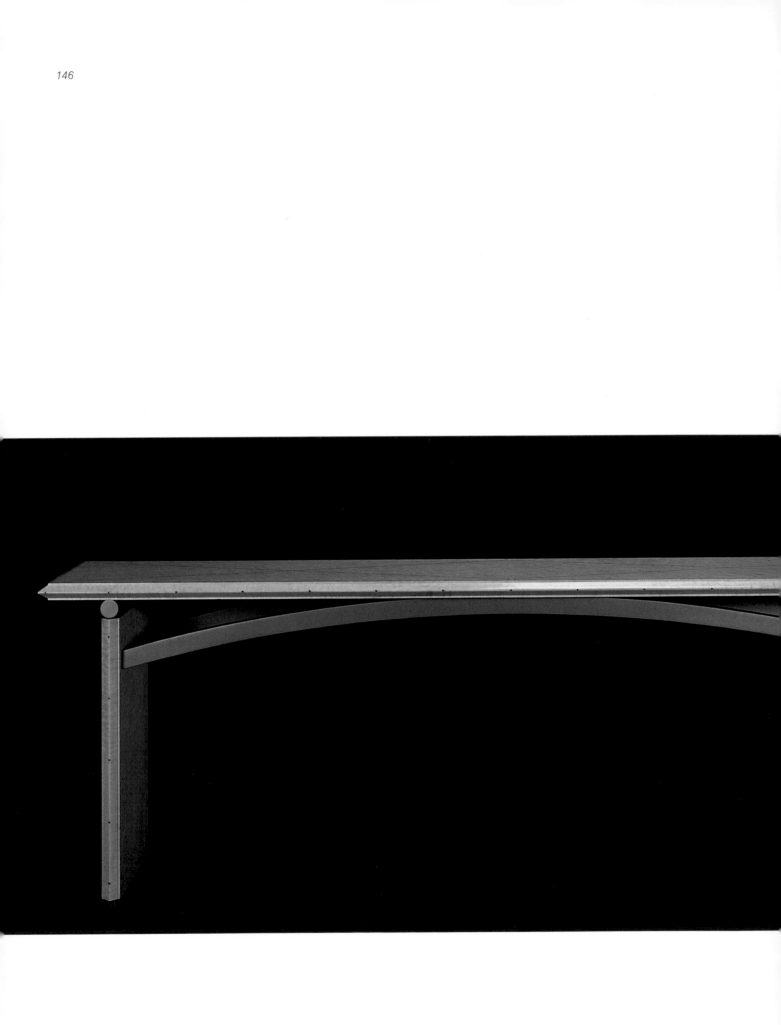

113   Dick Wickman   *Corridor Table*

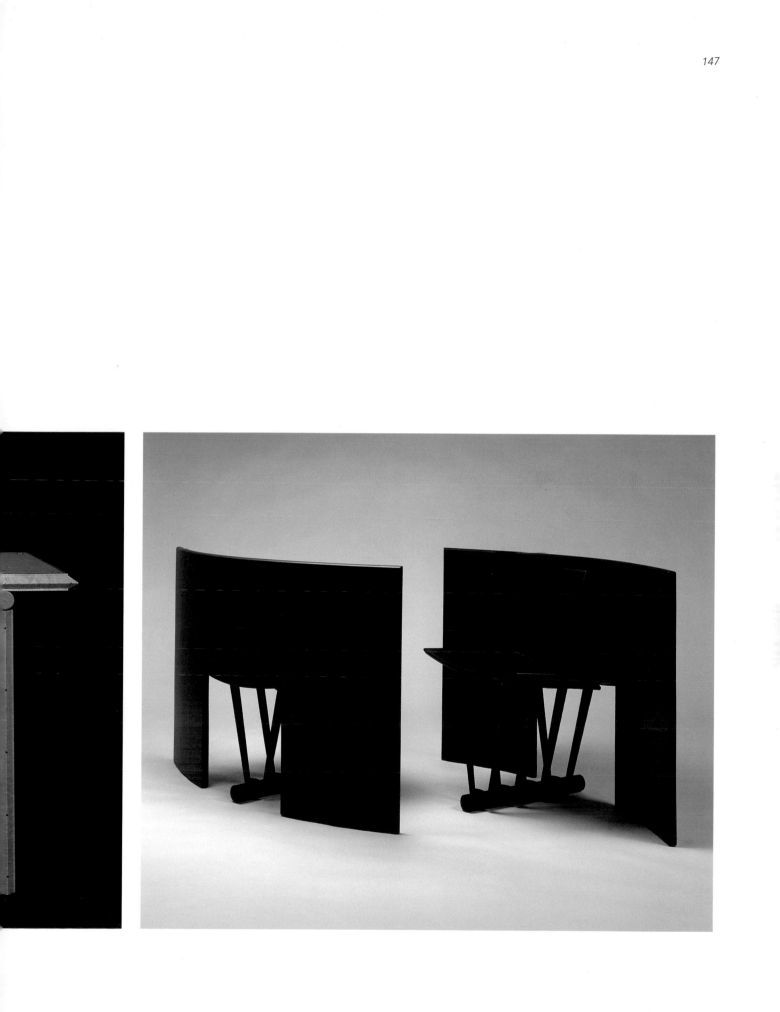

115 Peter S. Dean *Writing Desk*

116 Jere Osgood *Writing Desk*

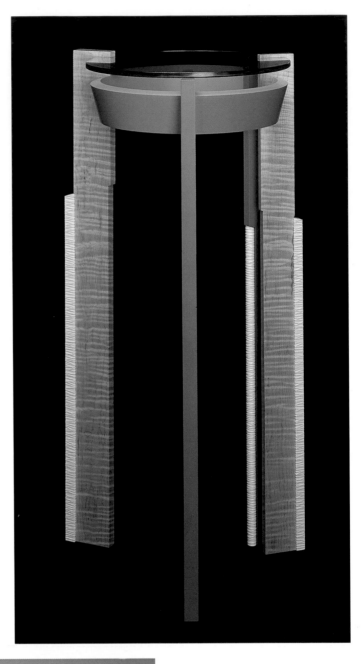

118   Mitch Ryerson   *Traveling Vanity*

117   Michael Pierschalla   *Table #41*

Opposite
119   Wendell Castle   *Ziggu*

120   Thomas Loeser   *Chest of Drawers*

Opposite
121   Peter Shire   *Rod an*
121a *Hourglass Teapot*

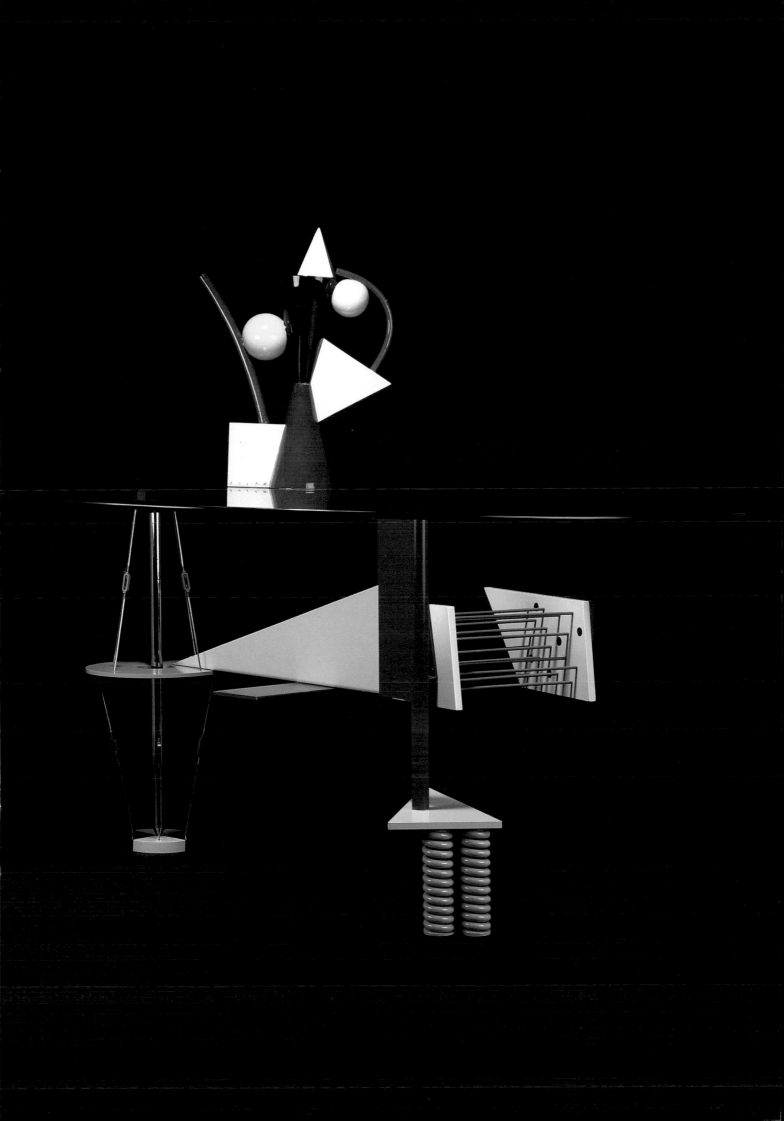

122 Garry Knox Bennett *Table Desk*

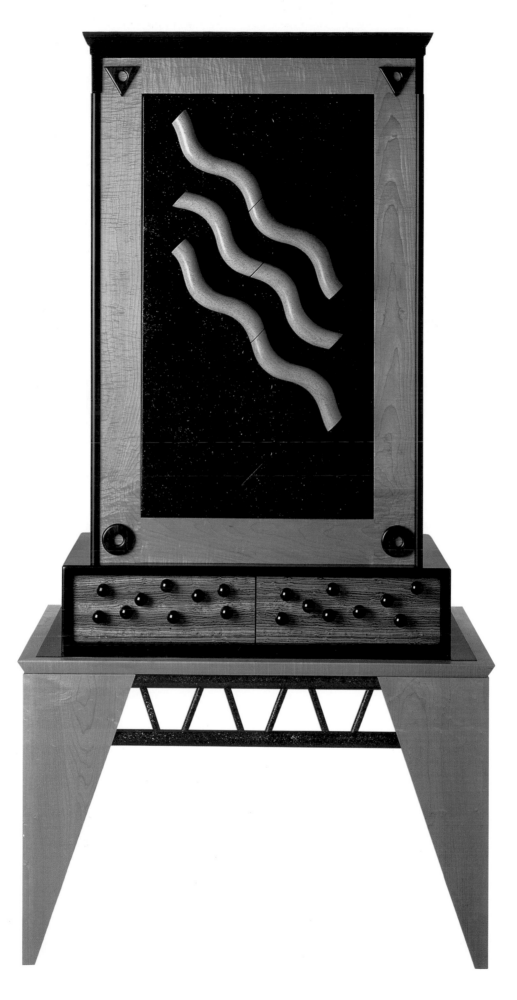

endy Maruyama   *Chest of Drawers*   124   Steven Madsen   *Three Worms Trying to Cross the Jagged Edge*

125 Bob Trotman *Table*

126 Judy Kensley McKie *Fox and Lizard Table*

127   Edward Zucca   *Table of the Future*

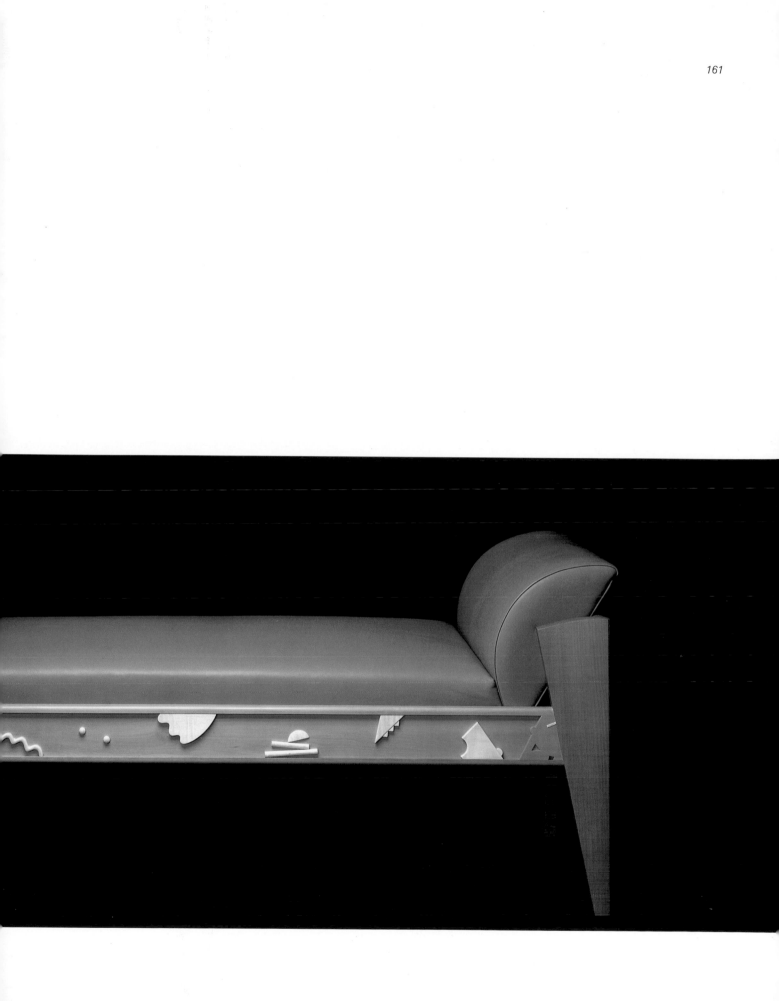

128   Rosanne Somerson   *Upholstered Bench*

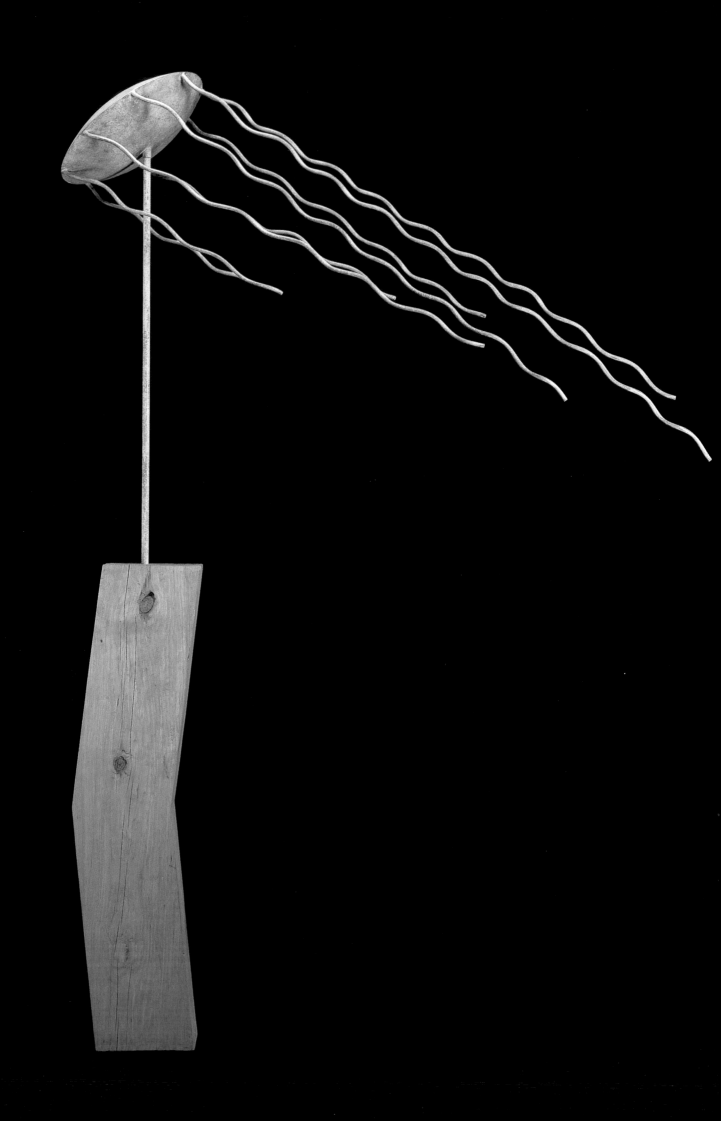

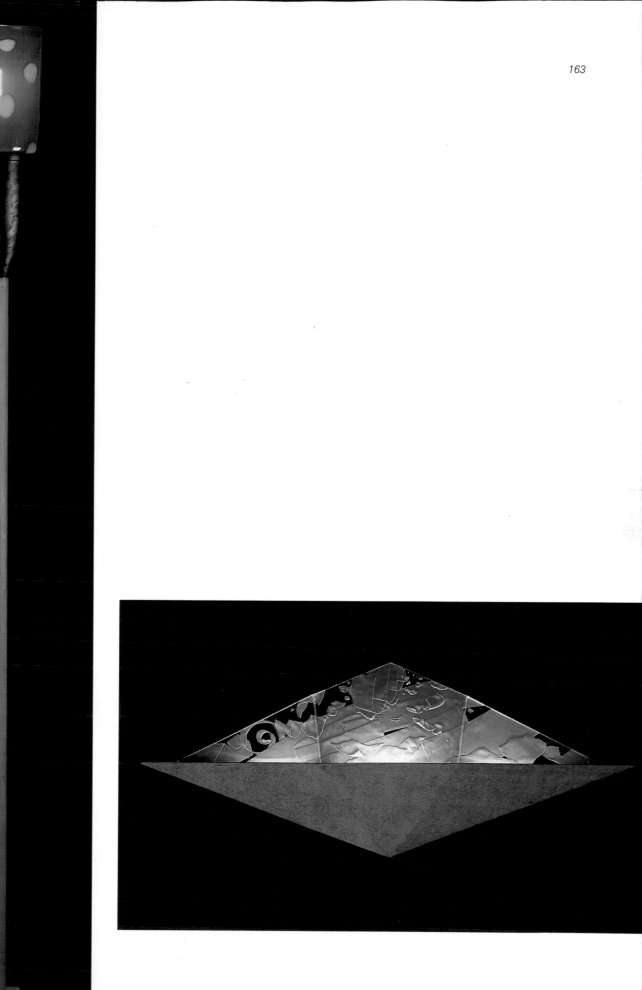

Opposite
129   Jonathan Bonner   *Weathervane*

130   Louis Mueller   *Lamp*

Above
131   Ray King   *Aurora Sconce*

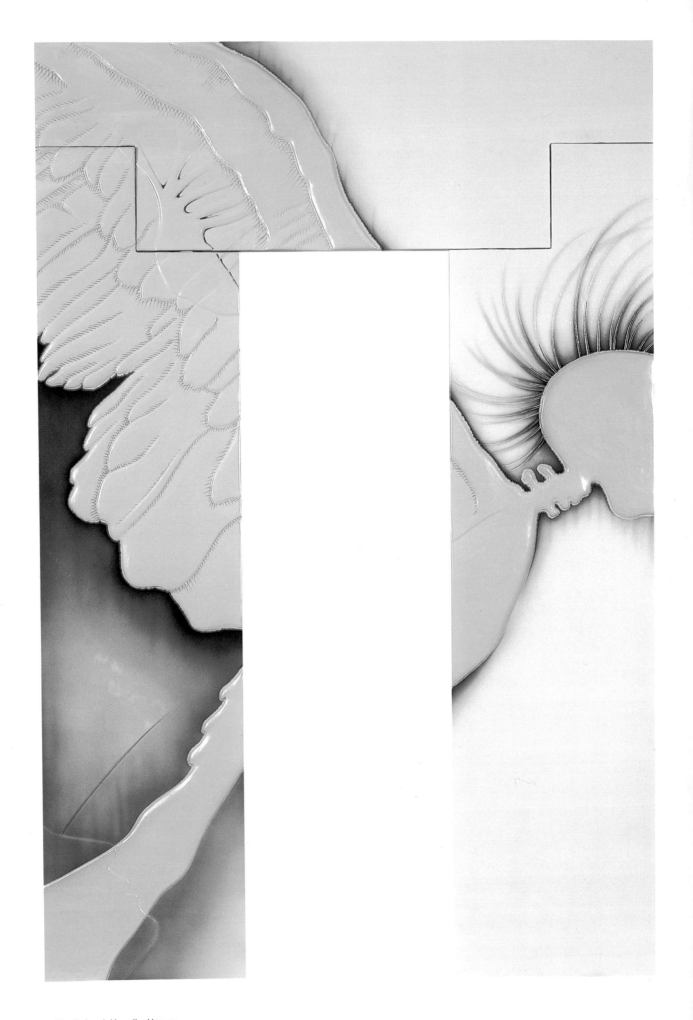

132 Deborah Horrell *Heaven*

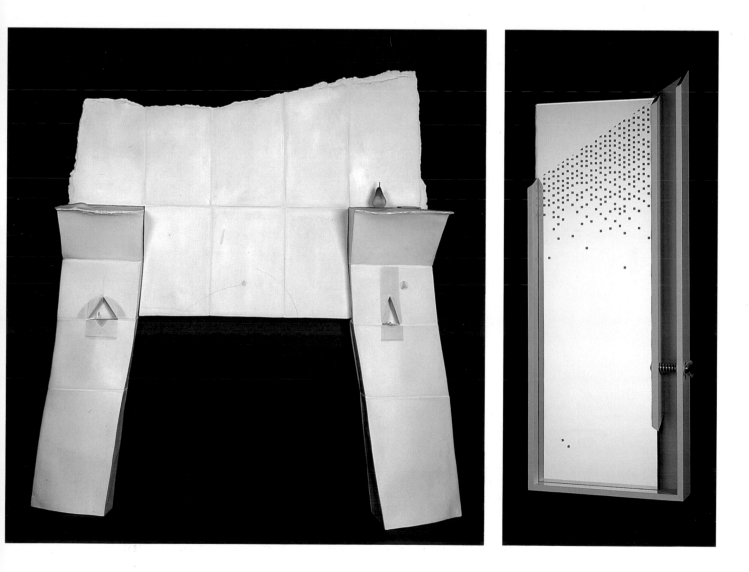

133 Paula Colton Winokur *Fireplace Site I*

134 Gail Fredell Smith *Citicorp Pink*

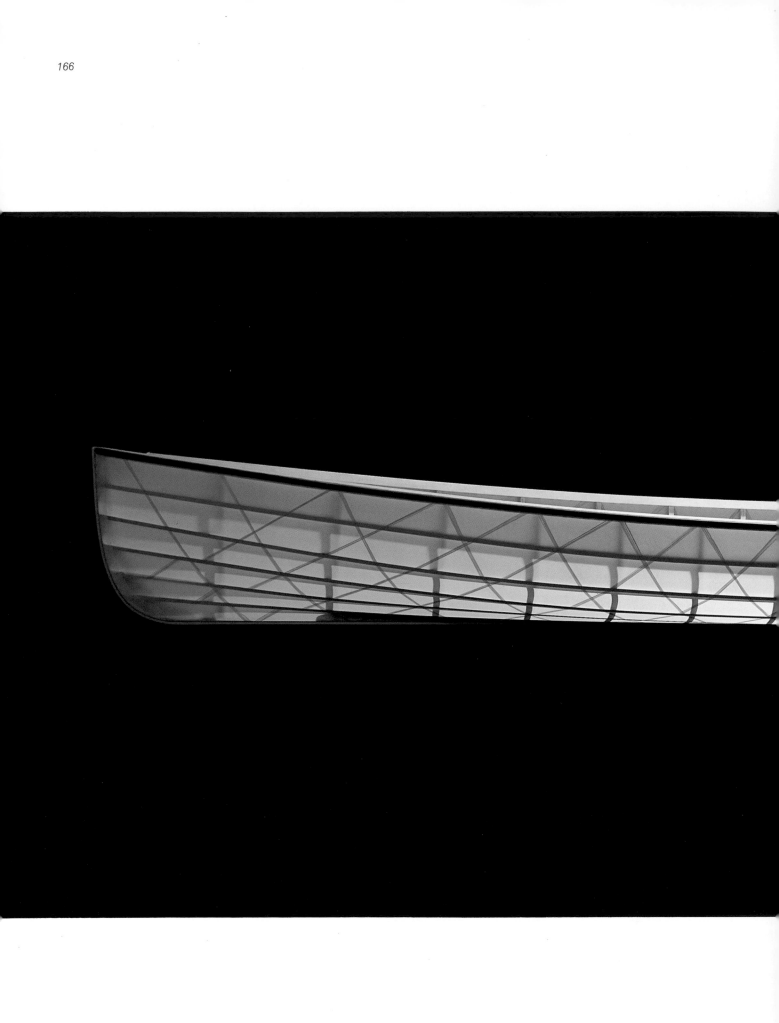

135 Platt Monfort *Snowshoe 12*

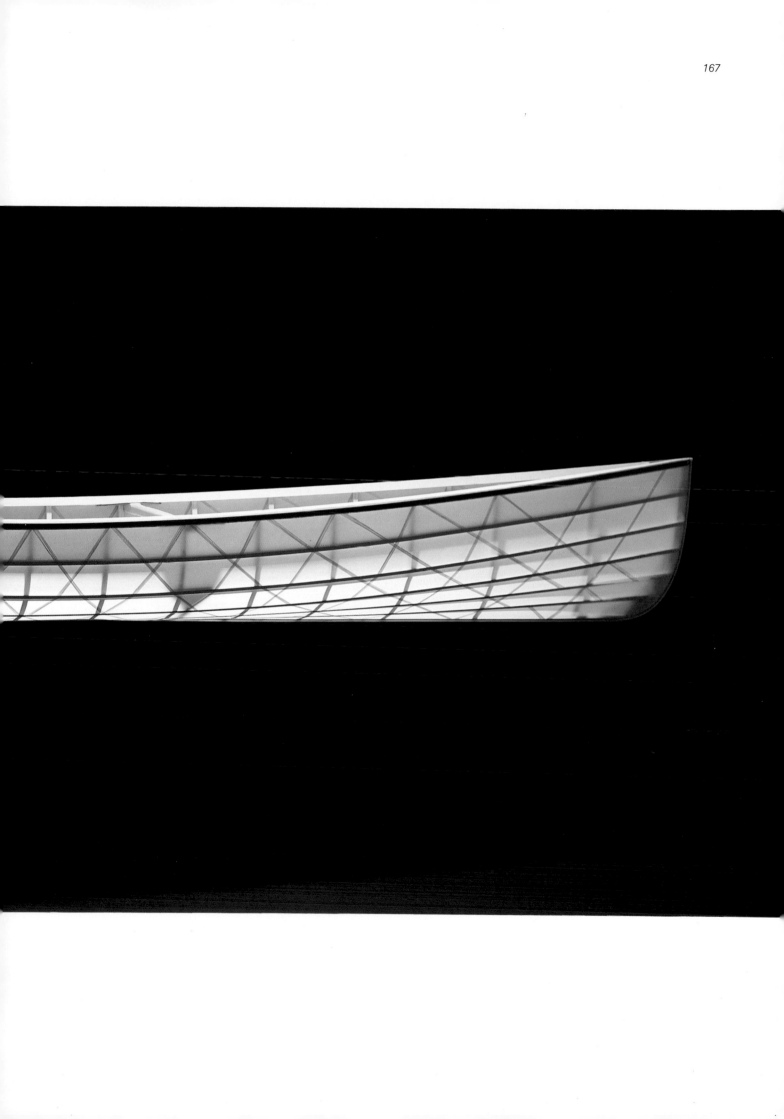

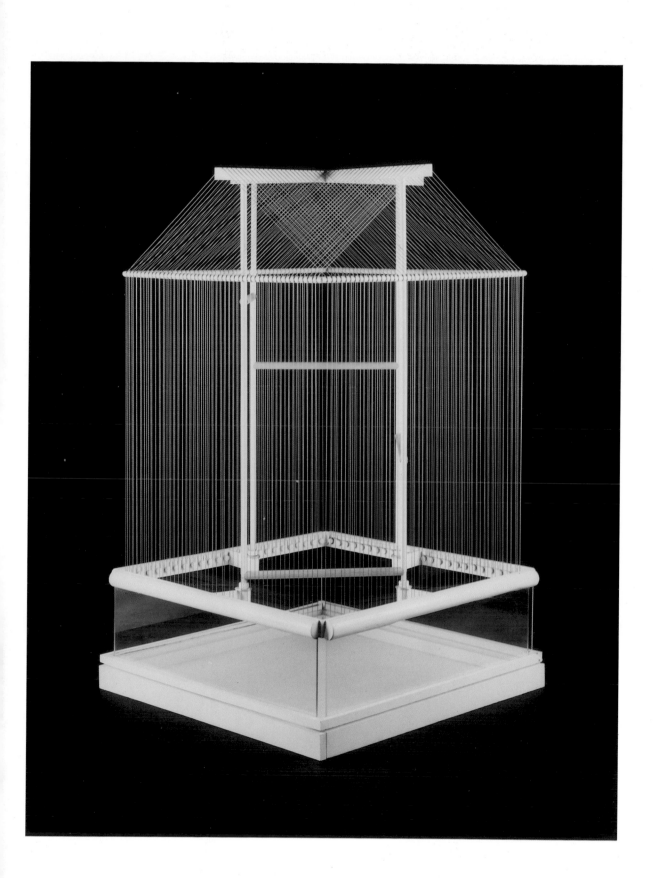

an Ohama   *Replica of Southampton, New York House*   137   Belmont Freeman   *Bird Cage*

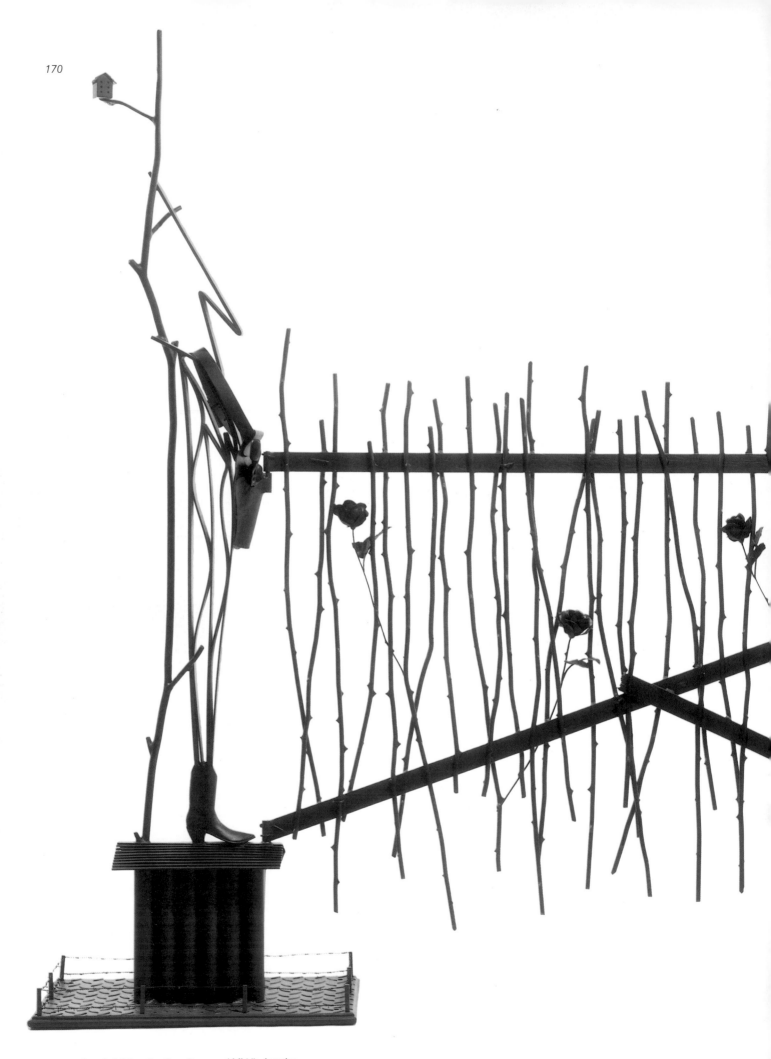

138   Gary S. Griffin   *Cap Gun, Roses and Middle America*

Detail of *Cap, Gun, Roses and Middle America*

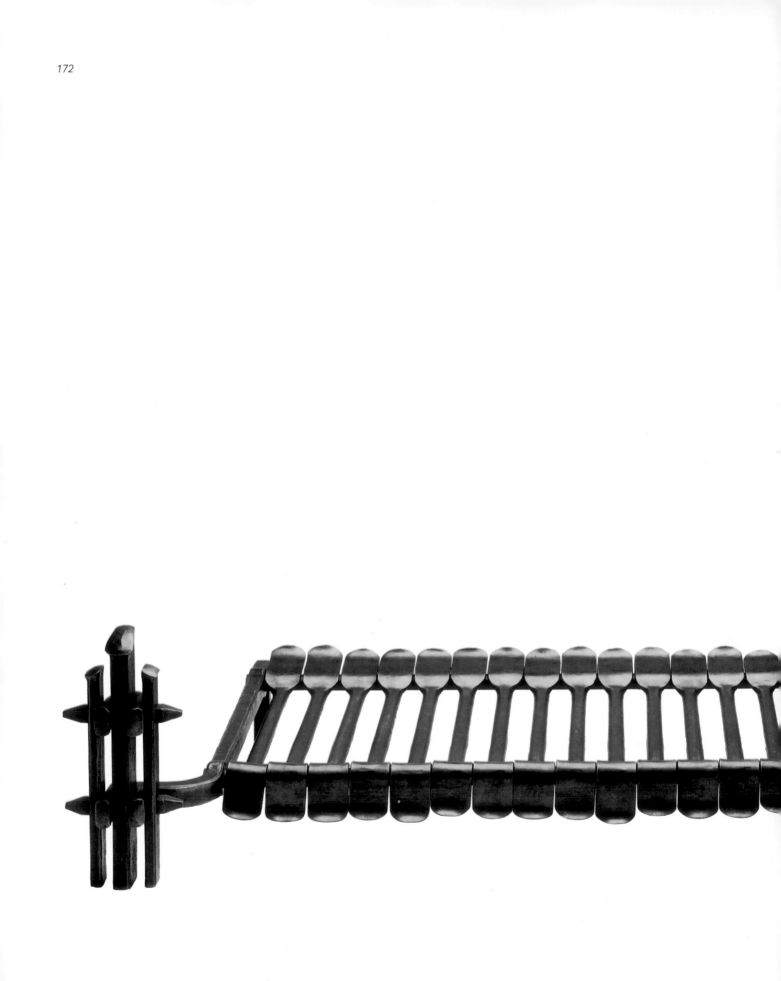

139   Tom Joyce   *Fire Hearth Grate*

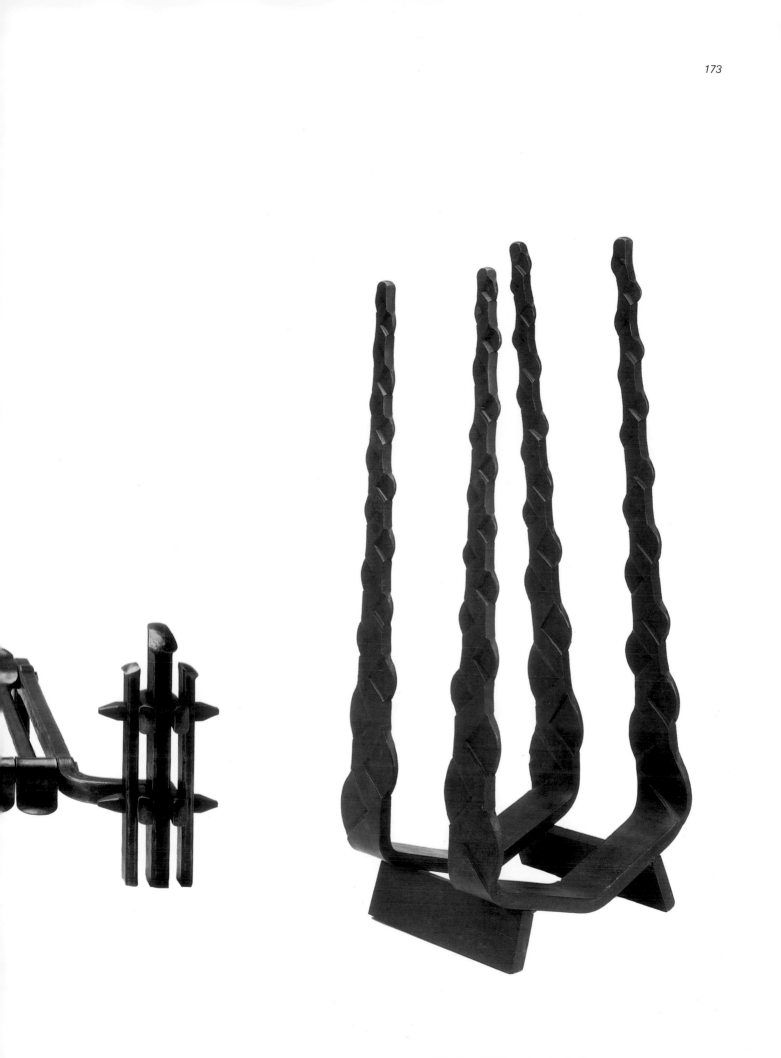

140   Russell C Jaqua Jr.   *Log Basket*

Detail of *Lectern*

141 Albert Paley *Lectern*

142 Gregory Litsios *Floor Standing Candelabrum*

143   Glen C. Simpson   *Number Two Shovel*

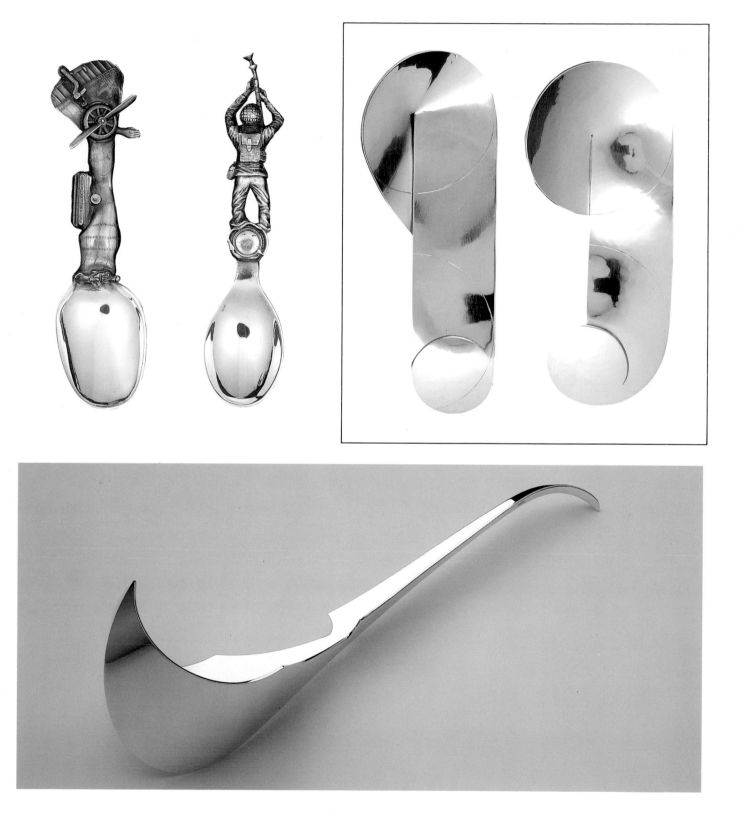

Above, left
144 J. Fred Woell   left, *Aero Setdown*
right, *All's Calm on the Western Front*

Above, right
145 John Prip *Spoons*

Below
146 Ronald Hayes Pearson *Ladle*

Above
147 Phillip Baldwin *Steak Knife Set II*

Below
148 Edward Frederick Burak *Smoking Pipes*

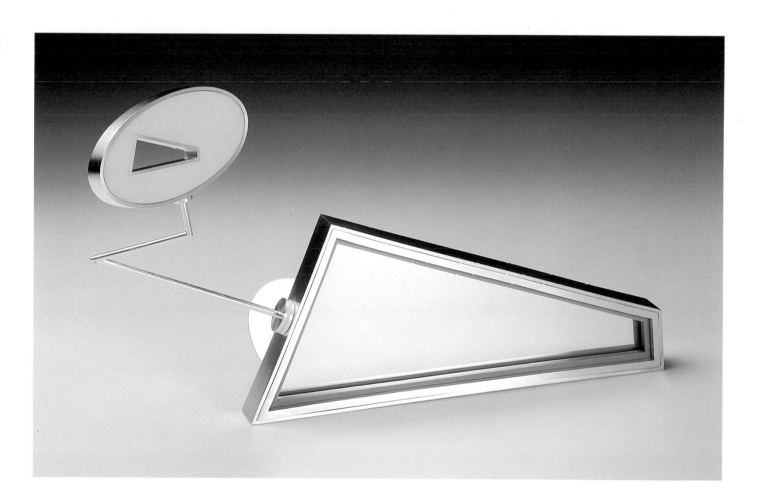

149   Billie Jean Theide   *Mirror Image*

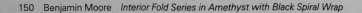

150   Benjamin Moore   *Interior Fold Series in Amethyst with Black Spiral Wrap*

151 William Bernstein/Katherine Bernstein *Face Goblets*

152 Stephen Smyers *Vienna Wine Goblets*

153 Steven Maslach *Lustre Stemmed Funnel Glasses*

154 Pat Flynn *Drinking Beakers*

155 Chunghi Choo *Fleur*

156 John C. Marshall   *Cocktail Server*

157 Fritz Dreisbach   *Crystal Optic Reversible Champagne and Cognac Goblets*

158   Karen Karnes   *Covered Vessel*

159 Byron Temple *Covered Jars*

188

Above
160 Rudolf Staffel *Light Gatherer*

Below
161 David Shaner *Pillow Form*

162   Val M. Cushing   *Covered Jar*

Above
163 Edward S. Eberle *A Dream; One Man Cup; A Bird, a Fox, and a Rabbit*

Below
164 James Makins *Dinnerware and Goblets*

Opposite
165 Harris Deller *Whit*

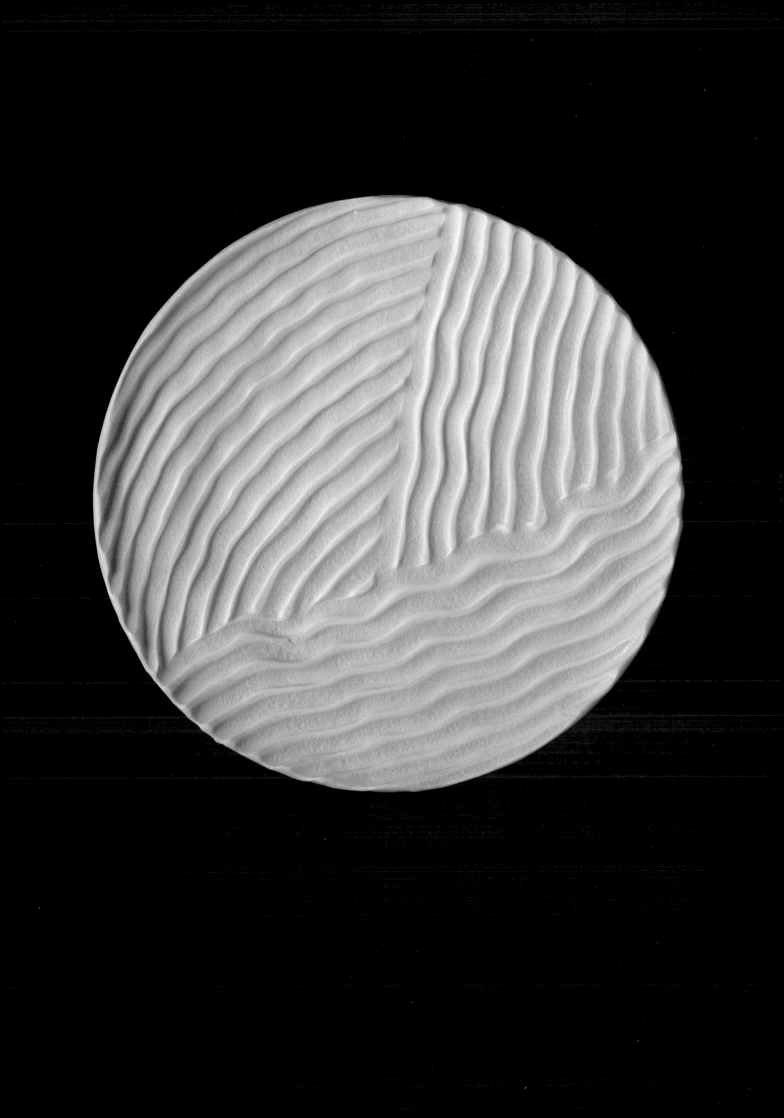

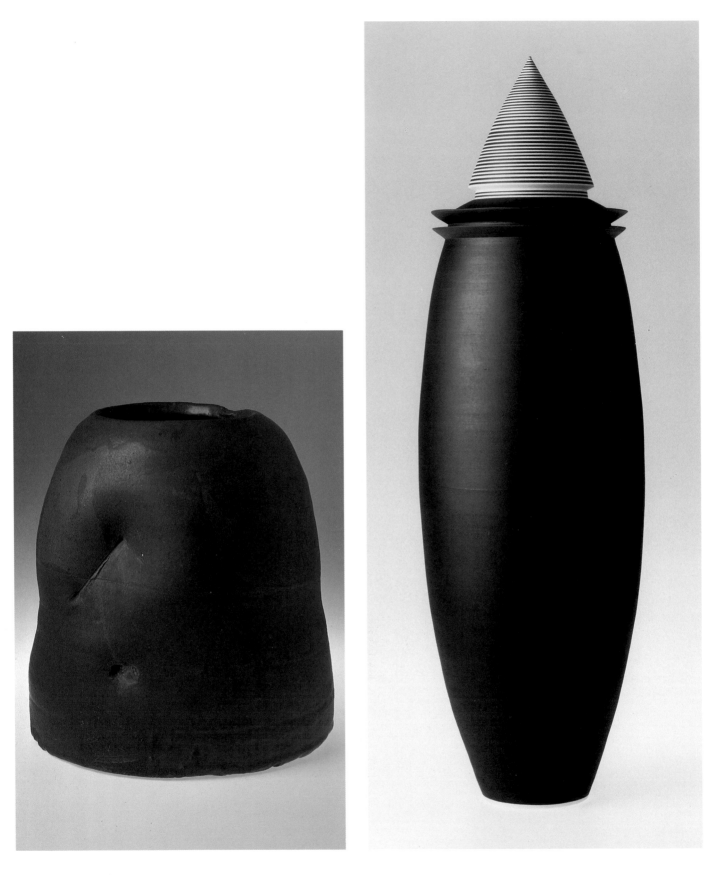

166   Robert Turner   *Dome Form*

167   Roseline Delisle   *L'Ogive*

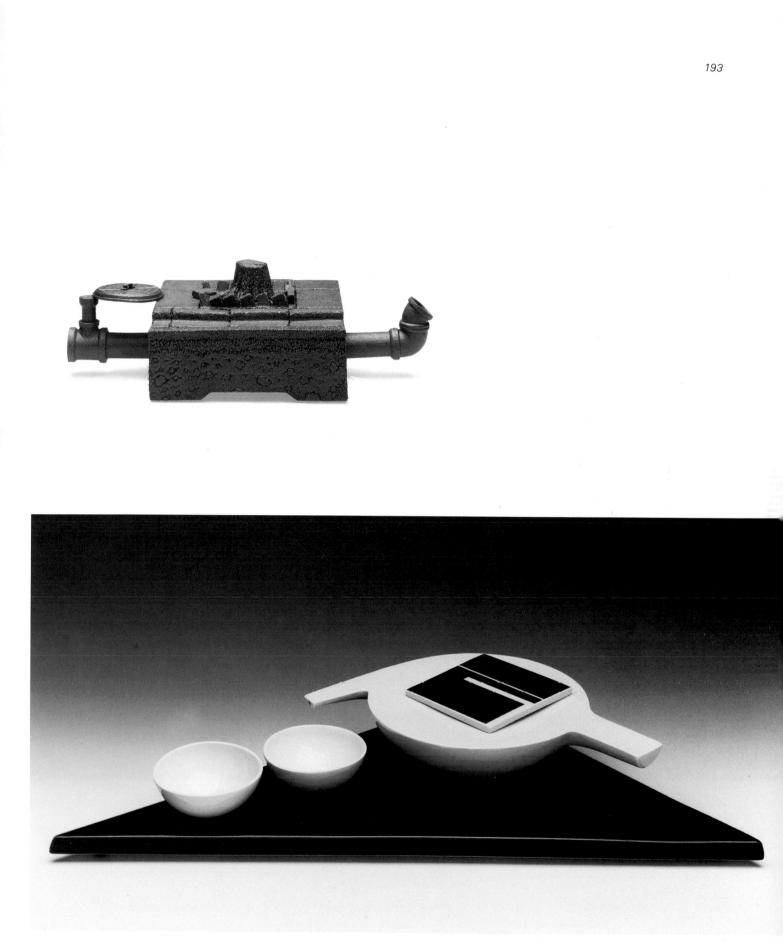

168　Richard Notkin　*Landform Teapot (Variation #12), Yixing Series*

Below
169　Marek Cecula　*Ceremonial Set*

Above
170 John Parker Glick   *Teapot*

Below
171 Chris Gustin   *Teapot*

174 Kenneth Ferguson *Basket*

175 Otto Natzler *Flaring Form*

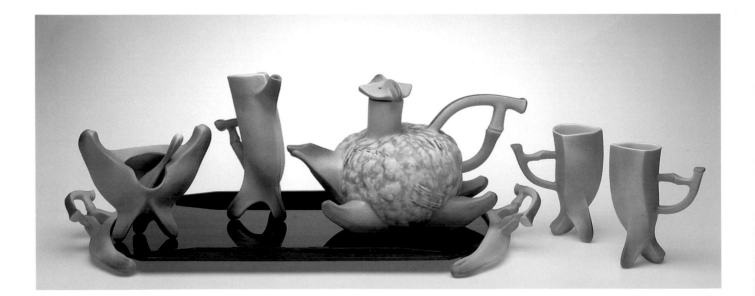

<table>
<tr><td>Above</td><td></td><td>Below</td><td></td><td>Opposite</td></tr>
</table>

179 William P. Daley *Turner's Court*

180   Elsa Rady   *Deductive Rigor*

181   Sylvia Seventy   *Breeder's Flock*

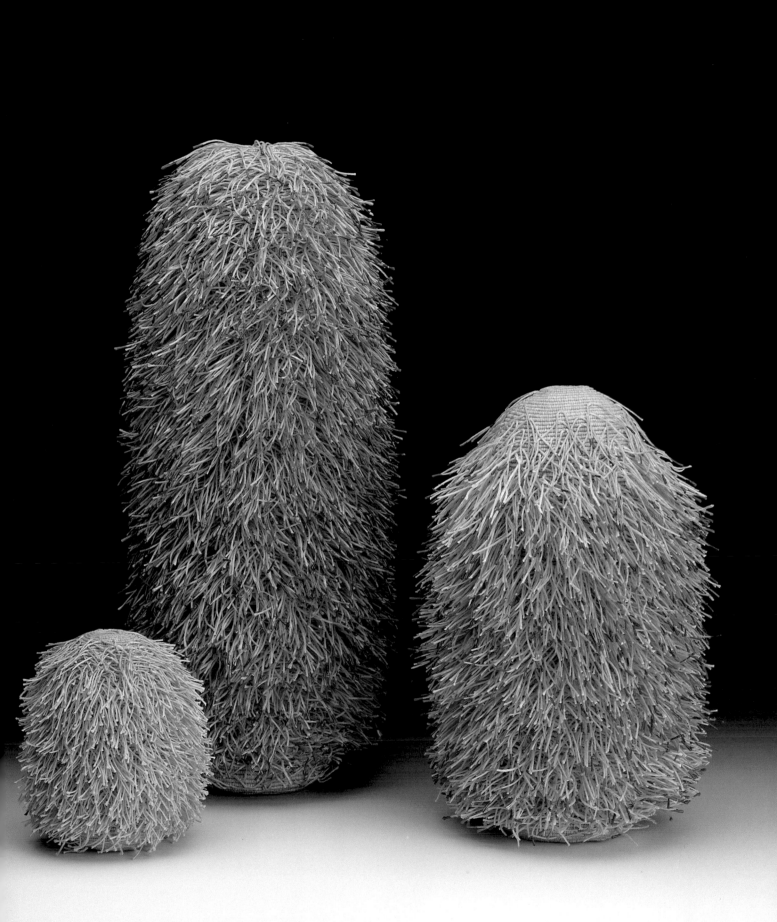

183 Del Stubbs *Manzanitas*

184 Bob Stocksdale *Salad Bowl*

Above
187 Stephen M. Paulsen *Scent Bottles*

Below
188 David Ellsworth *Signature Bowl #5*

Above
189 Lillian Elliott / Pat Hickman *Leaf Basket*

Below
190 Ruth Duckworth Untitled *(Five Porcelain Forms)*

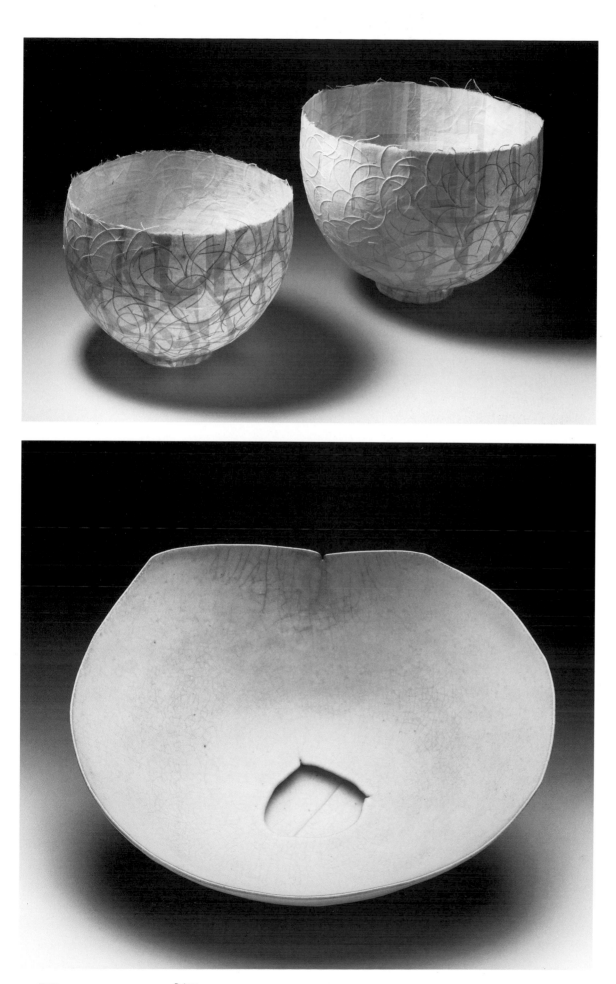

Above
191 Kay Sekimachi *Bowls*

Below
192 Richard E. DeVore *Bowl*

Above
193 Kevin Cannon *Begauge*

Below
194 Ed Rossbach *Red Hunk*

195   John McQueen   *Untitled Basket with Red String*

Above
196 Norma Minkowitz *Passage to Nowhere*

Below
197 Neil Prince and Fran Kraynek-Prince *Torrey Pine Olla*

198　Dorothy Gill Barnes　*Nova Scotia Spruce Basket*

Above
199 Dan Dailey *Garden of Oddities (Science Fiction Vase)*

Below
200 Joel Philip Myers *Contiguous Fragment Series*

Above
201 William Morris *Stone Vessel #3*   Below
202 Sonja Blomdahl *Tobak/Goldbraun/Black*

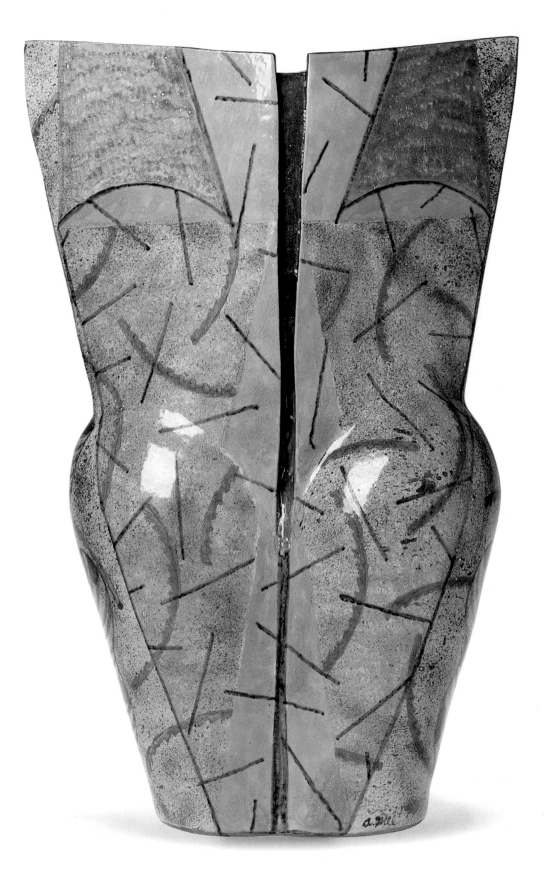

204   Andrea Gill   *Large Vase*

205 Mark Abildgaard *Ritual Vessel*

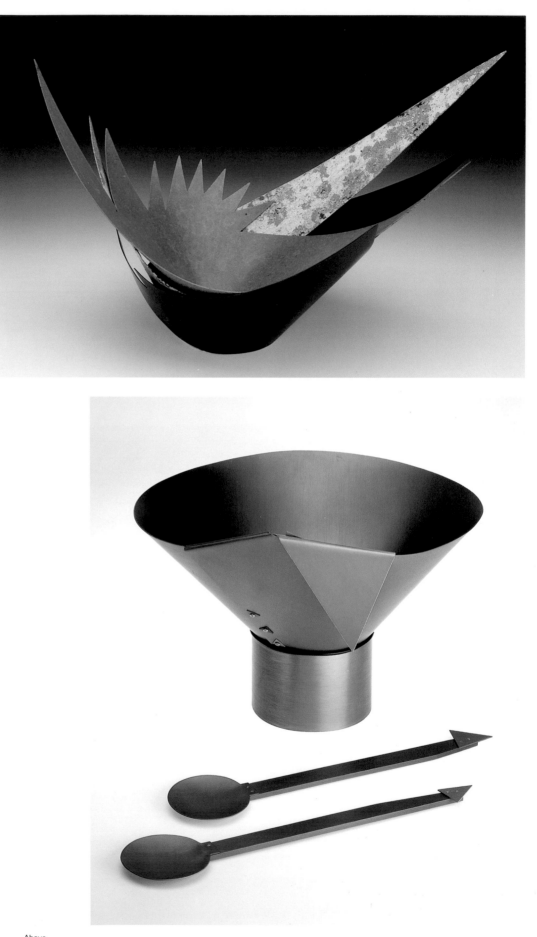

Above
208 Helen Shirk   *Vessel*

Below
209 David Tisdale   *Bowl with Serving Spoons*

Above
210 Randy Long   *Vessel for a Ring Master*

Below
211 Andrew Magdanz / Susan Shapiro   *Avery Series: Perfume Bottles*

212 John Donoghue *Plate*

Opposite
213 Ralph Bacerra

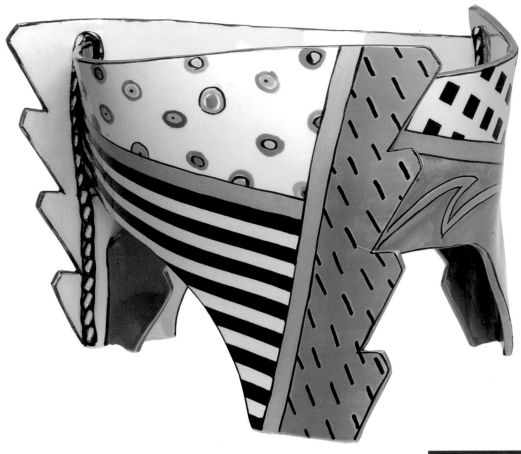

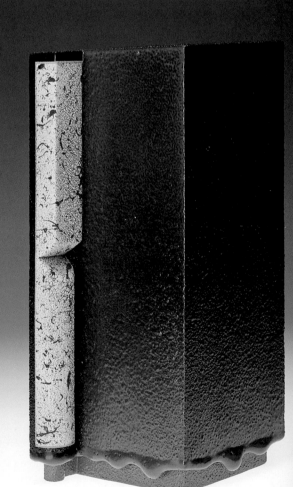

Above
214 Dorothy Hafner   *Lightening Bolt Punch Bowl*

Below
215 Ron Nagle   Untitled

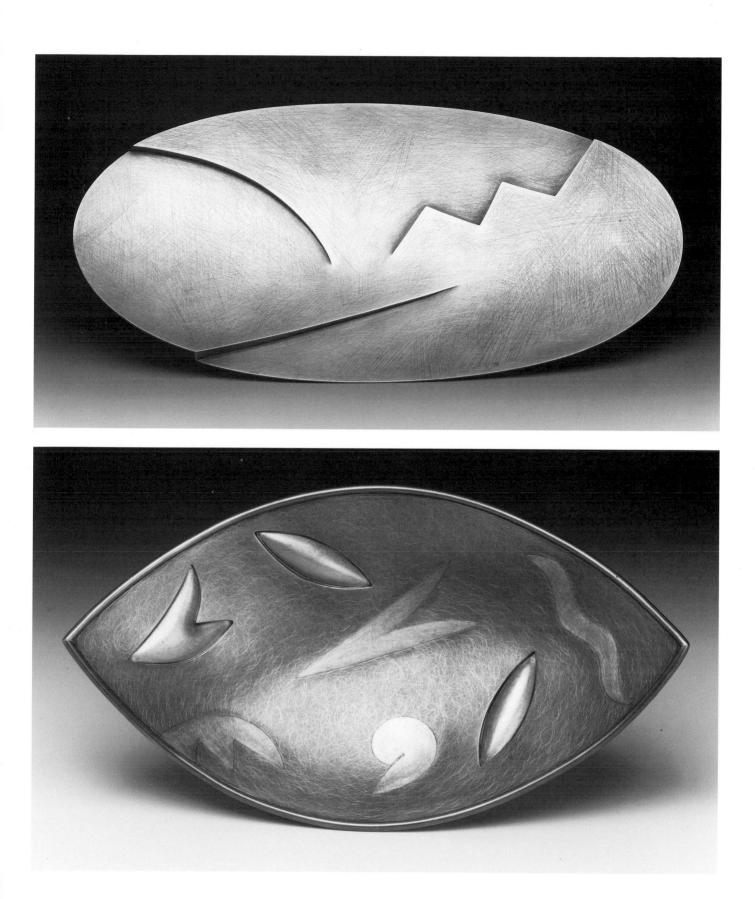

Above
218 Michael Frimkess *Kylix*

Below
219 Adrian Saxe *Untitled Gold Vessel*

Above
220   Rick Dillingham   Untitled

Below
221   Bennett Bean   *Bowl*

222 June Schwarcz *Bowl #917*

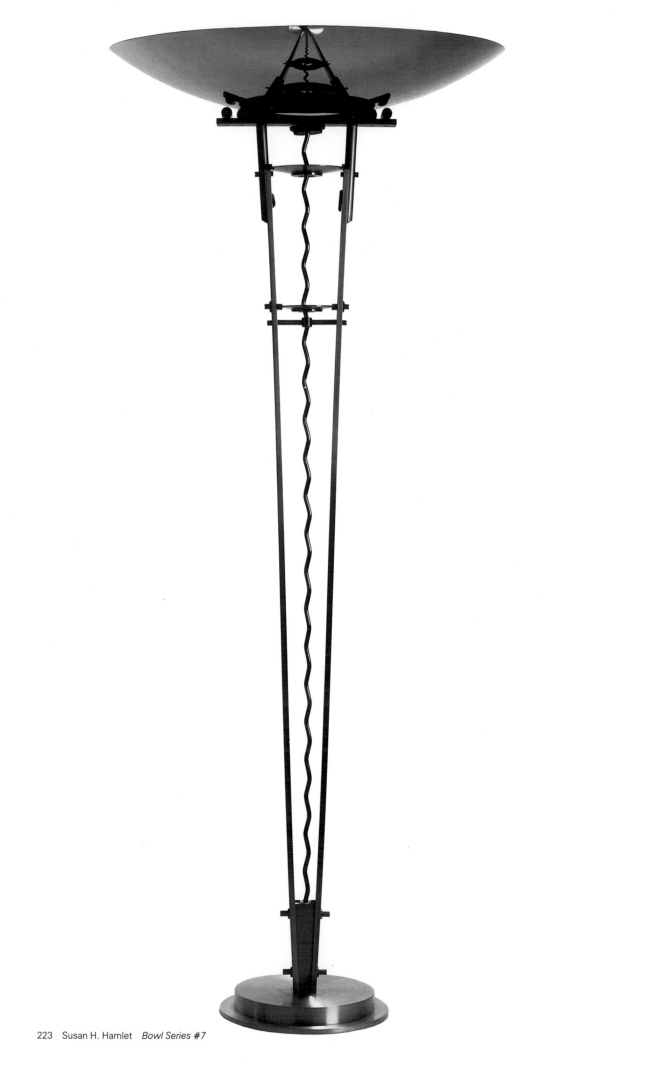

223   Susan H. Hamlet   *Bowl Series #7*

224 Peter Voulkos   Untitled

Opposite, above
225 Dennis M. Morinaka   *Wonder Blue*

Opposite, below
226 Wayne Higby   *Firewall Gap*

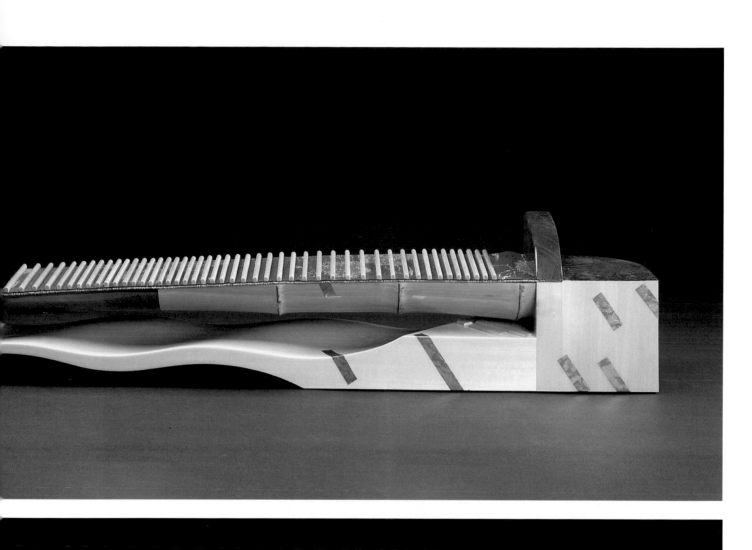

227   William Underhill   *Kabuto*

Opposite
228   Cliff Garten   *Sp*

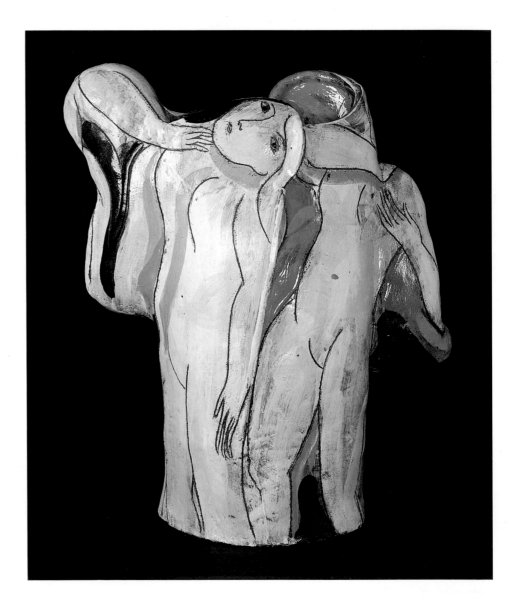

229 Rudy Autio *Going to the Sun*

Opposite
230 Arnold Zimmerman

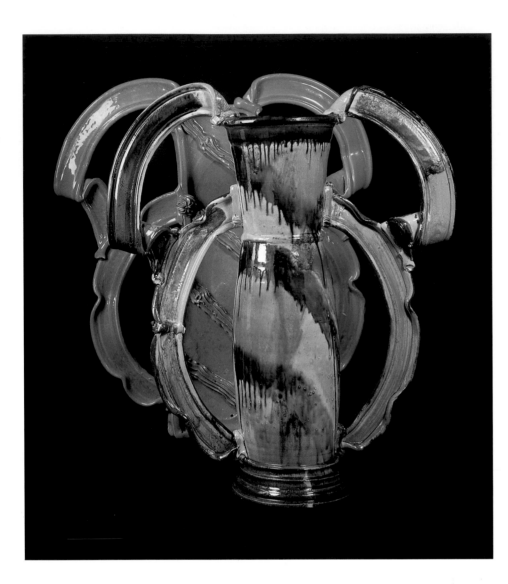

231   Betty Woodman   *Four Handled Vase with Green Shadow*

232   Margie Jervis / Susie Krasnican   *Landscape Vase*

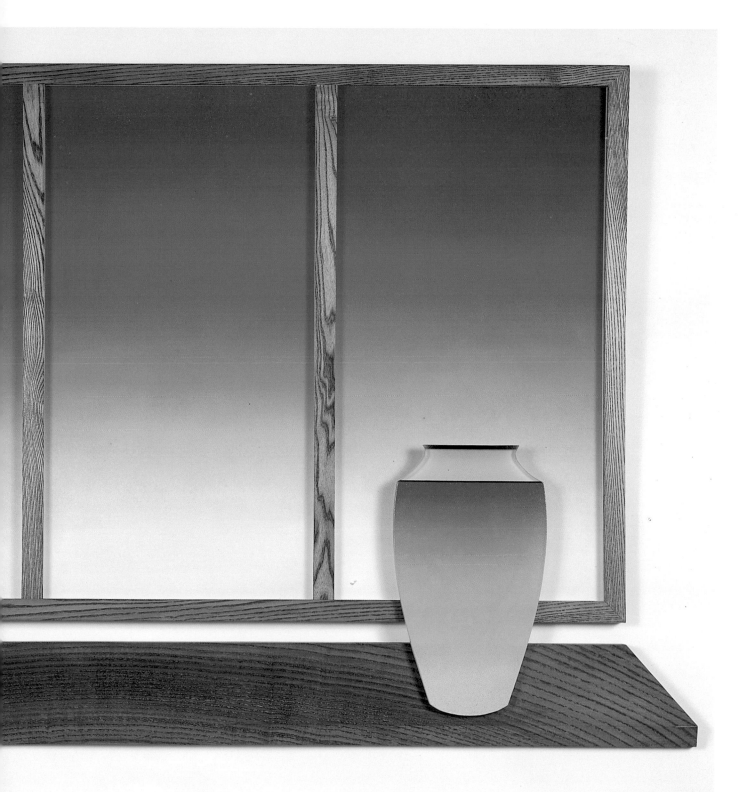

Overleaf
233 Tim Harding   *Memento Mori*

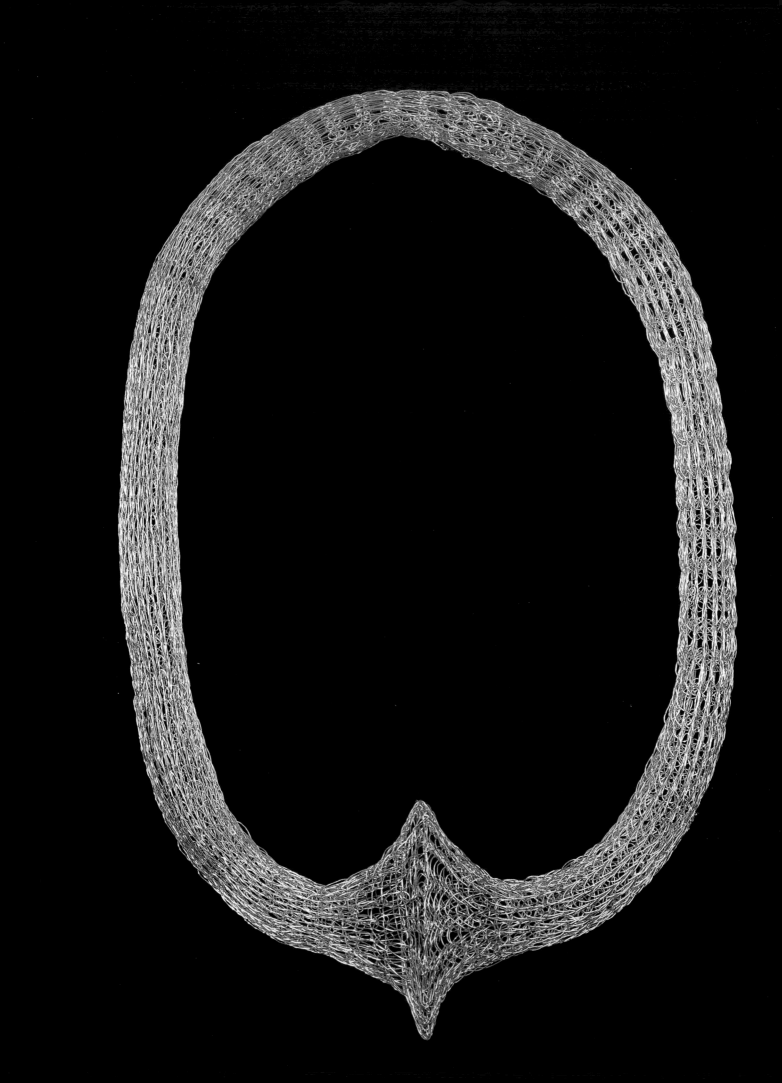

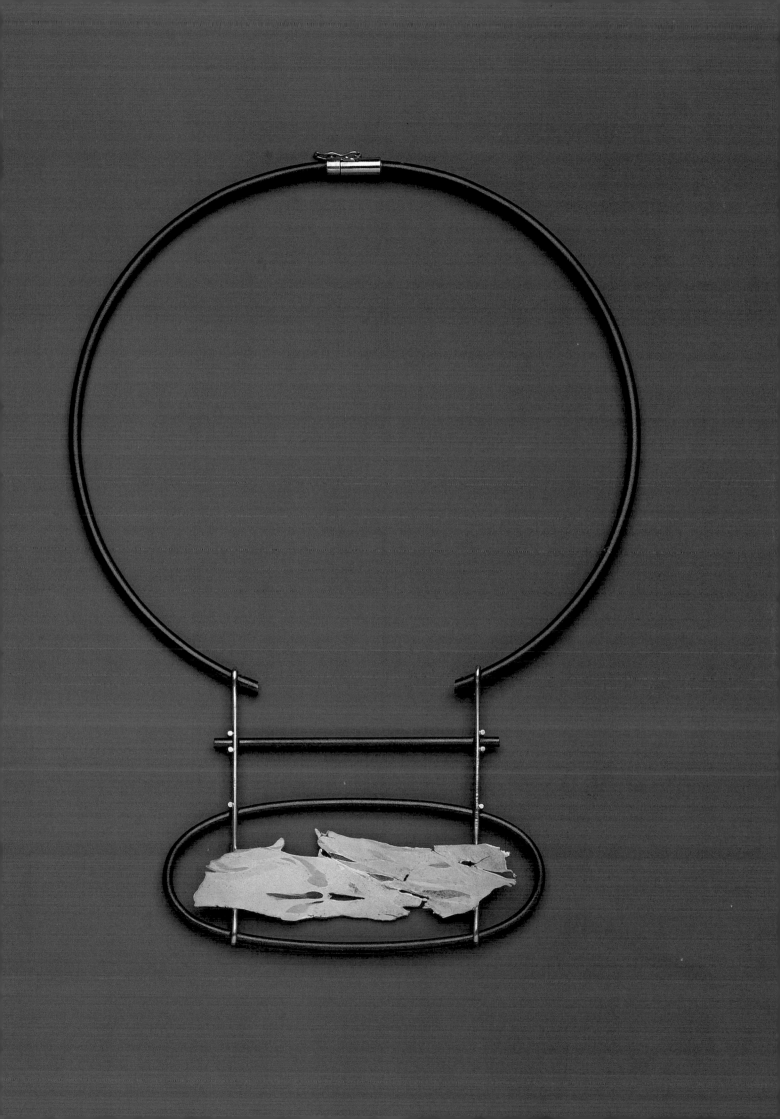

239   Hiroko Sato Pijanowski / Gene Pijanowski   *Neckpiece Gold No. 1, Bracelet Gold No. 1*

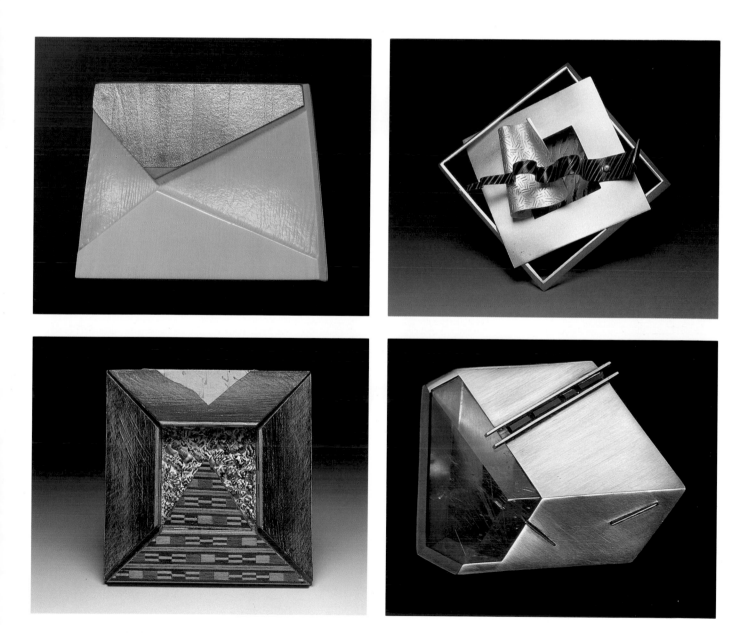

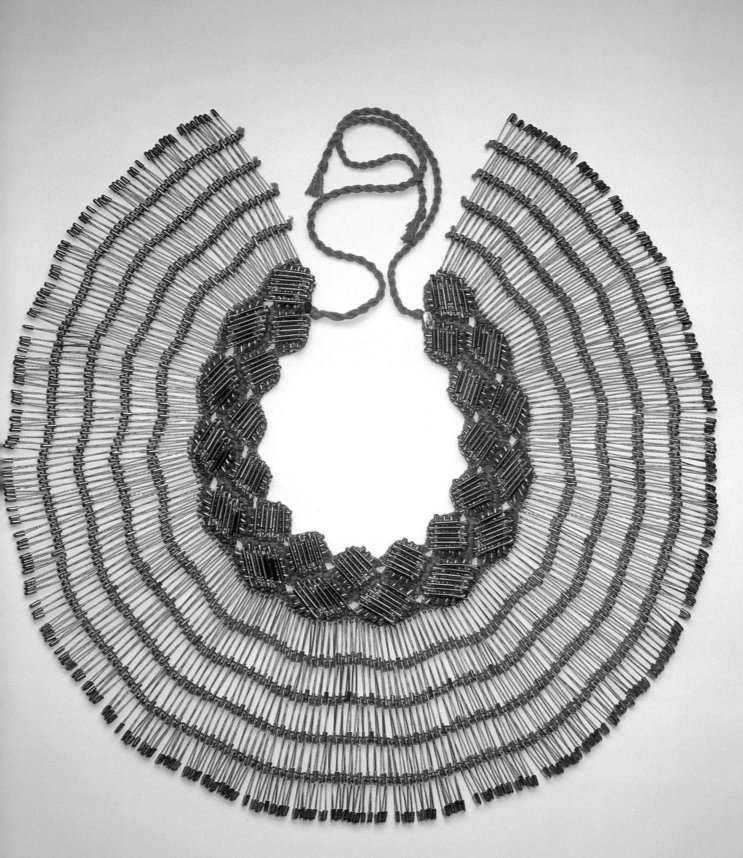

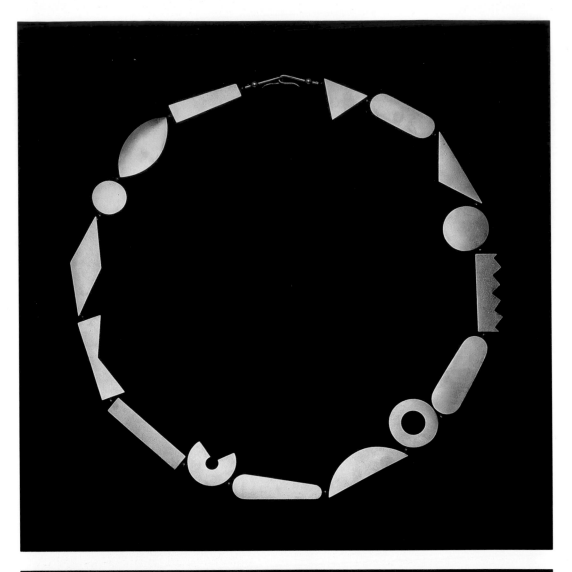

Above
246 Suzan Rezac   *Neckpiece*

Below
247 Rachelle Thiewes   *Grappelli Bracelet*

Opposite
248 Stanley Lechtzin   *Torque/Pendant*

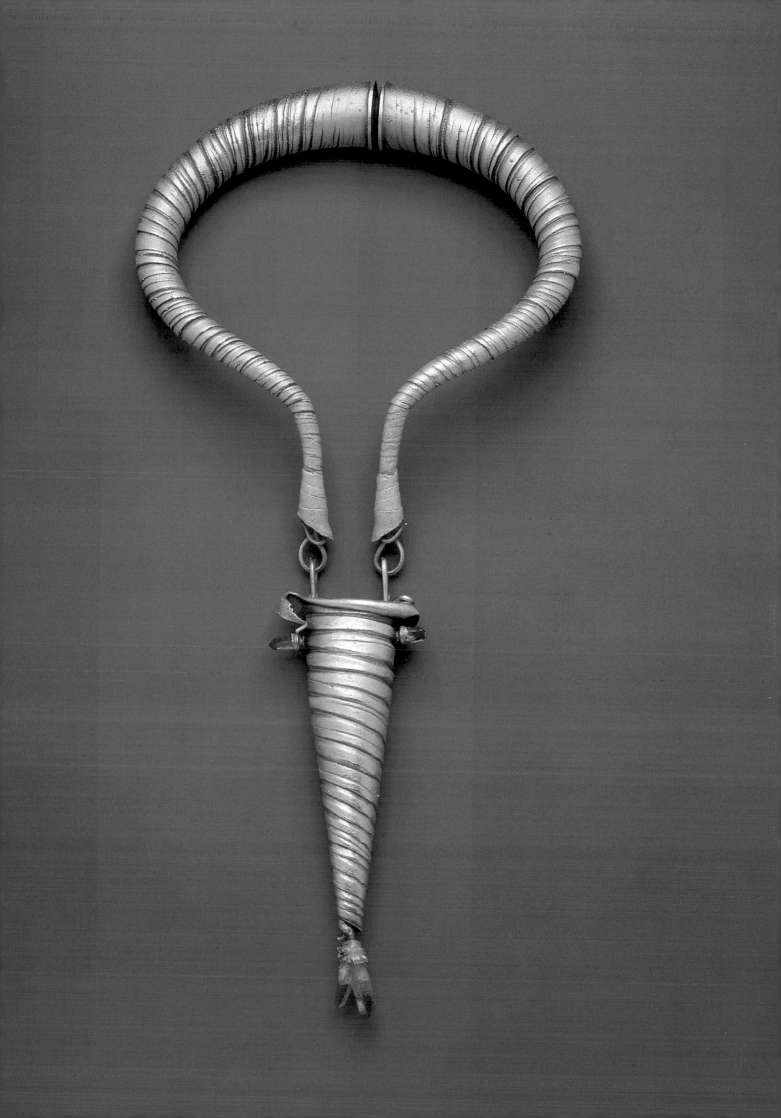

Above
249 Charles Loloma *Hopi Kachina*

Below, left
250 Ken Loeber *Brooch*

Below, right
251 Ann Young *Hummingbird Over My House*

Opposite
252 William Harper *The*

252

Above
253 Debra Rapoport *Found Metal Neckpiece 7/85*

Below, left
254 Martha Banyas *Brooch*

Below, right
255 Mary Ann Scherr *Waist-Monitor Belt Buckle*

Opposite
256 Sharon Church *Bead*

257   Gerhardt C. Herbst   *Collar and Bracelet*

Opposite
258   Ana Lisa Hedstrom   *Video Landscape*

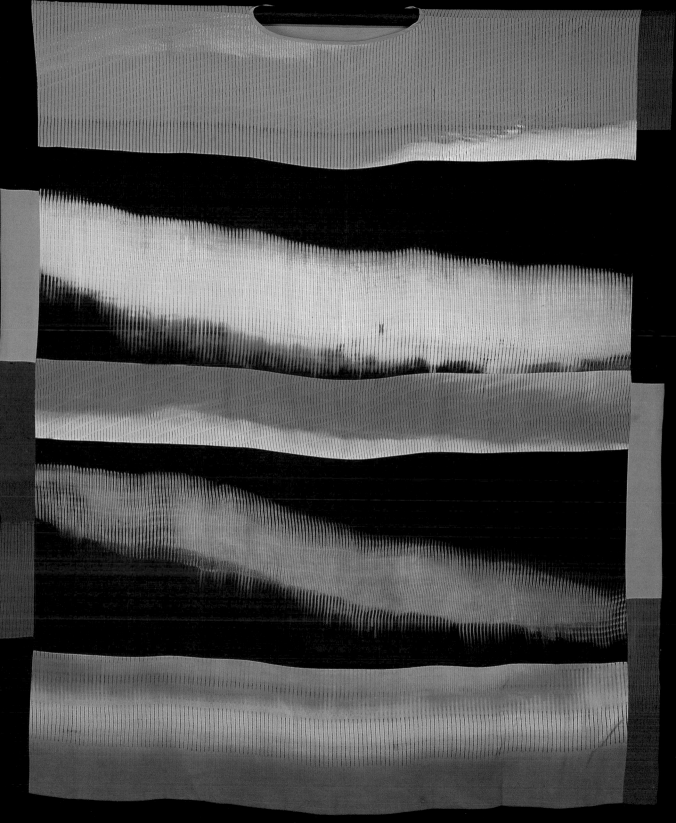

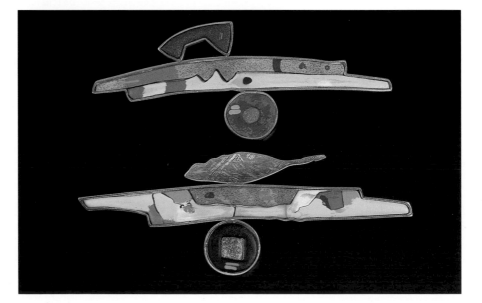

Above
259 Bruce Metcalf *Falling Figure with Background*

Below
260 Jamie Bennett *Brooches, from Deer Run Series*

Opposite, above
261 Colette *Pectoral #*

Opposite, below
262 Rebekah Laskin *Br*

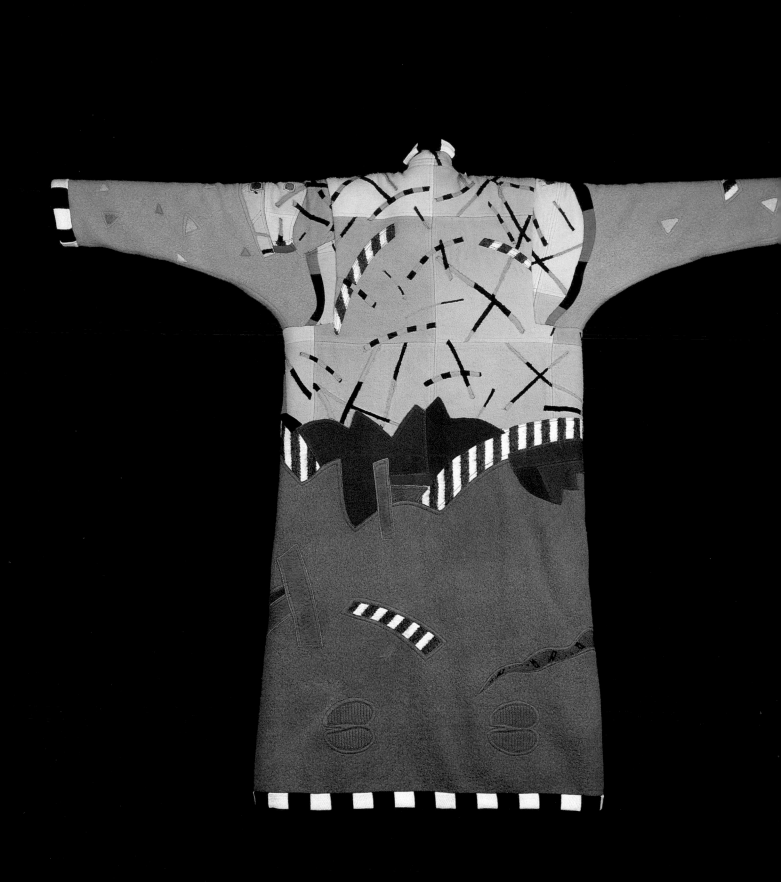

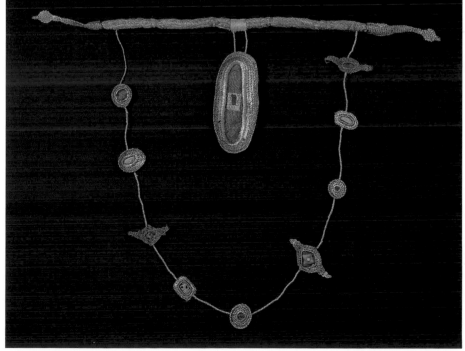

posite

an Williams Cacicedo   *Celebration Buffalo Coat*

Above
264   Randall Darwall   Detail of *Shawl*

Below
265   Ruth Nivola   *Adornment*

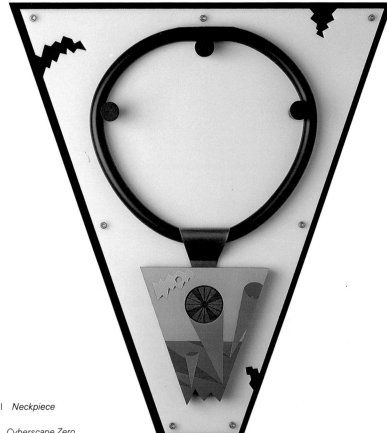

Above
266 Linda MacNeil   *Neckpiece*

Below
267 Vernon Reed   *Cyberscape Zero*

268   Marjorie Schick   *Neckpiece and Bracelet*

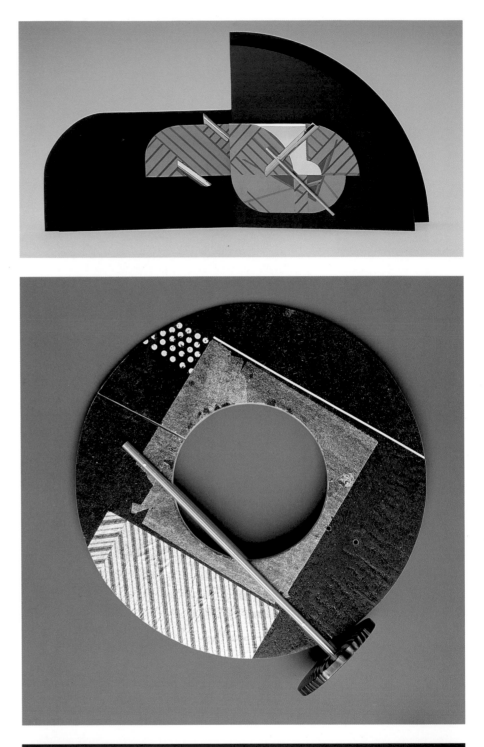

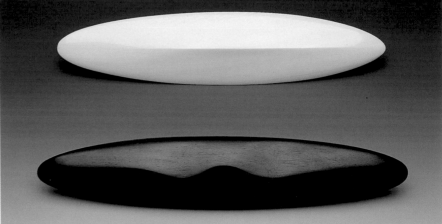

Top
269 Gretchen Raber   *9-Pieces-G*

Middle
270 Leslie Leupp   *Bracelet #485*

Below
271 Pavel Opočenský   *Pins*

Opposite
272 Alice H. Klein   *Calculation*

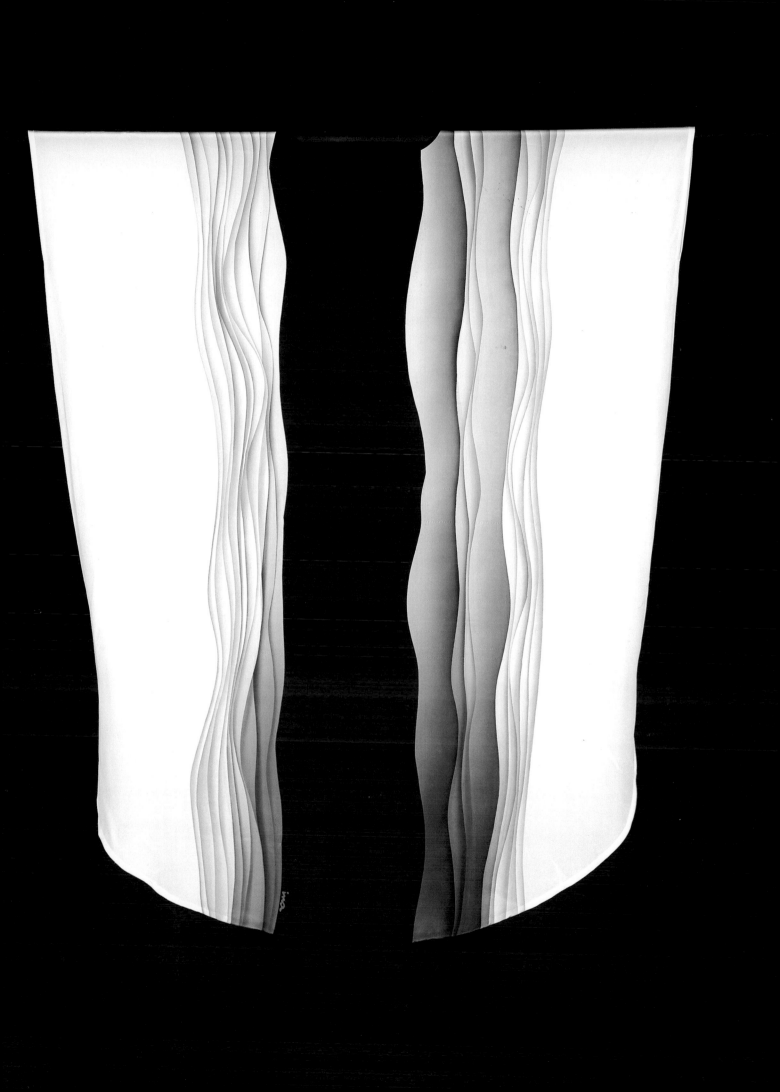

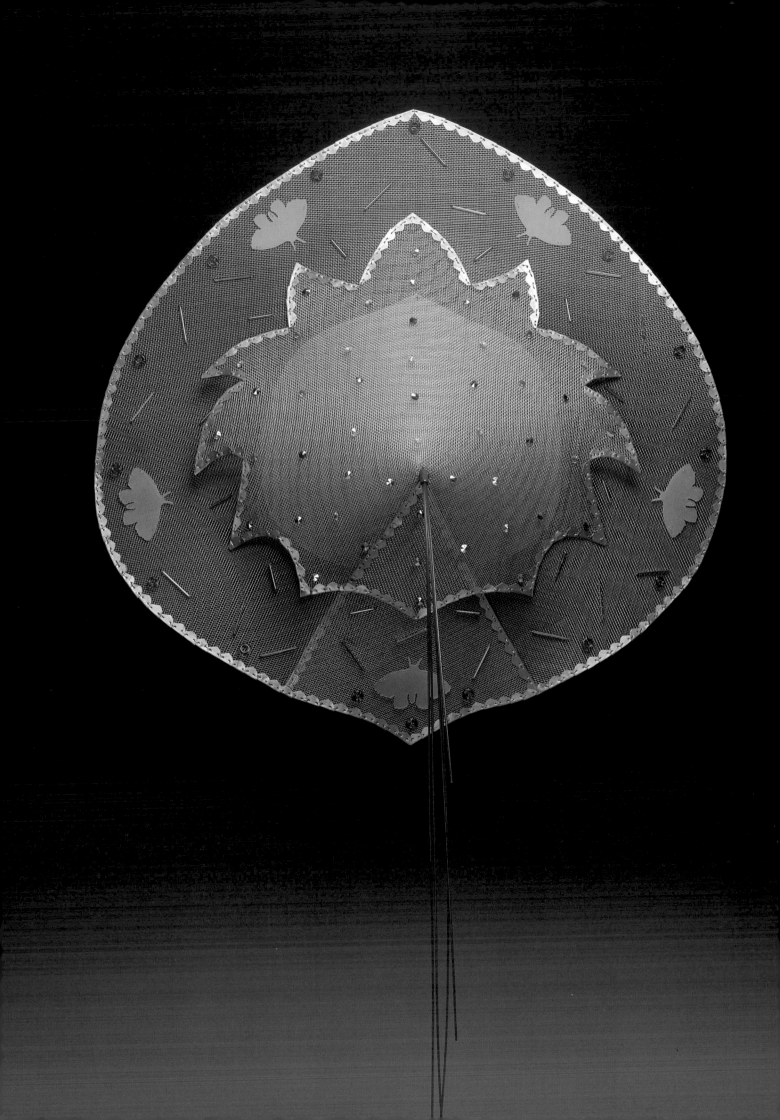

276   Gaza Bowen   *Never Say Never Again. Right, Den?*

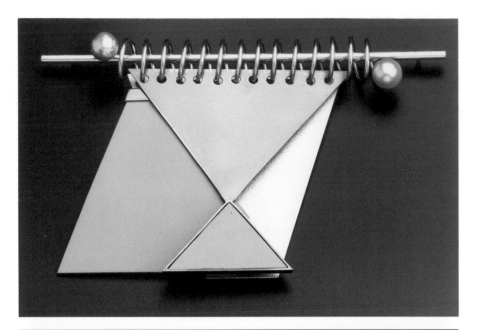

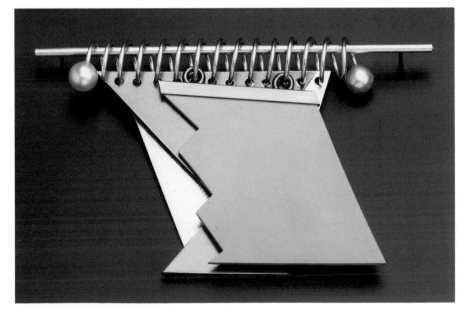

Preceding page, left
277   K. Lee Manuel   *Shinto Shards*
Preceding page, right
278   Julia Hill   Detail of *Africa*

279   Ivy Ross   *Flip It Brooch #2*

CHECKLIST OF THE EXHIBITION

Checklist order follows the sequence of plates in the catalogue.

All dimensions are given in inches and, unless otherwise noted, are listed in order of height, width, and depth.

All works have been loaned by the artist, unless otherwise credited.

1 **Fumio Yoshimura**
Three Bicycles, 1984–85
Linden
Laminated, carved
46 x 70⅛ x 114"

2 **Marilyn Levine**
H.R.H. Briefcase, 1985
Clay and mixed media
Handbuilt (slab constructed)
16 x 17½ x 6¾"
Courtesy of O.K. Harris Works of Art, New York, NY

3 **Douglas Anderson**
Boot Lace, 1985
Glass
Pâte de verre
9 x 12 x 6"
Private Collection

4 **Arturo Alonzo Sandoval**
State of the Union No. 4 (Return of the Hostages), 1984
Cotton, rayon, newspaper, plastic, posterboard, ink, acrylic polymer medium
Woven, collage
40¾ x 47 x ⅜"

5 **Richard Shaw**
V. Partch, D. Shaw, 1985
Porcelain, decal overglaze, china paint
Slip-cast, handbuilt
10½ x 8 x 8"
Courtesy of Braunstein Gallery, San Francisco, CA

6 **Louis B. Marak**
Green Rag Box, 1985
Low-fire clay
Handbuilt
22½ x 22¾ x 6"
Courtesy of Dorothy Weiss Gallery, San Francisco, CA

7 **Jack Thompson (a.k.a. Jugo de Vegetales)**
Snake Doggess, 1984
Whiteware, acrylic paint, acrylic lacquer
Handbuilt, painted, lacquered
27 x 20" diam.
Courtesy of Marian Locks Gallery, Philadelphia, PA

8 **Lizbeth Stewart**
Predator, 1984
Porcelain
Handbuilt, glazed, painted
23 x 44 x 15"
Courtesy of Helen Drutt Gallery, Philadelphia, PA

9 **Frank Fleming**
Screamer Goat #1, 1983–84
Porcelain
Handbuilt
52 x 14 x 14"

10 **Jack Earl**
For thou hast been a strength to the poor, a strength to the needy in his distress, a refuge from the storm, a shadow from the heat, when the blast of the terrible ones is as a storm against the wall, 1984
Clay, oil paint
Handbuilt (coiled), painted
27¾ x 15½ x 17¾"
Courtesy of Perimeter Gallery, Chicago, IL

11 **Michael Lucero**
Dream Developer, 1985
Low-fire clay, glazes
Handbuilt (slab constructed)
49 x 26 x 26"
Courtesy of Charles Cowles Gallery, New York, NY

12 **Robert Arneson**
Persistence, 1985
Clay, bronze
Handbuilt
72 x 21 x 21"
Courtesy of Allan Frumkin Gallery, New York, NY

13 **Patti Warashina**
Dinnerware Fiesta, 1984
Porcelain, mixed media
Cast, handbuilt
50 x 45½ x 6"

14 **Stephen De Staebler**
Seated Figure with Cleft, 1984
Clay
Handbuilt
83 x 15 x 24"
Courtesy of CDS Gallery, New York, NY

15 **Robert Brady**
Golfus, 1985
Stoneware, glaze, paint
Handbuilt (coiled)
64 x 36 x 24"
Courtesy of Braunstein Gallery, San Francisco, CA

16 **Nancy Carman**
Muerte Contra Mis Enemigos, 1985
Clay
Handbuilt, glazed, painted
96 x 84 x 1½"
Courtesy of Helen Drutt Gallery, Philadelphia, PA

17 **Jan Holcomb**
Freefall, 1984
Stoneware, paint
Handbuilt, painted
30 x 22 x 3"
Courtesy of Garth Clark Gallery, New York, NY

18 **Peter VandenBerge**
Zwartman, 1986
Clay, slips
Handbuilt (coiled)
45 x 14 x 17"
Courtesy of Rena Bransten Gallery, San Francisco, CA

19 **Viola Frey**
Leaning Man III, 1985
Clay, glazes
Handbuilt
102½ x 35 x 18"
Courtesy of Rena Bransten Gallery, San Francisco, CA

20 **Judy Moonelis**
Couple, 1985
Clay
Handbuilt
32 x 60 x 27"

21 **Patrick Siler**
Bourgeois Ceramicists, 1983
Clay
Handbuilt, stenciled
37 x 14 x 14"
Courtesy of Alternative Work Site, Bemis Project, Omaha, NB

22 **Howard Kottler**
Face Vase, 1985
Earthenware, paint, simulated gold leaf, dymo tape
Handbuilt
83 x 23 x 15"

23 **John Mason**
Counterpoint, 1985
Clay
Constructed from extruded forms
32 x 58 x 58"

24 **Kenneth Price**
Mungor, 1985
Clay, acrylic and metallic paint
Handbuilt, painted
7 x 6½ x 5"
Courtesy of Willard Gallery, New York, NY

25 **Scott Chamberlin**
Untitled, 1985
Terra cotta
Handbuilt
82 x 9" diam
Courtesy of Dorothy Weiss Gallery, San Francisco, CA

26 **Jun Kaneko**
Untitled, 1985
Clay
Handbuilt
17¾ x 29 x 20"

27 **John Roloff**
Night Ship/Double Horizon/The Frozen Sea, 1985
Clay, silica
Handbuilt, fused silica
13½ x 51 x 8"
Courtesy of Fuller Goldeen Gallery, San Francisco, CA

28 **Toshiko Takaezu**
"Ka Hua" #Seven, 1985
Clay
Handbuilt (coiled, slab constructed)
31 x 20 x 23"

29 **Tony Costanzo**
Dancing Winder, 1985
Slip, stains, fiberglass, wood
Painted, stained, constructed
25 x 69 x 1"
Courtesy of Braunstein Gallery, San Francisco, CA

30 **Graham Marks**
Untitled, 1984
Earthenware
Handbuilt (coiled), sandblasted
27 x 30 x 33"
Courtesy of Helen Drutt Gallery, Philadelphia, PA

31 **Mark Lindquist**
Silent Witness #1/Oppenheimer, 1983
Walnut, elm, pecan
Turned, incised
85 x 22" diam.

32 **Howard Werner**
Untitled, 1985
Spalted elm
Carved
39½ x 39 x 9½"
Courtesy of Snyderman Gallery, Philadelphia, PA

33 **Sam Hernandez**
St. Elmo's Fire, 1985
Wood, paint
Constructed, painted
51 x 47 x 12"
Courtesy of Rena Bransten Gallery,
San Francisco, CA

34 **Gerhardt Knodel**
The Pontiac Curtain, 1982
Cotton twill tape, mylar, metallic guimpe, linen
Painted, printed, woven
171 x 68"

35 **Michael Olszewski**
The Sin of Omission, 1985
Silk habutai, silk thread
Resist-painted, hand sewn
37 x 40 x 1"

36 **John Babcock**
Descending Angel, 1985
Pigmented cotton, abaca fiber
Free-cast paper
47 x 47½"

37 **Glenn Brill**
Now You Know, 1985
Wood, acrylic paint, modeling paste
Painted, constructed
64 x 108 x 160"
Courtesy of The Allrich Gallery,
San Francisco, CA

38 **Lia Cook**
Through the Curtain in Five Scenes Transposed,
1986
Rayon
Dyed, painted, woven, pressed
58 x 225½"
Courtesy of The Allrich Gallery,
San Francisco, CA

39 **Joan Sterrenburg**
Binary Barrier, 1984
Abaca pulp, pigments, wood
Hand papermaking (sheet formation),
constructed
46½ x 78 x 1"

40 **Adela Akers**
Compostela, 1985
Sisal, linen, wool, metallic thread
Woven (weft-faced weave with supplementary
weft)
60 x 180 x 6"

41 **Sheila Hicks**
Carving/Faceting/Masonry, 1985
Linen, wool, polished cotton
Embroidered (macro petit point)
72 x 144"
Collection of Itaka Schlubach and Cristobal
Zanartu, Paris, France

42 **Helena Hernmarck**
Framed Shadow, 1984-85
Linen, wool, cotton
Woven (eight harness twill and tabby discontinu-
ous wefts, double warp)
55 x 55 x ⅛"
Courtesy of Helena Hernmarck Tapestries, Inc.,
Ridgefield, CT

43 **Kris Dey**
Backwater, 1986
Cotton, textile paint, plastic tubing
Spray painted, wrapped
60 x 137 x 1"
Courtesy of The Allrich Gallery,
San Francisco, CA

44 **Tom Lundberg**
Lucky Steps, 1985
Cotton, silk, linen
Embroidered, quilted
26 x 26"

45 **Rebecca R. Medel**
Dawn, 1984
Linen, cotton
Indigo and ikat dyed, knotted
41 x 41 x 20"

46 **Glen Kaufman**
Kyoto: Nishijin Series VI, 1985
Silk, silver leaf
Twill woven, *nui haku* (metal leaf application)
7½ x 6⅜"
Collection of Page and Jeanne Paik Kaufman,
Ithaca, NY

47 **Lynn Basa**
Bias, 1984
Silk
Dyed, woven (Gobelin technique)
7¾ x 7¾"
Collection of King County Arts Commission,
Seattle, WA

48 **Mary Bero**
Self Portrait, 1983
Cotton, cotton floss
Embroidered
5½ x 6½"
Courtesy of Zolla/Lieberman Gallery, Chicago, IL

49 **Diane Itter**
Pattern Scape, 1985
Linen
Knotted
10 x 11 x 1/16"

50 **Nance O'Banion**
Shadow Wall: X, Speckle Spot Rock, Tom Rock,
and Shard Rock, 1985-86
Abaca paper, rattan, bamboo, aluminum mesh,
wire, acrylic paint, pastel
Hand papermaking, plaited, wired, painted
114 x 96 x 48"
Courtesy of The Allrich Gallery,
San Francisco, CA

51 **Jane Lackey**
Question Man, 1985
Telephone wire, rayon, wool, painted wood
Woven (warp-faced weave with supplementary
weft pile), constructed
80 x 22 x 3"

52 **Janice Lessman-Moss**
Passing Dreams II, 1984
Linen, cotton, wood, felt, paint
Woven, wrapped, knotted
40 x 46"

53 **Neda Alhilali**
The Serpent's Laughing Skin, 1985-86
Aluminum, paint
Constructed, painted
46 x 57 x 5"

54 **Harvey K. Littleton**
Opalescent Yellow Squared Pair, 1983
Glass
Hot worked, overlaid color, cased
10 x 6 x 13"; 12 x 6 x 15"
Courtesy of Heller Gallery, New York, NY

55 **Mark Peiser**
Pyramid, IS288, 1985
Glass
Cast, cut, polished
13 x 9 x 3"
Courtesy of Heller Gallery, New York, NY

56 **Robert Kehlmann**
Cloak, 1985
Glass, copper, brass
Sandblasted glass, brazed with copper and brass
32½ x 23 x 1½"
Courtesy of William Sawyer Gallery,
San Francisco, CA

57 **Marvin Lipofsky**
Pilchuck Series: Pacific Sunset, 1984-85
(Blown at the Pilchuck School with help from
Rich Royal and Robbie Miller. Finished in art-
ist's California studio.)
Glass
Semi-mold-blown, sandblasted, acid polished
13 x 18 x 14"

58 **Dale Chihuly**
Purple Violetta Macchia Set with Green Lip
Wraps, 1985
Glass
Hot worked
17 x 25½ x 31½"
Courtesy of Charles Cowles Gallery,
New York, NY

59 **Paul Seide**
Frosted Radio Light, 1985
Glass, mercury, argon
Blown, acid polished, charged with inert gases
19½ x 22 x 13"
Courtesy of Heller Gallery, New York, NY

60 **Richard Marquis**
Shard Rockets, 1985
Glass, silicone
Blown, fabricated
50 x 14 x 14"; 55 x 15 x 15"; 46 x 15 x 15"

61 **Jon F. Clark**
Leaning Tri-Form, 1984
Glass, steel, painted wood
Mold blown, constructed
43¼ x 23⅜ x 5¾"
Courtesy of Snyderman Gallery, Philadelphia, PA

62 **Ferne Jacobs**
Soft Paddle, 1983-85
Waxed linen thread
Coiled, twined
41½ x 7½ x 3"

63 **Joey Kirkpatrick**
Flora Mace
Figure with Ladder, 1984
Glass, wood, steel, wire
Hand and mold blown, etched, drilled, fabricated
53 x 8 x 8"

64 **Stephen Dale Edwards**
Man, 1985
Glass, concrete
Cast, constructed, electrically lit
43½ x 31 x 11"
Courtesy of Foster/White Gallery, Seattle, WA

65 **Hank Murta Adams**
Head with Flowers, 1986
Glass, copper
Cast, blown
26½ x 10 x 13½"

66 **Paul Marioni**
The Warriors, Shapers of Our Destiny, 1984
Glass, steel
Cast
20 x 24 x 1½"

67 **Steven I. Weinberg**
Untitled, 1985
Lead crystal
Cast, cut, polished, sandblasted
6 x 9½ x 9½"

68 **Amy Roberts**
Swami Dancer, 1985
Glass, wood, aluminum, paint
Blown glass, carved wood, painted
82½ x 15 x 5½"
Courtesy of Traver Sutton Gallery, Seattle, WA

69 **Michael Pavlik**
Vajra Transmutation Series, 1985
Glass
Cast, cut, ground, polished, laminated
12½ x 18 x 12"

70 **David Huchthausen**
Leitungs Scherbe 856, 1985
Architectural glass
Laminated, ground, optically polished
9¼ x 17 x 9"
Courtesy of Heller Gallery, New York, NY

71 **William Carlson**
Prägnänz Series, 1985
Glass, granite
Cast, laminated, cut, polished
18 x 12 x 8"

72 **Michael Cohn**
Roll Over Mondrian and Tell Brancusi the News #17, 1984
Glass, steel
Blown, cast, slumped, cut, fabricated
31 x 26 x 14½"

73 **Howard Ben Tré**
Column 22, 1985
Glass, copper
Cast, constructed
85 x 18 x 18"
Collection of American Craft Museum, New York, NY

74 **Susan Stinsmuehlen**
A Fancy Monitor, 1985
Glass, wood, metals, paint, mixed media
Blown, etched, painted, leaded
29 x 21 x 3"

75 **Henry Halem**
Blue Form, 1984
Vitrolite glass, brushed aluminum
Acid etched, constructed
39½" x 24 x 6"
Courtesy of Snyderman Gallery, Philadelphia, PA

76 **Jay Musler**
Voyage to Vogue, 1984
Plate glass, silicone, oil paint
Cut, sandblasted, painted
7 x 46 x 7"
Courtesy of Heller Gallery, New York, NY

77 **Albinas Elskus**
Four Columns, 1983
Antique glass, vitreous paint, lead, plexiglass
Painted, stained, fired, leaded
Stained glass: 18" diam
Plexiglass frame: 24 x 24"

78 **Carol Shaw-Sutton**
Surrender, 1985–86
Fruitwood, linen, pigment
Lashed
120 x 36 x 6"

79 **Faith Ringgold**
No More War Story Quilt Part II, 1985
Cotton canvas
Intaglio printed, resist-dyed, pieced
71½ x 101½"
Courtesy of Bernice Steinbaum Gallery, New York, NY

80 **Donald Reitz**
Given in Trust, 1986
Clay, vitreous engobes
Handbuilt
40 x 23 x 5"
Courtesy of Maurine Littleton Gallery, Washington, DC

81 **Dina Barzel**
Green Egg, 1984
Wool, silk, flax
Felted, stitched, hand papermaking
17 x 26 x 17"

82 **Winifred Lutz**
Leaf Covered Sun, Time In A Stone, A Corner, 1985
Handmade and cast kozo paper, gold leaf, redwood, fir, bamboo, cherry wood, fossilized stone
Hand papermaking (casting), assembled
92½ x 10⅞ x 12½"
Courtesy of Marilyn Pearl Gallery, New York, NY

83 **Lenore Tawney**
Indivisible Point, 1982
Cotton canvas, linen threads
Painted, knotted
108 x 72 x 72"

84 **James Bassler**
Skins, 1985
Silk, linen, sisal, plastic
Woven (painted warp/wedge weave technique)
48 x 45 x 2"

85 **Robert Sperry**
#565, 1983
Ceramic tile, glaze, slip
Slip applied over glaze on tiles
64 x 128 x 2½"

86 **Walter Nottingham**
Shrine, 1986
Handmade paper, natural fibers (reeds, willow, pine needles), linen, cotton, dyes
Hand papermaking, stitched, twined, glazed
55 x 33½ x 6"

87 **Katherine Westphal**
Past Splendor, 1985
Japanese handmade paper
Dyed, stamped, transfer printed with color xerox, machine stitched
84 x 84"

88 **Dominic Di Mare**
Domus Series #7, Darkest River, 1985
Horsehair, wood, photograph, feathers
Constructed
84 x 4 x 2"
Courtesy of Braunstein Gallery, San Francisco, CA

89 **Karyl Sisson**
Skins, 1984–85
Cotton twill, zippers, wooden clothespins
Dyed, twined, stitched
72 x 12" diam.; 43 x 9" diam.

90 **Cynthia Schira**
Dark Light, 1985
Cotton, linen, rayon
Woven (integrated triple cloth using painted warp, sectional and supplementary wefts)
63 x 59"
Courtesy of Miller/Brown Gallery, San Francisco, CA

91 **Claire Zeisler**
Tri-Color Arch, 1983–84
Hemp, synthetic fiber
Knotted, wrapped
74 x 11"; spill: 66 x 44"
Courtesy of Rhona Hoffman Gallery, Chicago, IL

92 **Anne Wilson**
China Spotted Fur I, 1985
Linen, abaca, oil paint
Woven, painted
40 x 22 x 11"
Courtesy of Miller/Brown Gallery, San Francisco, CA

93 **Patricia Campbell**
Column III, 1986
Anodized aluminum, cable
Constructed
192 x 48 x 24"

94 **L. Brent Kington**
Europa, 1985
Mild steel
Forged, welded
51¼ x 9 x 6½"

95 **Warren Seelig**
Brighton, 1983
Cotton, aluminum
Woven (grosgrain)
50 x 52"

96 **Nancy Crow**
Yellow Crosses IV, 1985
Cotton, cotton blends
Strip-pieced, pieced, hand quilted
82 x 82"

97 **Michael James**
Rhythm/Color: The Concord Cotillion, 1985
Cotton, silk
Machine pieced, machine quilted
100 x 100"

98 **Pamela Studstill**
Quilt #53, 1985
Cotton, textile paints
Machine pieced, hand quilted, painted
72 x 76"

99 **Sherri Smith**
Galaxy, 1985
Cotton webbing
Plaited
53 x 84 x 1"

100 **Jarmila Machova**
Nofret II, 1984
Pellon, nylon, ink
Drawn, laminated, cut
60 x 96 x 6" (four panels)

101 **John McNaughton**
It's Not Easy Keeping It Together, 1985
Poplar, ColorCore Formica
Carved, bent laminated, painted
85 x 16 x 12"

102 **Alphonse Mattia**
Primates, Geometric Valets, 1986
Oak, poplar, plywood
Carved, bleached, stained, painted
73 x 18 x 18", each

103 **Alan Siegel**
Aegean, 1986
Birch plywood, poplar, enamel paint
Laminated, carved, painted
83 x 18 x 23"
Courtesy of Nancy Hoffman Gallery, Inc., New York, NY

104 **Tommy Simpson**
Home Sweet Home, 1985
Woods (walnut, cherry, spalted maple, purpleheart, rosewood, ebony, osage orange, pine, lignum vitae, bird's-eye maple, ash), glass, shells, leather, feathers, fur, lead, steel, brass, tin, nylon, clay, sand, acrylic paint, photograph, lithograph, copper
Laminated, turned, carved, constructed
71½ x 22 x 18½"

105 **John Cederquist**
2-D Thonet, 1985
Birch plywood, maple
Laminated, joined
39 x 24 x 14"
Courtesy of The Gallery at Workbench, New York, NY

106 **Therman Statom**
Chair, 1983
Plate glass, mixed media
Painted, bonded
42 x 22 x 19"
Courtesy of New York Experimental Glass Workshop, New York, NY

107 **F. L. Wall**
Watching, 1985
Mahogany, rosewood, ebony, steel
Shaped, carved, welded
70 x 22 x 18"

108 **Jon Brooks**
Styx Ladderback Chairs, 1986
Maple, prisma color, lacquer
Dowel joined
84 x 18 x 18", each
Courtesy of Snyderman Gallery, Philadelphia, PA

109 **Sam Maloof**
Rocking Chair, 1985
Fiddleback hard rock maple, ebony
Constructed
46 x 26 x 46"

110 **James Schriber**
Pencil Post Bed, 1985
Curly maple
Joined, hand and machine shaped
84 x 60 x 80"
Original commissioned by W.R. Tingley

111 **Curtis Erpelding**
Coat Rack, 1985
White oak
Bent laminated
71 x 22" diam.

112 **James Krenov**
Cabinet on Stand, 1982
Spalted maple, oak, partridge wood, cedar of
Lebanon
Joined
67 x 27 x 11"
Courtesy of Pritam & Eames, East Hampton, NY

113 **Dick Wickman**
Corridor Table, 1985
Bird's-eye maple, lacquered wood, various inlays
Marquetry, lacquered, constructed
28 x 78 x 18"
Courtesy of Perimeter Gallery, Chicago, IL

114 **Thomas Hucker**
Side Chairs, 1985
Plywood, lacquer, wenge
Molded, lacquered, constructed
29½ x 46 x 19"
Courtesy of Pritam & Eames, East Hampton, NY

115 **Peter S. Dean**
Writing Desk, 1983
Bloodwood, pear, holly, maple, glass
Bent laminated
36½ x 46½ x 23½"

116 **Jere Osgood**
Writing Desk, 1986
Bubinga, ash
Laminated (legs), constructed
31½ x 59 x 22"

117 **Michael Pierschalla**
Table #41, 1984
Curly maple, hardwoods, lacquer, glass
Constructed, lacquered
35½ x 16½" diam.
Courtesy of Snyderman Gallery, Philadelphia, PA

118 **Mitch Ryerson**
Traveling Vanity, 1985
Wenge, Sitka spruce, birch veneer plywood, mir-
ror, oil paint
Joined, painted
12 x 15 x 10"
Collection of Anne and Ronald Abramson,
Rockville, MD

119 **Wendell Castle**
Ziggurat Clock, 1985
Gaboon ebony, curly koa veneer, leather, gold-
plated brass, weight-driven movement
Constructed
71 x 39 x 15"
Courtesy of Alexander F. Milliken Gallery,
New York, NY

120 **Thomas Loeser**
Chest of Drawers, 1984
Wood, Formica, enamel paint
Constructed, painted
62 x 36 x 32"

121 **Peter Shire**
Rod and Transit, 1984
Anodized aluminum, steel, glass
Fabricated
29 x 60" diam.
Courtesy of Hokin/Kaufman Gallery, Chicago, IL

121a *Hourglass Teapot,* 1983–84
Clay
Handbuilt
23 x 17 x 6"
Courtesy of Saxon/Lee Gallery,
Los Angeles, CA

122 **Garry Knox Bennett**
Table Desk, 1985
Goncalo alves, cocobolo, walnut, ebony,
watercolor paint, oil glaze
Constructed
30 x 94 x 37"

123 **Wendy Maruyama**
Chest of Drawers, 1985
Plywood, lacquers, lacewood, veneers
Joined, lacquered
60 x 20 x 18"
Collection of Anne and Ronald Abramson,
Rockville, MD

124 **Steven Madsen**
Three Worms Trying to Cross the Jagged Edge,
1986
Birch plywood, maple, plastic
Constructed
65½ x 33¾ x 22⅝"
Courtesy of Snyderman Gallery, Philadelphia, PA

125 **Bob Trotman**
Table, 1985
Mahogany
Carved, burned, painted
36 x 37 x 15"

126 **Judy Kensley McKie**
Fox and Lizard Table, 1985
Birch, paint, glass
Laminated, carved, painted
30 x 52 x 20"

127 **Edward Zucca**
Table of the Future, 1981
Curly maple, birch
Constructed
46 x 31 x 25"
Collection of Anne and Ronald Abramson,
Rockville, MD

128 **Rosanne Somerson**
Upholstered Bench, 1986
Swiss pearwood, bleached curly maple, aniline-
dyed leather
Joined, shaped, lacquered
23 x 58 x 22½"

129 **Jonathan Bonner**
Weathervane, 1985
Copper, pine
Fabricated, patinated
92 x 72 x 18"

130 **Louis Mueller**
Lamp, 1985
Bronze, oil paint, blown glass
Constructed
75½ x 10¼ x 10¼"
Courtesy of Helen Drutt Gallery, Philadelphia, PA

131 **Ray King**
Aurora Sconce, 1986
Optical glass, bronze (patina)
Carved, edge lit
24 x 60 x 10"

132 **Deborah Horrell**
Heaven, 1985
Clay
Fired panel, with clay added, carved, glazed, fired
108 x 72 x 1½"

133 **Paula Colton Winokur**
Fireplace Site I, 1985
Unglazed porcelain, sulfates, ceramic pencil
Handbuilt (slab constructed), assembled
66 x 58 x 11"
Courtesy of Helen Drutt Gallery, Philadelphia, PA

134 **Gail Fredell Smith**
Citicorp Pink, 1984
Wood, plywood, mirror
Joined (splined, mitered), lacquered, sandblasted
43 x 16½ x 3½"
Collection of Wendy Maruyama, Oakland, CA

135 **Platt Monfort**
Snowshoe 12, 1985
Spruce, ash, Kevlar, Dacron
Constructed
16 x 27 x 140"

136 **Jokan Ohama**
Replica of Southampton, New York House, 1985
White pine, spruce
Hand tooled. joined
33¾ x 79 x 43"
Promised gift of Jack Lenor Larsen to the
American Craft Museum

137 **Belmont Freeman**
Bird Cage, 1985
Steel, acrylic, stainless steel cable
Welded, fabricated, painted
32 x 20 x 20
Designed by Belmont Freeman; fabricated by
Donald Gratz, Treitel-Gratz Company, Inc., and
Chip McCloskey.
Prototype made possible by the Innovative
Design Fund.

138 **Gary S. Griffin**
Cap Gun, Roses and Middle America, 1984
Steel
Hammered, welded, ground
74 x 77 x 12"

139 **Tom Joyce**
Fire Hearth Grate, 1985
Mild steel
Forged
12 x 42 x 18"

139a *Wall-Mounted Hearth Tools,* 1985 (not
illustrated)
Mild steel, broomstraw
Forged
38 x 14 x 8"

140 **Russell C Jaqua Jr.**
Log Basket, 1985
Mild steel
Forged
35 x 14 x 12"

141 **Albert Paley**
Lectern, 1985
Mild steel, brass, copper
Forged, fabricated
46 x 32 x 24"
Courtesy of Fendrick Gallery, Washington, DC

142 **Gregory Litsios**
Floor Standing Candelabrum, 1986
Mild steel
Forged
68 x 18 x 18"

143 **Glen Simpson**
Number Two Shovel, 1982
Sterling silver, 14k gold, hickory
Formed, inlaid
16¾ x 3¾ x ⅝"

144 **J. Fred Woell**
All's Calm on the Western Front, 1984
Sterling silver
Lost-wax cast
5¼ x 1¼ x ½"

144a *Aero Setdown,* 1984
Sterling silver
Lost-wax cast
5¼ x 1½ x ½"

145 **John Prip**
Spoons, 1985 (from 1978 models)
Brass, silver
Fabricated
6" long, each

146 **Ronald Hayes Pearson**
Ladle, 1986
Sterling silver
Fabricated
11¼ x 3 x 2"

147 **Phillip Baldwin**
Steak Knife Set II, 1985–86
Pattern welded steel, wood, antler, bronze
Forged, fabricated
7 x 1⅛ x ⅜", each

149 **Billie Jean Theide**
Mirror Image, 1985
Sterling silver, plastic, mirror
Constructed
9 x 4 x 2"

148 **Edward Frederick Burak**
Smoking Pipes, 1983–85
Briarwood burl, para rubber
Constructed
Ranging in size from: 1¼ x 5⅜ x 2⅞" to
　2½ x 8⅛ x 1¼"
Courtesy of Connoisseur Pipe Shop, Ltd.,
　New York, NY

150 **Benjamin Moore**
*Interior Fold Series in Amethyst with Black Spiral
　Wrap,* 1985
Glass
Handblown
4¼ x 24" diam.
Courtesy of Traver Sutton Gallery, Seattle, WA

151 **William Bernstein
Katherine Bernstein**
Face Goblets, 1985
Glass
Blown, cane drawing
8 x 3" diam.
Courtesy of Maurine Littleton Gallery,
　Washington, DC

152 **Stephen Smyers**
Vienna Wine Goblets, 1986
Clear and colored glass
Handblown
8¼ x 3½" diam., each

153 **Steven Maslach**
*Lustre Stemmed Funnel, Hock, and Wine
　Glasses,* 1985
Crystal, lustre glass colored with precious metals
Handblown
Funnel glasses: 8 x 3" diam.
Hock glasses: 7 x 2¾" diam.
Wine glasses: 8¼ x 3" diam.

154 **Pat Flynn**
Drinking Beakers, 1985
Pewter, sterling silver, 18k and 24k gold
Formed, forged, soldered, oxidized, gold plated
3½ x 2½ x 2½", each

155 **Chunghi Choo**
Fleur, 1986
Silver-plated copper
Electroformed
18 x 10½ x 12"

156 **John C. Marshall**
Cocktail Server, 1983
Sterling silver, basalt, gold
Raised, formed, soldered
11 x 6" diam.

157 **Fritz Dreisbach**
*Crystal Optic Reversible Champagne and Cognac
　Goblets,* 1985
Glass
Blown
9⅛ x 3½" diam., each
Courtesy of Traver Sutton Gallery, Seattle, WA

158 **Karen Karnes**
Covered Vessel, 1985
Stoneware
Thrown, wood-fired
13 x 13" diam.

159 **Byron Temple**
Covered Jars, 1985
Stoneware
Thrown, wood-fired, salt glazed
　8 x 9" diam.; 6 x 6" diam.; 6 x 6½" diam.

160 **Rudolf Staffel**
Light Gatherer, 1985
Porcelain
Handbuilt, with overlapping elements
5¾ x 8¾ x 8"
Courtesy of Helen Drutt Gallery, Philadelphia, PA

161 **David Shaner**
Pillow Form, 1985
Stoneware, crystaline glaze
Handbuilt, glazed
5 x 11 x 11"

162 **Val M. Cushing**
Covered Jar, 1985
Stoneware, glazes, slips
Thrown, carved base
32 x 13" diam.

163 **Edward S. Eberle**
*A Dream; One Man Cup; A Bird, a Fox, and a
　Rabbit,* 1985
Porcelain, terra sigillata
Thrown, brush painted, sgraffito
Ranging in size from 3¼ x 3¾" diam. to 2¾ x 3"
　diam.

163a *Fantastic Landscape; City/Country; One Man
　Cup,* 1985 (not illustrated)
Porcelain, terra sigillata
Thrown, brush and finger painted, sgraffito
Ranging in size from 3½ x 3¼" diam. to 3⅜ x 3⅛"
　diam

164 **James Makins**
Dinnerware and Goblets, 1984–85
Porcelain
Thrown
Dinnerware, ranging in size from: 4¼ x 6½" diam.
　(cup and saucer) to 2 x 12" diam. (dinner plate)
Goblets, ranging in size from: 6½ x 3" diam.
　(white wine) to 6½ x 5½" diam. (champagne)

165 **Harris Deller**
White Platter, 1985
Porcelain
Thrown, carved
4 x 22" diam.

166 **Robert Turner**
Dome Form, 1983
Stoneware, glaze
Thrown, altered, reduction-fired, sandblasted
12¾ x 11¾" diam.
Courtesy of Exhibit A Inc., Chicago, IL

167 **Roseline Delisle**
L'Ogive, 1985
Porcelain
Thrown
15 x 4½" diam.
Courtesy of Dorothy Weiss Gallery,
　San Francisco, CA

168 **Richard Notkin**
Landform Teapot (Variation #12), Yixing Series,
　1985
Stoneware
Slip-cast, handbuilt, assembled
2½ x 7¾ x 3¾"
Courtesy of Traver Sutton Gallery, Seattle, WA

169 **Marek Cecula**
Ceremonial Set, 1984
Porcelain
Slip-cast, glazed, decal application
4 x 18 x 12"
Courtesy of Contemporary Porcelain,
　New York, NY

170 **John Parker Glick**
Teapot, 1985
Stoneware
Thrown
9 x 9 x 6¼"

171 **Chris Gustin**
Teapot, 1985
Stoneware, slip, glaze
Thrown, incised, altered, sandblasted
13 x 13½ x 7¼"
Courtesy of Garth Clark Gallery, New York, NY

172 **John Gill**
Ewer #1, 1985
Stoneware
Handbuilt
13¼ x 18 x 4"
Collection of Grace Borgenicht Brandt

173 **Mary Roehm**
Teapot, Reed, 1985
Porcelain
Thrown, constructed, wood-fired
9¼ x 11 x 13¼"

173a *Cups,* 1985 (not illustrated)
Porcelain
Thrown, wood-fired
2½ x 3½" diam., each

174 **Kenneth Ferguson**
Basket, 1984
Stoneware, Shino glaze
Thrown
16 x 16" diam.
Courtesy of Garth Clark Gallery, New York, NY

175 **Otto Natzler**
Flaring Form, 1980
Earthenware, glazes
Handbuilt, reduction-fired
8⅜ x 14⅛ x 3¾"
Courtesy of Jordan-Volpe Gallery, New York, NY

176 **Beatrice Wood**
Loving Cup, 1985
Earthenware, glaze
Thrown
6¾ x 10½ x 6¾"
Courtesy of Garth Clark Gallery, New York, NY

177 **Lynn Turner**
"Expresso" Set, 1982
Porcelain, porcelain slip, glaze, low-fire clay
Slip-cast, assembled, airbrushed, hand
　decorated
6 x 3 x 7"

178 **Paul Soldner**
Pedestal Piece 85–38, 1985
Clay, charred wood
Thrown, altered, low-fired
27 x 14 x 6"
Courtesy of Maurine Littleton Gallery,
　Washington, DC

179 **William P. Daley**
Turner's Court, 1983
Stoneware
Handbuilt
11¾ x 30 x 27½"
Courtesy of Helen Drutt Gallery, Philadelphia, PA

180 **Elsa Rady**
Deductive Rigor, 1985
Porcelain, enamel, granite
Thrown
9½ x 24 x 8"
Courtesy of Jan Turner Gallery, Los Angeles, CA

181 **Sylvia Seventy**
Breeder's Flock, 2, 1985
Handmade paper, wax, feathers, acrylic paint
Hand papermaking
4½ x 14" diam.
Courtesy of The Allrich Gallery,
　San Francisco, CA

182 **Jane Sauer**
Implications, 1985
Waxed linen, paint
Knotted
14 x 6" diam.; 8½ x 5" diam.; 3½ x 3½" diam.
Courtesy of B.Z. Wagman Gallery, St. Louis, MO

183 Del Stubbs
Manzanitas, 1986
Manzanita
Turned
6¼ x 1¼" diam.; 7½ x 1¼" diam.; 8 x 1¼" diam.

184 Bob Stocksdale
Salad Bowl, 1985
California black walnut
Turned
8 x 28½" diam.

185 Ronald E. Kent
Bowl I, 1985
Norfolk Island pine
Turned
10⅛ x 21⅜" diam.

186 Edward Moulthrop
Figured Tulipwood Spheroid, 1985
Tulipwood
Turned
25½ x 31" diam.

187 Stephen M. Paulsen
Scent Bottles, 1985
Ebony, tulipwood, orange ivorywood burl, maple
burl, pernambuco, antique ivory, Tagua ivory-
nut, purpleheart, Brazilwood, Arariba,
boxwood, walnut, jade
Machine and hand shaped, inlaid, carved, turned,
fabricated, chatterwork
Ranging in size from: 3 x ⅛ x ¾" to 7¾ x 3 x 1"

188 David Ellsworth
Signature Bowl #5, 1985
Redwood lace burl
Hollow-turned
18 x 16" diam.

189 Lillian Elliott
Pat Hickman
Leaf Basket, 1984
Natural materials, acrylic, graphite
Constructed
12½ x 11 x 8"

190 Ruth Duckworth
Untitled *(Five Porcelain Forms),* 1985
Porcelain
Thrown, altered, with slab elements
Ranging in size from 6 x 3½ x 3" to 8 x 7½ x 3½"
Courtesy of Helen Drutt Gallery, Philadelphia, PA

191 Kay Sekimachi
Bowls, 1985
Linen, Japanese handmade papers
Laminated
4¾ x 7" diam.; 6 x 8" diam.

192 Richard E. DeVore
Bowl, 1985
Stoneware, glazes
Thrown, handbuilt
7⅛ x 15 x 13½"

193 Kevin Cannon
Begauge, 1984
Leather, brass, acrylic paint, dye
Laminated, painted
4¼" x 6 x 7¼"
Courtesy of Charles Cowles Gallery,
New York, NY

194 Ed Rossbach
Red Hunk, 1985
Ash splints, rice paper, lacquer
Plaited, lacquered
13½ x 11" diam.

195 John McQueen
Untitled Basket with Red String, 1984
Ash, string
Sewn
18 x 9" diam.

196 Norma Minkowitz
Passage to Nowhere, 1985
Fiber, acrylic, pencil, shellac
Crocheted
7½ x 9¾" diam.

196a *Barrier,* 1985 (not illustrated)
Fiber, metal, acrylic, pencil, shellac
Crocheted
3⁵⁄₁₆ x 10" diam.

197 Neil Prince
Fran Kraynek-Prince
Torrey Pine Olla, 1985
Torrey Pine needles
Coiled helix
20 x 20" diam.

198 Dorothy Gill Barnes
Nova Scotia Spruce Basket, 1985
Red spruce bark
Plaited
18 x 15 x 10"

199 Dan Dailey
Garden of Oddities (Science Fiction Vase), 1985
Glass, enamels
Handblown, sandblasted, acid polished, fired
enamels
11¾ x 10" diam.
Courtesy of Foster/White Gallery, Seattle, WA

200 Joel Philip Myers
Contiguous Fragment Series, 1985
Glass
Blown, cut, sandblasted, acid etched
12 x 15 x 4"
Courtesy of Heller Gallery, New York, NY

201 William Morris
Stone Vessel #3, 1985
Glass, glass powders and shards
Handblown
18 x 16 x 5"
Courtesy of Heller Gallery, New York, NY

202 Sonja Blomdahl
Tobak/Goldbraun/Black, 1985
Glass
Handblown
8½ x 15" diam.
Courtesy of Traver Sutton Gallery, Seattle, WA

203 Dona Look
Basket #857, 1985
White birch bark, waxed silk thread
Woven, sewn, wrapped
6¼ x 19½ x 4½"

204 Andrea Gill
Large Vase, 1984
Low-fire terra cotta, vitreous slip, glaze
Handbuilt (press-molded), glazed
25½ x 15½ x 8½"
Collection of Robert L. Pfannebecker

205 Mark Abildgaard
Ritual Vessel, 1985
Glass
Blown, cast, sandblasted
18 x 11 x 11"

206 Mary Ann Toots Zynsky
Exotic Birds: American Dream Series, 1985
Glass threads
Filet de verre
4⅝ x 12" diam.
Courtesy of Theo Portnoy Gallery, New York, NY

207 Karla Trinkley
Herringbone Bowl, 1986
Glass
Pâte de verre
18 x 14" diam.

208 Helen Shirk
Vessel, 1984
Copper, brass
Formed, riveted, patinated
12 x 19 x 10"

209 David Tisdale
Bowl with Serving Spoons, 1985
Aluminum, rubber, steel screws
Anodized, fabricated
Bowl: 9 x 13" diam.
Spoons: 12½" long

210 Randy Long
Vessel for a Ring Master, 1983
Sterling silver, nickel silver
Sheet fabrication, married metal, sandblasted
6¼ x 5⅝ x 9¼"

211 Andrew Magdanz
Susan Shapiro
Avery Series: Perfume Bottles, 1985
Glass, enamels
Blown, cut, ground, enamel fired
Ranging in size from: 1¾ x 4½ x 1¾" to
5¾ x 1½ x 2½"

212 John Donoghue
Plate, 1985
Earthenware, underglazes
Thrown, glazed
3¼ x 19¾" diam.

213 Ralph Bacerra
Bowl, 1985
Porcelain, glaze, gold
Thrown
3 x 19" diam.
Courtesy of Garth Clark Gallery, New York, NY

214 Dorothy Hafner
Lightening Bolt Punch Bowl, 1985
Porcelain, underglaze
Handbuilt (slab constructed), glazed
Punch bowl: 8¾ x 13 x 12"
Ladle: 11½" long

215 Ron Nagle
Untitled, 1983
Clay, glazes
Slip-cast, glazed
7¾ x 3¼ x 3½"
Courtesy of Charles Cowles Gallery,
New York, NY

216 Robin Quigley
Oval Platter, 1984
Pewter
Fabricated
3 x 9 x 18"

217 Janet Prip
Bowl, 1985
Pewter, brass
Dapped, dye-formed, planished
11 x 6 x 1"

218 Michael Frimkess
Kylix, 1983
Stoneware, glaze, china paint
Thrown, painted
2½ x 9 x 5½"

219 Adrian Saxe
Untitled Gold Vessel, 1985
Stoneware, porcelain
Handbuilt
14 x 16"
Courtesy of Garth Clark Gallery, Los Angeles, CA

220 Rick Dillingham
Untitled, 1985
Clay, glazes, gold leaf
Broken, reassembled
16¼ x 10½" diam.
Courtesy of Nina Freudenheim Gallery,
Buffalo, NY

221 Bennett Bean
Bowl, 1985
White earthenware
Thrown, glazed, painted, applied gold leaf
7¼ x 13⅜" diam.

222 June Schwarcz
Bowl #917, 1984
Copper, enamel, iron
Electroplated, enameled
3½ x 6¼" diam.

223 **Susan H. Hamlet**
Bowl Series #7, 1985
Hastelloy, aluminum, copper, rubber, stainless
	steel
Fabricated, hydraulic-formed
42 x 17" diam.
Courtesy of Helen Drutt Gallery, Philadelphia, PA

224 **Peter Voulkos**
Untitled, 1982
Stoneware
Thrown, handbuilt
42 x 22" diam.
Collection of Modesto Lanzone,
	San Francisco, CA

225 **Dennis M. Morinaka**
Wonder Blue, 1982–84
Bamboo, poplar, copper leaf, redwood burl,
	Japanese cloth
Carved, leaf appliquéd, constructed, lacquered
6⅞ x 36½ x 5¼"
Courtesy of Susan Cummins Gallery,
	Mill Valley, CA

226 **Wayne Higby**
Firewall Gap, 1985
Earthenware
Handbuilt, raku-fired
12¼ x 32 x 6"
Courtesy of Helen Drutt Gallery, Philadelphia, PA

227 **William Underhill**
Kabuto, 1984
Bronze
Lost-wax cast
10 x 13 x 9½"

228 **Cliff Garten**
Spiral Vase, 1984
White earthenware, glazes
Thrown vessels, slip applied to tiles
46½ x 112½ x 9¾"
Courtesy of Helen Drutt Gallery, Philadelphia, PA

229 **Rudy Autio**
Going to the Sun, 1985
Stoneware
Handbuilt
35½ x 30 x 17"
Collection of Spencer-Scott, Weston, MA

230 **Arnold Zimmerman**
Untitled, 1985
Stoneware
Handbuilt, carved
102 x 44 x 42"

230a Untitled, 1985
Stoneware
Handbuilt, carved
113 x 48 x 44"

230b Untitled, 1985 (not illustrated)
Stoneware
Handbuilt, carved
110 x 45 x 42"
Courtesy of Objects Gallery, Chicago, IL

231 **Betty Woodman**
Four Handled Vase with Green Shadow, 1985
Earthenware, glazes
Thrown, assembled
Vase: 25 x 22 x 7½"
Shadow: 24 x 21½ x 3"
Courtesy of Max Protech Gallery, New York, NY

232 **Margie Jervis**
Susie Krasnican
Landscape Vases, 1985
Plate glass, wood, photograph
Constructed, enameled, painted
39½ x 61½ x 1½"
Courtesy of Heller Gallery, New York, NY

233 **Tim Harding**
Memento Mori, 1985
Cotton
Dyed, layered, quilted, slashed, frayed
54 x 66 x 2"

234 **Arline M. Fisch**
Necklace, 1985
18k gold, fine silver wire
Spool-knit
10 x 10 x 2½"
Courtesy of Helen Drutt Gallery, Philadelphia, PA

235 **Mary Lee Hu**
Choker #59, 1980
Fine and sterling silver
Twined, constructed
8¾ x 7½ x 1½"
Collection of Virginia K. Lewis, Richmond, VA

235a *Bracelet #34,* 1985 (not illustrated)
Fine and sterling silver, 18k gold
Soumak, constructed
¾ x 4" diam.

236 **John Paul Miller**
Bracelet, 1984
Oxidized 18k gold, pure gold
Fused, fabricated
1 x 2⅝ x 2⅛"
Private collection

237 **Alma Eikerman**
Set of Three Bracelets, 1984
Sterling silver, 14k gold
Formed, constructed
1¼ x 3½ x 2½"

238 **Gayle Saunders**
Neckpiece, 1982–85
14k yellow, pink, green, and white golds,
	18k yellow gold, mild steel
Fused, formed, constructed
7 x 4 x ¼"

238a *Brooch and Ring,* 1982–85 (not illustrated)
14k yellow, pink, green, and white golds, 18k
	yellow gold, mild steel
Fused, formed, constructed
Brooch: 1¼ x 4 x ¾"
Ring: 1 x 1 x ½"

239 **Hiroko Sato Pijanowski**
Gene Pijanowski
Neckpiece Gold No. 1, Bracelet Gold No. 1, 1985
Paper string, canvas
Constructed
Neckpiece: 9 x 23 x 1"
Bracelet: 3¼ x 10 x 1

240 **Donald Friedlich**
Tension Series, 1985
Ivory, 18k gold, titanium
Sandblasted, carved, roller printed, riveted,
	anodized
1¾ x 2⅛ x ⅜"
Courtesy of Helen Drutt Gallery, Philadelphia, PA

241 **Linda Threadgill**
Snake Pin, 1985
Sterling silver, brass
Constructed, spray etched
2¼ x 2¼ x 1"

242 **Robert Ebendorf**
Brooch, 1985
Wood, paper, paint, plexiglass
Assembled
3 x 3"

242a *Brooch* 1985 (not illustrated)
Silver, wood, shell
Assembled
1¼ x 3¾ x 1¼"

243 **Eleanor Moty**
Perspective Illusion Brooch, 1985
Sterling silver, 18k gold, topaz, rutilated quartz
Fabricated
2 x 2½ x ¾"

244 **Deborah Aguado**
Neckpiece, 1985
18k gold, sterling silver, golden beryl
Constructed, hinged
12 x 6 x ½"

245 **Tina Fung Holder**
Neckpiece, 2 Val7–785, 1985
Cotton yarn, safety pins, glass beads
Crocheted
14 x 12½"
Courtesy of Galerie 99, Bay Harbor Islands, FL

246 **Suzan Rezac**
Neckpiece, 1985
Vermeil
Constructed, gold plated
30 x 1½ x ¼"
Courtesy of Helen Drutt Gallery, Philadelphia, PA

247 **Rachelle Thiewes**
Grappelli Bracelet, 1984
Silver, 18k gold
Fabricated
1 x 6 x 7"

247a *Brooch,* 1985 (not illustrated)
Silver, 18k gold
Fabricated
⅜ x 8 x 3⅝"

248 **Stanley Lechtzin**
Torque/Pendant #68E, 1983
Silver, silver gilt, amethyst crystals
Electroformed
15½ x 7½ x 1½"

249 **Charles Loloma**
Hopi Kachina, 1985
Gold, lapis, coral, Lone Mountain turquoise
Constructed, inlaid
1¼ x 3"

250 **Ken Loeber**
Brooch, 1985
14k gold, black coral
Forged, fabricated
1½ x 3 x ½"

250a *Neckpiece,* 1985 (not illustrated)
Silk, 14k gold
Twined, forged, fabricated
30" long

251 **Ann Young**
Hummingbird Over My House, 1984
Fine silver, sterling silver, 22k gold, black opal,
	red glass
Constructed
1⅞ diam. x 1"
Courtesy of Helen Drutt Gallery, Philadelphia, PA

252 **William Harper**
The Seducer, 1984
Fine silver, 24k and 14k gold, sterling silver,
	enamel
Cloisonné enameled, fabricated
12 x 8 x 1½"
Courtesy of Alexander F. Milliken Gallery,
	New York, NY

253 **Debra Rapoport**
Found Metal Neckpiece 7/85, 1985
Metal, acrylic paint, paper cord, waxed linen
Fabricated
15½ x 5½ x 1"
Courtesy of Helen Drutt Gallery, Philadelphia, PA

254 **Martha Banyas**
Brooch, 1984
Enamel, copper, brass, silver
Fabricated, enameled
2½ x 3¼"

255 **Mary Ann Scherr**
Waist-Monitor Belt Buckle, 1985
Sterling silver, nu gold, electronics, leather
Appliquéd, constructed, engraved
Buckle: 3 x 2⅛"
Belt: 5 x 29"

256 **Sharon Church**
Beaded Collar, 1986
Jasper and glass beads, sterling silver, silk
Fabricated, strung
22" long

257 Gerhardt C. Herbst
Collar and Bracelet, 1985
Aluminum
Sandblasted, anodized
Collar: 6 diam. x 1"
Bracelet: 3 x 2½ x ¾"

258 Ana Lisa Hedstrom
Video Landscape Caftan, 1985
Silk crepe de chine
Resist-dyed
49 x 43½"

259 Bruce Metcalf
Falling Figure with Background, 1985
Silver, stainless steel, Plexiglas, photographic
   transparency
Fabricated
6¼ x 2½"

260 Jamie Bennett
Brooches, from Deer Run Series, 1985
Enamel, silver
Wet inlay enameled, fabricated
1 x 4¼ x ⅛", each

261 Colette
Pectoral #6, 1985
Sterling silver, fine silver, 24k and 14k gold,
   bronze
Cloisonné enameled, fabricated
9¼ x 3⅛ x ¼"

262 Rebekah Laskin
Brooch, 1985
Enamel on copper, sterling silver
Enameled, constructed
1¾ x 1¾"

Courtesy of Helen Drutt Gallery, Philadelphia, PA

263 Jean Williams Cacicedo
Celebration Buffalo Coat, 1985
Wool, cotton
Dyed, felted, woven, knitted, appliquéd, reverse
   appliquéd, quilted, lined
56 x 52 x ¼"

Courtesy of Julie: Artisans' Gallery, New
   York, NY

264 Randall Darwall
Shawl, 1985
Silk, wool, metallic thread, mohair, rayon
Warp-dyed, woven (three harness twill and five
   harness satin block weave)
96 x 23"

Courtesy of Julie: Artisans' Gallery,
   New York, NY

265 Ruth Nivola
Adornment, 1983
Metallic yarns, Indian silks
Crocheted, sewn, appliquéd, whipped,
   hammered
13½ x 9½"

266 Linda MacNeil
Neckpiece, 1986
Glass, gold, granite
Cut, ground, drilled, polished, fabricated
10⅛ x 6¾ x 1½"

267 Vernon Reed
Cyberscape Zero, 1985
Titanium, acrylic, rubber, microcomputer, liquid
   crystal display
Fabricated, programmed
12 x 10½ x 1½"

268 Marjorie Schick
Neckpiece and Bracelet, 1985
Wood, paint, rubber tubing
Riveted, painted
Neckpiece: 15¾ x 13 x 3½"
Bracelet: 5⅜ x 7 x 3"

Courtesy of Helen Drutt Gallery, Philadelphia, PA

269 Gretchen Raber
9-Pieces-G, 1985
Sterling silver, aluminum, niobium, rhodium
Constructed, anodized, plated
4 x 8 x 2"

270 Leslie Leupp
Bracelet #485, 1985
Paper, plastic, aluminum, paint
Assembled
5½ x 5½ x 9"

270a *Brooch #2285,* 1985 (not illustrated)
Paper, wood, plastic
Assembled
6 x ¾ x 1½"

271 Pavel Opočenský
Pins, 1985
Ebony, ivory
Carved
5½ x 1¼ x ½"; 5½ x 1¼ x ⅜"

272 Alice H. Klein
Calculation, 1984
Acrylic, cubic zirconia, peridot, amethyst, cul-
   tured pearls, gold-filled wire, mother-of-pearl,
   polyester resin
Fabricated, constructed
15 x 8¾ x 1½"

Courtesy of Helen Drutt Gallery, Philadelphia, PA

273 Risë Rice Nagin
Fog Area, 1985
Polyester chiffon and georgette, synthetic satin
   and shantung, cotton organdy, silk organza and
   habutai
Pieced, layered, appliquéd, embroidered, hand
   stitched
56¼ x 64½"

Courtesy of Helen Drutt Gallery, Philadelphia, PA

274 Ina Kozel
Snow Lake, 1982
Silk
Resist-painted
51½ x 43½"

275 Debra Chase
July Hat, 1984
Aluminum, acrylic, glass, steel
Fabricated
8 x 22 x 23"
Courtesy of Jayne H. Baum Gallery,
   New York, NY

275a *Winter Winds,* 1984 (not illustrated)
Aluminum, Delrin, acrylic, glass, steel
Fabricated, carved
12 x 10 x ¼"
Courtesy of Jayne H. Baum Gallery,
   New York, NY

276 Gaza Bowen
Never Say Never Again. Right, Den?, 1986
Ring lizard, Karung snake, kidskin, wood, acrylic
   paint
Cement lasting, inlaid, overlaid, wet-formed,
   painted
5 x 3 x 8", each

277 K. Lee Manuel
Shinto Shards, 1985
Feathers, leather
Painted, assembled
21" diam.

278 Julia Hill
Africa, 1985
Silk crepe de chine
Resist-painted
150 x 45"

279 Ivy Ross
Flip It Brooch #2, 1986
Sterling silver, pearls, ColorCore Formica
Fabricated
3 x 4 x ½"

This chronology records pivotal events in the
history of the American craft movement since
1851. Although by no means complete, it indi-
cates the nature and extent of craft-related
activity at various times. In the early years of th
movement, prominence is given to localized,
seminal events. In the post-World War II perio
when activity had accelerated, emphasis shift
from local and state events to those of regiona
national, and international scale. Certain even
occurring outside the United States are listed
because they were influential or because
American participation was significant.

Education
List comprises craft schools, teaching centers
craft programs in colleges and universities, an
governmental acts and other events influencir
education. Instructors who first taught the
courses listed are mentioned when known.

Organizations
List comprises artists' organizations, museum
and exhibiting centers and certain of their activ
ties; some influential craft businesses in the
early years; and relevant acts of legislatures ar
governmental agencies.

Periodicals
Locations are noted for periodicals that cease
publication prior to 1945 and for institutions
when listed. Founders are mentioned when
their careers are of particular importance and
publishers are mentioned when they are craf
organizations or museums. For more comple
information on current periodicals, consult th
bibliography.

Conferences
List comprises conferences, symposia, meet-
ings, and workshops.

Exhibitions
List comprises selected exhibitions of regior
and national significance. In the case of one
person exhibitions, only retrospectives are
listed. Institutions mentioned are the organ
unless otherwise specified.

CHRONOLOGY
American Craft 1851–1986

Compiled by Sharon K. Emanuelli

Education	Organizations and Institutions	Periodicals	Conferences
1856 Worcester Employment Society, MA, founded to educate women in sewing and lacemaking skills. Renamed Worcester Craft Center 1940. Professional Craft Studies program established 1976. **1871** Cincinnati School of Art, OH, offers first class in overglaze china painting under Benn Pitman. Wood carving and metalworking also taught about this time. **1874** California School of Design founded by San Francisco Art Association with courses in applied arts. Ceramics added 1935. Renamed Mark Hopkins Institute of Art 1893, California School of Design of the San Francisco Institute of Art 1906, and California School of Fine Arts 1917. Combined with San Francisco Art Association, renamed San Franciso Art Institute 1961. **1879** Washington U., St. Louis, MO, establishes Department of Art with courses in wood carving, bookbinding, and textile design, all discontinued by 1930, and ceramic decoration, pottery, and metalwork. **1880** Rookwood School for Pottery Decoration, Cincinnati, OH, established by Rookwood Pottery. School closed 1884. **1882** Western Reserve School of Design for Women, Cleveland, OH, founded. Renamed Cleveland School of Art and men officially admitted 1891. Renamed Cleveland Institute of Art 1945. Wood working program begun by G. E. Heidenreich 1882. Ceramics courses begun by Martha Tibbals Weaver 1909. Metalsmithing courses begun by Walter Adolph Heller 1915. **1884** Philadelphia College of Textiles and Science, PA, founded. School of the Museum of Fine Arts, Boston, MA, offers class in pottery decoration under C. Howard Walker. Department of Design organized by Walker with Katherine Child, assistant, by 1903, with courses in bookbinding taught by Mary Crease Sears, in furniture design and construction taught by Horace C. Dunham, and in stained glass, embroidery, and metalwork. **1887** Pratt Institute, Brooklyn, NY, founded by Charles Pratt with Art Department courses in wood carving and metalwork. Furniture design, weaving, basketry, and leather carving added 1903. **c. 1890** U. of Kansas, Lawrence, offers classes in weaving and bookbinding in Department of Design. Pottery and metalwork taught by Maria Benson 1919. Leatherwork and weaving taught by Marjorie Witney 1933. Furniture making and wood carving taught by Russell Lefferd 1946.	**1870** Metropolitan Museum of Art, NYC, founded, chartered to collect contemporary arts and to encourage art in industry. American Wing opened as a permanent gallery for modern decorative arts 1926. Museum of Fine Arts, Boston, MA, founded, chartered to exhibit industrially applied art. Contemporary crafts collection begun with silver pitcher from Louis C. Tiffany & Co. 1877. **1876** Pennsylvania Museum, Philadelphia, founded. Collection of art pottery begun early on under Edwin A. Barber, curator, who wrote the first history of American art pottery. Renamed Philadelphia Museum of Art 1938. **1877** Chicago Society of Decorative Arts, IL, organized. New York Society of Decorative Art, NYC, organized. **1879** Art Institute of Chicago, IL, founded. Crafts shown frequently in exhibitions organized by Chicago Architectural Club 1888–1928. Sales gallery maintained by Society of Decorative Arts of the Art Institute (now Antiquarian Society). American crafts collection begun by Bessie Bennett, curator, c. 1902, with purchases from annual national exhibitions organized by the Art Institute. Louis C. Tiffany & Co., Associated Artists, NYC, founded by Tiffany, Candace Wheeler, Lockwood DeForest, and Samuel Colman. Partnership dissolved and Tiffany Glass Co. established 1883. Renamed Tiffany Studios 1900. Women's Pottery Club, Cincinnati, OH, organized by Marie Louise McLaughlin. Disbanded c. 1890. **1880** Rookwood Pottery, Cincinnati, OH, founded by Maria Longworth Nichols, who retires 1889. Artist decorated ware discontinued late 1950s. Production ceased 1967. **c. 1885** Art Workers Guild, Providence, RI, organized. Reorganized as Handicraft Club 1904. **1888** Arts and Crafts Exhibition Society of London, England, organized partly in response to John Ruskin and William Morris, who favored the humanizing influence of handwork over industrialized production. Its members lecture in the United States, catalyzing many American organizations. American craft groups number in the thousands by the turn of the century. **1890** Keramic Club of San Francisco, CA, organized.	**1868** *Builder and Woodworker*, Chicago, IL.	

Education	Organizations and Institutions	Periodicals	Conferences
	1892 Chicago Ceramic Association, IL, organized. New York Society of Ceramic Arts, NYC, organized. **c. 1892** National League of Mineral Painters organized by Susan S. G. Frackelton.		
1893 Dr. William G. Frost, president of Berea College, KY, initiates program, soon known as Fireside Industries, to sell handwork of students and their families; income taken as tuition. Absorbed 1905 by Student Industries, a broader program in which all students participate.	**1893** Architects Charles Sumner Greene and Henry Mather Greene arrive in Pasadena, CA. Charles moves to Carmel 1916.	**1893** *Ornamental Iron*, Chicago, IL. Ceased 1895.	**1893** Ceramic Congress, Chicago, IL.
1894 Ohio State U., Columbus, establishes first North American university ceramics department in the College of Engineering under Edward Orton, Jr.	**c. 1894** Roycrofters Community, East Aurora, NY, founded by Elbert Hubbard. Community activities ceased 1938.		
1895 Newcomb Pottery, New Orleans, LA, established by Sophie Newcomb School for Girls (now Newcomb College, Tulane U.). Pottery closed 1930.	**1895** Allanstand Cottage Industries, Asheville, NC, informally founded by Frances L. Goodrich to sell crafts of Southern Appalachian region. Permanent salesroom opened 1908. Goodrich donates operation to Southern Highland Handicraft Guild 1931. Chalk and Chisel Club, Minneapolis, MN, organized. Renamed Minneapolis Arts and Crafts Society 1899. San Francisco Guild of Arts and Crafts, CA, organized.	**1895** *Ceramic Monthly*, Chicago, IL. Ceased 1900. **1896** *House Beautiful*. Continues.	
	1897 Chicago Arts and Crafts Society, IL, organized during a meeting in Hull House. Museum for the Arts of Decoration at Cooper Union, NYC, founded. Museum, its collections, and library transferred to Smithsonian Institution; renamed Cooper-Hewitt Museum; temporarily closed 1967. Museum reopened in new quarters, NYC, 1976. Society of Arts and Crafts, Boston, MA, organized. Members' sales outlet established 1900. New headquarters with exhibition space opened 1904. Vienna Secession, Austria, organized as artists' association in opposition to exhibition policies of Wiener Künstlerhaus (Vienna House of Artists). Exhibition building opened 1898.		
	1899 American Ceramic Society organized. Art Division established 1918, renamed Design Division c. 1930s. Industrial Art League, Chicago, IL, organized by Oscar Lovell Triggs. Disbanded 1904.	**1899** *Keramic Studio* founded by Adelaide A. Robineau, Syracuse, NY. Renamed *Design-Keramic Studio* 1924. Refocused and renamed *Design* 1930. Continues.	
1900 New York State School of Clayworking and Ceramics founded at Alfred U., NY, under Charles Fergus Binns. Renamed New York State College of Ceramics 1932, and New York State College of Ceramics at Alfred U. 1970s.	**1900** Guild of Arts and Crafts of New York, NYC, organized.		
1901 Rhode Island School of Design, Providence, offers first art metal classes under Laurin H. Marti. Jewelry department organized 1903 by Charles E. Hansen, foreman jeweler of Gorham Co., which uses the department to train employees. Textile courses initiated by Herman O. Werner 1903. Textile facility built 1908.	**1901** Rose Valley Association, Moylan, PA, founded by William L. Price. Disbanded 1909.	**1901** *Craftsman* founded and edited by Gustav Stickley, Syracuse, NY. Ceased 1916.	
1902 Handicraft Guild, Minneapolis, MN, founded. Courses offered in metalwork, leatherwork, needlework, wood working, and clay modeling. Pottery program organized by James T. Webb 1905. Absorbed by College of Education, U. of Minnesota 1918. New Jersey School of Clayworking and Ceramics founded at Rutgers U., New Brunswick. Rochester Athenaeum and Mechanics Institute, NY, establishes Department of Decorative Arts and Crafts under Theodore Handford Pond. Courses offered in carpet weaving, metalwork, furniture making, stained glass, book design, pottery, and embroidery. Department expanded and renamed Department of Applied and Fine Arts by 1910. School renamed Rochester Institute of Technology 1944.	**1902** Society of Arts and Crafts, Grand Rapids, MI, organized.	**1902** *Handicraft* published by Society of Arts and Crafts, Boston, MA. Ceased 1904. Revived by National League of Handicraft Societies, Boston, 1910. Ceased 1912.	
1903 School of the Art Institute of Chicago, IL, offers first china painting courses under Evelyn Beachy. Discontinued 1918. Pottery taught by Judson T. Webb. Discontinued 1905; revived 1910 under Stacey S. F. Philbrick. Weaving course added under Myrtle Merritt French 1921.	**1903** Frederick Carder arrives from England, founds Steuben Glass, Corning, NY, which becomes division of Corning Glass Works 1918. Morris Society, Chicago, IL, a.k.a. William Morris Society, organized.	**1903** *Artsman* published by Rose Valley Association, Moylan, PA. Ceased 1907.	

Education	Organizations and Institutions	Periodicals	Conferences
Jewelry course added under James H. Winn 1923. Crafts offered in art education and industrial design departments. Separate departments for ceramics and textiles established 1945.	National Ornamental Glass Manufacturers Association organized. Renamed Stained Glass Association of America 1925. Wiener Werkstätte (Vienna Workshop), Austria, "a manufacturing guild of craftsmen," founded. Disbanded 1932.		
1904 Arts and Crafts Department, Throop Polytechnic Institute, Pasadena, CA, organized by Ernest Batchelder. Throop reorganized as California Institute of Technology 1910; department discontinued.	**1904** U.S. Bureau of Labor publishes special report, "The Revival of Handicraft in America," on movement's growth, goals, and social effect.		
1905 College of Education, U. of Minnesota, Minneapolis, offers first courses in wood working under James M. Tate and weaving under Margaret Blair. Programs and personnel of Handicraft Guild of Minnesota absorbed 1918, creating Department of Art Education directed by Ruth Raymond.	**1905** Los Angeles Society of Arts and Crafts, CA, organized. Society of Printers, Boston, MA, organized.		
1906 Oregon School of Arts and Crafts, Portland, founded.	**1906** Detroit Society of Arts and Crafts, MI, founded by members of Arts and Crafts Exhibition Committee; gallery and salesroom opened. International crafts shown from 1907. Shop closed 1931. Gallery closed 1941. Guild of Book Workers, NYC, organized with international membership. National Society of Craftsmen, NYC, organized. Renamed New York Society of Craftsmen 1920. Merged with New York Society of Ceramic Arts c. 1948, forming Artist-Craftsmen of New York.		
1907 California School of Arts and Crafts, Berkeley, CA, founded. Relocated to Oakland, renamed California College of Arts and Crafts 1924.	**1907** Deutsche Werkbund, Munich, Germany, founded as association of artists, craftsmen, commercial firms, including Wiener Werkstätte. Disbanded 1933. National League of Handicraft Societies organized. Comprises 33 member groups from 20 states nationwide by 1908.*	**1907** *Ornamental Glass Bulletin* published by National Ornamental Glass Manufacturers Association (now Stained Glass Association of America). Renamed *Stained Glass* 1927. Continues.	**1907** Tenth Anniversary Conference, Society of Arts and Crafts, Boston, MA. Representatives from twenty-four other societies nationwide attend; National League of Handicraft Societies formed.
1909 Kansas City Art Institute, MO, offers classes in jewelry under Ada Rapp, metalwork under Delle Miller, leatherwork under Clarence Shepard, weaving under Catherine Wood, enameling, engraving, textile dying, batik, wood carving, and clay modeling. Department of Decorative Crafts established 1922.	**1909** Newark Museum, NJ, founded under directorship of John Cotton Dana, whose interest in design and industry influences other major museums. Contemporary design exhibitions, usually including handcrafts, begun 1910. Collection of art pottery begun 1911. Raymond Duncan, brother of Isadora Duncan and an early exponent of studio weaving, visits U.S. to lecture and demonstrate looms to craft groups in major cities. First built a loom and taught weaving in his Paris studio 1905.	**1909** *Arroyo Craftsman*, single issue edited by George Wharton James, Pasadena, CA, associated with Arroyo Guild of Craftsmen.	
1910 Academy of Fine Arts, People's U. of the American Woman's League, University City, MO, establishes ceramic art department under Taxile Doat, with instructors Katheryn E. Cherry, Adelaide A. and Samuel Robineau, and Frederick H. Rhead. Initially a correspondence school, exceptional students invited to university for personal instruction. Academy closed 1914.		**1910** *Claycrafter*, Dayton, OH. Ceased 1915.	
1912 Domestic Art Department, U. of California, Berkeley, first offers textile courses under [?] Kissell. Program discontinued after 1914, revived under Lea Van Pujmbroeck Miller in Decorative Arts Department 1941, transferred to College of Environmental Design late 1960s, and discontinued 1979. Pi Beta Phi Settlement School, Gatlinburg, TN, founded by the sorority; early program emphasizes spinning, dyeing, and weaving under directorship of Evelyn Bishop. Renamed Arrowmont School of Arts and Crafts 1945.	**1913** Society of Arts and Crafts, Boston, MA, awards its first medals for excellence in craftsmanship and service. **1915** Arroyo Guild of Craftsmen, Pasadena, CA, disbands. (Organization date unknown.)		
1916 Ceramics program initiated at San Jose State Normal School (now San Jose State U.), CA, by Albert Solon and at State Normal School at Arcata (now Humboldt State U.), CA, by Horace Jenkins. Clay and possibly other craft programs added to education courses in other state normal schools (now California State U. system) around this time. San Jose program wanes early 1930s; reinstated under Herbert Sanders 1938. U. of Washington, Seattle, offers first courses in pottery, metalwork, and needlework in Design Department c. 1916; courses taught by Annette Edens by 1917. Textile history program (including some technical instruction) organized by Grace Denny in Home Economics Department 1916. Pottery and sculpture taught by Eugenie Worman beginning 1920.	**1916** Wisconsin Designer Crafts Council organized. Renamed Wisconsin Designer/Craftsmen, date unknown. *For complete list of National League of Handicraft Societies' founding member organizations, see Allen H. Eaton, *Handicrafts of New England* (New York: Harper & Bros., 1949), 289.	**1916** *Potter* founded and edited by Frederick H. Rhead, Santa Barbara, CA. Ceased 1917.	

Education	Organizations and Institutions	Periodicals	Conferences
1918 Otis Art Institute of the Los Angeles County Museum of History, Science, and Art, CA, founded with craft departments. Pottery and textile decoration offered, wood carving taught by Emily Rutherford Mocine, and jewelry and metalwork taught by Douglas Donaldson by 1922. Separated from museum, renamed Los Angeles County Art Institute 1947. Renamed Otis Art Institute of Los Angeles County 1960. Merged with Parsons School of Design (NYC) 1978. **1919** Staatliches Bauhaus, Weimar, Germany, founded. Moved to Berlin, then to Dessau. Closed 1933. U. of California, Los Angeles, founded with Handicrafts and Elementary Industrial Arts Department offering weaving under Belle H. Whitice. Art Department established 1920, offering pottery under Olive Newcomb and leatherwork, basketry, bookbinding, metalcraft, and weaving. Except textiles, most courses lapsed 1930s. Ceramics revived by Laura Andreson 1936. **1923** Penland Weavers, NC, founded by Lucy Morgan. Pottery and metalwork classes added later. Renamed Penland Weavers and Potters Guild c. 1929, Penland School of Handicrafts 1938, and Penland School of Crafts 1984. **1925** John C. Campbell Folk School, Brasstown, NC, founded.		**1918** *American Ceramic Society Journal* published by American Ceramic Society. Continues.	
	1921 American Institute of Architects awards first Craftsmanship Medal. All institute awards consolidated, renamed Institute Honors 1975.	**1922** *American Ceramic Society Bulletin* published by American Ceramic Society. Continues. **1924** *Shuttle Craft* founded by Mary M. Atwater. Replaced by *Shuttle Craft Guild Monograph* 1960. Ceased 1967.	
	1925 Sandwich Home Industries, Center Sandwich, NH, founded by Mrs. Randolph Coolidge and local committee. Merged with League of New Hampshire Arts and Crafts 1931. San Francisco Womens Art Association, CA, organized by original members of Sketch Club (organized 1880s, merged with San Francisco Art Association 1915). Chartered to "support causes neglected by older art organizations in the Bay Area," including crafts. Renamed San Francisco Society of Women Artists c. 1928, and San Francisco Women Artists c. 1950. Established San Francisco Women Artists Gallery 1983.		
1926 Rudolf Schaeffer School of Rhythmo-Chromatic Design, San Francisco, CA, founded with courses in weaving and metalsmithing. Renamed Rudolf Schaeffer School of Design 1930s. Schaeffer's color theory especially influenced weavers of the region. Closed 1985. **1927** Cranbrook Academy of Art, Bloomfield Hills, MI, founded by George G. Booth, informally organized under Eliel Saarinen. Officially opened 1932. Weaving department organized by Loja Saarinen 1930. Ceramics first taught by Waylande Gregory 1932–33; department organized by Maija Grotell 1938. Metalwork initiated by Arthur Nevill Kirk in open studio 1927; metals department organized by Richard Thomas 1948.	**1926** American Ceramic Society first awards Charles Fergus Binns Medal for "notable contribution to the advancement of ceramic art," established 1925 by alumni of New York State School of Clayworking and Ceramics (now New York State College of Ceramics at Alfred U.). **1929** Southern Mountain Handicraft Guild, Asheville, NC, organized as an association of craft centers. Renamed Southern Highland Handicraft Guild 1933. **1930** Chicago Workshops, IL, founded as artist/designer cooperative modeled after the Austrian Werkbund. **1931** Governor appoints Commission of New Hampshire Arts and Crafts to develop the first government-sponsored program for assistance to the handicraft movement. Within six months the commission initiates the League of New Hampshire Arts and Crafts to provide training and to develop home industries. First annual exhibition and sale 1934.	**1931** *Annual of American Design 1931*, single issue published by American Union of Decorative Artists and Craftsmen, NYC.	**1928** Craft center representatives from Kentucky, Tennessee, and North Carolina meet to discuss common concerns, Penland, NC. Second meeting, Asheville, NC, 1929; Southern Mountain Handicraft Guild (now Southern Highland Handicraft Guild) formed.
1932 U. of Southern California, Los Angeles, offers first ceramics classes under Glenn Lukens, who organizes Ceramics Department in School of Architecture 1933. **1933** Black Mountain College, NC, founded by John Andrew Rice. Anni and Josef Albers, previously at Bauhaus, instrumental in college's organization. Ceramics program organized by Robert Turner 1949. Closed 1956. Craft Students League founded by YWCA of the City of New York with assistance from New York Society of Craftsmen. **1934** Scripps College, Claremont, CA, offers first ceramics course under William Manker.	**1932** Mountaineer Craftsmen's Cooperative Association, WV, established by American Friends Service Committee. Putnam County Products, NY, founded as a cooperative by Aileen Osborn Webb. **1935** Works Progress (later Projects) Administration's Federal Arts Project (WPA/FAP) established. **1936** Society of Connecticut Craftsmen organized.		**1932** First annual meeting, League of New Hampshire Arts and Crafts, State House, Concord.

Education	Organizations and Institutions	Periodicals	Conferences
1937 New Bauhaus, Chicago, IL, founded by Laszlo Maholy-Nagy with courses in weaving, woodworking, and ceramics. Closed 1938. Maholy-Nagy founds School of Design 1939; renamed Institute of Design 1944. Affiliated with Illinois Institute of Technology 1949.	**1937** Oregon Ceramic Studio, Portland, founded by Lydia Herrick Hodge. Renamed Contemporary Crafts Association and Gallery 1965.		
1938 Mills College, Oakland, CA, initiates ceramics, metalwork, and jewelry courses under F. Carlton Ball.	**1938** Arts and Crafts Association of Vermont organized. Renamed Society of Vermont Craftsmen 1947. Golden Gate Weavers Guild, San Francisco Bay Area, CA, organized. Vermont Handicraft Guild organized. **1939** American Handcraft Council, DE, organized by Anne Morgan. Handcraft League of Craftsmen organized by Aileen Osborn Webb at conference of groups from New York, New Jersey, and New England states. Merged with American Handcraft Council 1942, forming Handcraft Cooperative League of America. Renamed American Craftsmen's Cooperative Council 1942. American Craftsmen's Educational Council established to encompass educational programming for craftspeople and public 1942. American Craftsmen's Cooperative Council, primarily concerned with marketing, dissolved 1951; activities assumed by American Craftsmen's Educational Council. Renamed American Craftsmen's Council 1957, and American Craft Council 1979. Maine Crafts operated by state's Department of Education and Maine Development Commission to facilitate training of rural craftspeople and marketing of their products. Discontinued 1942. **1940** America House, NYC, established as sales outlet of Handcraft League of Craftsmen (later American Craftsmen's Cooperative Council) Made subsidiary of American Craftsmen's Educational Council 1951. Closed 1971.		
1942 Pond Farm Pottery, Guerneville, CA, founded by Marguerite Wildenhain as a summer workshop. Closed c. 1985.	**1941** Vermont Arts and Crafts Service, an advisory commission within the Department of Education, established by Vermont legislature.	**1941** *Craft Horizons* published by American Craftsmen's Educational Council (now American Craft Council). Renamed *American Craft* 1979. Continues.	
1944 Army Arts and Crafts Program authorized under General Federick Osborn, brother of Aileen Osborn Webb. Air Force Arts and Crafts Program begun as an offshoot when Armed Forces separate 1949–50. Congressional passage of Servicemen's Readjustment Act, popularly called "GI Bill of Rights," shortly precedes the proliferation of craft courses in colleges and universities nationwide. Bill grants World War II veterans most generous benefit package, including tuition subsidies and living expenses for advanced education, given to veterans of any American war. School for American Craftsmen founded by American Craftsmen's Educational Council (now American Craft Council) at Dartmouth College, Hanover, NH. Moved to Alfred U., NY, 1946, and to Rochester Institute of Technology, NY, 1950, when council relinquishes control.	**1944** Potomac Craftsmen, Washington, DC, organized. Association of San Francisco Potters, CA, organized.		
1945 Indiana U., Bloomington, ceramics program established. Jewelry and metalsmithing program begun by Alma Eikerman 1947. Weaving courses initiated 1948.	**1945** Massachussetts Association of Handicraft Groups organized.	**c. 1945** Pamphlets on metalsmithing topics published by Handy and Harman, NYC, metal refiners and suppliers. Ceased c. 1952.	
1946 Fulbright-Hayes Act passed by Congress enabling the Mutual Educational Exchange Program, commonly called "Fulbright grants," in support of international educational exchange. Various programs administered by U.S. Information Agency with assistance of U.S. Information Service, Institute of International Education, and American Council on Education. Montana State U., Bozeman, ceramics program begun by Frances Senska.	**1946** Allied Craftsmen of San Diego, CA, organized. Kiln Club of Washington, DC, organized. Pennsylvania Guild of Craftsmen organized. Walker Art Center, Minneapolis, MN, maintains Gallery of Everyday Art to exhibit handmade and industrial design, with library/reading room. Shop later added. Gallery closed c. 1955.	**1946** *Everyday Art Quarterly* published by Walker Art Center, Minneapolis, MN. Renamed *Design Quarterly* 1954. Continues.	
1947 Fletcher Farm Craft School, Ludlow, VT, founded by Society of Vermont Craftsmen.	**1947** California Design, Long Beach, CA, organized. Affiliated with Pasadena Art Museum 1957–74. Separately incorporated 1974. Disbanded 1976. Pacific Northwest Arts and Crafts Association organized; established Annual Pacific Northwest Arts and Crafts Fair, Bellevue, WA. Panaca established 1961 with shop, exhibitions, and rental gallery.		**1947** Free workshop/conferences on metalsmithing sponsored by Handy and Harman, NYC, at Rhode Island School of Design, Providence. Barron Eric Fleming (Sweden) leads workshop 1948. Discontinued 1951.

Education	Organizations and Institutions	Periodicals	Conferences
	1948 Michigan Silversmiths Guild organized. Seattle Clay Club, WA, organized. Disbanded early 1970s. First annual Southern Highland Craftsmen's Fair, Gatlinburg, TN, cosponsored by Southern Highland Handicraft Guild and Southern Highlanders, Inc., a craft marketing cooperative. **1949** English potter Bernard Leach first travels to U.S. to teach summer session at Mills College at invitation of F. Carlton Ball.		
1950 Haystack Mountain School of Crafts, Deer Isle, ME, founded by Mary Beason Bishop.	**1950** New Jersey Designer Craftsmen organized. **1951** Archie Bray Foundation, Helena, MT, founded by Archie Bray as artist-in-residence program. Corning Museum of Glass, NY, founded by Corning Glass Co. Metal Arts Guild, San Francisco Bay Area, CA, organized.	**1950** *Handweaver & Craftsman.* Ceased 1975.	
1952 Bernard Leach and Japanese potter Shoji Hamada visit U.S. together, conducting workshops in colleges across the country. Accompanied on 1953 visit by Soetsu Yanagi, founder of Japanese *mingei* movement. **1954** Brookfield Craft Center, CT, founded. Peter Voulkos heads newly formed Ceramics Department at Los Angeles County Art Institute (now Otis Art Institute of Parsons School of Design), Los Angeles, CA. Attracts dynamic student group, members of which become influential artists and teachers. Moved to Berkeley, CA, 1958.	**1952** Midwest Designer-Craftsmen organized. Disbanded 1963. Midwest Weavers Association organized. **1953** National Woodcarvers Association organized. **1954** Dard Hunter Paper Museum established by Institute of Paper Chemistry, Appleton, WI. Designer Craftsmen of California organized. Renamed Designer Craftsmen of Northern California 1957. Northshore Weavers' Guild, Evanston, IL, previously a study group, organized. **1955** Northwest Designer Craftsmen organized. **1956** Museum of Contemporary Crafts, NYC, established by American Craftsmen's Educational Council (now American Craft Council). Renamed American Craft Museum 1979.	**1953** *Ceramics Monthly.* Continues.	**1952** Dartington International Conference of Potters and Weavers, Dartington Hall, England. Informal gathering of weavers, U. of Kansas, Lawrence, leads to organization of Midwest Weavers Association. First annual conference 1954. **1954** *Craftsmen and Museum Relations*, conference organized by Art Institute of Chicago, IL.
1957 Clay Art Center, Portchester, NY, founded.	**1957** Southern California Designer Craftsmen organized. Disbanded c. 1978. **1958** Embroiderer's Guild of America organized. Minnesota Crafts Council organized. **1959** Arizona Designer/Craftsmen organized. **1960** Kentucky Guild of Artists and Craftsmen organized.		**1957** First National Conference of Craftsmen, American Craftsmen's Council (now American Craft Council), Asilomar Conference Center, Pacific Grove, CA. Themes: *The Socio-Economic Outlook, Professional Practices, Design--Its Importance and Its Relation to Techniques.* **1958** Second national conference, American Craftsmen's Council, Lake Geneva, WI. Theme: *Dimension of Design.* **1959** Third national conference, American Craftsmen's Council, Lake George, NY. Theme: *The Craftsman's World.* Symposium on Design and Silversmithing, organized by Southern Illinois U., Carbondale.
1962 Hot glass facility built by Harvey Littleton at Toledo Museum of Art, OH, with specifications and formulas provided by Dominic Labino. First workshops held March, June. U. of Wisconsin, Madison, offers first college-level hot glass program, initiated by Harvey Littleton in his studio during fall term. Formal courses offered 1963. Within ten years more than 50 college programs exist in U.S.	**1961** Design Section of Ceramic Educational Council of American Ceramic Society established. Design Section separated from American Ceramic Society 1966, first meeting held 1967, and renamed National Council on Education for the Ceramic Arts (NCECA). **1963** Northwest Crafts Center, Seattle, WA, founded. **1964** World Crafts Council organized. **1965** Friends of the Crafts, Seattle, WA, founded as educational organization with exhibition space. Closed 1975. Museum West of the American Craftsmens' Council, San Francisco, CA, established. Closed 1968.	**1962** *Guild of Book Workers Journal*, published by Guild of Book Workers. Continues.	**1961** Fourth national conference, American Craftsmen's Council, U. of Washington, Seattle. Theme: *Research in the Crafts.* **1964** First World Congress of Craftsmen, sponsored by American Craftsmen's Council at its fifth national conference, Columbia U., NYC; World Crafts Council formed. Themes: *Tradition and Progress, Vistas of the Future.*
1966 Anderson Ranch Craft Center, Aspen, CO, founded informally by Paul Soldner on land owned by Snowmass Corp. Anderson Ranch Foundation organized and property donated 1972. Pottery Northwest founded by Seattle Clay Club, WA.	**1966** Northeast Regional Assembly of American Craftsmen's Council (now American Craft Council) sponsors regional craft fair, Stowe, VT. Incorporated under ACC 1975. Renamed American Craft Enterprises, Ltd. 1977. Annual fairs operated in six locations nationwide by 1985. **1967** John Michael Kohler Arts Center, Sheboygan, WI, founded. Arts/Industry Program established with four-week artist residencies at ceramic facilities of Kohler Co. 1974.		**1966** *The Role of the Crafts in Education*, Niagara Falls, NY, conference organized by Office of Education, U.S. Department of Health, Education, and Welfare. Second World Congress of Craftsmen, World Crafts Council, Montreux, Switzerland. **1967** First annual conference, National Council on Education for the Ceramic Arts (NCECA), Michigan State U., East Lansing.

Education	Organizations and Institutions	Periodicals	Conferences
1968 Southwest Craft Center, San Antonio, TX, founded.			**1968** *Supermud*, annual clay symposium, organized by Pennsylvania State U., University Park. Discontinued 1978. Third World Congress of Craftsmen, World Craft Council, Lima, Peru. Theme: *The Cultural and Economic Functions of the Craftsman in a Changing World.*
	1969 Handweavers Guild of America organized. National Quilting Association organized. National Standards Council of American Embroiderers organized.	**1969** *Shuttle Spindle & Dyepot* published by Handweavers Guild of America. Continues.	**1969** *Focus*, sixth national conference, American Craftsmens's Council, Albuquerque, NM.
1970 Peters Valley Craft Village, Layton, NJ, founded as artist residence and teaching facility with support from National Park Service. Textile Workshops, Inc., Santa Fe, NM, founded as teaching facility by Mary Woodward Davis. Closed 1983.	**1970** American Craftsmen's Council (now American Craft Council) presents first Merit Awards, a.k.a. Gold Medal. Society of North American Goldsmiths organized.		**1970** Blacksmith workshop, organized by Southern Illinois U., Carbondale. First annual (organizing) conference, Society of North American Goldsmiths, St. Paul, MN. Fourth World Congress of Craftsmen, World Crafts Council, Dublin, Ireland. Theme: *The Craftsman as Creator.*
1971 Pilchuck Glass Center, Stanwood, WA, founded by Dale Chihuly and John Hauberg. Renamed Pilchuck School 1976.	**1971** Frog Hollow Craft Center, Middlebury, VT, founded. Renamed Vermont State Craft Center at Frog Hollow 1975, when governor grants honorary state sanction in recognition of service, making it first state craft center in U.S. Glass Art Society organized.		**1971** *Fiber as Medium*, international symposium, U. of California, Los Angeles. Exhibitions and related events at colleges, museums, and galleries in greater Los Angeles area.
1972 Pacific Basin Center for Textile Arts, Berkeley, CA, founded. Southern Illinois U., Carbondale, offers first major art department program in blacksmithing under Brent Kington.	**1972** Center for Folk Art and Contemporary Crafts, San Francisco, CA, founded. Reorganized as San Francisco Crafts and Folk Art Museum 1983. Renwick Gallery of the National Collection of Fine Arts (now National Museum of American Art) of the Smithsonian Institution, Washington, DC, established. The Wharton Esherick Museum, Paoli, PA, founded, encompassing the artist's home, studio, and personal collection.	**1972** *Glass Art*. Renamed *Glass* 1977. Ceased 1983. *Studio Potter*. Continues.	**1972** *Convergence '72*, first biennial convention, Handweavers Guild of America, Detroit, MI. *Glass, Art or Craft*, first international glass symposium, organized by Museum Bellerive, Zurich, Switzerland, in conjunction with exhibition, *Glass Today*. Fifth World Congress of Craftsmen, World Crafts Council, Tarabya, Turkey.
1973 Fiberworks, Center for the Textile Arts, Berkeley, CA, founded.	**1973** Artist-Blacksmith Association of North America organized. Ceramics Museum, Niagara Falls, NY, established by Carborundum Co. Renamed Crafts Museum 1975. Closed 1976. Craft and Folk Art Museum, Los Angeles, CA, founded by Edith R. Wyle, incorporating The Egg and the Eye gallery. Crafts Program established by National Endowment for the Arts under its Visual Arts Division; awards first fellowships. National Enamelist Guild organized.	**1973** *The Anvil's Ring* published by Artist-Blacksmith Association of North America. Continues.	**1973** Seventh national conference, American Craftsmen's Council, Fort Collins, CO. Theme: *Techniques and Materials.* Blacksmiths' convention, Westville Village, Lumpkin, GA. Artist-Blacksmith Association of North America formed.
1974 Center for Book Arts, NYC, founded by Richard Minsky.	**1974** Clayworks Studio Workshop, NYC, organized as artist-in-residence program using facilities of Hunter College. New facilities opened 1985.	**1974** *The Bead Journal*. Renamed *Ornament Magazine* 1979. Continues.	**1974** Tenth anniversary celebration at sixth World Congress of Craftsmen, World Crafts Council, York U., Toronto, Canada. Theme: *The Human Condition of the Craftsman.*
1975 Program in Artisanry established at Boston U., MA. Moved to Swain School of Art, New Bedford, MA, 1985.	**1975** Bellevue Art Museum, WA, established by Pacific Northwest Arts and Crafts Association. First Fellows of the American Craftsmen's Council named, based on artistic career and contributions to the field. National Ornamental Metals Museum, Memphis, TN, founded.	**1975** *The Crafts Report*. Continues. *Fine Woodworking*. Continues. *Golddust* published by Society of North American Goldsmiths. Renamed *Goldsmith's Journal* 1977 and *Metalsmith* 1981. Continues. *Interweave*. Ceased 1981.	**1975** First International Hand Papermakers Conference, organized by Joe Wilfer, at Institute of Paper Chemistry, Appleton, WI.
	1976 Ross C. Purdy Museum of Ceramics established by American Ceramic Society. Permanent space allotted in ACS headquarters, Columbus, OH, 1981. Surface Design Association organized.	**1976** *Fiberarts*. Continues. *Glass Art Society Newsletter* published by Glass Art Society. Renamed *Glass Art Society Journal* 1979. Continues.	**1976** First national conference, Artist-Blacksmith Association of North America, Southern Illinois U., Carbondale. Second International Hand Papermakers Conference, organized by Santa Barbara Museum of Art, CA. *New American Glass: Focus West Virginia*, conference and exhibition organized by Huntington Galleries, WV, culminate workshops with master glass artists conducted in nearby industrial glass facilities during preceding eighteen months. *Surface Design I*, first annual (organizing) conference, Surface Design Association, U. of Kansas, Lawrence. *Woodturning: Philosophy and Practice*, first in series of ten semiannual symposia organized by Alan Le Coff, Albert Le Coff, and Palmer Sharpless, at George School, Newtown, PA. Discontinued 1981. Seventh World Congress of Craftsmen, World Crafts Council, Oaxtepec, Mexico. Theme: *The Living Crafts: Tradition and Quality.*

Education	Organizations and Institutions	Periodicals	Conferences
1977 New York Experimental Glass Workshop, NYC, founded by Erik Erikson, Richard Yelle, and Joe Upham.		**1977** *Surface Design Journal* published by Surface Design Association. Continues.	**1977** Eighth national conference, American Craftsmen's Council, Winston-Salem, NC. Theme: *The Cultural and Industrial Heritage of the Southeast.* Third National Hand Papermakers Conference, organized by Center for Book Arts, NYC.
	1978 California Crafts Museum of the Palo Alto Cultural Center, CA, founded. Moved to San Francisco 1984. Mingei International Museum of World Folk Art, La Jolla, CA, founded by Martha Longenecker. National Council on Apprenticeship in Art and Craft organized.	**1978** *Glass Studio.* Continues.	**1978** *Craft, Art and Religion,* symposium, organized by Committee of Religion and Art in America, cosponsored by Smithsonian Institution and Vatican Museum in conjunction with exhibition of works by American artists, Vatican City, Italy. *Fiberworks Symposium* on international contemporary textile art, organized by Fiberworks, Center for Textile Arts, Berkeley, CA. National Craft Apprenticeship Conference, directed by Gerry Williams, at State U. of New York, Purchase. National Council on Apprenticeship in Art and Craft formed. *Paper: Art and Technology,* conference organized by San Francisco Museum of Modern Art and World Print Council, San Francisco, CA. Eighth World Congress of Craftsmen, World Crafts Council, Kyoto, Japan. Theme: *The Craftsman in Industrial Society—The Role of Handcraft.*
	1979 Society of American Woodworkers organized. Disbanded 1981.		**1979** *Wood Conference '79: State of the Art,* first (organizing) conference of Society of American Woodworkers, State U. of New York, Purchase. Second conference 1980. Discontinued.
1980 Joe L. Evins Appalachian Center for Crafts, Smithville, TN, founded with programs in clay, fiber, glass, metal, and wood. Wendell Castle Workshop, Scottsville, NY, founded by the artist to teach furniture making. Renamed Wendell Castle School 1985.	**1980** Michigan Glass Month established by resolution of legislature.	**1980** *Craft International* founded by Rose Slivka, published by Craft and Folk Art Museum, Los Angeles, CA. Publication transferred to World Craft Foundation of World Craft Council, NYC, 1983. Continues. *NCECA Journal* published by National Council on Education for the Ceramic Arts. Continues. *Neues Glas,* published in West Germany with international scope. English translation printed from 1981. Continues.	**1980** International Conference of Hand Papermakers, Boston, MA, organized by Carriage House Handmade Paperworks, cosponsored by Program in Artisanry of Boston U. and Massachusetts Association of Craftsmen. International Seminar for Wood Turners organized by Parnham House, Dorset, England. Ninth World Congress of Craftsmen, World Crafts Council, Vienna, Austria.
	1981 U.S. General Services Administration awards first commissions to craftspeople.	*New Glass Review* published by Corning Museum of Glass, NY. Continues. *New Work* published by New York Experimental Glass Workshop, NYC. Continues.	**1981** National Craft Planning Congress, Arvada, CO, organized by National Endowment for the Arts culminates National Craft Survey, a two-year information-gathering project. Symposium on Scholarship and Language in Craft Criticism, cosponsored by National Endowment for the Arts and National Endowment for the Humanities, Washington, DC.
	1982 American Craft Museum II established by American Craft Council, sponsored by International Paper Company at its corporate headquarters, NYC. Closed 1985. Leather Arts Network, an international association, organized by Marc Goldring.	**1982** *American Ceramics.* Continues.	**1982** *American Metalsmithing in the 1940s and '50s,* research conference, Washington, DC, cosponsored by Archives of American Art, Program in Artisanry of Boston U., *Metalsmith,* and Renwick Gallery, Smithsonian Institution. First Inter-American Meeting of Master Artisans, Washington, DC, organized by Organization of American States. First National Conference on Leather, organized by Arrowmont School of Arts and Crafts, Gatlinburg, TN, attracts international participants. Leather Arts Network formed.
	1983 Creative Glass Center of America established at Wheaton Village, Millville, NJ, as artist-in-residence facility.		**1983** First International Apprenticeship Conference, Sydney, Australia, organized by Australian Craft Council. *IPC'83JAPAN,* international paper conference, National Museum of Modern Art, Kyoto, Japan (primary sponsor). *The Textile Arts in America: Origins and Directions,* symposium organized by Fashion Institute of Technology, NYC.
	1984 First Leonard S. and Juliette K. Rakow Awards for Excellence in the Art of Glass given by Corning Museum of Glass. Woodworking Association of North America organized.		**1984** Second biennial International Conference on Leather, Leather Arts Network, Sawtooth Center for Visual Design, Winston-Salem, NC. Discontinued. Tenth World Congress of Craftsmen, World Crafts Council, Oslo, Norway.
	1985 American Association of Woodturners organized.		**1985** International Craft Conference, World Crafts Council, Jakarta, Indonesia. National Woodturning Conference organized by Arrowmont School of Arts and Crafts, Gatlinburg, TN. American Association of Woodturners formed.
			1986 *Art/Culture/Future,* ninth national conference, American Craft Council, Oakland Museum, CA.

Major Craft Exhibitions 1851–1986

1851
First Great International Exhibition celebrates Industrial Age at Crystal Palace, London, England.

1856
Annual *Mechanics Institute Fairs*, San Francisco, CA, include painting, sculpture, and handcrafts as well as industrial exhibits. Discontinued c. 1900.

1862
International Exhibition, South Kensington, England, gives first public recognition of [William] Morris, Marshall, Faulkner, and Co., Fine Art Workmen in Painting, Carving, Furniture, and Metals.

1876
Centennial Exposition, Philadelphia, PA, introduces European and Asian pottery to wide American audience.

1880
First annual exhibition, Cincinnati Women's Pottery Club, presented by Frederick Dallas of Hamilton Road Pottery, Cincinnati, OH. Discontinued 1889.

1887
Porcelain and Pottery Exhibition, Pennsylvania Museum of Art (now Philadelphia Museum of Art) and School of Industrial Art.

1889
World Exposition, Paris, France, awards gold medal to Rookwood Pottery and silver medal for china painting to Mary Louise McLaughlin.

1893
World's Columbian Exposition, Chicago, IL, serves as primary stimulus to American Arts and Crafts movement. Exposition includes building allotted to women's activities, with American and foreign craft exhibits. California pavilion includes exhibit of redwood objects by state's craftspeople.

1894
California Midwinter Fair and Exposition, San Francisco, showcases state's agriculture, industries, and crafts. China-painting exhibition presented in Women's Building.

1896
Bookbinding, illumination, graphics, and posters, subjects of first Guild of Arts and Crafts exhibition at J. A. G. Cartington's studio, San Francisco, CA

1897
First Exhibition of the Arts and Crafts, Representing the Application of Art to Industry and Comprising the Manufactured Articles and Original Designs for the Same, Copley and Allston Halls, Boston, MA, includes student work from School of the Museum of Fine Arts. Exhibition encourages organization of Society of Arts and Crafts, Boston.

1899
First annual *Exhibition of the Society of Arts and Crafts*, with *Loan Collection of Applied Art*, Copley and Allston Halls, Boston, MA. Exhibition's popularity prompts opening of salesroom and permanent exhibition space for members of the society. Museum of Fine Arts, Boston, first presents an exhibition for the society 1913. Annual juried exhibitions discontinued c. 1930.

1900
World Exposition, Paris, France, awards medal to Fireside Industries, Berea College, KY, for a coverlet. Rookwood Pottery awarded Grand Prix, other American potteries and individuals awarded medals. Major European museums purchase American ceramics.

1901
Pan-American Exposition, Buffalo, NY.

1902
Exhibition of Designs for Decorations and Examples of Art-Crafts Having Distinctive Merit, Art Institute of Chicago, IL. Renamed *Annual Exhibit of Applied Arts* 1903. Discontinued 1921.

1903
Arts and Crafts Exhibition, Syracuse Museum of Fine Arts (now Everson Museum of Art), NY.

1904
Arts and Crafts, Detroit Museum of Art (now Detroit Institute of Arts), MI, sponsored by Arts and Crafts Exhibition Committee. *Second Annual Exhibition of Applied Arts* organized 1905.

Louisiana Purchase International Exposition, St. Louis, MO. Division of Applied Arts dominated by members of Society of Arts and Crafts, Boston, MA. Louis C. Tiffany introduces Favrile pottery.

1906
American Silver: The Work of Seventeenth and Eighteenth Century Silversmiths, first museum exhibition of silversmithing, Museum of Fine Arts, Boston, MA.

1907
First annual exhibition, Guild of Book Workers, presented by Tiffany Studios, NYC. Exhibitions juried starting 1948.

1909
American Silver: The Hudson-Fulton Celebration, Metropolitan Museum of Art, NYC.

1911
Turin Exposition, Italy, awards Grand Prix and Diploma della Bene Merenza for porcelains to Adelaide Alsop Robineau and Grand Prix to People's University ceramics.

1912
Modern German Applied Arts, Newark Museum, NJ. Second exhibition presented 1922.

1915
Clay Products of New Jersey at the Present Time, Newark Museum, NJ.

Panama-Pacific International Exposition, celebrating opening of Panama Canal, presented in San Francisco, CA. Beaux-Arts extravaganza in Palace of Fine Arts marks end of Arts and Crafts era. The smaller *Panama-California Exposition* in San Diego introduces region's Spanish Colonial revival in architecture.

1919
Annual Exhibition of Work by Cleveland Artists and Craftsmen, regional competition, sponsored by Cleveland Art Association, organized by Cleveland Museum of Art, OH. Later known as *The May Show*. Continues.

1920
Modern British Arts and Crafts, Detroit Society of Arts and Crafts, MI, and national tour.

1921
Annual *Wisconsin Designer/Craftsmen Exhibition* presented in various museums and galleries within the state. Continues.

1925
Modern and Industrial Decorative Arts Exposition, Paris, France, focuses on Art Deco style in current European design. U.S. government declines to participate for lack of "modern" designers but sends observers. Exposition stimulates American industry to promote nontraditional design.

1926
First *Annual Exhibition of San Francisco Women Artists*, CA, held at various locations, including Women's City Club 1926–31, Palace of the Legion of Honor and M. H. De Young Memorial Museum (now Fine Arts Museums of San Francisco) 1932–35, San Francisco Museum of Art (now San Francisco Museum of Modern Art) 1936–70, and at various locations 1971–82. Discontinued in favor of permanent gallery program.

Exhibitions of objects selected from 1925 *Paris Exposition* organized by Metropolitan Museum of Art, NYC, and Newark Museum, NJ. Metropolitan's exhibition tours nationally.

1927
Swedish Contemporary Decorative Arts, Metropolitan Museum of Art, NYC.

1928
Decorative Native Arts, work by contemporary California artists, San Francisco Society of Women Artists, shown at Women's City Club, San Francisco, CA. Second exhibition presented 1929.

First International Exposition of Art in Industry organized by R. H. Macy and Co., NYC. Lord & Taylor, B. Altman, and Abraham and Straus also present design exhibitions, some with assistance of museum professionals.

International Exhibition of Ceramic Art, American Federation of Arts, tours nationally, introducing Americans to work of Wiener Werkstätte, Austria.

1929
Adelaide Alsop Robineau memorial exhibition, Metropolitan Museum of Art, NYC.

International Exhibition: Contemporary Glass and Rugs, American Federation of Arts, tours nationally.

Modern American Design in Metal, Newark Museum, NJ, shows new uses of familiar and unusual metals by thirty artists.

1930
Decorative Metalwork and Cotton Textiles: Third International Exhibition of Contemporary Industrial Art, American Federation of Arts, tours nationally.

1931
Exhibition of American Union of Decorative Artists and Craftsmen, Brooklyn Museum, NY.

1932
First *National Robineau Memorial Ceramic Exhibition*, Syracuse Museum of Fine Arts. Renamed *National Ceramic Exhibition* 1936 and *Ceramic National* 1948. Annual competition 1932–54, biennial 1954–72, then discontinued. In many years, exhibition tours nationally. Museum announces (1985) competition's reinstatement beginning 1987.

1933
Century of Progress Exposition, Chicago, IL, exhibits black pottery by Pueblo Indian Maria Martinez.

Exhibition of work from Southern Highland Handicraft Guild, Asheville, NC, organized by American Federation of Arts, tours nationally.

1935
Charles Fergus Binns memorial exhibition, Metropolitan Museum of Art, NYC.

1936
Old and New Paths in American Design 1720–1936, Newark Museum, NJ, exhibits photographs resulting from Works Progress Administration's Federal Art Project in historical scholarship, with new works of collaboration among painters, sculptors, designers, and craftspeople made for WPA/FAP programs.

1937
Selections from *Contemporary American Ceramics*, Syracuse Museum of Fine Art, NY, tours Scandinavia.

Rural Arts Exhibition, organized by Russell Sage Foundation, celebrates 75th anniversary of U.S. Department of Agriculture in its administration building, Washington, DC. Exhibition involves cooperation among Department of the Interior, Works Projects Administration, Farm Security Administration, National Youth Administration, Southern Highland Handicraft Guild, League of New Hampshire Arts and Crafts, and Society of Connecticut Craftsmen.

World Exposition, Paris, France, includes first exhibition of American crafts to travel abroad, organized by American Federation of Arts.

1938
First California Ceramic Exhibition, competition, organized by Fine Arts Gallery of San Diego (now San Diego Museum of Art), CA. Second exhibition organized 1939. Both tour statewide.

1939
Golden Gate International Exposition, San Francisco, CA, includes *Art in Action*, craft demonstrations organized by Dorothy Liebes.

New York World's Fair, NYC, exhibits Waylande Gregory's ceramic sculpture, *The Fountain of Atoms*, weighing more than twelve tons, commissioned by WPA's Federal Arts Project.

1941
Contemporary Ceramics of the Western Hemisphere celebrates tenth anniversary of *National Ceramic Exhibition*, Syracuse Museum of Fine Arts, NY.

Pacific Coast Ceramics and *Pacific Coast Textiles*, annual invitationals, City of Paris department store, San Francisco, CA. Discontinued 1954.

1942
Modern British Crafts, organized by British Council, London, tours U.S.

1943
Exhibition of Contemporary New England Handicrafts, Worcester Art Museum, MA.

1944
Annual International Textile Exhibitions, Weatherspoon Art Gallery, U. of North Carolina, Greensboro. Discontinued 1950.

1945
Scripps College Annual Ceramic Exhibition, invitational, Scripps College, Claremont, CA. Continues.

1946
Contemporary Jewelry, Museum of Modern Art, NYC.

First Biennial Exhibition of Textiles and Ceramics, Cranbrook Academy of Art Museum, Bloomfield Hills, MI. Tours nationally 1953, then discontinued.

Man and Clay, semipermanent installation, Walker Art Center, Minneapolis, MN. Dismantled c. 1948.

First annual *Michigan Artist-Craftsmen*, Detroit Institute of Arts, MI, organized by Detroit Artists Market. Renamed *Exhibition for Michigan Artist-Craftsmen* 1954. Discontinued 1971.

First *Wichita National Decorative Arts Competitive Exhibit*, Wichita Art Association, KS, annual through 1962, biennial 1964–72, then discontinued. Revived as annual event 1985. Continues.

1947
First *Annual Art Exhibition*, Fine Arts Building, Los Angeles County Fair, Pomona, CA, often focuses on crafts. Continues.

Maine Crafts and Decorative Arts, L. D. M. Sweat Memorial Art Museum, Portland, ME, organized by Portland Society of Arts.

Metalsmithing exhibitions circulated by Handy and Harman, NYC. Discontinued 1950.

c. 1947
2500° Fahrenheit: The Art and Technique of Modern Glass, Museum for the Arts of Decoration at Cooper Union (now Cooper-Hewitt Museum, Smithsonian Institution), NYC.

1948
Contemporary Swedish Decorative Arts, Worcester Art Museum, MA, and national tour.

Decorative Arts Today, Newark Museum, NJ.

Modern Jewelry under Fifty Dollars, Everyday Art Gallery, Walker Art Center, Minneapolis, MN, and national tour.

c. 1948
First biennial *American Craftsmen*, U. of Illinois, Urbana. Continues.

1949
First annual *Good Design*, Museum of Modern Art, NYC. Discontinued 1955.

1950
First *Annual Clay Competition*, western region, Oregon Ceramic Studio (now Contemporary Crafts Association and Gallery), Portland. Discontinued 1957.

Contemporary Form in Hand-wrought Silver, Metropolitan Museum of Art, NYC.

First *International Exhibition of Ceramic Art*, juried and invitational, National Collection of Fine Arts (now National Museum of American Art), Smithsonian Institution, organized by Kiln Club of Washington, DC, annual 1950–53, biennial 1953–57 and 1961–65. Moved to Division of Ceramics and Glass, National Museum of History and Technology (now National Museum of American History) 1961.

First *Young Americans*, recurring competition showing work of craftspeople under 30, America House, NYC. From 1971 continues at Museum of Contemporary Crafts (now American Craft Museum), NYC.

1951
First annual *Texas Crafts Exhibition*, Dallas Museum of Art, TX. Discontinued 1957.

1952
First biennial craft exhibition, *California I*, organized by Creative Arts League for E. B. Crocker Art Gallery (now Crocker Art Museum) Sacramento, CA. Renamed *California Crafts* 1959. Continues.

First biennial *Fiber-Clay-Metal* competition, St. Paul Gallery and School of Art (now Minnesota Museum of Art). Discontinued 1964.

5000 Years of Art in Clay, international loan and invitational exhibition, Fine Arts Building, Los Angeles County Fair, Pomona, CA.

Frederick Carder: His Life and Work, Corning Museum of Glass, NY.

Seattle Centennial Ceramic Exhibition, Henry Art Gallery, U. of Washington, Seattle, sponsored by Seattle Clay Club.

1953

Designer Craftsmen U.S.A., cosponsored by American Craftsmen's Educational Council, Brooklyn Museum, and Art Institute of Chicago, tours nationally.

New England Craft, Worcester Art Museum, MA, cosponsored by Junior League and Worcester Craft Center.

First *Northwest Craftsmen's Exhibition*, competition, Henry Art Gallery, U. of Washington, Seattle, sponsored by Seattle Weavers' Guild, Seattle Clay Club, and Lambda Rho Alumnae, annually 1953–65, and biennially 1965–77, then discontinued.

1954

American Craftsmen, U.S. Information Agency, tours internationally.

Decorated Book Papers: Seventeenth to Twentieth Centuries, Museum for the Arts of Decoration at Cooper Union, NYC.

Design in Scandinavia, American Federation of Arts, tours nationally.

Enamel: An Historic Survey to the Present Day, Museum for the Arts of Decoration at Cooper Union, NYC.

First annual *Kansas Designer-Craftsmen Show*, U. of Kansas, Lawrence.

First *Midwest Designer-Craftsmen* exhibition, Art Institute of Chicago, IL, in conjunction with its showing of *Designer Craftsmen U.S.A.*

1955

American Jewelry and Related Objects, Huntington Galleries, WV, and national tour.

First annual *California Design*, with juried and invitational sections, organized by California Design, at Pasadena Art Museum, CA, 1955–62, 1965, 1968, and 1972; at Pacific Design Center, Los Angeles, CA, 1976, then discontinued.

First biennial *Contemporary Handweaving*, six state invitational, M. Sheldon Memorial Art Gallery, U. of Nebraska, Lincoln. Discontinued 1963.

First *International Ceramics Exhibition*, Cannes, France, organized by International Academy of Ceramics, Geneva, Switzerland. Gold Medal awarded to Peter Voulkos.

1956

Craftsmanship in a Changing World, inaugural exhibition, Museum of Contemporary Crafts, NYC.

Textiles U.S.A., Museum of Modern Art, NYC.

1957

Designer Craftsmen of the West, M.H. De Young Memorial Museum and national and international tours.

Furniture by Craftsmen, Museum of Contemporary Crafts, NYC.

Twenty-four American Craftsmen, Henry Art Gallery, U. of Washington, Seattle.

1958

Brussels Worlds Fair, Belgium, includes *American Artists and Craftsmen* in American Pavilion.

Ceramic International celebrates twentieth anniversary of *Ceramic National*, Syracuse Museum of Fine Arts, NY.

Craftsmanship, juried regional exhibition, Los Angeles County Museum of Art, CA, cosponsored by Southern California Designer-Craftsmen. Second exhibition presented 1960.

Louis Comfort Tiffany 1848–1933, Museum of Contemporary Crafts, NYC, first retrospective exhibition of his work.

1959

Contemporary Enamels: A National Survey, Museum of Contemporary Crafts, NYC.

Furniture and Sculpture of Wharton Esherick, Museum of Contemporary Crafts, NYC.

Glass 1959, Corning Museum of Glass, NY.

Man and Clay, Art Galleries (now Frederick S. Wight Art Gallery), U. of California, Los Angeles.

First *Paris Biennial*, National Museum of Modern Art, France. Rodin Museum Prize for Sculpture awarded to Peter Voulkos.

The Second International Ceramics Exhibition, Ostend, Belgium, organized by International Academy of Ceramics, Geneva, Switzerland. Grand Prix des Nations awarded to U.S.

1960

American Keramik, Antwerp, Belgium.

Fabrics International, cosponsored by Museum of Contemporary Crafts and Philadelphia Museum College of Art, tours nationally.

First triennial *International Arts and Crafts Exhibition*, Stuttgart, W. Germany.

1961

Memorial Exhibition of Mariska Karasz and Katherine Choy, Museum of Contemporary Crafts, NYC.

1962

Century 21, Seattle World's Fair, includes *Adventures in Art*, exhibition of work in craft media, and *Northwest Designer-Craftsmen*.

Forms from the Earth: 1000 Years of American Pottery, Museum of Contemporary Crafts, NYC.

Third *International Ceramic Exhibition*, Prague, Czechoslovakia, organized by International Academy of Ceramics, Geneva, Switzerland.

1963

First biennial *American Jewelry Today*, Everhart Museum of Natural History, Science, and Art, Scranton, PA. Discontinued 1967.

First *International Biennial of Tapestry*, Cantonal Museum of Fine Arts, Lausanne, Switzerland. Continues.

Modern American Wall Hangings, Victoria and Albert Museum, London, England.

Works in Clay by Six Artists, San Francisco Art Institute, CA.

Woven Forms, Museum of Contemporary Crafts, NYC, first major exhibition of dimensional weaving.

1964

International Exhibition of Contemporary Ceramic Art, National Museum of Modern Art, Tokyo, Japan.

Thirteenth *Milan Triennial*, Italy. First time that American craftspeople widely represented.

1965

Clay: New Ceramic Forms, Museum of Contemporary Crafts, NYC.

The New England Silversmith: An Exhibition of New England Silver from the Mid-Seventeenth Century to the Present, Selected from New England Collections, Museum of Art, Rhode Island School of Design, Providence.

1966

Abstract Expressionist Ceramics, U. of California, Irvine.

The Ceramic Work of Gertrud and Otto Natzler: A Retrospective Exhibition, Los Angeles County Museum of Art.

Craftsmanship Defined, Philadelphia College of Art, PA.

First American Craftsmen's Invitational, Henry Art Gallery, U. of Washington, Seattle. Second exhibition presented 1968.

First biennial *Toledo Glass National*, competition, Toledo Museum of Art, OH. Discontinued 1970.

Twenty American Studio Potters, Victoria and Albert Museum, London, England.

1967

Air, Light, Form: New American Glass, Dallas Museum of Fine Arts, TX.

First Survey of Contemporary American Crafts, University Art Museum, U. of Texas, Austin.

Funk Art, University Art Museum, U. of California, Berkeley.

Maija Grotell, Galleries of Cranbrook Academy of Art, Bloomfield Hills, MI, and national tour.

1969

Fiber Structure '69, School of Fine Arts, U. of Wisconsin, Milwaukee.

Objects: USA, Johnson Collection of Contemporary Crafts, assembled by Johnson Wax, premieres at National Collection of Fine Arts, Washington, DC, tours nationally and internationally.

Twenty-five Years of Clay U.S.A. celebrates twenty-fifth anniversary of *Scripps College Annual Ceramic Exhibition*, Claremont, CA.

Wall Hangings, Museum of Modern Art, NYC.

1970

Dorothy Liebes Retrospective Exhibition, Museum of Contemporary Crafts, NYC.

Goldsmith '70, Minnesota Museum of Art, St. Paul, first of biennial exhibitions organized by various museums nationwide with cooperation of Society of North American Goldsmiths, tours nationally.

Laura Andreson: A Retrospective, Art Galleries, U. of California, Los Angeles.

Unfired Clay, University Museum, Southern Illinois U., Carbondale.

1971

Clayworks: Twenty Americans, Museum of Contemporary Crafts, NYC.

Contemporary Ceramic Art: Canada, U.S.A., Mexico, Japan, National Museum of Modern Art, Kyoto and Tokyo, Japan.

Deliberate Entanglements: An Exhibition of Fabric Forms, Art Galleries, U. of California, Los Angeles, centerpiece of *Fiber as Medium* Symposium.

Mary Ann Scherr Retrospective, Akron Art Institute, OH.

[Arthur and Lucia] Mathews: Masterpieces of the California Decorative Style, Oakland Museum, CA, and national tour.

The Metal Experience, Oakland Museum, CA, cosponsored by Art Guild of the Oakland Museum and Metal Arts Guild.

1972

American Glass Now, Museum of Contemporary Crafts, NYC, and Toledo Museum of Art, OH, and national tour.

The Arts and Crafts Movement in America: 1876–1916, Art Museum, Princeton U., NJ, first major survey of the period.

A Decade of Ceramic Art: 1962–1972, San Francisco Museum of Modern Art, CA.

Fabrications: Traditions of Tapestry Fabric Forms, international invitational, Galleries of Cranbrook Academy of Art, Bloomfield Hills, MI.

Glass Today, Museum Bellerive, Zurich, Switzerland.

International Ceramics, Victoria and Albert Museum, London, England.

First *International Textile Triennial*, Central Museum of Textiles, Lodz, Poland.

1973

Cranbrook Weavers—Pacesetters and Prototypes, Detroit Institute of Arts, MI, in conjunction with fiftieth anniversary of Cranbrook Institutions, Bloomfield Hills, MI.

International Ceramics '73, Alberta College of Art, Calgary, Canada, organized by International Academy of Ceramics, Geneva, Switzerland, cosponsored by Alberta Potter's Association.

International Glass Sculpture, Lowe Art Museum, U. of Miami, Coral Gables, FL.

1974

California Design 1910, Pasadena Art Museum, CA, organized by California Design.

Clay, Whitney Museum of American Art, NYC.

Clay Images, Frederick S. Wight Art Gallery, U. of California, Los Angeles.

Frans Wildenhain Retrospective, University Art Gallery, State U. of New York Binghampton.

In Praise of Hands, first contemporary world crafts exhibition, Ontario Science Center, Toronto, Canada, organized by World Crafts Council in conjunction with tenth-anniversary conference.

First biennial *International Exhibition of Miniature Textiles*, British Crafts Centre, London.

John Mason: Ceramic Sculpture, Pasadena Art Museum, CA.

Metal—74, State U. College at Brockport, NY.

Robert Arneson Retrospective 1961–1973, Museum of Contemporary Art, Chicago, IL.

1975

Clayworks in Progress, Los Angeles Institute of Contemporary Art, CA.

Contemporary Crafts of the Americas: 1975, Colorado State U., Fort Collins, and national tour.

Craft Multiples, Renwick Gallery of the National Collection of Fine Arts, Smithsonian Institution, Washington, DC.

Forms in Metal: 275 Years of Metalsmithing in America, shown in two parts: 1700–1940s at Finch College Museum of Art, NYC; 1940s–1975 at Museum of Contemporary Crafts, NYC. Traveled to Cranbrook Academy of Art, Bloomfield Hills, MI.

First *National Metals Invitational*, triennial (except 1983), Reese Bullen Gallery, Humboldt State U., Arcata, CA. Each exhibition retitled beginning 1983.

1976

American Crafts 76: An Aesthetic View, Museum of Contemporary Art, Chicago, IL.

Arts and Crafts in Detroit 1906–1976: The Movement, The Society, The School, Detroit Institute of Arts, MI.

Concepts in Clay: 10 Approaches, Dartmouth College Museum and Galleries, Hanover, NH.

First annual *Contemporary Glass*, Corning Museum of Glass, NY, all tour nationally. Discontinued 1978.

Fiber Structures, Heinz Gallery, Carnegie Institute Museum of Art, Pittsburgh, PA.

The Handwrought Object 1776–1976, Herbert E. Johnson Museum of Art, Cornell U., Ithaca, NY.

A History of Silver and Goldsmithing in America, Lowe Art Museum, U. of Miami, Coral Gables, FL.

Iron Solid Wrought U.S.A., University Museum, Southern Illinois U., Carbondale, first survey exhibition of contemporary forged iron.

The Jewelry of Margaret de Patta: A Retrospective Exhibition, Oakland Museum, CA.

First *New American Glass: Focus West Virginia* invitational, Huntington Galleries, WV, annual from 1978.

The North American Basket, 1790–1976, Worcester Craft Center, MA.

Structure in Textiles, Stedelijk Museum, Amsterdam, the Netherlands.

1977

California Women in Crafts, Craft and Folk Art Museum, Los Angeles, CA.

Dinnerware, glassware, and table decorations commissioned from American craftspeople by First Lady Rosalynn Carter for Senate Ladies Luncheon, May 16. Joan Mondale borrows fror American art museums for rotating displays in the Vice Presidential mansion, crafts are equitably represented. Discontinued 1981.

The Dyer's Art: Ikat, Batik, Plangi, Museum of Contemporary Crafts, NYC, and national tour.

Fiber Works: The Americas and Japan, Nation Museum of Modern Art, Kyoto and Tokyo, Japan.

Fiberworks, Cleveland Museum of Art, OH.

The Object as Poet, Renwick Gallery, Smithsonian Institution, Washington, DC.

Overglaze Imagery, Art Gallery, California Stat U., Fullerton.

1978

American Chairs: Form, Function, Fantasy, Joh Michael Kohler Arts Center, Sheboygan, WI.

American Crafts 1977, Philadelphia Museum c Art, PA.

Artist-craftsmen: An In-depth Look, Clevelan Institute of Art, OH.

The Biloxi Art Pottery of George Ohr, Mississippi State Historical Museum, Jackson.

Clay, Fiber, Metal by Women Artists, Bronx Museum, NY, sponsored by Women's Caucus for Art.

Clay from Molds: Multiples, Altered Castings, Combinations, John Michael Kohler Arts Cent Sheboygan, WI.

Craft, Art and Religion, exhibition of work by American artists, Vatican Museum, Italy, cosponsored by Smithsonian Institution, Was ington, DC, arranged by Committee of Religio and Art in America.

Hand Bookbinding Today: An International Ar San Francisco Museum of Modern Art, CA.

The Harmonious Craft: American Musical Instruments, Renwick Gallery, Smithsonian Institution, Washington, DC, and national tour

New Stained Glass: 10 American Artists, Museum of Contemporary Crafts, NYC.

Nine West Coast Clay Sculptors, Everson Museum of Art, Syracuse, NY.

Ornament in the Twentieth Century, Cooper-Hewitt Museum, Smithsonian Institution, NYC.

Peter Voulkos: A Retrospective 1948–1978, Museum of Contemporary Crafts, NYC, and national tour.

The Potters Art in California 1885–1955, Oakland Museum, CA.

1979

First triennial *Americans in Glass*, Leigh Yawkey Woodson Art Museum, Wausau, WI; 1985 exhibition tours internationally.

Another Side to Art: Ceramic Sculpture in the Northwest 1950–1979, Seattle Art Museum, WA.

A Century of Ceramics in the United States: 1878–1978, Everson Museum of Art, Syracuse, NY, and national tour.

Claire Zeisler—A Retrospective, Art Institute of Chicago, IL.

Functional Forms in Clay: Four Decades, Henry Art Gallery, U. of Washington, Seattle.

Goldsmith '79, Minnesota Museum of Art, St. Paul, with cooperation of Society of North American Goldsmiths, tours internationally.

Harrison McIntosh, Studio Potter: A Retrospective Exhibition, Rex W. Wignall Museum, Chaffey Community College, Alta Loma, CA.

New Glass: A Worldwide Survey, Corning Museum of Glass, NY.

Northern California Clay Routes: Sculpture Now, San Francisco Museum of Modern Art, CA.

Olaf Skoogfors, 20th-Century Goldsmith, Philadelphia College of Art, PA, and national tour.

First biennial *Quilt National*, competition, Dairy Barn, Athens, OH. Continues.

One Space/Three Visions, Albuquerque Museum, NM, includes contemporary crafts with traditional Hispanic and Native American sections. Contemporary section included in *New Mexico: Space and Imagos*, Craft and Folk Art Museum, Los Angeles.

1980

American Porcelain: New Expressions in an Ancient Art, Renwick Gallery, Smithsonian Institution, Washington, DC, tours nationally and internationally.

Art for Use, Winter Games, 23rd Olympiad, Lake Placid, NY, organized by American Craft Museum for National Fine Arts Committee.

Contemporary Ceramics: A Response to Wedgwood, Museum of Philadelphia Civic Center, PA.

Contemporary Glass, Indiana U. Art Museum, Bloomington, and national tour.

The Contemporary Potter: New Vessels, U. of Northern Iowa, Cedar Falls, and national tour.

Four Leaders in Glass, Craft and Folk Art Museum, Los Angeles, CA.

International Jewellery 1900–1980, House of Artists, Vienna, Austria.

Marguerite: A Retrospective Exhibition of the Work of Master Potter Marguerite Wildenhain, Herbert E. Johnson Museum of Art, Cornell U., Ithaca, NY.

Maximum Coverage: Wearables by Contemporary American Artists, John Michael Kohler Arts Center, Sheboygan, WI.

The Metalwork of Albert Paley, John Michael Kohler Arts Center, Sheboygan, WI.

1981

The Art Fabric: Mainstream, American Federation of Arts, tours nationally.

Ceramic Sculpture: Six Artists, San Francisco Museum of Modern Art and Whitney Museum of American Art, and national tour.

Contemporary Glass: Australia, Canada, U.S.A., and Japan, National Museum of Modern Art, Kyoto and Tokyo, Japan.

Enamels 50/80, organized by Brookfield Craft Center, CT, cosponsored by Manchester Institute of Arts and Sciences, NH, and Worcester Craft Center, MA.

Glass Art '81: International Exhibition, Kassel, W. Germany.

Glass: Artist and Influence, Jesse Besser Museum, Alpena, MI, and Detroit Institute of Arts, MI, and national tour.

Good as Gold: Alternative Materials in American Jewelry, Smithsonian Institution Traveling Exhibitions Service (SITES), tours nationally.

Innovative Furniture in America, Cooper-Hewitt Museum, Smithsonian Institution, NYC.

Made in LA: Contemporary Crafts '81, Craft and Folk Art Museum, Los Angeles, CA, celebrates Los Angeles bicentennial.

Matter, Memory and Meaning, Honolulu Academy of Art, HI, and national tour.

Old Traditions-New Directions, Textile Museum, Washington, DC.

Paint on Clay, John Michael Kohler Arts Center, Sheboygan, WI.

30 Years of Creative Textiles, Jack Lenor Larsen retrospective, Decorative Arts Museum, Palace of the Louvre, Paris, France.

Viola Frey Retrospective, organized by Creative Arts League of Sacramento for Crocker Art Museum, Sacramento, CA, as part of *California Crafts* series.

1982

Basketry: Tradition in New Form, Institute of Contemporary Art, Boston, MA, and national tour.

Douglass Morse Howell Retrospective, American Craft Museum, NYC.

Forms of Leather, Arrowmont School of Arts and Crafts, Gatlinburg, TN.

Glen Lukens: Pioneer of the Vessel Aesthetic, Fine Arts Gallery, California State U., Los Angeles, and national tour.

New American Paper Works, World Print Council, San Francisco, CA, national and international tours.

Papermaking USA: History, Process, Art, American Craft Museum II, tours nationally as *Making Paper*.

Pattern: An Exhibition of the Decorated Surface, American Craft Museum II, NYC.

The Tapestries of Trude Guermonprez: A Retrospective, Oakland Museum, CA.

Towards a New Iron Age, Victoria and Albert Museum, London, England, and U.S. tour.

The Wisconsin Movement—Glass in Form, Allen Priebe Gallery, U. of Wisconsin, Oshkosh, and national tour.

First triennial *World Glass Now*, Hokkaido Museum of Modern Art, Sapporo, Japan.

1983

The Art of Wood Turning, with historic and contemporary work, American Craft Museum II, NYC.

Art to Wear: New Handmade Clothing, American Craft Museum II, NYC, and national tour.

The Arts and Craft Movement in New York State 1890s–1920s, Gallery Association of New York State and Tyler Art Gallery, State U. of New York, Oswego, and statewide tour.

Beatrice Wood Retrospective, California State U., Fullerton, and national tour.

Design in America: The Cranbrook Vision 1925–1950, Detroit Institute of Arts, MI, and Metropolitan Museum of Art, NYC, and national tour.

The Diversions of Keramos: American Clay Sculpture 1925–1950, Everson Museum of Art, Syracuse, NY.

Echoes: Historical Reference in Contemporary Ceramics, Nelson-Atkins Museum of Art, Kansas City, MO.

Henry Varnum Poor 1887–1970, Museum of Art, Pennsylvania State U., University Park, and national tour.

International Directions in Glass Art, Art Gallery of Western Australia, Perth.

Rudy Autio Retrospective, School of Fine Arts, U. of Montana, Bozeman, Yellowstone Art Center, Billings, MT, and Montana Historical Society, Helena, and national tour.

Sculptural Glass, Tucson Museum of Art, AZ, and national tour.

1984

Art in Clay, Los Angeles Municipal Art Gallery, CA.

Contemporary Jewellery: The Americas, Australia, Europe and Japan, National Museum of Modern Art, Kyoto and Tokyo, Japan.

Directions in Contemporary American Ceramics, Museum of Fine Arts, Boston, MA.

Harvey K. Littleton: A Retrospective Exhibition, High Museum of Art, Atlanta, GA, and national tour.

Jewelry USA, competition cosponsored by Society of North American Goldsmiths, and *Jewelry International*, invitational, together at American Craft Museum, NYC. *Jewelry USA* tours nationally and internationally.

Precious Objects, Worcester Craft Center, MA.

Women in Clay: The Ongoing Tradition, Octagon Center for the Arts, Ames, IA.

1985

Chicago Furniture: Art, Craft and Industry, 1833–1983, Cooper-Hewitt Museum, Smithsonian Institution, NYC.

The Edward Jacobson Collection of American Turned Wood Bowls, Arizona State U. Art Collections, Tempe.

Enamels International 1985, competition, Long Beach Museum of Art, CA, organized by Enamel Guild: West.

Masterworks of Contemporary American Jewelry: Sources and Concepts, Victoria and Albert Museum, London, England.

Neda Alhillali: Selected Works 1968–1985, Los Angeles Municipal Art Gallery, CA.

Robert Sperry: A Retrospective, Bellevue Art Museum, WA, traveled to Cheney Cowles Memorial Museum, Spokane, WA.

Robert Turner: A Potter's Retrospective, Milwaukee Art Museum, WI.

The Thirteenth Chunichi International Exhibition of Ceramic Arts, Nagoya, Japan, devotes foreign section to contemporary U.S. ceramics for first time, using collection of Everson Museum of Art, Syracuse, NY.

Vivid Form: New Inventions, Kemper Gallery, Kansas City Art Institute, MO.

Woodturning Vision and Concept, Arrowmont School of Arts and Crafts, Gatlinburg, TN.

1986

The Art Quilt, Los Angeles Municipal Art Gallery, CA, and national tour.

Cast Glass Sculpture, California State U., Fullerton.

Fiber R/Evolution, Milwaukee Art Museum and University Art Museum, U. of Wisconsin, Milwaukee.

Perspectives in Glass: Present Tense, Craft and Folk Art Museum, Los Angeles, CA.

Robert Arneson: Sculpture and Drawings 1961–86, Des Moines Art Center, IA, and national tour.

The Woven and Graphic Art of Anni Albers, Renwick Gallery, Smithsonian Institution, Washington, DC, and national tour.

BIOGRAPHIES OF THE ARTISTS

Compiled by Terri Lonier

Mark Abildgaard
Davis, California

Born: San Francisco, California, 1957

Education: B.A., San Francisco State U., CA, 1979; M.F.A., U. of Hawaii, Honolulu, 1983

Award/Honor: Creative Glass Center of America Fellowship, 1985

Exhibitions: *Americans in Glass 1984*, Leigh Yawkey Woodson Art Museum, Wausau, WI, and tour, 1984; *Tokyo Glass Art Institute Group Show*, Tokyo, Japan, 1984; *Artists of Hawaii*, Honolulu Academy of Arts, HI, 1983, 1981; two-person exhibition, Contemporary Arts Center, Honolulu, HI, 1983

Collections: Contemporary Arts Center, Honolulu, HI; HI State Foundation on Culture and the Arts, Honolulu; Tokyo Glass Art Institute, Japan

Related Professional Experience: visiting artist, Tokyo Glass Art Institute, Notojima Glass Studio, Japan, 1984; artist-in-residence, Sculpture Space, Utica, NY, 1985

Hank Murta Adams
Smithville, Tennessee

Born: Philadelphia, Pennsylvania, 1956

Education: B.F.A., Rhode Island School of Design, Providence, 1978

Exhibitions: *Contemporary Blown Glass*, Museum of Fine Arts, St. Petersburg, FL, 1982; *Americans in Glass*, Leigh Yawkey Woodson Art Museum, Wausau, WI, and tour, 1981; *Contemporary Glass: Australia, Canada, U.S.A., and Japan*, National Museum of Modern Art, Kyoto and Tokyo, Japan, 1981; *Glass Routes*, DeCordova Museum, Lincoln, MA, 1981

Collections: Corning Museum of Glass, NY; Honolulu Academy of Art, HI; Leigh Yawkey Woodson Art Museum, Wausau, WI; Glass Museum, Fraunau, W. Germany

Related Professional Experience: faculty, Appalachian Center for Crafts, Smithville, TN, 1981–85; artist-in-residence, Artpark, Lewiston, NY, 1985

Deborah Aguado
New York, New York

Born: New York, New York, 1939

Education: B.A., Brooklyn College, NYC, 1972; M.A., New York U., NYC, 1982

Awards/Honors: NEA Fellowship, 1978; NY Foundation for the Arts Fellowship, 1985

Exhibitions: *Masterworks of Contemporary American Jewelry: Sources and Concepts,* Victoria and Albert Museum, London, England, 1985; *Jewelry USA,* American Craft Museum, NYC, and tour, 1984–86; *Art to Wear: New Handmade Clothing,* American Craft Museum, NYC, and tour, 1983–84; *Good As Gold: Alternative Materials in American Jewelry,* SITES tour, 1981–84; *Clay, Fiber, Metal by Women Artists,* Bronx Museum, NYC, 1978; *Jewelry '77—Tendencies,* Jewelry Museum, Pforzheim, W. Germany, 1977

Collections: American Craft Museum, NYC; Smithsonian Institution, Washington, DC

Related Professional Experience: faculty, Parsons School of Design/New School, NYC, 1971–present

Adela Akers
Philadelphia, Pennsylvania

Born: Santiago de Compostela, Spain, 1933

Education: School of the Art Institute of Chicago, IL, 1957–60; Cranbrook Academy of Art, Bloomfield Hills, MI, 1960–61, 1962–63

Awards/Honors: NEA grant, 1969, 1971; NJ State Council on the Arts grant, 1971; NEA Fellowship, 1974, 1980; PA Council on the Arts grant, 1983

Exhibitions: solo exhibition, Philadelphia Academy of Fine Arts, PA, 1986; *Jacquard Textiles*, Rhode Island School of Design Museum of Art, Providence, and SITES tour, 1982; *Fiber: Thread and Cloth Forms*, Dayton Art Institute, OH, 1981; *8 Artists*, Philadelphia Museum of Art, PA, 1978; *Young Americans 1962*, Museum of Contemporary Crafts, NYC, 1962

Collections: American Craft Museum, NYC; Chase Manhattan Bank, NYC; Equitable Life Assurance Society, NYC and Milford, CT; Everson Museum of Art, Syracuse, NY; Hewlett-Packard, Palo Alto, CA; Providence Museum of Art, RI

Related Professional Experience: faculty, Tyler School of Art, Philadelphia, PA, 1972–present

Neda Alhilali
Santa Monica, California

Born: Cheb, Czechoslovakia, 1938

Education: B.F.A., M.F.A., U. of California, Los Angeles, 1966, 1968

Awards/Honors: NEA Fellowship, 1974, 1979

Exhibitions: *Mixed Media/Fiber*, Southwest Crafts Center, San Antonio, TX, 1985; *Neda Alhilali: Selected Works 1968–1985*, Los Angeles Municipal Art Gallery, CA, 1985; *On and Off the Wall*, Oakland Museum, CA, and tour, 1983–84; *Neda Alhilali: Paper Constructions*, Seattle Art Museum, WA, 1982; *The Art Fabric: Mainstream*, American Federation of Arts national tour, 1981–83; *Made in L.A.*, Craft and Folk Art Museum, Los Angeles, CA, 1981; *American Crafts: An Aesthetic View*, Museum of Contemporary Art, Chicago, IL, 1976; *International Biennial of Tapestry*, Cantonal Museum of Fine Arts, Lausanne, Switzerland, 1971; *Objects: USA*, Johnson Collection of Contemporary Crafts, national and international tour, 1969–72

Collections: American Express, NYC; International Paper, NYC; Xerox, Torrance, CA; Banff Center, Canada; Central Museum of Textiles, Lodz, Poland

Related Professional Experience: faculty, Scripps College, Claremont, CA, 1969–present

Douglas Anderson
Mount Vernon, Ohio

Born: Erie, Pennsylvania, 1952

Education: B.F.A., Columbus College of Art and Design, OH, 1975; M.F.A., Rochester Institute of Technology, NY, 1980

Award/Honor: OH Arts Council Fellowship, 1985

Exhibitions: *Contemporary American and European Glass*, Oakland Museum, CA, 1986; *Glass Now '84*, Yamaha Corporation, Tokyo, Japan, 1984; *Sculptural Glass*, Tucson Museum of Art, AZ, 1983

Collections: Corning Museum of Glass, NY; Goodyear Tire and Rubber, Akron, OH

Related Professional Experience: Rakow commission, Corning Museum of Glass, NY, 1986

Robert Arneson
Benicia, California

Born: Benicia, California, 1930

Education: B.A., California College of Arts and Crafts, Oakland, 1954; M.F.A., Mills College, Oakland, CA, 1958

Exhibitions: *Robert Arneson: Sculpture and Drawings 1961–86*, Des Moines Arts Center, IA, Hirshhorn Museum and Sculpture Garden, Smithsonian Institution, Washington, DC, and Portland Art Museum, OR, 1986–87; *Ceramic Sculpture: Six Artists*, Whitney Museum of American Art, NYC, and San Francisco Museum of Modern Art, CA, 1981–82; *The Clay Figure*, American Craft Museum, NYC, 1981; *A Century of Ceramics in the United States: 1878–1978*, Everson Museum of Art, Syracuse, NY, 1979; *Biennial Exhibition,* Whitney Museum of American Art, NYC, 1979, 1970; *Robert Arneson: A Ret-rospective*, Museum of Contemporary Art, Chicago, IL, and San Francisco Museum of Modern Art, CA, 1974; *Objects: USA*, Johnson Collection of Contemporary Crafts, national and international tour, 1969–72

Publications: *Robert Arneson*, monograph to accompany retrospective exhibition, Museum of Contemporary Art, Chicago, IL, 1974; *My Head in Ceramics*, self-published, 1972

Collections: American Craft Museum, NYC; Hirshhorn Museum and Sculpture Garden, Smithsonian Institution, Washington, DC; Oakland Museum, CA; Philadelphia Museum of Art, PA; San Francisco Museum of Modern Art, CA; Santa Barbara Museum of Art, CA; Stedelijk Museum, Amsterdam, Netherlands

Related Professional Experience: faculty, U. of California, Davis, 1962–present

Rudy Autio
Missoula, Montana

Born: Butte, Montana, 1926

Education: B.S., Montana State U., Bozeman, 1950; M.F.A., Washington State U., Pullman, 1952

Awards/Honors: Tiffany grant, 1963; Honorary Member, National Council on Education for the Ceramic Arts, 1977; Fellow, American Craft Council, 1978; American Ceramic Society art award, 1978; NEA Fellowship, 1980; Montana governor's award, 1980

Exhibitions: *Directions in Contemporary Ceramics*, Museum of Fine Arts, Boston, MA, 1983; *Rudy Autio: A Retrospective*, School of Fine Arts, U. of Montana, Missoula, and tour, 1983; *A Century of Ceramics in the United States: 1878–1978*, Everson Museum of Art, Syracuse, NY, and tour, 1979; *Objects: USA*, Johnson Collection of Contemporary Crafts, national and international tour, 1969–72; *American Studio Potters*, Victoria and Albert Museum, London, England, 1966

Publications: *Rudy Autio: A Retrospective*, monograph to accompany exhibition, U. of Montana, Missoula, 1983

Collections: American Craft Museum, NYC; Brooklyn Museum, NYC; Portland Art Museum, OR; Toledo Art Museum, OH; Applied Arts Museum, Helsinki, Finland

Related Professional Experience: founding codirector (with Peter Voulkos) and resident artist, Archie Bray Ceramics Foundation, Helena, MT, 1952–57; faculty, U. of Montana, Missoula, 1957–85

John Babcock
Davenport, California

Born: Miami, Florida, 1941

Education: B.A., M.F.A., San Francisco State U., 1966; M.F.A., Academy of Arts and Humanities, Seaside, CA, 1976

Exhibitions: *Works in Paper*, Monterey Peninsula Museum of Art, CA, 1984; *Hand Cast Paper*, Los Gatos Museum, CA, 1982; *Papermaking USA*, American Craft Museum, NYC, 1982; *Paper Art*, Crocker Art Museum, Sacramento, CA, 1981; *The Handmade Paper Object*, Santa Barbara Museum of Art, CA, and tour, 1976–77; *Prints and Unique Works on Handmade Paper*, Museum of Modern Art, NYC, 1976

Collections: American Craft Museum, NYC; Cargill, Minneapolis, MN; Center for the Book Arts, NYC; Chubb Insurance Group, Warren, NJ; Detroit Institute of Arts, MI; Gulf Oil, Houston, TX; International Paper, NYC

Ralph Bacerra
Los Angeles, California

Born: Garden Grove, California, 1938

Education: B.F.A., Chouinard Art School, Los Angeles, CA, 1961

Exhibitions: *Echoes: Historical Reference in Contemporary Ceramics*, Nelson-Atkins Museum of Art, Kansas City, MO, 1983; *The Animal Image: Contemporary Objects and the Beast*, Renwick Gallery, Smithsonian Institution, Washington, DC, 1981; *American Porcelain: New Expressions in an Ancient Art*, Renwick Gallery, Smithsonian Institution, Washington, DC, and SITES tour, 1980–84; *California Design IX*, Pasadena Art Museum, CA, 1974; *A Decade of Ceramic Art: 1962–72*, San Francisco Museum of Modern Art, CA, 1972; *International Ceramics*, Victoria and Albert Museum, London, England, 1972; *Objects: USA*, Johnson Collection of Contemporary Crafts, national and international tour, 1969–72

Collections: American Craft Museum, NYC; Everson Museum of Art, Syracuse, NY; Museum of Modern Art, Kyoto, Japan

Related Professional Experience: faculty, Chouinard Art School, Los Angeles, CA, 1961–72; Otis/Parsons Art Institute, Los Angeles, 1983–present

Phillip Baldwin
Seattle, Washington

Born: New York, New York, 1953

Education: B.A., State U. of New York, College at Potsdam, 1976; M.F.A., Southern Illinois U., Carbondale, 1979

Exhibitions: *Design in America*, USIA tour, 1986–88; *Towards a New Iron Age*, Victoria and Albert Museum, London, England, 1982; *The Cutting Edge*, Kentucky Arts Commission tour, 1981–82; *Young Americans: Metal*, Museum of Contemporary Crafts, NYC, 1980; *Statements in Sterling*, Lever House, NYC, 1979

Collections: Oregon School of Arts and Crafts, Portland; Southern Illinois U., Carbondale

Related Professional Experience: artist-in-residence, Oregon School of Arts and Crafts, Portland, 1979–81; visiting faculty, U. of Washington, Seattle, 1984

Martha Banyas
Portland, Oregon

Born: Cincinnati, Ohio, 1944

Education: B.S., Miami U., Oxford, OH, 1966; M.A., Ohio U., Athens, 1968

Award/Honor: OR Arts Commission Fellowship, 1984

Exhibitions: *Forum for Jewelry and Design*, Cologne Craft Guild, W. Germany, 1985; *Metals and Enamels*, Kyoto Municipal Museum of Traditional Industry, Japan, 1983; *Oregon Biennial*, Portland Art Museum, 1983, 1981; *The Animal Image: Contemporary Objects and the Beast*, Renwick Gallery, Smithsonian Institution, Washington, DC, 1981; *Northwest Enamelists*, Museum of Art, Eugene, OR, and Visual Arts Resources tour, 1979–81; *Testimony to a Process*, Portland Art Museum, OR, 1973

Collections: Kaiser Permanente, Portland, OR; Mt. Hood Medical Center, Portland, OR; Oregon Institute of Technology, Klamath Falls

Related Professional Experience: faculty, Mt. Hood Community College, Portland, OR, 1971–present

Dorothy Gill Barnes
Worthington, Ohio

Born: Strawberry Point, Iowa, 1927

Education: B.A., M.A., U. of Iowa, Iowa City, 1949, 1951

Awards/Honors: OH Arts Council Fellowship, 1984, 1986

Exhibitions: *International Miniature Textiles Exhibition*, British Crafts Centre, London, England, 1980, 1978

Related Professional Experience: faculty, Capital U., Columbus, OH, 1965–present

Dina Barzel
Bellevue, Washington

Born: Iara, Romania, 1931

Education: B.A., Hebrew University, Jerusalem, Israel, 1957; U. of Washington and Factory of Visual Art, Seattle; Camden Institute, London, England, 1964–71

Exhibitions: *Washington Craft Forms 1950–1980*, State Capitol Museum, Olympia, WA, 1982; *Felting: Contemporary Work and Historical Precedent*, American Craft Museum, NYC, 1980; *Northwest '77*, Seattle Art Museum, WA, 1977; *Bodycraft*, Portland Art Museum, OR, 1973

Collection: Seattle City Light Portable Works, WA

Related Professional Experience: public commission, Seattle Municipal Building, 1977

Lynn Basa
Seattle, Washington

Born: Pittsburgh, Pennsylvania, 1954

Education: B.A., Indiana U., Bloomington, 1977; M.A., U. of Washington, Seattle, 1981

Exhibitions: solo exhibition, Tacoma Art Museum, WA, 1986; *Regional Crafts: A Contemporary Perspective*, Bellevue Art Museum, WA, 1984

Related Professional Experience: corporate art curator, Safeco Insurance, 1981–present

James Bassler
Los Angeles, California

Born: Santa Monica, California, 1933

Education: B.A., M.A., U. of California, Los Angeles, 1963, 1968

Awards/Honors: NEA Fellowship, 1977, 1984; NEA Apprentice Fellowship, 1981

Exhibitions: *Made in L.A.*, Craft and Folk Art Museum, Los Angeles, CA, 1981; *The Dyer's Art: Ikat, Batik, Plangi*, Museum of Contemporary Crafts, NYC, and tour, 1976–78; *Frontiers in Contemporary American Weaving/Fiber*, Lowe Museum of Art, Miami, FL, 1976; *Fabrications*, Cranbrook Academy of Art, Bloomfield Hills, MI, and tour, 1972

Collections: Chubb Insurance Group, NYC; State of California, Sacramento; State of Kansas, Wichita; *USA Today*, Arlington, VA

Related Professional Experience: faculty, U. of California, Los Angeles, 1975–80; Appalachian Center for Crafts, Smithville, TN, 1980–82; U. of California, Los Angeles, 1982–present

Bennett Bean
Blairstown, New Jersey

Born: Cincinnati, Ohio, 1941

Education: B.A., Iowa State U., Ames, 1963; M.F.A., Claremont Graduate School, CA, 1966

Awards/Honors: NJ State Council on the Arts Fellowship, 1978; NEA Fellowship, 1980

Exhibitions: *Bennett Bean: Recent Works*, New Jersey State Museum, Trenton, 1984; *Raku and Smoke*, Newport Art Museum, RI, and American Craft Museum, NYC, 1984; *Pattern: An Exhibition of the Decorated Surface*, American Craft Museum, NYC, 1982; *Contemporary American Sculpture*, Whitney Museum of American Art, NYC, 1968; *Craftsmen USA 1966*, Museum of Contemporary Crafts, NYC, 1966

Collections: Newark Museum, NJ; New Jersey State Museum, Trenton; St. Louis Art Museum, MO; Whitney Museum of American Art, NYC

Related Professional Experience: artist-in-residence, Artpark, Lewiston, NY, 1980; Sun Valley Center for the Arts, ID, 1981

Garry Knox Bennett
Alameda, California

Born: Alameda, California, 1934

Education: California College of Arts and Crafts, Oakland, 1959–62

Award/Honor: NEA Fellowship, 1984

Exhibitions: *Material Evidence: New Color Techniques in Handmade Furniture*, Renwick Gallery, Smithsonian Institution, Washington, DC, 1985; *California Woodworking*, Oakland Museum, CA, 1980; *New Handmade Furniture: American Furniture Makers Working in Hardwood*, American Craft Museum, NYC, 1979; solo exhibition, Craft and Folk Art Museum, Los Angeles, CA, 1973; *Metal Experience*, Oakland Museum, CA, 1971; *Sculpture Annual*, San Francisco Museum of Modern Art, CA, 1961, 1960

Collections: Best Products, Richmond, VA; Judah Magnes Memorial Museum, Berkeley, CA; Oakland Museum, CA

Jamie Bennett
Cambridge, Massachusetts

Born: Philadelphia, Pennsylvania, 1948

Education: B.B.A., U. of Georgia, Athens, 1970; M.F.A., State U. of New York, College at New Paltz, 1974

Awards/Honors: NEA Fellowship, 1973, 1979; MA Arts Council Artists' Fellowship, 1980, 1984

Exhibitions: *Masterworks of Contemporary American Jewelry: Sources and Concepts*, Victoria and Albert Museum, London, England, 1985; *Contemporary Jewelry: The Americas, Australia, Europe and Japan*, National Museum of Modern Art, Kyoto and Tokyo, Japan, 1984; *Jewelry USA*, American Craft Museum, NYC, and tour, 1984–86; *Contemporary Metals: Focus on Idea*, Museum of Art, Washington State U., Pullman, 1981; *Good As Gold: Alternative Materials in American Jewelry*, SITES tour, 1981–84; *Jewelry International 1900–1980*, House of Artists, Vienna, Austria, 1980

Collections: Brockton Art Museum, MA; Renwick Gallery, Smithsonian Institution, Washington, DC; Museum of Applied Arts, Trondheim, Norway

Related Professional Experience: faculty, Program in Artisanry, Boston U., MA, 1979–85; State U. of New York, College at New Paltz, NY, 1985–present

Howard Ben Tré
Providence, Rhode Island

Born: Brooklyn, New York, 1949

Education: B.F.A., Portland State College, OR, 1978; M.F.A., Rhode Island School of Design, Providence, 1980

Awards/Honors: RI State Council on the Arts grant, 1979, 1984; NEA Fellowship, 1980, 1984

Exhibitions: *World Glass Now*, Hokkaido Museum of Modern Art, Sapporo, Japan, 1985, 1982; *Hot Stuff*, St. Louis Art Museum, MO, 1984; *Howard Ben Tre and Dale Chihuly*, Newport Art Museum, RI, 1983; *Columns, Ornament and Structure*, Cooper-Hewitt Museum, NYC, 1982; *50 Americans*, Leigh Yawkey Woodson Art Museum, Wausau, WI, 1981, 1978; *New Glass: A Worldwide Survey*, Corning Museum of Glass, NY, 1979

Collections: American Craft Museum, NYC; Corning Museum of Glass, NY; High Museum of Art, Atlanta, GA; Leigh Yawkey Woodson Art Museum, Wausau, WI; Metropolitan Museum of Art, NYC; National Museum of American History, Smithsonian Institution, Washington, DC; Philadelphia Museum of Art, PA; National Museum of Modern Art, Tokyo, Japan

Katherine Bernstein (works collaboratively with William Bernstein)
Burnsville, North Carolina

Born: Newark, New Jersey, 1945

Education: B.F.A., Philadelphia College of Art, PA, 1967

Exhibitions: *Glass Now '84*, Yamaha Corporation, Tokyo, Japan, 1984; *Piedmont Craftsmen*, Renwick Gallery, Smithsonian Institution, Washington, DC, 1983

Collections: Asheville Art Museum, NC; Smithsonian Institution, Washington, DC; Hokkaido Museum of Modern Art, Sapporo, Japan

Related Professional Experience: artist-in-residence, Penland School of Crafts, NC, 1968–70

William Bernstein (works collaboratively with Katherine Bernstein)
Burnsville, North Carolina

Born: Newark, New Jersey, 1945

Education: B.F.A., Philadelphia College of Art, PA, 1968

Awards/Honors: NEA Fellowship, 1974; Tiffany grant, 1975; NEA grant, 1976; NC Arts Council Fellowship, 1983

Exhibitions: *Glass Now '84*, Yamaha Corporation, Tokyo, Japan, 1984; *New Glass: A Worldwide Survey*, Corning Museum of Glass, NY, 1979; *American Crafts in the White House*, Washington, DC, and tour, 1977; *Craft Multiples*, Renwick Gallery, Smithsonian Institution, Washington, DC, 1975; *Baroque '74*, Museum of Contemporary Crafts, NYC, 1974; *American Glass Now*, Museum of Contemporary Crafts, NYC, Toledo Museum of Art, OH, and tour, 1972

Collections: Corning Museum of Glass, NY; Craft and Folk Art Museum, Los Angeles, CA; Mint Museum of Art, Charlotte, NC; National Collection of Fine Art, Smithsonian Institution, Washington, DC; Glass Museum, Fraunau, W. Germany

Related Professional Experience: artist-in-residence, Penland School of Crafts, NC, 1968–70

Mary Bero
Madison, Wisconsin

Born: Two Rivers, Wisconsin, 1949

Education: B.S., Stout State U., Menomonie, WI, 1971

Awards/Honors: Arts Midwest/NEA Fellowship, 1985; WI Arts Board Fellowship, 1986

Exhibitions: *Fiber R/Evolution*, Milwaukee Art Museum, WI, 1986; *Textile Properties*, Minneapolis Art Institute, MN, 1985; *Needle Expressions '84*, Greenville County Museum of Art, SC, 1984; *Miniatures '82*, Triton Museum of Art, Santa Clara, CA, 1982; solo exhibition, Triton Museum of Art, Santa Clara, CA, 1981

Collection: Continental Bank, Chicago, IL

Sonja Blomdahl
Seattle, Washington

Born: Waltham, Massachusetts, 1952

Education: B.F.A., Massachusetts College of Art, Boston, 1974; Glass School, Orrefors Glass Factory, Orrefors, Sweden, 1976

Exhibitions: *Design in America*, USIA tour, 1986–88; *American Glass Now*, Yamaha Corporation, Yamaha, Japan, and tour, 1981–86; *American Glass: Northwest*, international tour,1982; *New Glass*, Bellevue Art Museum, WA, 1981

Collections: Corning Museum of Glass, NY; Fine Arts Museum of the South, Mobile, AL; Safeco Corporation, Seattle, WA; Seattle Arts Commission, WA; Washington State Arts Commission, Seattle

Related Professional Experience: faculty, Pratt Fine Arts Center, Seattle, WA, 1980–84; Pilchuck School, Stanwood, WA, 1985; Appalachian Center for Crafts, Smithville, TN, 1986

Jonathan Bonner
Providence, Rhode Island

Born: Princeton, New Jersey, 1947

Education: B.F.A., Philadelphia College of Art, PA, 1971; M.F.A., Rhode Island School of Design, Providence, 1973

Award/Honor: NEA Fellowship, 1974

Exhibition: *Pattern: An Exhibition of the Decorated Surface*, American Craft Museum, NYC, 1982

Collections: New England Institute of Technology, Providence, RI; Wichita State U., KS

Related Professional Experience: faculty, Philadelphia College of Art, PA, 1976; Rhode Island School of Design, Providence, 1978; Rhode Island School of Design Continuing Education, 1978–present

Gaza Bowen
Santa Cruz, California

Born: Memphis, Tennessee, 1944

Education: Antioch College, Yellow Springs, OH, 1962–65

Exhibitions: *Body Adornment*, Wichita Art Museum, KS, 1986; *Beyond Wearables*, California Crafts Museum, San Francisco, 1985; *Wearable Art for the Collector*, Evansville Museum of Arts and Sciences, IN, 1985; solo exhibition, San Francisco Craft and Folk Art Museum, CA, 1984; *Quintet in Art*, Art Museum of Santa Cruz County, CA, 1983; *Art Couture, Haute Couture*, Pittsburgh Center for the Arts, PA, 1981; *The Great American Foot*, Museum of Contemporary Crafts, NYC, and tour, 1978

Robert Brady
Benicia, California

Born: Reno, Nevada, 1946

Education: B.F.A., California College of Arts and Crafts, Oakland, 1968; M.F.A., U. of California, Davis, 1975

Awards/Honors: NEA Fellowship, 1981; NEA/Southeast Center for Contemporary Art grant, 1981

Exhibitions: *Modern Masks*, Whitney Museum of American Art, NYC, 1984; two-person exhibition, Huntsville Museum, AL, 1984; *The Animal Image: Contemporary Objects and the Beast*, Renwick Gallery, Smithsonian Institution, Washington, DC, 1981; *Northern California Clay Routes: Sculpture Now*, San Francisco Museum of Modern Art, CA, 1979; solo exhibition, Crocker Art Museum, Sacramento, CA, 1979; solo exhibition, Newport Museum of Art, CA, 1979

Collections: AT&T, NYC; San Francisco Museum of Modern Art, CA; Utah Museum of Art, Salt Lake City; Stedelijk Museum, Amsterdam, Netherlands

Related Professional Experience: faculty, California State U., Sacramento, 1975–80, 1982–85; master craftsman, Appalachian Center for Crafts, Smithville, TN, 1980–82

Glenn Brill
Oakland, California

Born: New York, New York, 1949

Education: B.A., Moravian College, Bethlehem, PA, 1970; B.F.A., California College of Arts and Crafts, Oakland, 1973; M.F.A., Cranbrook Academy of Art, Bloomfield Hills, MI, 1979

Award/Honor: NEA Fellowship, 1982

Exhibitions: *The Creative Spirit: A Celebration of Contemporary American Craft*, Maier Museum of Art, Lynchburg, VA, 1985; solo exhibition, San Jose Museum of Art, CA, 1985; *Pattern: An Exhibition of the Decorated Surface*, American Craft Museum, NYC, 1982; *Singular, Multiple, Multiple, Multiple*, World Print Council, San Francisco, CA, 1981; *21st Print National*, Brooklyn Museum, NYC, 1978

Collections: Brooklyn Museum, NYC; IBM, Atlanta, GA, Boca Raton, FL, and San Jose, CA; Phoenix Art Museum, AZ; San Jose Museum of Art, CA; Tamarind Collection, Albuquerque, NM; U. of Iowa Museum, Iowa City; *US News & World Report*, Washington, DC

Related Professional Experience: faculty, San Francisco State U., CA, 1983–present

Jon Brooks
New Boston, New Hampshire

Born: Manchester, New Hampshire, 1944

Education: B.F.A., M.F.A., Rochester Institute of Technology, NY, 1966, 1967

Award/Honor: MA Arts Council grant, 1985

Exhibitions: solo exhibition, Craft Council of Tasmania, 1984; *Elements of Contrast*, DeCordova Museum, Lincoln, MA, 1975; *First World Craft Exhibition*, Ontario Science Center, Toronto, Canada, 1974

Collections: Brockton Art Museum, MA; Queen Victoria and Albert Museum, Launceston, Tasmania

Related Professional Experience: faculty, St. Anselm's College, Manchester, NH, 1970–78; artist-in-residence, Artpark, Lewiston, NY, summers, 1975–78; faculty, U. of Tasmania, Hobart, Tasmania, 1983–84

Edward Frederick Burak
New York, New York

Born: New York, New York, 1943

Education: School of Visual Arts, NYC, 1961–64; apprentice to Austrian pipe maker Paul Fischer, 1964–69

Collections: Mastercraft Pipe, NYC; Museum of Modern Art, NYC

Related Professional Experience: pipe designer and owner, Connoisseur Pipe Shop, NYC, 1969–present

Jean Williams Cacicedo
Berkeley, California

Born: Orange, New Jersey, 1948

Education: B.F.A., Pratt Institute, Brooklyn, NY, 1970

Award/Honor: NEA Fellowship, 1976

Exhibitions: *Body Adornment*, Wichita Art Museum, KS, 1986; *Wearable Art*, Phoenix Art Museum, AZ, 1985; *Art to Wear*, American Craft Museum USIA

Asian tour, 1984–85; *Art to Wear: New Handmade Clothing*, American Craft Museum, NYC, and tour, 1983–84; *Wearable Works of Art*, Craft and Folk Art Museum, Los Angeles, CA, 1983; *Approaches to Collecting*, American Craft Museum, NYC, 1982; *Wearable Art*, Chrysler Museum, Norfolk, VA, 1979; *Wearables*, Philadelphia Museum of Art, PA, 1977; *Baroque '74*, Museum of Contemporary Crafts, NYC, 1974

Collections: Coyote Point Museum, San Mateo, CA; Security Pacific Bank, Los Angeles, CA

Related Professional Experience: faculty, Fiberworks, Center for Textile Arts, JFK U., Berkeley, CA, 1984–present

Patricia Campbell
Saco, Maine

Born: Concord, New Hampshire, 1943

Education: B.A., Colby College, Waterville, ME, 1965; M.F.A., U. of Georgia, Athens, 1971; M.F.A., Cranbrook Academy of Art, Bloomfield Hills, MI, 1979

Awards/Honors: NEA Fellowship, 1979; PA Council on the Arts Fellowship, 1982

Exhibitions: *The Presence of Light*, Meadows Museum, Dallas, TX, 1984; *International Biennial of Tapestry*, Cantonal Museum of Fine Arts, Lausanne, Switzerland, 1983; *The Art Fabric: Mainstream*, American Federation of Arts national tour, 1981–83; *International Textile Triennial*, Central Museum of Textiles, Lodz, Poland, 1981

Collections: H & R Block, Kansas City, MO; Hurculon Collection, Wilmington, DE; U. of Connecticut School of Law, Hartford; Westin Hotel, Dallas, TX

Related Professional Experience: weaving instructor, Peace Corps, Paraiba, Brazil, 1966–68; faculty, Kansas City Art Institute, MO, 1973–76; Tyler School of Art, Temple U., Philadelphia, PA, 1979–83; Cleveland Institute of Art, OH, 1984–85

Kevin Cannon
New York, New York

Born: New York, New York, 1948

Education: A.A., City College of New York, NYC, 1971

Collection: Cincinnati Art Museum, OH

William Carlson
Champaign, Illinois

Born: Dover, Ohio, 1950

Education: B.F.A., Cleveland Institute of Art, OH, 1973; M.F.A., New York State College of Ceramics at Alfred U., NY, 1976

Award/Honor: NEA Fellowship, 1981

Exhibitions: *American Glass Art: Evolution and Revolution*, Morris Museum of Arts and Sciences, Morristown, NJ, 1982; *World Glass Now*, Hokkaido Museum of Modern Art, Sapporo, Japan, 1982; *Americans in Glass*, Leigh Yawkey Woodson Art Museum, Wausau, WI, and tour, 1981; *Beyond Tradition: 25th Anniversary*, Museum of Contemporary Crafts, NYC, 1981; *Contemporary Glass: Australia, Canada, U.S.A. and Japan*, National Museum of Modern Art, Kyoto and Tokyo, Japan, 1981

Collections: Columbus Museum of Art, OH; Metropolitan Museum of Art, NYC; Hokkaido Museum of Modern Art, Sapporo, Japan; Museum of Decorative Arts, Lausanne, Switzerland; National Museum of Modern Art, Kyoto, Japan

Related Professional Experience: faculty, U. of Illinois, Champaign-Urbana, 1976–present

Nancy Carman
San Francisco, California

Born: Tucson, Arizona, 1950

Education: B.A., U. of California, Davis, 1969–72; San Francisco Art Institute 1972–74; M.F.A., U. of Washington, Seattle, 1974–76

Award/Honor: NEA Fellowship, 1980

Exhibitions: *Contemporary Arts: An Expanding View*, Monmouth Museum of Art, Lincroft, NJ, 1986; *Clay National*, Erie Art Museum, PA, 1985; *Soup Soup Beautiful Soup*, Campbell Museum, Camden, NJ, 1983; *Contemporary Ceramics: A Response to Wedgwood*, Museum of Philadelphia Civic Center, PA, 1980;

Young Americans: Clay/Glass, American Craft Museum, NYC, and tour, 1978

Collections: Home Savings & Loan, San Francisco, CA; U. of Washington, Seattle

Related Professional Experience: faculty, San Francisco Art Institute, 1978–79; California State College, Hayward, 1980–81; visiting artist, U. of California, Los Angeles, 1982; School of the Art Institute, Chicago, 1985–86

Wendell Castle
Scottsville, New York

Born: Emporia, Kansas, 1932

Education: B.F.A., M.F.A., U. of Kansas, Lawrence, 1958, 1961

Awards/Honors: Tiffany grant, 1972; NEA grant, 1973, 1975, 1976; honorary Ph.D., Maryland Institute of Art, Baltimore, 1979; NY Foundation for the Arts Fellowship, 1986

Exhibitions: *Masterpieces of Time*, Renwick Gallery, Smithsonian Institution, Washington, DC, 1985; solo exhibition, Taft Museum, Cincinnati, OH, 1985; *Tradition and Innovation*, Laguna Gloria Art Museum, Austin, TX, 1985; *Ornamentalism: The New Decorativeness in Architecture and Design*, Hudson River Museum, Yonkers, NY, 1983; *New Handmade Furniture: American Furniture Makers Working in Hardwood*, Museum of Contemporary Crafts, NYC, 1979; *Craft, Art and Religion*, Vatican Museum, Italy, 1978; *Objects: USA*, Johnson Collection of contemporary Crafts, national and international tour, 1969–72

Publications: *The Wendell Castle Book of Wood Lamination*, Van Nostrand Reinhold, NYC, 1980

Collections: American Craft Museum, NYC; Art Institute of Chicago, IL; Houston Museum of Fine Arts, TX; Metropolitan Museum of Art, NYC; Museum of Fine Arts, Boston, MA; Museum of Modern Art, NYC; Philadelphia Museum of Art, PA, Smithsonian Institution, Washington, DC; Museum of Applied Arts, Oslo, Norway

Related Professional Experience: president, Wendell Castle School, Scottsville, NY, 1980–present; artist-in-residence, Rochester Institute of Technology, NY, 1984–present

Marek Cecula
New York, New York

Born: Kielce, Poland, 1944

Education: School of Applied Arts, Kielce, Poland, 1959; private studies, Jerusalem, Israel, 1960, 1964–65

Exhibitions: *American Ceramic National*, Downey Museum, CA, 1985; *Containers '80* Fort Wayne Museum of Art, IN, 1980; *For the Tabletop*, American Craft Museum, NYC, 1980; *A Century of Ceramics in the United States: 1878–1978*, Everson Museum of Art, Syracuse, NY, and tour, 1979

Collection: Museum of Fine Arts, Boston, MA

Related Professional Experience: artist-in-residence, Schmidt Porcelain, Curtiba, Brazil, 1975; owner, Contemporary Porcelain, studio/showroom, NYC, 1978–present; Arts/Industry program, Kohler Co., WI, 1982; faculty, Parsons School of Design/New School, 1984–present

John Cederquist
Capistrano Beach, California

Born: Altadena, California, 1946

Education: B.A., M.A., California State U., Long Beach, 1969, 1971

Award/Honor: NEA Fellowship, 1975

Exhibitions: *Post-Modern Colour*, Victoria and Albert Museum, London, England, 1984; *Deceptions*, Craft and Folk Art Museum, Los Angeles, and Laguna Beach Museum of Art, CA, 1983; *California Woodworking*, Oakland Museum, CA, 1980; *New Handmade Furniture: American Furniture Makers Working in Hardwood*, Museum of Contemporary Crafts, NYC, 1979; *American Crafts: An Aesthetic View*, Museum of Contemporary Art, Chicago, IL, 1976; *Craft Multiples*, Renwick Gallery, Smithsonian Institution, Washington, DC, and tour, 1975–79

Collections: Craft and Folk Art Museum, Los Angeles, CA; Renwick Gallery, Smithsonian Institution, Washington, DC

Related Professional Experience: faculty, Saddleback Community College, Mission Viejo, CA, 1976–present

Scott Chamberlin
Boulder, Colorado

Born: Orange, California, 1948

Education: B.A., California State U., San Francisco, 1973; M.F.A., New York State College of Ceramics at Alfred U., NY, 1976

Exhibitions: *California Art 1984*, Laguna Beach Museum of Art, CA, 1984; *Sculpture of Scott Chamberlin*, Dordrecht Museum of Art, Netherlands, 1980; *Northern California Clay Routes: Sculpture Now*, San Francisco Museum of Modern Art, CA, 1979; *California Ceramics and Glass*, Oakland Museum, CA, 1974

Publications: *Sculpture of Scott Chamberlin*, monograph to accompany exhibition, Dordrecht Museum, Netherlands, 1980

Related Professional Experience: faculty, Camberwell School of Art, London, England, 1976–78, 1982–83; visiting artist, New York State College of Ceramics at Alfred U., NY, 1983; San Francisco State U., CA, 1984; U. of Colorado, Boulder, 1985

Debra Chase
New York, New York

Born: Rochester, New York, 1954

Education: B.S., Nazareth College, Rochester, NY, 1977; M.F.A., School for American Craftsmen, Rochester Institute of Technology, NY, 1982

Exhibitions: *Jewelry USA*, American Craft Museum, NYC, and tour, 1984–86; *Wearable Art Fashion Show*, Albright-Knox Art Gallery, Buffalo, NY, 1984; *Pattern: An Exhibition of the Decorated Surface*, American Craft Museum, NYC, 1982

Related Professional Experience: artist-in-residence, Artpark, Lewiston, NY, 1983

Dale Chihuly
Seattle, Washington

Born: Tacoma, Washington, 1941

Education: B.A., U. of Washington, Seattle, 1965; M.S., U. of Wisconsin, Madison, 1967; M.F.A., Rhode Island School of Design, Providence, 1968

Awards/Honors: Tiffany grant, 1967; Fulbright Fellowship, 1968; NEA Master Craftsman/Apprenticeship grant, 1975; NEA Fellowship, 1977

Exhibitions: *Americans in Glass*, Leigh Yawkey Woodson Art Museum, Wausau, WI, and tour, 1984; *Chihuly: A Decade of Glass*, Bellevue Art Museum, WA, 1984; solo exhibitions, Phoenix Art Museum, AZ, Tucson Museum of Art, AZ, San Diego Museum of Art, CA, 1982; *Contemporary Glass: Australia, Canada, U.S.A. and Japan*, National Museum of Modern Art, Kyoto and Tokyo, Japan, 1981; solo exhibition, Haaretz Museum, Tel Aviv, Israel, 1980; *New Glass: A Worldwide Survey*, Corning Museum of Glass, NY, 1979; solo exhibition, Renwick Gallery, Smithsonian Institution, Washington, DC, 1978; *American Glass Now*, Museum of Contemporary Crafts, NYC, 1973; *Objects: USA*, Johnson Collection of Contemporary Crafts, national and international tour, 1969–72

Publications: *Chihuly Glass*, by Linda Norden, Providence, RI, 1982; *Chihuly: A Decade of Glass*, by Karen S. Chambers and Jack Cowart, to accompany exhibition, Bellevue Art Museum, WA, 1984; *Chihuly: Color, Glass and Form*, by Dale Chihuly, Henry Geldzahler and Michael Monroe, Kodansha, Tokyo/NYC, 1986

Collections: American Craft Museum, NYC; Cooper-Hewitt Museum, NYC; Corning Museum of Glass, NY; Los Angeles County Museum of Art, CA; Metropolitan Museum of Art, NYC; Museum of Fine Arts, Boston, MA; Renwick Gallery, Smithsonian Institution, Washington, DC; National Museum of Modern Art, Kyoto, Japan; Victoria and Albert Museum, London, England

Related Professional Experience: faculty, Rhode Island School of Design, Providence, 1968–80; artist-in-residence, RISD, 1981–present; co-founder and artist-in-residence, Pilchuck School, Stanwood, WA, 1971–present

Chunghi Choo
Iowa City, Iowa

Born: Inchon, Korea, 1938

Education: B.F.A., Ewha Women's U., Seoul, Korea, 1961; M.F.A., Cranbrook Academy of Art, Bloomfield Hills, MI, 1965

Award/Honor: NEA Fellowship, 1981

Exhibitions: *For the Tabletop*, American Craft Museum, NYC, 1980; *The Dyer's Art: Ikat, Batik, Plangi*, Museum of Contemporary Crafts, NYC, and tour, 1976–78; *Forms in Metal: 275 Years of Metalsmithing in America*, Museum of Contemporary Crafts, NYC, and tour, 1975–76; *North American Goldsmiths*, Renwick Gallery, Smithsonian Institution, Washington, DC, with Minnesota Museum of Art, and tour, 1974–77; *Fabric Vibrations/Tie and Fold-dye Wall Hangings and Environments*, Museum of Contemporary Crafts, NYC, and SITES international tour, 1972–75

Collections: American Craft Museum, NYC; Cooper-Hewitt Museum, NYC; Metropolitan Museum of Art, NYC; Museum of Modern Art, NYC; Museum of Decorative Arts, Paris, France

Related Professional Experience: faculty, U. of Iowa, Iowa City, 1968–present

Sharon Church
Philadelphia, Pennsylvania

Born: Richland, Washington, 1948

Education: B.S., Skidmore College, Saratoga Springs, NY, 1970; M.F.A., School for American Craftsmen, Rochester Institute of Technology, NY, 1973

Award/Honor: NEA Fellowship, 1978

Exhibitions: *Jewelry USA*, American Craft Museum, NYC, and tour, 1984–86; *Metal*, State U. of New York, Brockport, 1981, 1974; *Eight Contemporary Metalsmiths*, Bradley U., Peoria, IL, 1976; *Contemporary Crafts of the Americas: 1975*, Colorado State U., Fort Collins, 1975

Collection: Delaware Art Museum, Wilmington

Related Professional Experience: faculty, crafts dept., Philadelphia Colleges of the Arts, PA, 1985–present

Jon F. Clark
Elkins Park, Pennsylvania

Born: Waterloo, Wisconsin, 1947

Education: B.S., U. of Wisconsin, River Falls, 1970; M.A., Royal College of Art, London, England, 1972

Awards/Honors: NEA Fellowship, 1981; PA Council for the Arts Fellowship, 1984

Exhibitions: *World Glass Now*, Hokkaido Museum of Modern Art, Sapporo, Japan, 1985; *Americans in Glass*, Leigh Yawkey Woodson Art Museum, Wausau, WI, and tour, 1984, 1981, 1978; *International Directions in Art Glass*, Art Gallery of Western Australia, Perth, and tour, 1982–83; *Explorations in Glass*, Southern Alleghenies Museum of Art, Loretto, PA, 1981; *National Crafts '81*, Greenville County Museum of Art, SC, 1981

Collections: Archie Bray Foundation, Helena, MT; Leigh Yawkey Woodson Art Museum, Wausau, WI; Museum of Art, Dusseldorf, W. Germany; Art Gallery of Art of Western Australia, Perth

Related Professional Experience: faculty, Tyler School of Art, Temple U., Philadelphia, PA, 1973–present; Pilchuck School, Stanwood, WA, 1983; founding board member, Creative Glass Center of America, Millville, NJ, 1983–present

Michael Cohn
Emeryville, California

Born: Long Beach, California, 1949

Education: B.A., U. of California, Berkeley, 1972

Awards/Honors: NEA Fellowship, 1977, 1984

Exhibitions: *Glass As Sculpture*, Tampa Museum, FL, 1985; *Americans in Glass*, Leigh Yawkey Woodson Art Museum, Wausau, WI, 1984; *Sculptural Glass*, Tucson Museum of Art, AZ, 1983; *Beyond Tradition: 25th Anniversary Exhibition*, Museum of Contemporary Crafts, NYC, 1982; *World Glass Now*, Hokkaido Museum of Modern Art, Sapporo, Japan, 1982; *New Glass: A Worldwide Survey*, Corning Museum of Glass, NY, 1979; *Modern Glass of America, Europe and Japan*, Museum of Applied Arts, Frankfurt, W. Germany, 1976; *California Glass and Ceramics*, Oakland Museum, CA, 1974

Collections: Corning Museum of Glass, NY; High Museum of Art, Atlanta, GA; Toledo Museum of Art, OH; Oakland Museum, CA; Hokkaido Museum of Modern Art, Sapporo, Japan; Kestner Museum, Hanover, W. Germany; National Museum of Modern Art, Kyoto, Japan

Colette
Berkeley, California

Born: Oakland, California, 1937

Education: self-taught

Exhibitions: *Contemporary Metals USA*, Downey Museum of Art, CA, 1985; *Enamels International 1985*, Long Beach Museum of Art, CA, 1985; *Masterworks of Contemporary American Jewelry: Sources and Concepts*, Victoria and Albert Museum, London, England, 1985; *Jewelry: USA*, American Craft Museum, NYC, and tour, 1984–86; *The Animal Image: Contemporary Objects and the Beast*, Renwick Gallery, Smithsonian Institution, Washington, DC, 1981

Collections: American Craft Museum, NYC; Mendocino Museum, CA; Oakland Museum, CA

Lia Cook
San Francisco, California

Born: Ventura, California, 1942

Education: B.A., U. of California, Berkeley, 1965; M.A., U. of California, Berkeley, 1973

Awards/Honors: NEA Fellowship, 1974, 1977; NEA grant, special projects, 1981

Exhibitions: *Jacquard Textiles*, Cooper-Hewitt Museum, NYC, 1982; *Pattern: An Exhibition of the Decorated Surface*, American Craft Museum, NYC, 1982; ten-year retrospective, National Gallery of Tapestry and Textile Art, Beauvais, France, 1982; two-person exhibition, Renwick Gallery, Smithsonian Institution, Washington, DC, 1980; *Fiber Works: The Americas and Japan*, National Museum of Modern Art, Kyoto and Tokyo, Japan, 1977; *International Biennial of Tapestry*, Cantonal Museum of Fine Arts, Lausanne, Switzerland, 1977, 1975, 1973

Collections: American Craft Museum, NYC; AT&T, NY; Itel, San Francisco, CA; Museum of Modern Art, NYC; U. of Texas Art Museum, Austin; National Collection, Paris, France

Related Professional Experience: faculty, California College of Arts and Crafts, Oakland, 1976–present

Tony Costanzo
Oakland, California

Born: Schenectady, New York, 1948

Education: B.F.A., San Francisco Art Institute, CA, 1971; M.F.A., Mills College, Oakland, CA, 1973

Award/Honor: NEA grant, 1978

Exhibitions: *Contemporary American Ceramics: Twenty Artists*, Newport Harbor Art Museum, Newport Beach, CA, 1985; ten-year survey exhibition, De Saisset Museum, Santa Clara, CA, 1984; *Clay for Walls*, Renwick Gallery, Smithsonian Institution, Washington, DC, 1983; *Pacific Currents*, San Jose Museum of Art, CA, 1982; *A Century of Ceramics in the United States: 1878–1978*, Everson Museum of Art, Syracuse, NY, and tour, 1979; *Northern California Clay Routes: Sculpture Now*, San Francisco Museum of Modern Art, CA, 1979; *Young Americans: Clay/Glass*, Museum of Contemporary Crafts, NYC, 1978; *California Ceramics and Glass*, Oakland Museum, CA, 1974

Collections: Oakland Museum, CA; San Francisco Museum of Modern Art, CA

Nancy Crow
Baltimore, Ohio

Born: Loudonville, Ohio, 1943

Education: B.F.A., M.F.A., Ohio State U., Columbus, OH, 1965, 1969

Awards/Honors: NEA Fellowship, 1980; OH Arts Council Fellowship, 1980, 1982, 1985

Exhibitions: *Fabrications*, Missoula Museum of Art, MT, 1985; *Quilt National*, Athens, OH, 1985; *Contemporary American Quilts*, touring France, 1984–85; *Contemporary American Quilts in Japan*, touring Japan, 1984–85

Collections: American Craft Museum, NYC; Ashland Chemical, Dublin, OH; General Foods, Rye, NY; Islamabad Consulate, Washington, DC; Massillon Museum of Art, OH; Museum of American Folk Art, NYC; Ohio Bell Telephone, Cleveland, OH

Related Professional Experience: originator/organizer, *Quilt National*, biennial exhibition of contemporary quilts, Athens, OH, 1978–present

Val M. Cushing
Alfred Station, New York

Born: Rochester, New York, 1931

Education: B.F.A., M.F.A., New York State College of Ceramics at Alfred U., NY, 1952, 1956

Awards/Honors: Fellow, National Council on Education for the Ceramic Arts, 1974; Fulbright grant, 1975; NEA Fellowship, 1983

Exhibitions: *American Clay Artists '85*, Port of History Museum, Philadelphia, PA, 1985; *Contemporary Ceramics: A Response to Wedgwood*, Museum of Philadelphia Civic Center, PA, 1980; *For the Tabletop*, Museum of Contemporary Crafts, NYC, 1980; *A Century of Ceramics in the United States: 1878–1978*, Everson Museum of Art, Syracuse, NYC, and tour, 1979; *National Ceramics Exhibition*, Carborundum Museum of Ceramics, Niagara Falls, NY, 1975; *Objects: USA*, Johnson Collection of Contemporary Crafts, national and international tour, 1969–72; *Syracuse Ceramic National*, Everson Museum of Art, Syracuse, NY, biennial, 1956–68; *Young Americans 1958*, Museum of Contemporary Crafts, NYC, 1958

Collections: American Craft Museum, NYC; Everson Museum of Art, Syracuse, NY; Museum of New Mexico, Santa Fe

Related Professional Experience: faculty, New York State College of Ceramics at Alfred U., NY, 1957–present; founding member, National Council on Education for the Ceramic Arts, 1962; president, 1981–82

Dan Dailey
Amesbury, Massachusetts

Born: Philadelphia, Pennsylvania, 1947

Education: B.F.A., Philadelphia College of Art, PA, 1969; M.F.A., Rhode Island School of Design, Providence, 1972

Awards/Honors: Fulbright Hayes Fellowship, 1972; MIT Center for Advanced Visual Studies Fellowship, 1975–79; NEA Fellowship, 1979; MA Council on the Arts Fellowship, 1980

Exhibitions: *Glass Art*, Museum of Fine Arts, Rouen, France, 1985; *Glass Now*, Culture House, Stockholm, Sweden, 1985; *World Glass Now*, Hokkaido Museum of Modern Art, Sapporo, Japan, 1985, 1982; *Americans in Glass*, Leigh Yawkey Woodson Museum of Art, Wausau, WI, and tour, 1984, 1981, 1978; *Sculptural Glass*, Tucson Museum of Art, AZ, 1983; *Contemporary Glass: Australia, Canada, U.S.A. and Japan*, National Museum of Modern Art, Kyoto and Tokyo, Japan, 1981; *New Glass: A Worldwide Survey*, Corning Museum of Glass, NY, 1979

Collections: American Craft Museum, NYC; Corning Museum of Glass, NY; Metropolitan Museum of Art, NYC; Philadelphia Museum of Art, PA; Smithsonian Institution, Washington, DC; Kestner Museum, Hanover, W. Germany; National Gallery of Victoria, Australia; National Museum of Modern Art, Kyoto, Japan

Related Professional Experience: faculty, Massachusetts College of Art, Boston, 1975–present; independent artist/designer, Cristallerie Daum, Paris, and Nancy, France, 1976–present

William P. Daley
Elkins Park, Pennsylvania

Born: Hastings-on-Hudson, New York, 1925

Education: B.S., Massachusetts College of Art, Boston, 1950; M.A., Columbia U., NYC, 1951

Awards/Honors: NEA Fellowship, 1977; Honorary Member, National Council on Education for the Ceramic Arts, 1983

Exhibitions: *Contemporary Arts: An Expanding View*, Monmouth Museum of Art, Lincroft, NJ, 1986; *Echoes: Historical Reference in Contemporary Ceramics*, Nelson-Atkins Museum of Art, Kansas City, MO, 1983; *Beyond Tradition: 25th Anniversary Exhibition*, Museum of Contemporary Crafts, NYC, 1981; *A Century of Ceramics in the United States: 1878–1978*, Everson Museum of Art, Syracuse, NY, and tour, 1979; *Three Centuries of American Art in Philadelphia*, Philadelphia Museum of Art, PA, 1975

Collections: Campbell Museum, Camden, NJ; Everson Museum of Art, Syracuse, NY; Museum of Philadelphia Civic Center, PA; Philadelphia Museum of Art, PA; St. Louis Art Museum, MO; Museum of Contemporary Art, Hertogenbosch, Netherlands; Victoria and Albert Museum, London, England

Related Professional Experience: faculty, Philadelphia College of Art, 1957–present

Randall Darwall
South Yarmouth, Massachusetts

Born: Alexandria, Virginia, 1948

Education: B.A., Harvard U., Cambridge, MA, 1970; M.A., Rhode Island School of Design, Providence, 1973

Exhibitions: *Art To Wear*, American Craft Museum USIA Asian tour, 1984–85; *Celebration 84! A Sense of Occasion*, Ontario Crafts Council, Toronto, Canada, 1984; *Art To Wear: New Handmade Clothing*, American Craft Museum, NYC, and tour, 1983–84

Collections: IBM, Essex Junction, VT; Eko Hotel, Nigeria, Africa

Related Professional Experience: faculty, Cambridge School, Weston, MA, 1973–81; designer/craftsman of handwoven silks for apparel, 1981–present

Peter S. Dean
Newton Highlands, Massachusetts

Born: Boston, Massachusetts, 1951

Education: B.F.A., Rhode Island School of Design, Providence, 1977; M.F.A., Boston U., MA, 1984

Exhibition: *Material Evidence: New Color Techniques in Handmade Furniture*, Renwick Gallery, Smithsonian Institution, Washington, DC, and tour, 1985

Roseline Delisle
Venice, California

Born: Quebec, Canada, 1952

Education: diploma of professional studies, College of Old Montreal, Canada

Exhibition: *Roseline Delisle: Porcelain Work and Drawings*, Triton Museum of Art, Santa Clara, CA, 1986

Collection: San Francisco Museum of Modern Art, CA

Related Professional Experience: commissions, John Paul Getty Center for the History of Arts and Humanities, Santa Monica, CA, 1985; Frost/Tsuji architects, San Francisco, CA, 1985

Harris Deller
Carbondale, Illinois

Born: Brooklyn, New York, 1947

Education: B.A., California State U., Northridge, 1971; M.F.A., Cranbrook Academy of Art, Bloomfield Hills, MI, 1973

Awards/Honors: Fulbright Hayes Fellowship, 1981

Exhibitions: *Design in the Service of Tea*, Cooper-Hewitt Museum, NYC, 1984; *American Porcelain: New Expressions in an Ancient Art*, Renwick Gallery, Smithsonian Institution, Washington, DC, and SITES tour, 1980–84; *Contemporary Ceramics: A Response to Wedgwood*, Museum of Philadelphia Civic Center, PA, 1980; *For the Tabletop*, American Craft Museum, NYC, 1980; *Soup Tureens*, Campbell Museum, Camden, NJ, 1976; *Artists in Georgia*, High Museum of Art, Atlanta, GA, 1975

Collections: Evansville Museum of Art, IN; Illinois State Museum, Springfield; State of Illinois Building, Chicago; Korean-American Education Commission, Seoul, South Korea

Related Professional Experience: faculty, Southern Illinois U., Carbondale, 1975–present

Stephen De Staebler
San Francisco, California

Born: St. Louis, Missouri, 1933

Education: B.A., Princeton U., Princeton, NJ, 1954; M.A., U. of California, Berkeley, 1961

Awards/Honors: Fulbright scholarship, 1954; NEA Fellowship, 1979, 1981; Guggenheim Fellowship, 1983

Exhibitions: *Stephen De Staebler*, Emily Carr College of Art with the Art Museum Association of America, Vancouver, Canada, and international tour, 1983–85;

Art and/or Craft, Arts Museum, Kanazawa, Japan, and international tour, 1982–84; *100 Years of California Sculpture*, Oakland Museum, CA, 1982; *The Clay Figure*, American Craft Museum, NYC, 1981; *Twenty American Artists*, San Francisco Museum of Modern Art, CA, 1980; *A Century of Ceramics in the United States: 1878–1978*, Everson Museum of Art, Syracuse, NY, and tour, 1979; solo exhibition, Oakland Museum, CA, 1974

Publications: *Stephen De Staebler*, monograph to accompany exhibition, Emily Carr College of Art, Vancouver, Canada, 1983

Collections: Minneapolis Art Institute, MN; Oakland Museum, CA

Related Professional Experience: faculty, San Francisco Art Institute, CA, 1961–67; San Francisco State U., 1967–present; numerous commissions for works in public spaces around the country

Richard E. DeVore
Fort Collins, Colorado

Born: Toledo, Ohio, 1933

Education: B.Ed., U. of Toledo, OH, 1955; M.F.A., Cranbrook Academy of Art, Bloomfield Hills, MI, 1957

Awards/Honors: NEA grant, 1976, 1980

Exhibitions: *Currents 3: Richard DeVore 1972–82*, Milwaukee Art Museum, WI, and tour, 1983; *Echoes: Historical Reference in Contemporary Ceramics*, Nelson-Atkins Museum of Art, Kansas City, MO, 1983; *A Century of Ceramics in the United States: 1878–1978*, Everson Museum of Art, Syracuse, NY, and tour, 1979; *American Crafts: An Aesthetic View*, Museum of Contemporary Art, Chicago, IL, 1976

Collections: American Craft Museum, NYC; High Museum of Art, Atlanta, GA; Nelson-Atkins Museum of Art, Kansas City, MO; Philadelphia Museum of Art, PA; St. Louis Art Museum, MO; Boymans and Van Beuningen Museum, Rotterdam, Netherlands; Victoria and Albert Museum, London, England

Kris Dey
Diamond Springs, California

Born: Buffalo, New York, 1949

Education: B.A., M.A., M.F.A., U. of California, Los Angeles, 1972, 1974, 1976

Award/Honor: NEA Fellowship, 1978

Exhibitions: *Art and/or Craft*, Arts Museum, Kanazawa, Japan, and international tour, 1982–84; *Pattern: An Exhibition of the Decorated Surface*, American Craft Museum, NYC, 1982; *The Art Fabric: Mainstream*, American Federation of Arts national tour, 1981–83; *Old Traditions—New Directions*, Textile Museum, Washington, DC, 1981; *The New Classicism*, Museum of Modern Art, NYC, 1977

Collections: Atlantic Richfield, Los Angeles, CA; Fluor, Irvine, CA; IBM, San Jose, CA; Pacific Mutual Insurance, San Francisco, CA; Price Waterhouse, Austin, TX; Standard Oil, San Ramon, CA

Rick Dillingham
Santa Fe, New Mexico

Born: Lake Forest, Illinois, 1952

Education: B.F.A., U. of New Mexico, Albuquerque, 1974; M.F.A., Claremont Graduate School, Scripps College, CA, 1976

Awards/Honors: NEA Fellowship, 1977, 1982

Exhibitions: ten-year survey exhibition, St. John's College, Santa Fe, NM, 1984; *Echoes: Historical Reference in Contemporary Ceramics*, Nelson-Atkins Museum of Art, Kansas City, MO, 1983; *Approaches to Collecting*, American Craft Museum, NYC, 1982; *Contemporary Ceramics: A Response to Wedgwood*, Museum of Philadelphia Civic Center, PA, 1980; *New Mexico: Space and Images*, Craft and Folk Art Museum, Los Angeles, CA, 1979; *One Space/Three Visions*, Museum of Albuquerque, NM, 1979

Collections: Brooklyn Museum, NYC; Everson Museum of Art, Syracuse, NY; Utah Museum of Fine Arts, Salt Lake City

Related Professional Experience: guest curator, *Seven Families in Pueblo Pottery*, Maxwell Museum of Anthropology, U. of New Mexico, Albuquerque, NM, 1974

Dominic Di Mare
Tiburon, California

Born: San Francisco, California, 1932

Education: self-taught

Awards/Honors: NEA Fellowship, 1977, 1981

Exhibitions: *Contemporary Arts: An Expanding View*, Monmouth Museum of Art, Lincroft, NJ, 1986; *Papermaking USA*, American Craft Museum, NYC, 1982; *The Art Fabric: Mainstream*, American Federation of Arts national tour, 1981–83; *Paper Art*, Crocker Art Museum, Sacramento, CA, 1981; *The Object As Poet*, Renwick Gallery, Smithsonian Institution, Washington, DC, and tour, 1977; *The Handmade Paper Object*, Santa Barbara Museum of Art, CA, and tour, 1976–77; *Objects: USA*, Johnson Collection of Contemporary Crafts, national and international tour, 1969–72; *Dominic Di Mare—Woven Forms*, Museum of Contemporary Crafts, NYC, 1965

Collections: American Craft Museum, NYC; International Paper, NYC; Portland Art Museum, OR

John Donoghue
St. Louis, Missouri

Born: Rochester, Minnesota, 1952

Education: B.F.A., Memphis Academy of Art, TN, 1976; M.F.A., Cranbrook Academy of Art, Bloomfield Hills, MI, 1979

Exhibitions: *Cranbrook Ceramics 1950–80*, Cranbrook Academy of Art Museum, Bloomfield Hills, MI, 1983; *Echoes: Historical Reference in Contemporary Ceramics*, Nelson-Atkins Museum of Art, Kansas City, MO, 1983

Collections: Cranbrook Academy of Art Museum, Bloomfield Hills, MI; Detroit Institute of Arts, MI; Monsanto, St. Louis, MO; Prudential Insurance, Dallas, TX; St. Louis Art Museum, MO

Related Professional Experience: faculty, Southern Illinois U., Edwardsville, 1982–83

Fritz Dreisbach
Penland, North Carolina

Born: Cleveland, Ohio, 1941

Education: B.A., Hiram College, OH, 1962; M.F.A., U. of Wisconsin, Madison, 1967

Exhibitions: *Wine: Celebration and Ceremony*, Cooper-Hewitt Museum, NYC, 1985; *The Animal Image: Contemporary Objects and the Beast*, Renwick Gallery, Smithsonian Institution, Washington, DC, 1981; *Glass—Artist and Influence*, Detroit Institute of Arts, MI, 1981; *Baroque '74*, Museum of Contemporary Crafts, NYC, 1974; *Objects: USA*, Johnson Collection of Contemporary Crafts, national and international tour, 1969–72; solo exhibition, Toledo Museum of Art, OH, 1969; *Young Americans*, Museum of Contemporary Crafts, NYC, 1969

Collections: American Craft Museum, NYC; Cooper-Hewitt Museum, NYC; Corning Museum of Glass, NY; High Museum of Art, Atlanta, GA; St. Louis Art Museum, MO; Smithsonian Institution, Washington, DC; Toledo Museum of Art, OH

Related Professional Experience: faculty, Toledo Museum School, OH, 1967–70; Penland School of Crafts, NC, 1967–84; Ohio U., Athens, 1974–78; guest faculty, Kent State U., OH, 1986

Ruth Duckworth
Chicago, Illinois

Born: Hamburg, W. Germany, 1919

Education: Liverpool School of Art, England, 1936–40; Central School of Art and Crafts, London, England, 1956–60

Award/Honor: honorary Ph.D., DePaul U., Chicago, IL, 1982

Exhibitions: *Contemporary Arts: An Expanding View*, Monmouth Museum of Art, Lincroft, NJ, 1986; *Ten Years of Collecting at the Museum of Contemporary Art*, Museum of Contemporary Art, Chicago, IL, 1984; solo exhibition, Museum of Arts and Crafts, Hamburg, W. Germany, 1976; *Objects: USA*, Johnson Collection of Contemporary Crafts, national and international tour, 1969–72; *Three Artists*, Art Institute of Chicago, IL, 1969

Collections: American Craft Museum, NYC; Art Institute of Chicago, IL; Museum of Contemporary Art, Chicago, IL; Philadelphia Museum of Art, PA; National

Museum of Modern Art, Kyoto, Japan; Stedelijk Museum, Amsterdam, Netherlands; Stuttgart Museum, W. Germany

Related Professional Experience: faculty, U. of Chicago, Midway Studios, 1964–65, 1967–77; numerous public commissions in Chicago area

Jack Earl
Lakeview, Ohio

Born: Uniopolis, Ohio, 1934

Education: B.A., Bluffton College, OH, 1956; M.A., Ohio State U., Columbus, 1964

Awards/Honors: NEA Fellowship, 1974; OH Council on the Arts grant, 1983

Exhibitions: *The Clay Figure*, American Craft Museum, NYC, 1981; *Jack Earl: Narrative Sculptures*, Akron Art Museum, OH, 1981–82; *Jack Earl—Porcelains*, Museum of Contemporary Crafts, NYC, 1971; *Objects: USA*, Johnson Collection of Contemporary Crafts, national and international tour, 1969–72; group exhibition, Everson Museum of Art, Syracuse, NY, 1968

Publications: *Jack Earl: The Genesis and Triumphant Survival of an Underground Ohio Artist*, by Lee Nordness, Perimeter Press, Chicago, IL, 1985

Collections: American Craft Museum, NYC; Kohler Co., WI

Related Professional Experience: faculty, Toledo Museum of Art, OH, 1964–72; Virginia Commonwealth U., Richmond, 1972–78; artist-in-residence, Kohler Co., WI, 1974, 1976, 1977, 1978, 1979

Robert Ebendorf
Highland, New York

Born: Topeka, Kansas, 1938

Education: B.F.A., M.F.A., U. of Kansas, Lawrence, 1958, 1963

Awards/Honors: Fulbright grant, 1963; Tiffany grant, 1965; NEA Fellowship, 1970

Exhibitions: *Masterworks of Contemporary American Jewelry: Sources and Concepts*, Victoria and Albert Museum, London, England, 1985; *Contemporary Jewellery: The Americas, Australia, Europe and Japan*, National Museum of Modern Art, Kyoto and Tokyo, Japan, 1984; *Design in the Service of Tea*, Cooper-Hewitt Museum, NYC, 1984; *Jewelry USA*, American Craft Museum, NYC, and tour, 1984–86; *Silver in American Life*, Yale U., New Haven, CT, 1978

Collections: Cooper-Hewitt Museum, NYC; Metropolitan Museum of Art, NYC; Renwick Gallery, Smithsonian Institution, Washington, DC; Museum of Applied Arts, Oslo, Norway; Museum of Applied Arts, Trondheim, Norway; Jewelry Museum, Pforzheim, W. Germany; Victoria and Albert Museum, London, England

Related Professional Experience: founding member, Society for North American Goldsmiths, 1969; faculty, State U. of New York, College at New Paltz, 1970–present; president, 1972–77; staff designer and consultant, David-Andersen, Oslo, Norway, 1978–80

Edward S. Eberle
Pittsburgh, Pennsylvania

Born: Tarentum, Pennsylvania, 1944

Education: B.S., Edinboro State College, PA, 1967; M.F.A., New York State College of Ceramics at Alfred U., NY, 1971

Exhibitions: solo exhibition, Museum of Art, Carnegie Institute, Pittsburgh, PA, 1980; *Pennsylvania '74*, William Penn Memorial Museum, Harrisburg, PA, and tour, 1974; *27th Ceramics International*, media section/slides, Everson Museum of Art, Syracuse, NY, 1972

Collections: Museum of Art, Carnegie Institute, Philadelphia, PA; Westmoreland Museum of Art, Greensburg, PA

Related Professional Experience: faculty, Philadelphia College of Art, PA, 1971–75; Carnegie-Mellon U., Pittsburgh, PA, 1975–85

Stephen Dale Edwards
Kirkland, Washington

Born: Fort Worth, Texas, 1948

Education: B.F.A., California College of Arts and Crafts, Oakland, 1972; M.A., M.F.A., U. of Iowa, Iowa City, 1974

Exhibitions: *Northwest Crafts*, Museum of History and Industry, Seattle, WA, 1982; *American Glass Now*, Yamaha Corporation, Tokyo, Japan, and tour, 1981–82; *The Animal Image: Contemporary Objects and the Beast*, Renwick Gallery, Smithsonian Institution, Washington, DC, 1981; *Governor's Invitational: Washington Artists*, State Capitol Museum, Olympia, WA, 1980; *New American Glass*, Huntington Galleries, WV, 1980

Collections: Corning Museum of Glass, NY; Safeco Insurance, Seattle, WA; Seattle Arts Commission, WA; Brierley Hill Glass Centre, Brierley Hill, England; International Glass Museum, Ebeltoft, Denmark

Related Professional Experience: faculty, Bellevue Art Museum, WA, 1977–78; Pratt Fine Art Center, Seattle, WA, 1980–86; Miasa Bunka Center, Nagano, Japan, 1984; freelance designer, Steuben Glass, Corning, NY, 1985

Alma Eikerman
Bloomington, Indiana

Born: Pratt, Kansas

Education: B.S., Kansas State College, Emporia, 1934; M.S., Columbia U., NYC, 1942

Awards/Honors: Carnegie grant, 1968; NEA grant, 1975; Fellow, American Craft Council, 1978; Ford Foundation grant, 1980, 1983

Exhibitions: *Reflections: A Tribute to Alma Eikerman*, Indiana U. Art Museum, Bloomington, 1985; *Jewelry and Beyond*, Mitchell Museum, Mt. Vernon, IL, 1984; *Beyond Tradition: 25th Anniversary Exhibition*, Museum of Contemporary Crafts, NYC, 1981; *Copper 2*, U. of Arizona Museum of Art, Tucson, 1980; *The Metalsmith*, Phoenix Art Museum, AZ, 1977; *Forms in Metal: 275 Years of Metalsmithing in America*, Museum of Contemporary Crafts, NYC, and tour, 1975–76; *American Metalsmiths*, DeCordova Museum, Lincoln, MA, 1974; *Objects: USA*, Johnson Collection of Contemporary Crafts, national and international tour, 1969–72

Publications: monograph to accompany exhibition, Indiana U. Art Museum, Bloomington, 1985

Collections: American Craft Museum, NYC; Indiana U. Art Museum, Bloomington; Sheldon Memorial Art Gallery, Lincoln, NE

Related Professional Experience: faculty, Wichita U., KS, 1941–47; Indiana U., Bloomington, 1947–1978; founding member, Society of North American Goldsmiths, 1969

Lillian Elliott (works collaboratively with Pat Hickman)
Berkeley, California

Born: Detroit, Michigan, 1930

Education: B.A., Wayne State U., Detroit, MI, 1952; M.F.A., Cranbrook Academy of Art, Bloomfield Hills, MI, 1955

Awards/Honors: Tiffany grant, 1964; NEA Fellowship, 1976; CA Arts Council grant, 1977, 1979, 1980

Exhibitions: *Fiber Art '85*, Museum of Decorative Arts, Paris, France, 1985; *International Biennial of Tapestry*, Cantonal Museum of Fine Arts, Lausanne, Switzerland, 1985; *Tapestry—Tradition and Technique*, Los Angeles County Museum of Art, CA, 1971; *Objects: USA*, Johnson Collection of Contemporary Crafts, national and international tour, 1969–72; *Collage*, Museum of Applied Arts, Zurich, Switzerland, 1968; *Fabric Collage*, Museum of Contemporary Crafts, NYC, 1965

Collections: American Craft Museum, NYC; Detroit Institute of Arts, MI; Renwick Gallery, Smithsonian Institution, Washington, DC

Related Professional Experience: fabric designer, Ford Motor Co., Dearborn, MI, 1955–59; faculty, U. of California, Berkeley, 1966–72; California College of Arts and Crafts, Oakland, 1972–76; Pacific Basin School of Textile Arts, Berkeley, CA, 1981–present

David Ellsworth
Quakertown, Pennsylvania

Born: Iowa City, Iowa, 1944

Education: B.F.A., M.F.A., U. of Colorado, Boulder, 1971, 1973

Awards/Honors: CO Artist/Craftsman award, 1977; NEA Fellowship, 1984

Exhibitions: *Contemporary Arts: An Expanding View*, Monmouth Museum of Art, Lincroft, NJ, 1986; *The Art of Woodturning*, American Craft Museum, NYC, 1983; solo exhibition, Sheldon Memorial Art Museum, Lincoln, NE, 1980

Collections: Museum of Fine Arts, Boston, MA; Denver Art Museum, CO; High Museum of Art, Atlanta, GA; Sheldon Memorial Art Museum, Lincoln, NE

Related Professional Experience: artist-in-residence, Anderson Ranch Art Center, Aspen, CO, 1974–75; Artpark, Lewiston, NY, 1983; visiting faculty, Rochester Institute of Technology, NY, 1985

Albinas Elskus
New York, New York

Born: Kaunas, Lithuania, 1926

Education: diploma, Academy of Arts and Crafts, Freiburg, W. Germany, 1949; Academy of Fine Arts, Paris, France, 1952–53

Award/Honor: NEA Fellowship, 1980

Exhibitions: *Pilchuck Glass*, Aspen Art Museum, CO, 1986; *Glass Routes*, DeCordova Museum, Lincoln, MA, 1981; *Contemporary Stained Glass*, Jacksonville Art Museum, FL, 1980; *Craft, Art and Religion*, Vatican Museum, Italy, 1978; *New Stained Glass*, Museum of Contemporary Crafts, NYC, 1978

Collection: Corning Museum of Glass, NY

Related Professional Experience: numerous commissions of stained glass windows for churches throughout the United States

Curtis Erpelding
Seattle, Washington

Born: Fort Dodge, Iowa, 1950

Education: B.S., U. of Colorado, Boulder, 1972

Award/Honor: NEA grant, 1980

Exhibitions: *Woodworkers' Invitational*, Whatcom Museum of History and Art, Bellingham, WA, 1984; *Componental Furniture: Studies in Knockdown Design*, Oregon School of Arts and Crafts, Portland, 1982; *Natural Fibers*, Bellevue Art Museum, WA, 1980

Kenneth Ferguson
Kansas City, Missouri

Born: Elwood, Indiana, 1928

Education: B.F.A., Carnegie Institute of Technology, Pittsburgh, PA, 1952; M.F.A., New York State College of Ceramics at Alfred U., NY, 1958

Awards/Honors: Tiffany grant, 1967; NEA Fellowship, 1973, 1980; Honorary Member, National Council on Education for the Ceramic Arts, 1981

Exhibitions: *Echoes: Historical Reference in Contemporary Ceramics*, Nelson-Atkins Museum of Art, Kansas City, MO, 1983; *A Century of Ceramics in the United States: 1878–1978*, Everson Museum of Art, Syracuse, NY, and tour, 1979; *Objects: USA*, Johnson Collection of Contemporary Crafts, national and international tour, 1969–72

Collections: American Craft Museum, NYC; Brooklyn Museum, NYC; Carnegie Museum, Pittsburgh, PA; Nelson-Atkins Museum of Art, Kansas City, MO; Smithsonian Institution, Washington, DC; St. Louis Art Museum, MO; Victoria and Albert Museum, London, England

Related Professional Experience: resident artist and manager, Archie Bray Foundation, Helena, MT, 1958–64; faculty, Kansas City Art Institute, MO, 1964–present

Arline M. Fisch
San Diego, California

Born: Brooklyn, New York, 1931

Education: B.S., Skidmore College, Saratoga Springs, NY, 1952; M.A., U. of Illinois, Champaign-Urbana, 1954

Awards/Honors: Fulbright grant, 1956, 1966, 1982; NEA Fellowship, 1974; NEA workshop/project grant, 1974, 1976, 1979, 1981; NEA apprentice grant, 1977; Fellow, American Craft Council, 1979

Exhibitions: *Contemporary Arts: An Expanding View*, Monmouth Museum of Arts, Lincroft, NJ, 1986; *Jewelry USA*, American Craft Museum, NYC, and tour, 1984–86; solo exhibition, Museum of Applied Arts, Vienna, Austria, 1982; *Fourth Tokyo Triennial*, Tokyo, Japan, 1979; *Jewelry '77*, Jewelry Museum, Pforzheim, W. Germany, 1977; *Objects: USA*, Johnson Collection of Contemporary Crafts, national and international tour, 1969–72; solo exhibition, Museum of Contemporary Crafts, NYC, 1968; solo exhibition, Pasadena Museum of Art, CA, 1962; *Young Americans 1958*, Museum of Contemporary Crafts, NYC, and tour, 1958–59

Publication: *Textile Techniques in Metal*, Van Nostrand Reinhold, NYC, 1975

Collections: American Craft Museum, NYC; Minnesota Museum of Art, St. Paul; Jewelry Museum, Pforzheim, W. Germany; Museum of Applied Arts, Trondheim, Norway; National Museum of Modern Art, Kyoto, Japan; Royal Scottish Museum, Edinburgh, Scotland; Vatican Museum, Italy; Worshipful Company of Goldsmiths, London, England

Related Professional Experience: faculty, San Diego State U., CA, 1961–present; founding member, 1969, and president, 1982–85, Society of North American Goldsmiths; vice-president, World Crafts Council, 1976–80

Frank Fleming
Birmingham, Alabama

Born: Bear Creek, Alabama, 1940

Education: B.S., Florence State College, AL, 1962; M.A., M.F.A., U. of Alabama, Tuscaloosa, 1969, 1973

Exhibitions: *The Animal Image: Contemporary Objects and the Beast*, Renwick Gallery, Smithsonian Institution, Washington, DC, 1981; *Contemporary Ceramics: A Response to Wedgwood*, Museum of Philadelphia Civic Center, PA, 1980; *The Great American Foot*, Museum of Contemporary Crafts, NYC, 1978; *35 Artists in the Southeast*, High Museum of Art, Atlanta, GA, 1976

Collections: Birmingham Museum of Art, AL; Hunter Museum of Art, Chattanooga, TN; Nelson-Atkins Museum of Art, Kansas City, MO; Smithsonian Institution, Washington, DC; Utah Museum of Fine Arts, Salt Lake City

Pat Flynn
New Paltz, New York

Born: Edinboro, Pennsylvania, 1954

Education: B.F.A., State U. of New York, College at New Paltz, NY, 1978

Award/Honor: NEA Fellowship, 1984

Exhibitions: *Jewelry USA*, American Craft Museum, NYC, and tour, 1984–86; *Contemporary Metals: Focus on Idea*, Washington State U. Museum of Art, Pullman, 1981; *Good As Gold: Alternative Materials in American Jewelry*, SITES tour, 1981–84; *Copper 2*, U. of Arizona Museum of Art, Tucson, AZ, 1980; *Young Americans: Metal*, Museum of Contemporary Crafts, NYC, 1980

Collection: Museum of Applied Arts, Trondheim, Norway

Related Professional Experience: faculty, Parsons School of Design/New School, NYC, 1983–present

Belmont Freeman
New York, New York

Born: Washington, DC, 1951

Education: B.A., Yale U., New Haven, CT, 1973; M. Arch., U. of Pennsylvania, Philadelphia, 1976

Award/Honor: Innovative Design Fund/NEA Fellowship, 1984

Related Professional Experience: associate, Davis, Brody & Associates architectural firm, NYC, 1977–present

Viola Frey
Oakland, California

Born: Lodi, California, 1933

Education: B.F.A., California College of Arts and Crafts, Oakland, 1956; M.F.A., Tulane U., New Orleans, LA, 1958

Award/Honor: NEA Fellowship, 1978

Exhibitions: *It's All Part of the Clay: Viola Frey*, Moore College of Art, Philadelphia, PA and tour, 1984; solo exhibition, Whitney Museum of American Art, NYC, 1984; *100 Years of California Sculpture*, Oakland Museum, CA, 1982; *The Clay Figure*, American Craft Museum, NYC, 1981; *Viola Frey: A Retrospective*, Crocker Art Museum, Sacramento, CA, and tour, 1981–84; *Young Americans 1962*, Museum of Contemporary Crafts, NYC, 1962

Publications: *Viola Frey: A Retrospective*, monograph to accompany exhibition, Crocker Art Museum, Sacramento, CA, 1981; *It's All Part of the Clay: Viola Frey*, monograph with Moore College of Art exhibition, Philadelphia, PA, 1984

Collections: Everson Museum of Art, Syracuse, NY; Minneapolis Institute of the Arts, MN; Oakland Museum, CA; San Francisco Museum of Modern Art, CA

Related Professional Experience: faculty, California College of Arts and Crafts, Oakland, 1970–present

Donald Friedlich
Providence, Rhode Island

Born: Montclair, New Jersey, 1954

Education: B.F.A., Rhode Island School of Design, Providence, 1982

Award/Honor: Young Alumnus award, Rhode Island School of Design, Providence, 1985

Exhibitions: *Body Adornment*, Wichita Art Museum, KS, 1986; *Affordable Frills*, Renwick Gallery, Smithsonian Institution, Washington, DC, 1985; *American Jewelry Now*, American Craft Museum USIA Asian tour, 1985; *Contemporary Metals USA*, Downey Museum of Art, CA, 1985; *Jewelry Today*, Craft and Folk Art Museum, Los Angeles, CA, 1985; group exhibition, Hudson River Museum, Yonkers, NY, 1984; *Jewelry USA*, American Craft Museum, NYC, and tour, 1984–86; *Selections from the Washington Craft Show*, Renwick Gallery, Smithsonian Institution, Washington, DC, 1983

Michael Frimkess
Venice, California

Born: Los Angeles, California, 1937

Education: Otis Art Institute, Los Angeles, CA, 1954–57

Awards/Honors: NEA Fellowship, 1977; U.S./U.K. Bicentennial Exchange Fellowship, 1979

Exhibitions: *Teapots*, Arkansas Arts Center, Little Rock, 1985; *Echoes: Historical Reference in Contemporary Ceramics*, Nelson-Atkins Museum of Art, Kansas City, MO, 1983; *Continuity and Change: Three Generations of American Potters*, Southern Alleghenies Museum of Art, Loretto, PA, and SITES tour, 1981–83; *A Century of Ceramics in the United States: 1878–1978*, Everson Museum of Art, Syracuse, NY and tour, 1979; *California Ceramics and Glass*, Oakland Museum, CA, 1974; *International Ceramics 1972*, Victoria and Albert Museum, London, England, and tour, 1972; *Contemporary Ceramic Art: Canada, U.S.A., Mexico, Japan*, National Museum of Modern Art, Kyoto and Tokyo, Japan, 1971; *Objects: USA*, Johnson Collection of Contemporary Crafts, national and international tour, 1969–72

Collections: American Craft Museum, NYC; National Museum of Modern Art, Kyoto, Japan

Related Professional Experience: faculty, William Grant Still Community Learning Center, Los Angeles, CA, 1983–86

Cliff Garten
St. Paul, Minnesota

Born: Ridgewood, New Jersey, 1952

Education: B.F.A., New York State College of Ceramics at Alfred U., NY, 1974; M.F.A., Rhode Island School of Design, Providence, 1978

Awards/Honors: MN State Arts Board grant, 1980; Arts Midwest/NEA grant, 1985

Exhibitions: *Contemporary Arts: An Expanding View*, Monmouth Museum of Art, Lincroft, NJ, 1986; *Architectural Ceramics: Eight Concepts*, Washington U. Gallery of Art, St. Louis, MO, and American Craft Museum, NYC, 1985; *Minnesota Ceramics*, Tweed Museum of Art, Duluth, MN, 1982; *Westwood Clay National*, Downey Museum of Art, CA, 1981; *Young Americans: Clay/Glass*, Museum of Contemporary Crafts, NYC, 1978

Collection: Plains Art Museum, Moorhead, MN

Related Professional Experience: faculty, Hamline U., St. Paul, MN, 1978–present

Andrea Gill
Alfred, New York

Born: Newark, New Jersey, 1948

Education: B.F.A., Rhode Island School of Design, Providence, 1971; M.F.A., New York State College of Ceramics at Alfred U., NY, 1976

Awards/Honors: NEA Fellowship, 1978, 1984; OH Arts Council Individual Artist grant, 1981, 1982, 1984

Exhibitions: *Contemporary Arts: An Expanding View*, Monmouth Museum of Art, Lincroft, NJ, 1986; *Echoes: Historical Reference in Contemporary Ceramics*, Nelson-Atkins Museum of Art, Kansas City, MO, 1983; *Pattern: An Exhibition of the Decorated Surface*, American Craft Museum, NYC, 1982; two-person exhibition, Akron Art Museum, and Massillon Museum, OH, 1981; *Contemporary Ceramics: A Response to Wedgwood*, Museum of Philadelphia Civic Center, PA, 1980; *Young Americans: Clay/Glass*, Museum of Contemporary Crafts, NYC, 1978

Collections: Massillon Museum, OH; Museum of Art, Rhode Island School of Design, Providence; Museum of Contemporary Art, Druithuis, Netherlands; Victoria and Albert Museum, London, England

Related Professional Experience: faculty, New York State College of Ceramics at Alfred U., NY, 1984–present

John Gill
Alfred, New York

Born: Renton, Washington, 1949

Education: B.F.A., Kansas City Art Institute, MO, 1973; M.F.A., New York State College of Ceramics at Alfred U., NY, 1976

Award/Honor: NEA Fellowship, 1979

Exhibitions: *Beyond Tradition: 25th Anniversary Exhibition*, American Craft Museum, NYC, 1981; *Contemporary Ceramics: A Response to Wedgwood*, Museum of Philadelphia Civic Center, PA, 1980; *Young Americans: Clay/Glass*, Museum of Contemporary Crafts, NYC, 1978; *The Collector*, Museum of Contemporary Crafts, NYC, 1974

John Parker Glick
Farmington, Michigan

Born: Detroit, Michigan, 1938

Education: B.F.A., Wayne State U., Detroit, MI, 1960; M.F.A., Cranbrook Academy of Art, Bloomfield Hills, MI, 1962

Awards/Honors: Tiffany grant, 1961, 1972; NEA project grant, 1974; NEA Fellowship, 1977

Exhibitions: *26th National Exhibition of New Zealand Society of Potters*, Duneden City Museum, New Zealand, 1984; *Cranbrook Ceramics, 1950–1980*, Cranbrook Academy of Art Museum, Bloomfield Hills, MI, 1983; *A Century of Ceramics in the United States: 1878–1978*, Everson Museum of Art, Syracuse, NY, and tour, 1979; *Eight Independent Production Potters*, Kansas City Art Institute, MO, 1976

Collections: Craft and Folk Art Museum, Los Angeles, CA; Cranbrook Academy of Art Museum, Bloomfield Hills, MI; Delaware Art Museum, Wilmington; Detroit Institute of Arts, MI; Everson Museum of Art, Syracuse, NY; Hunter Museum of Art, Chattanooga, TN

Related Professional Experience: owner, Plum Tree Pottery, 1964–present

Gary S. Griffin
Bloomfield Hills, Michigan

Born: Wichita Falls, Texas, 1945

Education: B.A., California State U., Long Beach, 1968; M.F.A., Tyler School of Art, Temple U., Philadelphia, PA, 1974

Awards/Honors: NEA grant, 1976; NEA Fellowship, 1977

Exhibitions: *Gary S. Griffin: Recent Works in Steel*, Cranbrook Academy of Art Museum, Bloomfield Hills, MI, 1985; *Contemporary Jewellery: The Americas, Australia, Europe and Japan*, National Museum of Modern Art, Kyoto and Tokyo, Japan, 1984; *Modern Jewelry: 1964–84*, Montreal Museum of Decorative Arts, Canada, and tour, 1984–87

Publications: monograph to accompany exhibition,

Cranbrook Academy of Art Museum, Bloomfield Hills, MI, 1985

Related Professional Experience: artist-in-residence and head of metalsmithing, Cranbrook Academy of Art, Bloomfield Hills, MI, 1984–present

Chris Gustin
South Dartmouth, Massachusetts

Born: Chicago, Illinois, 1952

Education: B.F.A., Kansas City Art Institute, MO, 1975; M.F.A., New York State College of Ceramics at Alfred U., NY, 1977

Awards/Honors: NEA Fellowship, 1978; CT Commission on the Arts Fellowship, 1980

Exhibitions: *American Potters Today*, Victoria and Albert Museum, London, England, 1985; *Design in the Service of Tea*, Cooper-Hewitt Museum, NYC, 1984; *Westwood Clay National*, Downey Museum of Art, CA, 1980; *Young Americans: Clay/Glass*, Museum of Contemporary Crafts, NYC, 1978

Collection: Victoria and Albert Museum, London, England

Related Professional Experience: faculty, Program in Artisanry, Boston U., MA, 1980–1985; Swain School of Design, New Bedford, MA, 1985–present

Dorothy Hafner
New York, New York

Born: Woodbridge, Connecticut, 1952

Education: B.S., Skidmore College, Saratoga Springs, NY, 1974

Award/Honor: Westerwald Industrial Design award, Hohr-Grenzhausen, W. Germany, 1985

Exhibitions: *Design in the Service of Tea*, Cooper-Hewitt Museum, NYC, 1984; *Ornamentalism: The New Decorativeness in Architecture and Design*, Hudson River Museum, Yonkers, NY, 1983; *Soup Soup Beautiful Soup*, Campbell Museum, Camden, NJ, 1983; *Pattern: An Exhibition of the Decorated Surface*, American Craft Museum, NYC, 1982; *Function and Ritual*, Museum of Art, Rhode Island School of Design, Providence, 1981; *American Porcelain: New Expressions in an Ancient Art*, Renwick Gallery, Smithsonian Institution, Washington, DC, and SITES tour, 1980–84; *For the Tabletop*, American Craft Museum, NYC, 1980

Collections: Museum of Applied Arts, Berlin, W. Germany; Victoria and Albert Museum, London, England

Related Professional Experience: owner/operator, Art for Dining, NYC, 1979–present; faculty, Parsons School of Design/New School, NYC, 1980–85; designer, Rosenthal AG, Selb, W. Germany, 1982–present

Henry Halem
Kent, Ohio

Born: New York, New York, 1938

Education: B.F.A., Rhode Island School of Design, Providence, 1960; M.F.A., George Washington U., Washington, DC, 1968

Exhibitions: *American Glass Art*, Morris Museum of Arts and Sciences, Morristown, NJ, 1982; *World Glass Now*, Hokkaido Museum of Modern Art, Sapporo, Japan, 1982; *Americans in Glass*, Leigh Yawkey Woodson Art Museum, Wausau, WI, 1981; *New Glass: A Worldwide Survey*, Corning Museum of Glass, NY, 1979; *Objects Are...*, Museum of Contemporary Crafts, NYC, 1968; solo exhibition, National Gallery, Smithsonian Institution, Washington, DC, 1966; solo exhibition, Virginia Museum of Fine Arts, Richmond, 1964; *Young Americans 1962*, Museum of Contemporary Crafts, NYC, 1962

Collections: Cleveland Museum of Art, OH; Corning Museum of Glass, NY; High Museum of Art, Atlanta, GA; Philadelphia Museum of Art, PA; National Gallery, Smithsonian Institution, Washington, DC; Australian Council for the Arts, Perth

Related Professional Experience: faculty, Kent State U., OH, 1969–present

Susan H. Hamlet
Stillwater, Oklahoma

Born: Evanston, Illinois, 1954

Education: B.A., Mount Holyoke College, South Hadley, MA, 1976; M.F.A., School for American Craftsmen, Rochester Institute of Technology, NY, 1978

Award/Honor: NEA Fellowship, 1979

Exhibitions: *Contemporary Arts: An Expanding View*, Monmouth Museum of Art, Lincroft, NJ, 1986; *Contemporary Jewellery: The Americas, Australia, Europe and Japan*, National Museum of Modern Art, Kyoto and Tokyo, Japan, 1984; *Jewelry USA*, American Craft Museum, NYC, and tour, 1984–86; *Modern Jewelry: 1964–1984*, Montreal Museum of Decorative Arts, Canada, and tour, 1984–87; *Ferrous Finery*, National Ornamental Metal Museum, Memphis, TN, 1983; *Young Americans: Metal*, Museum of Contemporary Crafts, NYC, 1980

Collection: National Museum of Modern Art, Kyoto, Japan

Related Professional Experience: faculty, Oklahoma State U., Stillwater, OK, 1981–present

Tim Harding
St. Paul, Minnesota

Born: St. Croix Falls, Wisconsin, 1950

Education: B.A., Hamline U., St. Paul, MN, 1973; Minneapolis College of Art and Design, MN, 1976

Award/Honor: NEA/Arts Midwest Regional Fellowship, 1985

Exhibitions: *Handmade Clothing: 10 American Artists*, British Crafts Centre, London, England, 1985; *Textile Properties*, Minneapolis Institute of Arts, MN, 1985; *Art To Wear*, American Craft Museum USIA Asian tour, 1984–85; *Contemporary Wearable Art*, Newark Museum, NJ, 1984; *Art To Wear: New Handmade Clothing*, American Craft Museum, NYC, and tour, 1983–84; *Arango International Design Competition*, Metropolitan Museum of Art, Miami, FL, 1980; *Maximum Coverage: Wearables by Contemporary American Artsists*, John Michael Kohler Arts Center, Sheboygan, WI, and tour, 1980–81

Collections: Hyatt Regency Hotel, Los Angeles, CA, and Minneapolis, MN; Minnesota Historical Society, St. Paul

William Harper
Tallahassee, Florida

Born: Bucyrus, Ohio, 1944

Education: B.A., M.S., Western Reserve U., Cleveland, OH, 1966, 1967

Awards/Honors: NEA grant, 1974, 1978, 1979; FL Arts Council Individual Artist Fellowship, 1985

Exhibitions: *Contemporary Arts: An Expanding View*, Monmouth Museum of Art, Lincroft, NJ, 1986; *Masterworks of Contemporary American Jewelry: Sources and Concepts*, Victoria and Albert Museum, London, England, 1985; *Jewelry USA*, American Craft Museum, NYC, and tour, 1984–86; solo exhibition, Phoenix Art Museum, AZ, 1982; group exhibition, Goldsmiths' Hall, London, England, 1978; solo exhibition, Renwick Gallery, Smithsonian Institution, Washington, DC, 1977

Publications: *Step by Step Enameling*, Western Publishing, NYC, 1973

Collections: Cleveland Museum of Art, OH; Metropolitan Museum of Art, NYC; Renwick Gallery, Smithsonian Institution, Washington, DC; Yale U., New Haven, CT; Jewelry Museum, Pforzheim, W. Germany; Vatican Museum, Italy

Related Professional Experience: faculty, Florida State U., Tallahassee, 1974–present

Ana Lisa Hedstrom
Emeryville, California

Born: Detroit, Michigan, 1943

Education: B.A., Mills College, Oakland, CA, 1965

Award/Honor: NEA Fellowship, 1982

Exhibitions: *Art to Wear*, American Craft Museum USIA Asian tour, 1984–85; *Celebration 84! A Sense of Occasion*, Ontario Crafts Council, Toronto, Canada, 1984; *Traditional Japanese and Contemporary Japanese and American Textiles*, Takeda Kahei Shoten, Tokyo, Japan, 1984; *Art to Wear: New Handmade Clothing*, American Craft Museum, NYC, and tour, 1983–84; *Fiber as Art*, Metropolitan Museum of the Philippines, Manila, 1980; *The New Fabric Surface*, Renwick Gallery, Smithsonian Institution, Washington, DC, 1978; *Third International Exhibition of Miniature Textiles*, British Crafts Centre, London, England, 1978

Gernardt C. Herbst
San Diego, California

Born: Ontario, Canada, 1959

Education: B.A., San Diego State U., CA, 1983

Exhibitions: *Jewelry USA*, American Craft Museum, NYC, and tour, 1984–86; *California Crafts*, Crocker Art Museum, Sacramento, CA, 1983; *International Jewelry Exhibition*, Craft Fair, Munich, W. Germany, 1983; *Statements in Sterling*, Nelson-Atkins Museum of Art, Kansas City, MO, 1981

Related Professional Experience: independent jewelry designer/manufacturer, San Diego, CA, 1984–present

Sam Hernandez
Hayward, California

Born: Hayward, California, 1948

Education: B.A., California State U., Hayward, 1970; M.F.A., U. of Wisconsin, Madison, 1974

Award/Honor: NEA Fellowship, 1984

Exhibitions: *Contemporary American Wood Sculpture*, Crocker Art Museum, Sacramento, CA, and tour, 1984; solo exhibition, San Jose Museum of Art, CA, 1984; *The Animal Image: Contemporary Objects and the Beast*, Renwick Gallery, Smithsonian Institution, Washington, DC, 1981; *Five Decades: Recent Work by Alumni of the Department of Art*, Elvejhem Museum of Art, Madison, WI, 1981; *James D. Phelan Award Exhibition*, San Francisco Museum of Modern Art, CA, 1980; *New Acquisitions*, New Orleans Museum of Art, LA, 1978

Helena Hernmarck
Ridgefield, Connecticut

Born: Stockholm, Sweden, 1941

Education: Swedish State School of Art, Craft and Design, Stockholm, 1959–63

Award/Honor: American Institute of Architects craftsmanship medal, 1973

Exhibitions: solo exhibitions, Danish Museum of Decorative Arts, Copenhagen, Denmark, 1977; National Museum, Stockholm, Sweden, 1976; Los Angeles County Museum of Art, CA, 1974; Museum of Modern Art, NYC, 1973

Collections: Dallas Centre, TX; Federal Reserve Bank, Boston, MA; Los Angeles County Museum of Art, CA; Museum of Modern Art, NYC; Pitney-Bowes, Stamford, CT; Warner-Lambert, Morris Plains, NJ; Weyerhaeuser, Tacoma, WA; Cunard Steamship, London, England; National Gallery of Victoria, Melbourne, Australia; National Museum, Stockholm, Sweden; Swedish State Council for the Arts, Stockholm

Pat Hickman (works collaboratively with Lillian Elliot)
Berkeley, California

Born: Ft. Morgan, Colorado, 1941

Education: B.A., U. of Colorado, Boulder, 1962; M.A., U. of California, Berkeley, 1977

Award/Honor: Canada Arts Council grant, 1984

Exhibitions: *Fiber Art '85*, Museum of Decorative Arts, Paris, France, 1985; *International Biennial of Tapestry*, Cantonal Museum of Fine Arts, Lausanne, Switzerland, 1985; *K18–Stoffwechsel Projecktgruppe Textilforum*, Kassel, W. Germany, 1982

Collections: Renwick Gallery, Smithsonian Institution, Washington, DC; Pierre Pauli Foundation, Lausanne, Switzerland; Savaria Museum, Szombathely, Hungary

Related Professional Experience: faculty, U. of California, Davis, 1978–81, 1984–85; Pacific Basin School of Textile Arts, Berkeley, CA, 1980–86; San Francisco State U., CA, 1983–86

Sheila Hicks
New York, New York

Born: Hastings, Nebraska, 1934

Education: B.F.A., M.F.A., Yale U., New Haven, CT, 1957, 1959

Awards/Honors: gold medal, American Institute of Architects, 1972; Fellow, Art Academy, The Hague, Netherlands, 1978; American Craft Council, 1983; honorary Ph.D., Rhode Island School of Design, 1984

Exhibitions: solo exhibitions, Museum of Applied Arts, Oslo, Norway, 1983; Museum of Fine Art, Rennes, France, 1981; Museum of Tapestry, Aix-en-

Provence, France, 1979; retrospective exhibitions, Stedelijk Museum, Amsterdam, Netherlands, 1974; Museum of Decorative Arts, Nantes, France, 1973; *New Acquisitions*, Museum of Modern Art, NYC, 1967, 1960

Collections: American Craft Museum, NYC; Art Institute of Chicago, IL; Cooper-Hewitt Museum, NYC; Metropolitan Museum of Art, NYC; Museum of Modern Art, NYC; American embassies, Abidjan, Ivory Coast; Moscow, USSR; New Delhi, India; Rabat, Morocco; Tunis, Tunisia; Centre Georges Pompidou, Paris, France; Museum of Modern Art, Kyoto and Tokyo, Japan; Stedelijk Museum, Amsterdam, Netherlands

Related Professional Experience: publisher and editor-in-chief, *American Fabrics and Fashions*, 1980–83; faculty, School of Architecture and Music, Fontainbleau, France, 1980–present

Wayne Higby
Alfred Station, New York

Born: Colorado Springs, Colorado, 1943

Education: B.F.A., U. of Colorado, Boulder, 1966; M.F.A., U. of Michigan, Ann Arbor, 1968

Awards/Honors: NEA Fellowship, 1973, 1977; NY Foundation for the Arts Fellowship, 1985

Exhibitions: *Contemporary Arts: An Expanding View*, Monmouth Museum of Art, Lincroft, NJ, 1986; *International Ceramics*, Taipei Fine Arts Museum, Taiwan, 1985; *Directions in Contemporary Ceramics*, Museum of Fine Arts, Boston, MA, 1984; *Echoes: Historical Reference in Contemporary Ceramics*, Nelson-Atkins Museum of Art, Kansas City, MO, 1983; *A Century of Ceramics in the United States: 1878–1978*, Everson Museum of Art, Syracuse, NY, and tour, 1979; *American Crafts: An Aesthetic View*, Museum of Contemporary Art, Chicago, IL, 1976; solo exhibition, Museum of Contemporary Crafts, NYC, 1973; *Objects: USA*, Johnson Collection of Contemporary Crafts, national and international tour, 1969–72; *Young Americans*, Museum of Contemporary Crafts, NYC, 1969

Collections: American Craft Museum, NYC; Museum of Fine Arts, Boston, MA; Brooklyn Museum, NYC; Everson Museum of Art, Syracuse, NY; Metropolitan Museum of Art, NYC; Philadelphia Museum of Art, PA

Related Professional Experience: faculty, New York State College of Ceramics at Alfred U., NY, 1973–present

Julia Hill
New York, New York

Born: Frankfurt, West Germany, 1947

Education: B.A., M.A., Kunsthochschule, Offenbach, W. Germany, 1968, 1969

Exhibitions: *Art to Wear*, American Craft Museum USIA Asian tour, 1984–85; *Art To Wear: New Handmade Clothing*, American Craft Museum, NYC, and tour, 1983–84; *Poetry for the Body, Clothing for the Spirit*, Richmond Art Center, VA, 1983; *Maximum Coverage: Wearables by Contemporary American Artists*, John Michael Kohler Arts Center, Sheboygan, WI, and tour, 1980–81; *East-West*, San Francisco Museum of Modern Art, CA, 1979; *Surface Design*, Renwick Gallery, Smithsonian Institution, Washington, DC, 1978

Related Professional Experience: owner, Art & Textile Lab, NYC, 1983–present

Jan Holcomb
Pascoag, Rhode Island

Born: Seattle, Washington, 1945

Education: B.A., B.F.A., U. of Michigan, Ann Arbor, 1968, 1975; M.A., California State U., Sacramento, 1977

Award/Honor: NEA Fellowship, 1979

Exhibitions: *Contemporary American Ceramics: Twenty Artists*, Newport Harbor Art Museum, CA, 1985; *Sculpture Invitational*, College of Wooster Art Museum, OH, 1984; *Contemporary Ceramics: A Response to Wedgwood*, Museum of Philadelphia Civic Center, PA, 1980; *California Crafts X*, Crocker Art Museum, Sacramento, CA, 1977

Related Professional Experience: faculty, Rhode Island School of Design, Providence, 1977–present

Tina Fung Holder
Chicago, Illinois

Born: Bartica, Guyana, 1946

Education: B.F.A., M.F.A., School of the Art Institute of Chicago, IL, 1974, 1977

Exhibitions: *Jewelry USA*, American Craft Museum, NYC, and tour, 1984–86; *Convergence '76*, Museum of Art, Carnegie Institute, Pittsburgh, PA, 1976; *Frontiers in Contemporary Weaving*, Florida U., Coral Gables, FL, 1976; *Beaux Arts*, Museum of Fine Arts, Columbus, OH, 1975; *Chicago and Vicinity Show*, Art Institute of Chicago, IL, 1973

Related Professional Experience: independent jewelry designer, 1977–present

Deborah Horrell
Columbus, Ohio

Born: Phoenix, Arizona, 1953

Education: B.F.A., Arizona State U., Tempe, 1975; M.F.A., U. of Washington, Seattle, 1979

Awards/Honors: Ford Foundation grant, 1979; OH Arts Council Individual Artist Fellowship, 1984

Exhibitions: *Pacific Currents*, San Jose Museum of Art, CA, 1982; *The Animal Image: Contemporary Objects and the Beast*, Renwick Gallery, Smithsonian Institution, Washington, DC, 1981; *Westwood Clay National*, Downey Museum of Art, CA, 1981; *American Porcelain: New Expressions in an Ancient Art*, Renwick Gallery, Smithsonian Institution, Washington, DC and SITES tour, 1980–84; *Birds in Art*, Tacoma Art Museum, WA, 1979

Collection: Tucson Museum of Art, AZ

Related Professional Experience: artist-in-residence, Arts/Industry program, Kohler Co., WI, summers, 1983, 1984; faculty, Ohio State U., Columbus, 1983–present

Mary Lee Hu
Seattle, Washington

Born: Lakewood, Ohio, 1943

Education: B.F.A., Cranbrook Academy of Art, Bloomfield Hills, MI, 1965; M.F.A., Southern Illinois U., Carbondale, 1967

Awards/Honors: NEA Fellowship, 1976, 1984

Exhibitions: *Masterworks of Contemporary American Jewelry: Sources and Concepts*, Victoria and Albert Museum, London, England, 1985; *Jewelry International 1900–1980*, House of Artists, Vienna, Austria, 1980; two-person exhibition, Columbus Museum of Fine Arts, OH, 1977; *Goldsmith '74*, Renwick Gallery, Smithsonian Institution, DC, and Minnesota Museum of Art, St. Paul, MN, and tour, 1974–76; *Young Americans*, Museum of Contemporary Crafts, NYC, 1969

Collections: American Craft Museum, NYC; Columbus Museum of Fine Arts, OH; Renwick Gallery, Smithsonian Institution, Washington, DC; Worshipful Company of Goldsmiths, London, England

Related Professional Experience: president, Society of North American Goldsmiths, 1977–80; faculty, U. of Washington, Seattle, 1980–present

David Huchthausen
Smithville, Tennessee

Born: Wisconsin Rapids, Wisconsin, 1951

Education: B.S., U. of Wisconsin, Madison, 1974; M.F.A., Illinois State U., Normal, 1976

Awards/Honors: Fulbright research scholarship, 1977; NEA Fellowship, 1982

Exhibitions: *World Glass Now*, Hokkaido Museum of Modern Art, Sapporo, Japan, 1985; *A Decade Apart*, Boise Museum of Art, ID, 1984; solo exhibition, St. Louis Art Museum, MO, 1984; *Pattern: An Exhibition of the Decorated Surface*, American Craft Museum, NYC, 1982; *New Glass: A Worldwide Survey*, Corning Museum of Glass, NY, 1979

Collections: Corning Museum of Glass, NY; Metropolitan Museum of Art, NYC; St. Louis Art Museum, MO; Smithsonian Institution, Washington, DC; Glass Museum, Fraunau, W. Germany; Glass Museum, Liege, Belgium; Lobmeyr Museum, Vienna, Austria; Museum of Arts and Crafts, Hamburg, W. Germany; Museum of Decorative Arts, Prague, Czechoslovakia

Related Professional Experience: curatorial consultant, Leigh Yawkey Woodson Art Museum, Wausau, WI, 1976–present; faculty, Tennessee Tech U., Smithville, TN, 1980–present

Thomas Hucker
Charlestown, Massachusetts

Born: Bryn Mawr, Pennsylvania, 1955

Education: certificate of mastery, Program in Artisanry, Boston U., MA, 1980

Awards/Honors: NEA apprenticeship grant, 1981; NEA Fellowship, 1983

Exhibitions: *Bent Wood Furniture*, Rhode Island Museum of Art, Providence, 1984; *Center for the Arts Faculty*, Columbia Museum, SC, and Huntsville Museum of Art, AL, 1982; *New Handmade Furniture: American Furniture Makers Working in Hardwood*, Museum of Contemporary Crafts, NYC, and tour, 1979–80; *Young Americans: Fiber/Wood/Plastic/Leather*, Museum of Contemporary Crafts, NYC, and tour, 1977–79

Collection: Museum of Fine Arts, Boston, MA

Related Professional Experience: faculty, Center for the Arts, Smithville, TN, 1980–82; artist-in-residence, Tokyo U. of Fine Arts, Japan, 1982; Boston U. Program in Artisanry, MA, 1982–83

Diane Itter
Bloomington, Indiana

Born: Summit, New Jersey, 1946

Education: B.A., U. of Pittsburgh, PA, 1969; M.F.A., Indiana U., Bloomington, 1974

Awards/Honors: NEA Fellowship, 1977, 1979, 1984

Exhibitions: *Contemporary Arts: An Expanding View*, Monmouth Museum of Art, Lincroft, NJ, 1986; *Pattern: An Exhibition of the Decorated Surface*, American Craft Museum, NYC, 1982; *Threads: Seven American Artists and Their Miniature Textile Pictures*, Renwick Gallery, Smithsonian Institution, Washington, DC, 1982; *The Art Fabric: Mainstream*, American Federation of Arts national tour, 1981–83

Collections: American Craft Museum, NYC; Indianapolis Museum of Art, IN; Prudential Insurance, Newark, NJ; Royal Scottish Museum, Edinburgh, Scotland

Related Professional Experience: artist-in-residence, Fabric Workshop, Philadelphia, PA, 1977, 1983; Jacquard loom project, Rhode Island School of Design, Providence, 1981

Ferne Jacobs
Los Angeles, California

Born: Chicago, Illinois, 1942

Education: Art Center College of Design, Los Angeles, CA, 1960–63; Pratt Institute, New York, NY, 1964–65; M.F.A., Claremont Graduate School, CA, 1976

Awards/Honors: NEA grant, 1973, 1977

Exhibitions: *Basketry: Tradition in New Form*, Institute of Contemporary Art, Boston, MA, and tour, 1982; *Old Traditions—New Directions*, Textile Museum, Washington, DC, 1981; ten-year retrospective exhibition, Chaffey Community College, Alta Loma, CA, 1980; *Fiberworks*, Cleveland Museum of Art, OH, 1977; *American Crafts: An Aesthetic View*, Museum of Contemporary Art, Chicago, IL, 1976; *Fibre Structures*, Denver Art Museum, CO, 1972; *Sculpture in Fiber*, Museum of Contemporary Crafts, NYC, 1971

Related Professional Experience: lectures/workshops on off-loom techniques and textiles, nationwide, 1975–present; tutorial staff, International College, Los Angeles, CA, 1978–present

Michael James
Somerset Village, Massachusetts

Born: New Bedford, Massachusetts, 1949

Education: B.A., Southeastern Massachusetts U., North Dartmouth, MA, 1971; M.F.A., Rochester Institute of Technology, NY, 1973

Award/Honor: NEA Fellowship, 1978

Exhibitions: *Contemporary American Quilts,* Chateau d'Annecy, France, and tour, 1984–85; *Michael James: Quiltmaker*, ten-year retrospective, Worcester Craft Center, MA, 1983; *Pattern: An Exhibition of the Decorated Surface*, American Craft Museum, NYC, 1982; *American Quiltmakers*, Stedelijk Museum, Amsterdam, Netherlands, 1979; *Young Americans: Fiber/Wood/Plastic/Leather*, Museum of Contemporary Crafts, NYC, 1977

Publications
The Quiltmaker's Handbook and *The Second Quiltmaker's Handbook*, Prentice-Hall, Inc., Englewood Cliffs, NJ, 1978, 1981

Collections: IBM, Essex Junction, VT, and Marietta, GA; Newark Museum, NJ

Russell C Jaqua Jr.
Port Townsend, Washington

Born: Detroit, Michigan, 1947

Education: Alma College, MI, 1965–67; Penland School of Crafts, NC, 1973–74

Exhibitions: *A Decade of American Blacksmithing*, National Ornamental Metal Museum, Memphis, TN, 1986; *Ferrous Finery*, National Ornamental Metal Museum, Memphis, TN, 1984; *Jewelry USA*, American Craft Museum, NYC, and tour, 1984–86

Collection: Timberline Lodge, Mt. Hood, OR

Related Professional Experience: owner-operator, Nimba Forge, Port Townsend, WA, 1976–85

Margie Jervis (works collaboratively with Susie Krasnican)
Falls Church, Virginia

Born: Washington, DC, 1956

Education: B.F.A., Rhode Island School of Design, Providence, 1978

Award/Honor: NEA Fellowship, 1980

Exhibitions: *Americans in Glass*, Leigh Yawkey Woodson Art Museum, Wausau, WI, 1984; *Sculptural Glass*, Tucson Museum of Art, AZ, 1983; *Approaches to Collecting*, American Craft Museum, NYC, 1982; *World Glass Now*, Hokkaido Museum of Modern Art, Sapporo, Japan, 1982; *Contemporary Glass: Australia, Canada, U.S.A. and Japan*, National Museum of Modern Art, Kyoto and Tokyo, Japan, 1981; *Young Americans: Clay/Glass*, Museum of Contemporary Crafts, NYC, 1978

Collections: Corning Museum of Glass, NY; Johnson Wax Collection, Racine, WI; Renwick Gallery, Smithsonian Institution, Washington, DC; Leigh Yawkey Woodson Art Museum, Wausau, WI; Kestner Museum, Hanover, W. Germany; Museum of Art, Dusseldorf, W. Germany

Related Professional Experience: collaborative artist/designer, 1977–present

Tom Joyce
Santa Fe, New Mexico

Born: Tulsa, Oklahoma, 1956

Education: self-educated

Exhibitions: *A Decade of American Blacksmithing*, National Ornamental Metal Museum, Memphis, TN, 1986; *Steel the Show*, Institute of History and Art, Albany, NY, 1985

Collections: Kansas Museum of History, Topeka; Museum of New Mexico, Albuquerque

Related Professional Experience: guest lecturer, Boston Institute of Art and Design, MA, 1984; Boston U., MA, 1984; International Blacksmithing Conference, Artist Blacksmith Association of North American, St. Norbert College, Green Bay, WI, 1984; Ironbridge Gorge International Blacksmithing Symposium, British Artist Blacksmith Association, Coalbrookdale, England, 1985; Southern Illinois U., Edwardsville, 1985

Jun Kaneko
Bloomfield Hills, Michigan

Born: Nagoya, Japan, 1942

Education: Chouinard Art Institute, Los Angeles, CA, 1964; U. of California, Berkeley, 1966; Claremont College, CA, 1970

Awards/Honors: NEA Fellowship, 1979, 1984

Exhibitions: *Contemporary Arts: An Expanding View*, Monmouth Museum of Art, Lincroft, NJ, 1986; *New Directions in Contemporary American Ceramics*, Museum of Fine Arts, Boston, MA, 1984; *Jun Kaneko: Parallel Sounds*, Contemporary Arts Museum, Houston, TX, 1981; *Material Pleasures: The Fabric Workshop at ICA, Philadelphia*, Museum of Contemporary Art, Chicago, IL, 1980; *A Century of Ceramics in the United States: 1878–1978*, Everson Museum of Art, Syracuse, NY, and tour, 1979; *Contemporary Ceramic Art: Canada, U.S.A., Mexico, Japan*, National Museum of Modern Art, Kyoto and Tokyo, Japan, 1971; *Objects:*

USA, Johnson Collection of Contemporary Crafts, national and international tour, 1969–72

Collections: American Craft Museum, NYC; Everson Museum of Art, Syracuse, NY; Philadelphia Museum of Art, PA; Japan Foundation, Tokyo, Japan

Related Professional Experience: faculty, Cranbrook Academy of Art, Bloomfield Hills, MI, 1979–1986

Karen Karnes
Morgan, Vermont

Born: New York, New York, 1925

Education: Brooklyn College, NYC, 1946; New York State College of Ceramics at Alfred U., NY, 1951–52

Awards/Honors: Tiffany Fellowship, 1958; Fellow, American Craft Council, 1976; NEA Fellowship, 1976; Fellow, National Council on Education for the Ceramic Arts, 1980

Exhibitions: *High Styles: Twentieth-Century American Design*, Whitney Museum of American Art, NYC, 1985; *Contemporary Ceramics: A Response to Wedgwood*, Museum of Philadelphia Civic Center, PA, 1980; *For the Tabletop*, American Craft Museum, NYC, 1980; *A Century of Ceramics in the United States: 1878–1978*, Everson Museum of Art, Syracuse, NY, and tour, 1979; *Objects: USA*, Johnson Collection of Contemporary Crafts, national and international tour, 1969–72; *American Studio Pottery*, Victoria and Albert Museum, London, England, 1968; *Designed for Production: The Craftsman's Approach*, Museum of Contemporary Crafts, NYC, 1964

Collections: American Craft Museum, NYC; Delaware Museum of Art, Wilmington; Everson Museum of Art, Syracuse, NY; Philadelphia Museum of Art, PA; St. Louis Art Museum, MO; Victoria and Albert Museum, London, England

Glen Kaufman
Athens, Georgia

Born: Fort Atkinson, Wisconsin, 1932

Education: B.S., U. of Wisconsin, Madison, 1954; M.F.A., Cranbrook Academy of Art, Bloomfield Hills, MI, 1959

Exhibitions: *International Exhibition of Miniature Textiles*, British Crafts Centre, London, England, and international tour, 1980, 1978, 1976, 1974; *American Crafts 1977*, Philadelphia Museum of Art, PA, 1977; *Artists in the Southeast*, High Museum of Art, Atlanta, GA, and tour, 1976–78; *Pacesetters and Prototypes: Weavers and Fabrics*, Detroit Institute of Arts, MI, 1973; *Modern American Textile Sculptures and Tapestries*, Museum of Applied Arts, Oslo, Norway, and tour, 1972; *Objects: USA*, Johnson Collection of Contemporary Crafts, national and international tour, 1969–72; solo exhibition, Museum of Contemporary Crafts, NYC, 1967

Publications: *Design on Fabrics*, with Meda Johnston, Van Nostrand Reinhold, NYC, 1967

Collection: American Craft Museum, NYC

Related Professional Experience: faculty, U. of Georgia, Athens, 1972–present

Robert Kehlmann
Berkeley, California

Born: Brooklyn, New York, 1942

Education: B.A., Antioch College, Yellow Springs, OH, 1963; M.A., U. of California, Berkeley, 1966

Awards/Honors: NEA Fellowship, 1977, 1978

Exhibitions: *Americans in Glass*, Leigh Yawkey Woodson Art Museum, Wausau, WI, 1984, 1981, 1978; *Sculptural Glass*, Tucson Museum of Art, AZ, 1983; *Pictures in Glass*, County Museum, Darmstadt, W. Germany, 1979; *New Glass: A Worldwide Survey*, Corning Museum of Glass, NY, 1979

Collections: American Craft Museum, NYC; Corning Museum of Glass, NY; Hokkaido Museum of Modern Art, Sapporo, Japan; International Glass Museum, Ebeltoft, Denmark; Museum of Decorative Arts, Lausanne, Switzerland

Related Professional Experience: faculty, California College of Arts and Crafts, Oakland, 1978–80; editor, *Glass Art Society Journal*, 1981–84

Ronald E. Kent
Honolulu, Hawaii

Born: Chicago, Illinois, 1931

Education: B.S., U. of California, Los Angeles, 1957

Exhibitions: *American Woodturners*, Brookfield Craft Center, CT, 1986; *Crafts: National*, Buffalo State College, NY, 1985; *The Art of Woodturning*, American Craft Museum, NYC, 1983

Collections: American Craft Museum, NYC; Albrecht Art Museum, St. Joseph, MO; Honolulu Academy of Arts, HI; Metropolitan Museum of Art, NYC; Museum of Fine Arts, Boston, MA; State Foundation for Culture and the Arts, Honolulu, HI

Related Professional Experience: by profession, an executive and stockbroker with Paine Webber

Ray King
Philadelphia, Pennsylvania

Born: Philadelphia, Pennsylvania, 1950

Education: apprenticed with Philadelphia artist Marco Zubar in stained glass, 1970–71; studied with Patrick Reyntiens, Burleighfield House, Buckinghamshire, England, 1975–76

Awards/Honors: Tiffany grant, 1975; PA Council on the Arts Fellowship, 1979; NEA Fellowship, 1982, 1984

Exhibitions: *Ray King: Maquettes and Drawings of Commissioned Works, 1980–1986*, Royal Institute of British Architects, London, England, 1986; *New American Glass*, Culture House, Stockholm, Sweden, 1985; *Ornamentalism: The New Decorativeness in Architecture and Design*, Hudson River Museum, Yonkers, NY, 1983; *Pattern: An Exhibition of the Decorated Surface*, American Craft Museum, NYC, 1982; *World Glass Now*, Hokkaido Museum of Modern Art, Sapporo, Japan, 1982

Collections: Corning Museum of Glass, NY; National Museum of American Art, Smithsonian Institution, Washington, DC; Victoria and Albert Museum, London, England

Related Professional Experience: major commissions for architectural glass in public spaces throughout the United States

L. Brent Kington
Makanda, Illinois

Born: Topeka, Kansas, 1934

Education: B.F.A., U. of Kansas, Lawrence, 1957; M.F.A., Cranbrook Academy of Art, Bloomfield Hills, MI, 1961

Awards/Honors: NEA Fellowship, 1975, 1982; Fellow, American Craft Council, 1978; IL Arts Council Fellowship, 1985

Exhibitions: *Jewelry USA*, American Craft Museum, NYC, and tour, 1984–86; solo exhibition, National Ornamental Metal Museum, Memphis, TN, 1984; *Toward a New Iron Age*, American Craft Museum, NYC, 1983; *Good As Gold: Alternative Materials in American Jewelry*, SITES tour, 1981–84; solo exhibition, Illinois State Museum, Springfield, 1980; *Goldsmiths*, Phoenix Art Museum, AZ, 1977; *American Crafts: An Aesthetic View*, Museum of Contemporary Art, Chicago, IL, 1976; *American Metalsmiths*, DeCordova Museum, Lincoln, MA, 1974; solo exhibition, Museum of Contemporary Crafts, NYC, 1969; *Young Americans 1962*, Museum of Contemporary Crafts, NYC, 1962

Collections: American Craft Museum, NYC; Illinois State Museum, Springfield; National Ornamental Metal Museum, Memphis, TN; Minnesota Museum of Art, St. Paul

Related Professional Experience: faculty, Southern Illinois U., Carbondale, 1961–present

Joey Kirkpatrick (works collaboratively with Flora Mace)
Seattle, Washington

Born: Des Moines, Iowa, 1952

Education: B.F.A., U. of Iowa, Iowa City, 1975; Iowa State U., Ames, 1978–79

Exhibitions: *New American Glass: Focus West Virginia*, Huntington Galleries, WV, 1985; *World Glass Now*, Hokkaido Museum of Modern Art, Sapporo, Japan, 1985; *Americans in Glass*, Leigh Yawkey Woodson Art Museum, Wausau, WI, 1984, 1981; *International Directions in Glass Art*, Art Gallery of Western Australia, Perth, and tour, 1982–83

Collections: Corning Museum of Glass, NY; Leigh Yawkey Woodson Art Museum, Wausau, WI; Broadfield Museum of England, London, England; International Glass Museum, Ebeltoft, Denmark; Museum of Decorative Arts, Lausanne, Switzerland

Related Professional Experience: faculty, Pilchuck School, Stanwood, WA, 1981–83, 1986; Lobmeyr, Vienna, Austria, 1985; lecturer, Nordisk Glass, Reykjavik, Iceland, 1985

Alice H. Klein
Milwaukee, Wisconsin

Born: Waukesha, Wisconsin, 1956

Education: B.F.A., U. of Wisconsin, Milwaukee, 1978; M.F.A., Tyler School of Art, Temple U., Philadelphia, PA, 1980

Award/Honor: WI Arts Board Fellowship, 1986

Exhibitions: *Contemporary Arts: An Expanding View*, Monmouth Museum of Art, Lincroft, NJ, 1986; *Contemporary Jewellery: The Americas, Australia, Europe and Japan*, National Museum of Modern Art, Kyoto and Tokyo, Japan, 1984; *Pattern: An Exhibition of the Decorated Surface*, American Craft Museum, NYC, 1982; *Good As Gold: Alternative Materials in American Jewelry*, SITES tour, 1981–84; *Young Americans: Metal* Museum of Contemporary Crafts, NYC, 1980

Collection: Cooper-Hewitt Museum, NYC

Related Professional Experience: self-employed, T.K.O. Contemporary Jewelry, 1980–present

Gerhardt Knodel
Bloomfield Hills, Michigan

Born: Milwaukee, Wisconsin, 1940

Education: B.A., U. of California, Los Angeles, 1962; M.A., California State U., Long Beach, 1970

Awards/Honors: NEA Fellowship, 1976; Japan/United States Friendship Commission Fellowship, 1984

Exhibitions: *International Biennial of Tapestry*, Cantonal Museum of Fine Arts, Lausanne, Switzerland, 1983, 1977, 1975; *Gerhardt Knodel Makes Places to Be*, Cranbrook Academy of Art Museum, Bloomfield Hills, MI, 1982; *The Art Fabric: Mainstream*, American Federation of Arts national tour, 1981–83; *Across the Nation—Fine Art for Federal Buildings*, National Collection of Fine Arts, Smithsonian Institution, Washington, DC, 1980; *Miniature Fiber Arts: A National Exhibition*, Textile Museum, Washington, DC, and tour, 1979–80; *Printed, Painted and Dyed: The New Fabric Surface*, Renwick Gallery, Smithsonian Institution, Washington, DC, 1978; *Fiberworks*, Cleveland Museum of Art, OH, 1977; *Young Americans*, Museum of Contemporary Crafts, NYC, 1969

Publications: *Gerhardt Knodel Makes Places to Be*, catalogue to accompany exhibition, Cranbrook Academy of Art Museum, Bloomfield Hills, MI, 1982

Collections: Cranbrook Academy Museum of Art, Bloomfield Hills, MI; Minneapolis Museum of Art, MN; National Collection of Fine Arts, Smithsonian Institution, Washington, DC

Related Professional Experience: artist-in-residence and director, fiber dept., Cranbrook Academy of Art, Bloomfield Hills, MI, 1970–present

Howard Kottler
Seattle, Washington

Born: Cleveland, Ohio, 1930

Education: B.A., M.A., Ohio State U., Columbus, 1952, 1956; M.F.A., Cranbrook Academy of Art, Bloomfield Hills, MI, 1957; Ph.D., Ohio State U., Columbus, 1964

Awards/Honors: Fulbright grant, 1957; NEA Fellowship, 1975; Japan/United States Friendship Commission grant, 1978

Exhibitions: *Grant Wood: The Regionalist Vision*, Whitney Museum of American Art, NYC, 1983; *For the Tabletop*, Museum of Contemporary Crafts, NYC, 1980; *A Century of Ceramics in the United States: 1878–1978*, Everson Museum of Art, Syracuse, NY, and tour, 1979; *Ornament of the 20th Century*, Cooper-Hewitt Museum, NYC, 1978; *Clay*, Whitney Museum of American Art, NYC, 1974; *International Exhibition of Ceramics*, Victoria and Albert Museum, London, England, 1972; *Contemporary Ceramic Art: Canada, U.S.A., Mexico, Japan*, National Museum of Modern

Art, Kyoto and Tokyo, Japan, 1971; *Objects: USA*, Johnson Collection of Contemporary Crafts, national and international tour, 1969–72

Collections: American Craft Museum, NYC; Cooper-Hewitt Museum, NYC; Cleveland Museum of Art, OH; Detroit Institute of Arts, MI; National Museum of Modern Art, Kyoto, Japan; Victoria and Albert Museum, London, England

Related Professional Experience: faculty, U. of Washington, Seattle, 1964–present

Ina Kozel
Oakland, California

Born: Tanevezys, Lithuania, 1944

Education: B.S., Cleveland Institute of Art and Case Western Reserve U., OH, 1966

Exhibitions: *Art to Wear*, American Craft Museum USIA Asian tour, 1984–85; *Art to Wear: New Handmade Clothing*, American Craft Museum, NYC, and tour, 1983–84; *Pattern: An Exhibition of the Decorated Surface*, American Craft Museum, NYC, 1982; *Art Clothing*, Art Textile Center, Berlin, W. Germany, 1981; *Art for Wearing*, San Francisco Museum of Modern Art, CA, 1979; *The Dyer's Art: Ikat, Batik, Plangi*, Museum of Contemporary Crafts, NYC, and tour, 1976–78; *Wearable Art*, Mint Museum, Charlotte, NC, 1976

Related Professional Experience: travels through Southeast Asia and Europe, 1969–73; study of traditional dyeing and resist techniques, Kyoto, Japan, 1975–76; commissions for large-scale fabric installations suspended in corporate atriums, 1981–present

Susie Krasnican (works collaboratively with Margie Jervis)
Falls Church, Virginia

Born: Alliance, Ohio, 1954

Education: B.F.A., Cleveland Institute of Art, OH, 1978

Award/Honor: NEA Fellowship, 1980

Exhibitions: *Americans in Glass*, Leigh Yawkey Woodson Art Museum, Wausau, WI, 1984; *Sculptural Glass*, Tucson Museum of Art, AZ, 1983; *Approaches to Collecting*, American Craft Museum, NYC, 1982; *World Glass Now*, Hokkaido Museum of Modern Art, Sapporo, Japan, 1982; *Contemporary Glass: Australia, Canada, U.S.A. and Japan*, National Museum of Modern Art, Kyoto and Tokyo, Japan, 1981; *Young Americans: Clay/Glass*, Museum of Contemporary Crafts, NYC, 1978

Collections: Corning Museum of Glass, NY; Johnson Wax Collection, Racine, WI; Renwick Gallery, Smithsonian Institution, Washington, DC; Leigh Yawkey Woodson Art Museum, Wausau, WI; Kestner Museum, Hanover, W. Germany; Museum of Art, Dusseldorf, W. Germany

Related Professional Experience: collaborative artist/designer, 1977–present

Fran Kraynek-Prince (works collaboratively with Neil Prince)
Encinitas, California

Born: Pittsburgh, Pennsylvania, 1943

Education: A.A., Point Park College, Pittsburgh, PA, 1962

Exhibitions: *Fiber Individualists*, Charles A. Wustum Museum of Fine Arts, Racine, WI, 1986; *American Crafts in Iceland*, National Art Museum, Reykjavik, Iceland, 1983

Collections: Arizona State U. Art Museum, Tempe; Fine Arts Museum of the South, Mobile, AL; Sheldon Art Museum, Lincoln, NE

James Krenov
Fort Bragg, California

Born: Siberia, USSR, 1920

Education: studies in design and furniture-making with Carl Malmsten, Stockholm, Sweden

Publications: *A Cabinetmaker's Notebook* (1976), *The Impractical Cabinetmaker* (1979), *James Krenov: Worker in Wood* (1981)—all published by Van Nostrand Reinhold, NYC

Collections: Museum of Applied Arts, Trondheim, Norway; Museum of Arts and Crafts, Tokyo, Japan; National Museum, Stockholm, Sweden

Related Professional Experience: faculty, College of the Redwoods, Fort Bragg, CA, 1981–present

Jane Lackey
Kansas City, Missouri

Born: Chattanooga, Tennessee, 1948

Education: B.F.A., California College of Arts and Crafts, Oakland, 1974; M.F.A., Cranbrook Academy of Art, Bloomfield Hills, MI, 1979

Award/Honor: NEA Fellowship, 1984

Exhibitions: *Fiber R/Evolution*, University Art Museum, U. of Wisconsin, Milwaukee, 1986; *Art for the Collector*, Museum of Rhode Island School of Design, Providence, 1983; *The Dyer's Art*, Pacific Design Center, Los Angeles, CA, 1982; *Mid-Four Art Exhibition*, Nelson-Atkins Museum of Art, Kansas City, MO, 1981; *Fiberworks: Michigan*, Flint Institute of Arts, MI, 1980

Collections: Chubb Insurance Group, Warren, NJ; Corpus Christi National Bank, TX; Sigal Corp., Washington, DC; United Telephone Systems, Altamonte, FL

Related Professional Experience: faculty, Kansas City Art Institute, MO, 1980–present

Rebekah Laskin
New Paltz, New York

Born: New York, New York, 1955

Education: B.F.A., State U. of New York, College at New Paltz, 1982

Exhibitions: *Contemporary Arts: An Expanding View*, Monmouth Museum of Art, Lincroft, NJ, 1986; *American Jewelry Now*, American Craft Museum USIA Asian tour, 1985; *Enamels International*, Long Beach Museum of Art, CA, 1985; *Jewelry USA*, American Craft Museum, NYC, and tour, 1984–86; *Good As Gold: Alternative Materials in American Jewelry*, SITES tour, 1981–84

Collections: Cooper-Hewitt Museum, NYC; Museum of Applied Arts, Trondheim, Norway; Museum of Applied Arts, Oslo, Norway

Related Professional Experience: artist-in-residence, Oregon School of Arts and Crafts, Portland, 1981–82; faculty, New York U., NYC, 1985–present

Stanley Lechtzin
Melrose Park, Pennsylvania

Born: Detroit, Michigan, 1936

Education: B.F.A., Wayne State U., Detroit, MI, 1960; M.F.A., Cranbrook Academy of Art, Bloomfield Hills, MI, 1962

Awards/Honors: Tiffany grant, 1967; NEA Fellowship, 1973, 1976, 1984; PA Governor's Award/Hazlett Memorial Award, 1984

Exhibitions: *Masterworks of Contemporary American Jewelry: Sources and Concepts*, Victoria and Albert Museum, London, England, 1985; solo exhibitions, Southern Alleghenies Museum of Art, Loretto, PA, 1984; William Penn Museum, Harrisburg, PA, 1984; *Good As Gold: Alternative Materials in American Jewelry*, SITES tour, 1981–84; solo exhibition, Goldsmiths' Hall, London, England, 1973; *Objects: USA*, Johnson Collection of Contemporary Crafts, national and international tour, 1969–72; solo exhibition, Museum of Contemporary Crafts, NYC, 1965; *Young Americans 1958*, Museum of Contemporary Crafts, NYC, 1958

Collections: American Craft Museum, NYC; Detroit Institute of Arts, MI; Philadelphia Museum of Art, PA; Goldsmiths' Hall, London, England; Jewelry Museum, Pforzheim, W. Germany

Related Professional Experience: faculty, Tyler School of Art, Temple U., Philadelphia, PA, 1962–present

Janice Lessman-Moss
Ravenna, Ohio

Born: Pittsburgh, Pennsylvania, 1954

Education: A.S., Endicott College, Beverly, MA, 1974; B.F.A., Tyler School of Art, Temple U., Philadelphia, PA, 1979; M.F.A., U. of Michigan, Ann Arbor, 1981

Award/Honor: OH Arts Council Fellowship, 1983

Exhibitions: *Have a Heart*, Akron Art Museum, OH, 1985; *May Show*, Cleveland Museum of Art, OH, 1985, 1984, 1982; *Visual Reservoirs: Objects and Images of In-Of-Under-About Surface*, Monterey Peninsula Museum of Art, CA, 1985; *Fiber Structure National*, Downey Museum of Art, CA, 1984; *Focus:*

Fiber, Cleveland Museum of Art, OH, 1983; *September Competition*, Alexandria Museum, LA, 1983

Related Professional Experience: faculty, Kent State U., OH, 1981–present

Leslie Leupp
Lubbock, Texas

Born: Archbold, Ohio, 1944

Education: A.A., Hesston Junior College, Hesston, KS, 1966; B.A., Bethel College, North Newton, KS, 1968; M.F.A., Indiana U., Bloomington, 1973

Awards/Honors: NEA Fellowship, 1984; Ford Foundation grant, 1980, 1981

Exhibitions: *Contemporary Metals USA*, Downey Museum of Art, CA, 1985; *Jewelry USA*, American Craft Museum, NYC, and tour, 1984–86; *National Jewelry and Unique Objects Invitational*, Fine Arts Center of Tempe, AZ, 1984; solo exhibition, Idaho State U., Pocatello, ID, 1981; *Off the Body*, Bradley U., Peoria, IL, 1980; *The Metalsmith*, Phoenix Art Museum, AZ, and tour, 1977; *Forms in Metal: 275 Years of Metalsmithing in America*, Museum of Contemporary Crafts, NYC, and tour, 1975–76

Related Professional Experience: faculty, Ball State U., Muncie, IN, 1973–78; Indiana U., Bloomington, 1978–83; Texas Tech U., Lubbock, 1983–present

Marilyn Levine
Oakland, California

Born: Medicine Hat, Canada, 1935

Education: B.S., M.S., U. of Alberta, Edmonton, Canada, 1957, 1959; M.A., M.F.A., U. of California, Berkeley, 1970, 1971

Awards/Honors: Canada Arts Council grant, 1973; NEA Fellowship, 1976, 1980

Exhibitions: *Marilyn Levine: A Ten-Year Survey*, Institute of Contemporary Art, Boston, MA, 1981; *Nine West Coast Clay Sculptors*, Everson Museum of Art, Syracuse, NY, 1978; *A Decade of Ceramic Art: 1962–72*, San Francisco Museum of Modern Art, CA, 1972; *Clayworks: 20 Americans*, Museum of Contemporary Crafts, NYC, 1971

Collections: Everson Museum of Art, Syracuse, NY; Museum of Contemporary Art, Chicago, IL; Oakland Museum, CA; San Francisco Museum of Modern Art, CA; International Museum of Ceramics, Faenza, Italy; Montreal Museum of Fine Arts, Canada; National Museum of Modern Art, Kyoto and Tokyo, Japan

Related Professional Experience: faculty, U. of Utah, Salt Lake City, 1973–76; U. of California, Berkeley, 1975–80

Mark Lindquist
Quincy, Florida, and Henniker, New Hampshire

Born: Oakland, California, 1949

Education: B.A., New England College, Henniker, NH, 1971

Awards/Honors: NH Commission on the Arts grant, 1984; MA Council on the Arts and Humanities grant, 1985

Exhibitions: *The Art of Woodturning*, American Craft Museum, NYC, 1983; two-person exhibition with Melvin Lindquist, Columbus Museum of Art, OH, 1982; *New Handmade Furniture: American Furniture Makers Working in Hardwood*, Museum of Contemporary Crafts, NYC, 1979; solo exhibition, Greenville County Museum of Art, SC, 1979; *The Art of the Turned Bowl*, Renwick Gallery, Smithsonian Institution, Washington, DC, 1978; *Twentieth-Century Decorative Art*, Metropolitan Museum of Art, NYC, 1978; *Bed and Board*, DeCordova Museum, Lincoln, MA, 1975

Collections: Dallas Museum of Art, TX; High Museum of Art, Atlanta, GA; Metropolitan Museum of Art, NYC; National Museum of American Art, Smithsonian Institution, Washington, DC; Philadelphia Museum of Art, PA

Marvin Lipofsky
Berkeley, California

Born: Barrington, Illinois, 1938

Education: B.F.A., U. of Illinois, Champaign-Urbana, 1961; M.S., M.F.A., U. of Wisconsin, Madison, 1964

Awards/Honors: NEA Fellowship, 1974, 1976; honorific prize, Vincointer '83, Valencia, Spain, 1983

Exhibitions: *World Glass Now*, Hokkaido Museum of Modern Art, Sapporo, Japan, 1982; *Three Glass Mas-*

ters, Renwick Gallery, Smithsonian Institution, Washington, DC, 1980; *New Glass: A Worldwide Survey*, Corning Museum of Glass, NY, 1979; *Objects: USA*, Johnson Collection of Contemporary Crafts, national and international tour, 1969–72; *Young Americans*, Museum of Contemporary Crafts, NYC, 1969

Collections: American Craft Museum, NYC; Corning Museum of Glass, NY; Detroit Institute of Arts, MI; High Museum of Art, Atlanta, GA; Oakland Museum, CA; Arts and Crafts Museum, Prague, Czechoslovakia; Museum of Contemporary Art, Skopje, Yugoslavia; National Museum of Glass, Leerdam, Holland; National Museum of Modern Art, Kyoto, Japan

Related Professional Experience: faculty, U. of California, Berkeley, 1964–72; California College of Arts and Crafts, Oakland, 1967–present

Gregory Litsios
Rochester, New Hampshire

Born: Hackensack, New Jersey, 1953

Education: B.F.A., Syracuse U., NY, 1976

Exhibitions: *Crafts USA*, National Art Museum, Reykjavik, Iceland, 1983; *Young Americans: Award Winners*, American Craft Museum, NYC, 1982; *Beyond Tradition: 25th Anniversary Exhibition*, American Craft Museum, NYC, 1981; *For the Tabletop*, American Craft Museum, NYC, 1980; *Young Americans: Metal*, Museum of Contemporary Crafts, NYC, 1980

Related Professional Experience: artist-in-residence, Culverbrook Restoration Society, Branchville, NJ, 1977–79; assistant, Albert Paley studio, Rochester, NY, 1979–81; artist-in-residence, Stissing Hollow Craftworks, Pine Plains, NY, 1981–83

Harvey K. Littleton
Spruce Pine, North Carolina

Born: Corning, New York, 1922

Education: B.D., U. of Michigan, Ann Arbor, 1947; M.F.A., Cranbrook Academy of Art, Bloomfield Hills, MI, 1951

Awards/Honors: Tiffany grant, 1970; Honorary Member, National Council on Education for the Ceramic Arts, 1972; Fellow, American Craft Council, 1975; Honorary Life Membership, Glass Art Society, 1976; NEA Fellowship, 1978; honorary Ph.D., Philadelphia College of Art, 1982

Exhibitions: *Harvey K. Littleton: Retrospective Exhibition*, High Museum of Art, Atlanta, GA and tour, 1984–85; *Americans in Glass*, Leigh Yawkey Woodson Art Museum, Wausau, WI, 1982, 1978; *World Glass Now*, Hokkaido Museum of Modern Art, Sapporo, Japan, 1982; *New Glass: A Worldwide Survey*, Corning Museum of Glass, NY, 1979; *Objects: USA*, Johnson Collection of Contemporary Crafts, national and international tour, 1969–72; solo exhibition, Museum of Contemporary Crafts, NYC, 1964; Art Institute of Chicago, IL, 1963

Publications: *Glassblowing—A Search for Form*, Van Nostrand Reinhold, NYC, 1971

Collections: American Craft Museum, NYC; Cooper-Hewitt Museum, NYC; Corning Museum of Glass, NY; Metropolitan Museum of Art, NYC; Museum of Modern Art, NYC; Museum of Modern Art, Tokyo, Japan; Victoria and Albert Museum, London, England

Related Professional Experience: faculty, U. of Wisconsin, Madison, 1951–1977; professor emeritus, 1977–present

Ken Loeber
Algoma, Wisconsin

Born: Milwaukee, Wisconsin, 1948

Education: B.F.A., M.F.A., U. of Wisconsin, Milwaukee, 1970, 1978

Award/Honor: NEA Regional Fellowship, 1985

Exhibitions: *American Jewelry Now*, American Craft Museum USIA Asian tour, 1985; *Designed and Made for Use*, American Craft Museum, NYC, 1985; *Jewelry USA*, American Craft Museum, NYC, and tour, 1984–86; *Crafts in the Carnegie Mansion*, Cooper-Hewitt Museum, NYC, 1982, 1981

Related Professional Experience: design partner, Loeber/Look Studio, Algoma, WI, 1980–present

Thomas Loeser
Cambridge, Massachusetts

Born: Boston, Massachusetts, 1956

Education: B.A., Haverford College, PA, 1979; B.F.A., Program in Artisanry, Boston University, MA, 1982

Awards/Honors: MA Council on the Arts Fellowship, 1984; NEA Fellowship, 1984

Exhibitions: *Material Evidence: New Color Techniques in Handmade Furniture*, Renwick Gallery, Smithsonian Institution, Washington, DC, 1985; *Post-Modern Colour—New Furniture by British, American and French Designers*, Victoria and Albert Museum, London, England, 1984; *Ornamentalism: The New Decorativeness in Architecture and Design*, Hudson River Museum, Yonkers, NY, 1983; *Pattern: An Exhibition of the Decorated Surface*, American Craft Museum, NYC, 1982

Collection: Cooper-Hewitt Museum, NYC

Related Professional Experience: artist-in-residence, Appalachian Center for Crafts, Smithville, TN, 1983, 1986; Artpark, Lewiston, NY, 1984; faculty, Penland School of Crafts, NC, 1986

Charles Loloma
Hotevilla, Arizona

Born: Hotevilla, Arizona, 1921

Education: certificate, New York State College of Ceramics at Alfred U., NY, 1947

Awards/Honors: NEA grant, 1974, 1978; Fellow, American Craft Council, 1976

Exhibitions: *In Beauty I Create*, San Diego Museum of Man, CA, 1984; *The Center Space: Pueblo Indian Architecture*, Museum of New Mexico, Santa Fe, NM, 1983; solo exhibitions, Museum of Contemporary Crafts, NYC, 1974; Heard Museum, Phoenix, AZ, 1971; *Objects: USA*, Johnson Collection of Contemporary Crafts, national and international tour, 1969–72

Collections: Denver Art Museum, CO; M. H. DeYoung Memorial Museum, San Francisco, CA; Heard Museum, Phoenix, AZ; Millicent Rodgers Museum, Taos, NM

Related Professional Experience: faculty, Institute of American Indian Arts, Santa Fe, NM, 1962–65

Randy Long
Bloomington, Indiana

Born: Tarentum, Pennsylvania, 1951

Education: B.A., M.A., San Diego State U., CA, 1974, 1977; M.F.A., California State U., Long Beach, 1983

Awards/Honors: IN Arts Commission Fellowship, 1985; NEA Fellowship, 1983, 1984

Exhibitions: *Jewelry USA*, American Craft Museum, NYC, 1984; *North American Metalwork Invitational*, Kyoto Municipal Museum of Traditional Industry, Japan, 1983; *Young Americans: Metal*, American Craft Museum, NYC, 1980; *Clay, Fiber, Metal by Women Artists*, Bronx Museum, NY, 1978; *Goldsmith '74*, Renwick Gallery, Smithsonian Institution, Washington, DC, and Minnesota Museum of Art, St. Paul, 1974

Collections: Marietta College, OH; Museum of Art, U. of Iowa, Iowa City, IA; San Diego State U., CA

Related Professional Experience: faculty, Drake U., Des Moines, IA, 1978–83; Indiana U., Bloomington, 1983–present

Dona Look
Algoma, Wisconsin

Born: Mequon, Wisconsin, 1948

Education: B.A., U. of Wisconsin, Oshkosh, 1970

Exhibitions: *Designed and Made for Use*, American Craft Museum, NYC, 1985; *Art for the Table*, American Craft Museum, NYC, 1984

Related Professional Experience: faculty, Sydney and Tamworth, New South Wales, Australia, 1976–78; design partner, Look & Heaney Studio, Byron Bay, New South Wales, Australia, 1978–80; design partner, Loeber/Look Studio, Algoma, WI, 1980–present

Michael Lucero
New York, New York

Born: Tracy, California, 1953

Education: B.A., Humboldt State U., Arcata, CA, 1975; M.F.A., U. of Washington, Seattle, 1978

Award/Honor: NEA Fellowship, 1979

Exhibitions: *American Ceramics*, Ceramics Museum, Barcelona, Spain, 1985; *New York Art Now: Correspondences*, Laforet Museum, Tokyo, Japan, 1985; *American Sculpture: Three Decades*, Seattle Art Museum, WA, 1984; *Bay Area Collects: A Diverse Sampling*, San Francisco Museum of Modern Art, CA, 1983; *Still Modern After All These Years*, Chrysler Museum, Norfolk, VA, 1982; *The Clay Figure*, American Craft Museum, NYC, 1981; *The Figure: A Celebration*, Museum of South Texas, Corpus Christi, 1981; *Contemporary Ceramics: A Response to Wedgwood*, Museum of Philadelphia Civic Center, PA, 1980; *Another Side to Art*, Seattle Art Museum, WA, 1979; *Young Americans: Clay/Glass*, Museum of Contemporary Crafts, NYC, 1978

Collections: Metropolitan Museum of Art, NYC; Seattle Art Museum, WA

Tom Lundberg
Fort Collins, Colorado

Born: Belle Plaine, Iowa, 1953

Education: B.F.A., U. of Iowa, Iowa City, 1975; M.F.A., Indiana U., Bloomington, 1979

Awards/Honors: Ford Foundation grant, 1978; CO Council on the Arts and Humanities Creative Fellowship, 1986

Exhibitions: *Needle Expressions '84*, Greenville County Museum of Art, SC, and tour, 1984; *Needle Expressions '82*, Tennessee State Museum, Nashville, 1982; *Threads: Seven American Artists and Their Miniature Textile Pictures*, Renwick Gallery, Smithsonian Institution, Washington, DC, and international tour, 1982–84; *First Biennial Thread and Fiber Competition*, Alexandria Museum of Art, LA, 1978; *Third International Exhibition of Miniature Textiles*, British Crafts Centre, London, England and international tour, 1978

Related Professional Experience: faculty, Indiana U., Bloomington, 1976–79; Colorado State U., Fort Collins, 1979–present

Winifred Lutz
Huntingdon Valley, Pennsylvania

Born: Brooklyn, New York, 1942

Education: B.F.A., Cleveland Institute of Art, OH, 1965; M.F.A., Cranbrook Academy of Art, Bloomfield Hills, MI, 1968

Award/Honor: NEA grant, 1984

Exhibitions: group exhibition, Arad Museum, Israel, 1986; *Paper Now: Bent, Molded, and Manipulated*, Cleveland Museum of Art, OH, 1986; *Paper as Image*, Arts Council of Great Britain tour, 1983; *New American Paperworks*, National Museum of Fine Art, Kyoto, Japan, and Asian tour, 1982; *Papermaking USA*, American Craft Museum, NYC, 1982; *With Paper, About Paper*, Albright-Knox Art Gallery, Buffalo, NY, 1980; *Paper*, SITES tour, 1978; *New Ways with Paper*, National Collection of Fine Arts, Smithsonian Institution, Washington, DC, 1977; *Handmade Paper, Prints and Unique Works*, Museum of Modern Art, NYC, 1976; *The Handmade Paper Object*, Santa Barbara Museum of Art, CA, 1975; solo exhibition, International Ceramic Center, Rome, Italy, 1966

Collections: Albright-Knox Art Gallery, Buffalo, NY; Art Institute of Chicago, IL; Cleveland Museum of Art, OH; International Paper, NYC; Newark Museum, NJ

Related Professional Experience: faculty, Yale U., New Haven, CT, 1975–82; Tyler School of Art, Temple U., Philadelphia, PA, 1982–present

Flora Mace (works collaboratively with Joey Kirkpatrick)
Seattle, Washington

Born: Hampton, New Hampshire, 1949

Education: B.S., Plymouth State College, New Hampshire, 1972; M.F.A., U. of Illinois, Champaign-Urbana, 1976

Exhibitions: *New American Glass: Focus West Virginia*, Huntington Galleries, WV, 1985; *World Glass Now*, Hokkaido Museum of Modern Art, Sapporo, Japan, 1985; *Americans in Glass*, Leigh Yawkey Woodson Art Museum, Wausau, WI, 1984, 1981; *International Directions in Glass Art*, Art Gallery of Western Australia, Perth, and tour, 1982–83

Collections: Corning Museum of Glass, NY; Leigh Yawkey Woodson Art Museum, Wausau, WI;

Broadfield Museum of England, London, England; International Glass Museum, Ebeltoff, Denmark; Museum of Decorative Arts, Lausanne, Switzerland

Related Professional Experience: faculty, U. of Illinois, Champaign-Urbana, 1981–82; Pilchuck School, Stanwood, WA, 1981–83, 1986; Lobmeyr, Vienna, Austria, 1985; lecturer, Nordisk Glass, Reykjavik, Iceland, 1985

Jarmila Machova
Los Angeles, California

Born: Poprad, Czechoslovakia, 1923

Education: M.F.A., College of Applied Arts, Prague, Czechoslovakia, 1963; M.F.A., U. of California, Los Angeles, 1980

Exhibitions: *Fiber Structure National,* Downey Museum of Art, CA, 1984; *California Crafts XIII,* Crocker Art Museum, Sacramento, CA, 1983; *International Biennial of Tapestry,* Cantonal Museum of Fine Arts, Lausanne, Switzerland, 1983; *Silver Jubilee Retrospective,* Downey Museum of Art, CA, 1983

Collections: Columbia National Bank, Santa Monica, CA; Epson Computer, Los Angeles, CA; Hyatt Regency Hotel, Flint, MI, and Oakland, CA; Security Pacific National Bank, Carmichael, CA, Glendale, CA, and San Diego, CA

Related Professional Experience: restoration studies of ancient tapestries, National Gallery, Prague, Czechoslovakia, 1964

Linda MacNeil
Amesbury, Massachusetts

Born: Boston, Massachusetts, 1954

Education: B.F.A., Rhode Island School of Design, Providence, 1976

Awards/Honors: MA Council on the Arts Fellowship, 1979; NEA Fellowship, 1984

Exhibitions: *Jewelry USA,* American Craft Museum, NYC, and tour, 1984–86; *Sculptural Glass,* Tucson Museum of Art, AZ, 1983; *International Directions in Glass Art,* Art Gallery of Western Australia, Perth, and tour, 1982–83; *Americans in Glass,* Leigh Yawkey Woodson Art Museum, Wausau, WI, 1981; *Glass Routes,* DeCordova Museum, Lincoln, MA, 1981; *Good As Gold: Alternative Materials in American Jewelry,* SITES tour, 1981–84; *Art for Use,* Olympic Winter Games, Lake Placid, NY, and American Craft Museum, NYC, 1980

Collections: Corning Museum of Glass, NY; Renwick Gallery, Smithsonian Institution, Washington, DC

Steven Madsen
Albuquerque, New Mexico

Born: Oxnard, California, 1947

Education: Utah State U., Logan, 1967; U. of New Mexico, Albuquerque, 1973

Award/Honor: NEA Fellowship, 1981

Exhibitions: *Pattern: An Exhibition of the Decorated Surface,* American Craft Museum, NYC, 1982; *Art for Use,* Olympic Winter Games, Lake Placid, NY, and American Craft Museum, NYC, 1980; *Here and Now: 35 Artists in New Mexico,* Museum of Albuquerque, 1980; *New Handmade Furniture: American Furniture Makers Working in Hardwood,* Museum of Contemporary Crafts, NYC, 1979; *New Mexico: Space and Images,* Craft and Folk Art Museum, Los Angeles, CA, 1979; *One Space/Three Visions,* Museum of Albuquerque, NM, 1979; *Six West Coast Craftsmen,* San Jose State Museum, CA, 1978

Collections: Museum of Albuquerque, NM; U. of Texas, El Paso

Andrew Magdanz (works collaboratively with Susan Shapiro)
Cambridge, Massachusetts

Born: River Falls, Wisconsin, 1951

Education: B.S., M.A., U. of Wisconsin, Madison, 1975, 1976; M.F.A., California College of Arts and Crafts, Oakland, 1978

Award/Honor: NEA Master Craftsman apprentice grant, 1979

Exhibitions: *Americans in Glass,* Leigh Yawkey Woodson Art Museum, Wausau, WI, 1984, 1981, 1978; *Reflections on the California Craft Collection,* Oakland Museum, CA, 1984; *Glass Routes,* DeCordova Museum, Lincoln, MA, 1981; *Introduc-*

tions, Craft and Folk Art Museum, Los Angeles, CA, 1981; *Pilchuck Glass Invitational,* Seattle Art Museum, WA, 1976

Collections: Corning Museum of Glass, NY; Greenville Museum of Art, NC; Oakland Museum, CA; Roanoke Museum of Fine Arts, VA; Wheaton Museum of Glass, Millville, NJ

James Makins
New York, New York

Born: Johnstown, Pennsylvania, 1946

Education: B.F.A., Philadelphia College of Art, PA, 1968; M.F.A., Cranbrook Academy of Art, Bloomfield Hills, MI, 1973

Awards/Honors: NEA artist-in-residence grant, 1975, 1978–80; NEA Fellowship, 1976, 1980; NY Foundation for the Arts Fellowship, 1986

Exhibitions: *Contemporary Arts: An Expanding View,* Monmouth Museum of Art, Lincroft, NJ, 1986; *Centering on Contemporary Clay,* U. of Iowa Museum of Art, Iowa City, 1981; *American Porcelain: New Expressions in an Ancient Art,* Renwick Gallery, Smithsonian Institution, Washington, DC, and SITES tour, 1980–84; *For the Tabletop,* American Craft Museum, NYC, 1980; *Attitudes,* Brooklyn Museum, NYC, 1977; *Soup Tureens,* Campbell Museum, Camden, NJ, 1976; *Salt Glaze Ceramics,* Museum of Contemporary Crafts, NYC, 1972

Collections: Everson Museum of Art, Syracuse, NY; Philadelphia Museum of Art, PA; Rhode Island Museum, Providence; Boymans and van Beuningen Museum, Rotterdam, Netherlands

Sam Maloof
Alta Loma, California

Born: Chino, California, 1916

Education: Chino High School, 1934

Awards/Honors: Tiffany grant, 1969; Fellow, American Craft Council, 1975; NEA Fellowship, 1984; MacArthur Foundation Fellowship, 1985

Exhibitions: *California Crafts XIV: Living Treasures of California,* Crocker Art Museum, Sacramento, CA, 1985; *High Styles: Twentieth-Century American Design,* Whitney Museum of American Art, NYC, 1985; *California Woodworker,* Oakland Museum, CA, 1981; *New Handmade Furniture: American Furniture Makers Working in Hardwood,* Museum of Contemporary Crafts, 1979; *Crafts, Art, and Religion,* Smithsonian Institution, Washington, DC, and Vatican Museum, Italy, 1978; *American Crafts: An Aesthetic View,* Museum of Contemporary Art, Chicago, IL, 1976; *Woodenworks,* Renwick Gallery, Smithsonian Institution, Washington, DC, 1971; *Objects: USA,* Johnson Collection of Contemporary Crafts, national and international tour, 1969–72; *California Design, I–XI,* Pasadena Art Museum, CA, 1954–1971

Publications: *Sam Maloof Woodworker,* Kodansha International, Tokyo/NYC, 1983

Collections: American Craft Museum, NYC; Craft and Folk Art Museum, Los Angeles, CA; Minnesota Art Museum, St. Paul; Museum of Fine Arts, Boston, MA; Oakland Museum, CA; Philadelphia Museum of Art, PA; St. Louis Art Museum, MO; Vice-President's Residence, Washington, DC; White House, Washington, DC

K. Lee Manuel
Santa Cruz, California

Born: Loma Linda, California, 1936

Education: U. of California, Los Angeles, 1956; B.F.A., San Francisco Art Institute, CA, 1959

Exhibitions: *Beyond Wearables,* California Craft Museum, San Francisco, 1985; *Crafts America,* Craft Council of England and Wales, London, England, 1985; *New Furniture,* Triton Art Museum, San Jose, CA, 1985; *Art to Wear,* American Craft Museum USIA Asian tour, 1984–85; *Celebration 84! A Sense of Occasion,* Ontario Crafts Council, Toronto, Canada, 1984; *Art to Wear: New Handmade Clothing,* American Craft Museum, NYC, and tour, 1983–84; *Poetry for the Body, Clothing for the Spirit,* Richmond Art Museum, CA, 1983

Louis B. Marak
Eureka, California

Born: Shawnee, Oklahoma, 1942

Education: B.F.A., U. of Illinois, Champaign-Urbana, 1965; M.F.A., New York State College of Ceramics at Alfred U., New York, 1967

Award/Honor: NEA Fellowship, 1975

Exhibitions: *Soup Soup Beautiful Soup,* Campbell Museum, Camden, NJ, 1983; *American Porcelain: New Expressions in an Ancient Art,* Renwick Gallery, Smithsonian Institution, Washington, DC, and SITES tour, 1980–84; *Contemporary Ceramics: A Response to Wedgwood,* Museum of Philadelphia Civic Center, PA, 1980; *Northern California Clay Routes: Sculpture Now,* San Francisco Museum of Modern Art, CA, 1979; *Young Americans,* Museum of Contemporary Crafts, NYC, 1969

Collection: Krannert Art Museum, Champaign, IL

Related Professional Experience: faculty, Humboldt State U., Arcata, CA, 1969–83

Paul Marioni
Seattle, Washington

Born: Cincinnati, Ohio, 1941

Education: B.A., San Francisco State U., Ca, 1964

Awards/Honors: NEA Fellowship, 1975, 1982

Exhibitions: *New Glass: A Worldwide Survey,* Corning Museum of Glass, NY, 1979; *Americans in Glass,* Leigh Yawkey Woodson Art Museum, Wausau, WI, 1978; *New Stained Glass,* Museum of Contemporary Crafts, NYC, and tour, 1978

Collections: Corning Museum of Glass, NY; Oakland Museum, CA; Portable Works Collection, City of Seattle, WA; Hessisches County Museum, Darmstadt, W. Germany

Related Professional Experience: faculty, Pilchuck School, Stanwood, WA, 1974–86; director, glass program, Summervail, Vail, CO, 1979–84

Graham Marks
Scottsville, New York

Born: New York, New York, 1951

Education: B.F.A., Philadelphia College of Art, PA, 1974; M.F.A., New York State College of Ceramics at Alfred U., NY, 1976

Awards/Honors: NEA Fellowship, 1978, 1984; NY Foundation for the Arts Fellowship, 1985

Exhibitions: *Contemporary Arts: An Expanding View,* Monmouth Museum of Art, Lincroft, NJ, 1986; *Contemporary American Ceramics: Twenty Artists,* Newport Harbor Art Museum, Newport Beach, CA, 1985; *Who's Afraid of American Pottery?* Museum of Contemporary Art, Hertogenbosch, Netherlands, and tour, 1983; *Contemporary Ceramics: A Response to Wedgwood,* Museum of Philadelphia Civic Center, PA, 1980; *Young Americans: Clay/Glass,* Museum of Contemporary Crafts, NYC, and tour, 1978

Collections: American Craft Museum, NYC; Kohler Co., WI; New York State College of Ceramics at Alfred U., NY; U. of Iowa Museum of Art, Iowa City, IA

Related Professional Experience: faculty, Kansas State U., Manhattan, KS, 1976–78; School for American Craftsmen, Rochester Institute of Technology, Rochester, NY, 1980–84

Richard Marquis
Freeland, Washington

Born: Bumblebee, Arizona, 1945

Education: B.A., M.A., U. of California, Berkeley, 1969, 1971

Awards/Honors: NEA grant, 1974, 1978, 1981; Australian Craft Council grant, 1974, 1975, 1976; Fulbright grant, 1969, 1981

Exhibitions: *Transparent Motives: Glass on a Large Scale,* Cincinnati Art Center, OH, 1985; *World Glass Now,* Hokkaido Museum of Modern Art, Sapporo, Japan, 1985; *Pacific Glass '83,* Govett-Brewser Art Gallery, New Plymouth, New Zealand, 1983

Collections: American Craft Museum, NYC; Corning Museum of Glass, NY; Philadelphia Museum of Art, PA; Smithsonian Institution, Washington, DC; Toledo Art Museum, OH; Finnish National Glass Museum, Rihimaki; Museum of Art, Auckland, New Zealand; Museum of Art, Dusseldorf, W. Germany; National

Glass Museum, Leerdam, Netherlands; Queen Victoria Art Museum, Launceston, Australia

Related Professional Experience: faculty, U. of California, Los Angeles, 1977–82

John C. Marshall
Edmonds, Washington

Born: Pittsburgh, Pennsylvania, 1936

Education: B.F.A., Cleveland Institute of Art, OH, 1965; M.F.A., Syracuse U., NY, 1967

Exhibitions: *Contemporary Metals USA,* Downey Museum of Art, Downey, CA, 1985; *Masterworks of Contemporary American Jewelry: Sources and Concepts,* Victoria and Albert Museum, London, England, 1985; *Fire Arts '79,* Bellevue Art Museum, Bellevue, WA, 1979; *American Metalsmiths,* DeCordova Museum, Lincoln, MA, 1974; *Objects: USA,* Johnson Collection of Contemporary Crafts, national and international tour, 1969–72

Collection: American Craft Museum, NYC

Related Professional Experience: faculty, Syracuse U., NY, 1965–70; founding member, Society of North American Goldsmiths, 1969; U. of Washington, Seattle, 1970–present; numerous liturgical commissions

Wendy Maruyama
San Francisco, California

Born: La Junta, California, 1952

Education: B.A., San Diego State U., CA, 1975; M.F.A., School for American Craftsmen, Rochester Institute of Technology, NY, 1980

Awards/Honors: NEA Fellowship, 1982, 1984; TN Arts Commission Artist Fellowship, 1983

Exhibitions: *Material Pleasures: Furniture for a Postmodern Age,* Queens Museum, NYC, 1985; *Ornamentalism: The New Decorativeness in Architecture and Design,* Hudson River Museum, Yonkers, NY, 1983; *Appalachian Center Faculty,* Huntsville Museum of Art, AL, 1982; *Pattern: An Exhibition of the Decorated Surface,* American Craft Museum, NYC, 1982

Related Professional Experience: head, woodworking and furniture design program, Appalachian Center for Crafts, Smithville, TN, 1980–1985; artist-in-residence, Artpark, Lewiston, NY, 1983; Program in Artisanry, Boston U., MA, 1984; faculty, California College of Arts and Crafts, Oakland, 1985–present

Steven Maslach
Greenbrae, California

Born: San Francisco, California, 1950

Education: California College of Arts and Crafts, Oakland, 1969–70

Exhibitions: *Glass: Multiple and Singular,* California Crafts Museum, San Francisco, 1985; *Studio Glass: A Contemporary American Survey Exhibition,* Redding Museum, Ca, 1985; *Sculptural Glass,* Tucson Museum of Art, AZ, 1983; *For the Tabletop,* American Craft Museum, NYC, 1980; *First Annual Mid-America Glass Festival,* Evansville Museum of Arts and Science, IN, 1979; *Americans in Glass,* Leigh Yawkey Woodson Art Museum, Wausau, WI, 1978; *American Crafts in the White House,* Renwick Gallery, Smithsonian Institution, Washington, DC, and tour, 1977

Collections: Corning Museum of Glass, NY; Smithsonian Institution, Washington, DC

John Mason
Los Angeles, California

Born: Madrid, Nebraska, 1927

Education: Otis Art Institute, Los Angeles, CA, 1952; Chouinard Art Institute, Los Angeles, CA, 1954

Exhibitions: *Art and Clay: 1950s–1980s in Southern California,* Los Angeles Municipal Gallery, CA, 1984; *Twentieth Century: San Francisco Museum of Modern Art Collection,* San Francisco Museum of Modern Art, CA, 1984; *100 Years of California Sculpture,* Oakland Museum, CA, 1982; *Ceramic Sculpture: Six Artists,* Whitney Museum of American Art, NYC, 1981; *California Painting and Sculpture: The Modern Era,* San Francisco Museum of Modern Art, CA, 1976; *200 Years of American Sculpture,* Whitney Museum of American Art, NYC, 1976; *John Mason Ceramic Sculpture,* retrospective exhibition, Pasadena Art Museum, CA, 1974

Publications: monograph to accompany exhibition, Pasadena Museum of Art, CA, 1974

Collections: American Craft Museum, NYC; Art Institute of Chicago, IL; Nelson-Atkins Museum of Art, Kansas City, MO; Oakland Museum, CA; Pasadena Art Museum, CA; San Francisco Museum of Modern Art, CA; National Museum of Modern Art, Kyoto, Japan

Related Professional Experience: faculty, Hunter College, NYC, 1974–85; California Arts Council public sculpture commission, Sacramento, CA, 1982; NEA public sculpture commission, Boise, ID, 1982

Alphonse Mattia
Boston, Massachusetts

Born: Phildadelphia, Pennsylvania, 1947

Education: B.F.A., Philadelphia College of Art, Pennslyvnaia, 1969; M.F.A., Rhode Island School of Design, Providence, 1973

Award/Honor: NEA Fellowship, 1984

Exhibitions: *Contemporary Arts: An Expanding View,* Monmouth Museum of Art, Lincroft, NJ, 1986; *Bentwood Today,* Museum of Rhode Island School of Design, Providence, 1984; *Ornamentalism: The New Decorativeness in Architecture and Design,* Hudson River Museum, Yonkers, NY, 1983; *Contemporary Work by Master Craftsmen,* Museum of Fine Arts, Boston, MA, 1977; *Peace Show,* Philadelphia Museum of Art, PA, 1970

Related Professional Experience: faculty, Virginia Commonwealth U., Richmond, 1973–76; Program in Artisanry, Boston U., MA 1976–85; Swain School of Design, New Bedford, MA, 1985–present

Judy Kensley McKie
Cambridge, Massachusetts

Born: Boston, Massachusetts, 1944

Education: B.F.A, Rhode Island School of Design, 1966

Awards/Honors: NEA Fellowship, 1979, 1982; MA Artists Foundation Fellowship, 1980

Exhibitions: *Material Evidence: New Color Techniques in Handmade Furniture,* Renwick Gallery, Smithsonian Institution, Washington, DC, 1985; *Ornamentalism: The New Decorativeness in Architecture and Design,* Hudson River Museum, Yonkers, NY, 1983; *Approaches to Collecting,* American Craft Museum, NYC, 1982; *New Acquisitions,* Museum of Fine Arts, Boston, MA, 1979; *New Handmade Furniture: American Furniture Makers Working in Hardwood,* American Craft Museum, NYC, 1979

Collections: Brockton Art Museum, MA; Museum of Fine Arts, Boston, MA; Museum of Rhode Island School of Design, Providence, RI; Vice-President's Residence, Washington, DC

John McNaughton
Evansville, Indiana

Born: Winchester, Indiana, 1943

Education: B.S., M.A., Ball State U., Muncie, IN, 1965, 1969; M.F.A., Bowling Green State U., OH, 1970

Awards/Honors: NEA Fellowship, 1976; IN Arts Commission grant, 1984

Exhibitions: *Sculpture in the Space Age,* Lafayette Art Museum, IN, 1985; two-person exhibition, Fort Wayne Museum of Art, IN, 1980; *New Handmade Furniture: American Furniture Makers Working in Hardwood,* Museum of Contemporary Crafts, NYC, 1979; solo exhibition, Owensboro Museum, KY, 1979; *Art on Paper,* Indianapolis Museum of Art, IN, 1972; *Mid-States Crafts Exhibition,* Evansville Museum of Art, IN, annually, 1970–85;

Collections: Evansville Museum of Art, IN; Formica, Wayne, NJ

Related Professional Experience: industrial designer, General Motors Technical Center, Warren, MI, 1965–68; faculty, Indiana State U., Evansville, 1970–present

John McQueen
Alfred Station, New York

Born: Oakland, Illinois, 1943

Education: B.A., U. of South Florida, Tampa, 1971; M.F.A., Tyler School of Art, Temple U., Philadelphia, PA, 1975

Awards/Honors: NEA Fellowship, 1977, 1979;

Japan/United States Friendship Commission Exchange Fellowship, 1980

Exhibitions: *The Art Fabric: Mainstream,* American Federation of Arts national tour, 1981–83; *Beyond Tradition: 25th Anniversary Exhibition,* Museum of Contemporary Crafts, NYC, 1981; *Twentieth-Century Design: Recent Acquisitions,* Philadelphia Museum of Art, PA, 1979; *Fiber Works: The Americas and Japan,* National Museum of Modern Art, Tokyo, Japan, 1977

Collections: Cooper-Hewitt Museum, NYC; Herbert F. Johnson Museum, Cornell U., Ithaca, NY; Philadelphia Museum of Art, PA

Related Professional Experience: artist-in-residence, Artpark, Lewiston, NY, 1979; Fabric Workshop, Philadelphia, PA, 1978, 1980

Rebecca R. Medel
Smithville, Tennessee

Born: Denver, Colorado, 1947

Education: B.F.A., Arizona State U., Tempe, 1970; M.F.A., U. of California, Los Angeles, 1982

Awards/Honors: NEA scholarship grant, 1976; Southern Arts Federation/NEA grant, 1985

Exhibitions: *5th International Triennial of Tapestry,* Central Museum of Textiles, Lodz, Poland, 1985; *International Biennial of Tapestry,* Cantonal Museum of Fine Arts, Lausanne, Switzerland, 1985, 1983; *Threads in Space: An Environmental Installation,* North Dakota Museum of Art, Grand Forks, ND, 1985; *The Presence of Light,* Meadows Museum, Dallas, TX, 1984; *Vehta Biennial,* Romanesque church at Vichte, West Flanders, Belgium, 1984; *Miniatures,* Redlands Art Museum, CA, 1980; *Arizona Crafts,* Tucson Museum of Art, AZ, 1975

Collections: Museum of Tapestry, Aix-en-Provence, France; Museum of Decorative Arts, Lausanne, Switzerland; Museum Bellerive, Zurich, Switzerland; Stedelijk Museum, Amsterdam, Netherlands

Related Professional Experience: faculty, Appalachian Center for Crafts, Tennessee Technological U., Smithville, TN, 1983–present

Bruce Metcalf
Kent, Ohio

Born: Amherst, Massachusetts, 1949

Education: B.F.A., Syracuse U., NY, 1972; M.F.A., Tyler School of Art, Temple U., Philadelphia, PA, 1977

Awards/Honors: NEA Fellowship, 1977; MA Artists Foundation Fellowship, 1980; OH Arts Foundation Fellowship, 1983, 1984

Exhibitions: *Jewelry USA,* American Craft Museum, NYC, and tour, 1984–86; *Focus on Bruce Metcalf,* Akron Art Museum, OH, 1983; *Contemporary Metals: Focus on Idea,* Western Association of Art Museums tour, 1981–83; *Good As Gold: Alternative Materials In American Jewelry,* SITES tour, 1981–84; *Copper 2,* U. of Arizona Museum of Art, Tucson, AZ, 1980; *Introductions,* Craft and Folk Art Museum, Los Angeles, CA, 1980; *Young Americans: Metal,* Museum of Contemporary Crafts, NYC, 1980

Collection: Philadelphia Museum of Art, PA

Related Professional Experience: faculty, Kent State U., OH, 1981–present

John Paul Miller
Brecksville, Ohio

Born: Huntingdon, Pennsylvania, 1918

Education: diploma, Cleveland Institute of Art, OH, 1940

Exhibitions: *Masterworks of Contemporary American Jewelry: Sources and Concepts,* Victoria and Albert Museum, London, England, 1985; *Jewelry USA,* American Craft Museum, NYC, and tour, 1984–86; *American Crafts: An Aesthetic View,* Museum of Contemporary Art, Chicago, IL, 1976; *Objects: USA,* Johnson Collection of Contemporary Crafts, national and international tour, 1969–72; solo exhibition, Museum of Contemporary Crafts, NYC, 1964; solo exhibition, Art Institute of Chicago, IL, 1957

Collections: American Craft Museum, NYC; Cleveland Museum of Art, OH; Minnesota Museum of Art, St. Paul

Related Professional Experience: faculty, Cleveland Institute of Art, OH, 1940–83

Norma Minkowitz
Westport, Connecticut

Born: New York, New York, 1937

Education: certificate degree, Cooper Union, NYC, 1958

Award/Honor: Women in Design International award, 1981

Exhibitions: *Fiber R/Evolution,* University Art Museum, U. of Wisconsin, Milwaukee, 1986; solo exhibition, Monterey Peninsula Museum of Art, CA, 1986; *Fiber Structure National,* Downey Museum of Art, CA, 1984; *The Flexible Medium: Art Textiles from the Museum Collection,* Renwick Gallery, Smithsonian Institution, Washington, DC, 1984; *The New Elegance: Contemporary Wearable Art,* Newark Museum of Art, NJ, 1984; *Art to Wear: New Handmade Clothing,* American Craft Museum, NYC, 1983; *Fiberworks,* Cleveland Museum of Art, OH, 1977; *Wearable Art,* Philadelphia Museum of Art, PA, 1977

Collections: American Craft Museum, NYC; Metropolitan Museum of Art, NYC; Renwick Gallery, Smithsonian Institution, Washington, DC

Platt Monfort
Wiscasset, Maine

Born: Huntington, New York, 1921

Education: Pratt Institute, 1941–43

Related Professional Experience: liaison engineer, Fairchild Guided Missile Division, 1949–62; inventor and patentee of innovative techniques and lightweight materials for boatbuilding

Judy Moonelis
New York, New York

Born: Jackson Heights, New York, 1953

Education: B.F.A., Tyler School of Art, Temple U., Philadelphia, PA, 1975; M.F.A., New York State College of Ceramics at Alfred U., NY, 1978

Awards/Honors: NEA Fellowship, 1980; NY Foundation for the Arts Fellowship, 1985

Exhibitions: *Architectural Ceramics: Eight Concepts,* Washington U. Art Gallery, St. Louis, MO, and American Craft Museum, NYC, 1985; *Contemporary Clay Sculpture: Works by Judy Moonelis,* Heckscher Museum, Huntington, NY, 1983; *Contemporary Ceramics: A Response to Wedgwood,* Museum of the Philadelphia Civic Center, PA, and tour, 1980–83; *Young Americans: Clay/Glass,* Museum of Contemporary Crafts, NYC, and tour, 1978

Collections: Heckscher Museum, Huntington, NY; Illinois State Museum, Springfield; Pennsylvania Academy of the Fine Arts, Philadelphia

Related Professional Experience: artist-in-residence, Clayworks Studio Workshop, NYC, 1980; Omaha Brickworks, NE, 1982; Artpark, Lewiston, NY, 1983; Heckscher Museum, Huntington, NY, 1983; faculty, Parsons School of Design/New School, NYC, 1984–present

Benjamin Moore
Seattle, Washington

Born: Olympia, Washington, 1952

Education: B.F.A., California College of Arts and Crafts, Oakland, 1974; M.F.A., Rhode Island School of Design, Providence, 1977

Exhibitions: *Americans in Glass,* Leigh Yawkey Woodson Art Museum, Wausau, WI, 1981; *New Glass: A Worldwide Survey,* Corning Museum of Glass, NY, 1979; *Young Americans: Clay/Glass,* Museum of Contemporary Crafts, NYC, 1978

Collections: Corning Museum of Glass, NY; Fraunau Museum, W. Germany; Lobmeyr Museum, Vienna, Austria; Venini Collection, Venice, Italy

Related Professional Experience: faculty and educational coordinator, Pilchuck School, Stanwood, WA, summers, 1974–85; designer, Fostoria Glass, Moundsville, WV, 1977; Venini, Venice, Italy, 1978–79; Lobmeyr, Vienna, Austria, 1980–81; Glass Eye Studio, Seattle, WA, 1982–84; designer and owner, Benjamin Moore, Inc., Seattle, WA, 1984–present

Dennis M. Morinaka
Oakland, California

Born: Sterling, Colorado, 1945

Education: B.F.A., M.F.A., California College of Arts and Crafts, Oakland, 1968, 1970

Awards/Honors: NEA Fellowship, 1982, 1984

Exhibitions: *Best of the West,* Wing Luke Memorial Museum, Seattle, WA, 1985; *Twentieth-Century Acquisitions,* Oakland Museum, CA, 1985; two-person exhibition, California Crafts Museum, San Francisco, 1984; *American Crafts: A Pacific Heritage,* California State Fairgrounds, Sacramento, CA, 1983; *California Crafts XIII,* Crocker Art Museum, Sacramento, CA, 1983; *Crafts Now,* Coos Art Museum, Coos Bay, OR, 1982; *Vessels,* Minneapolis Institute of the Arts, MN, 1982

Collection: Oakland Museum, CA

William Morris
Stanwood, Washington

Born: Carmel, California, 1957

Education: California State U., Chico, 1975–76; Central Washington U., Ellensburg, 1977–78; Pilchuck School, Stanwood, WA, 1978–79

Exhibitions: solo exhibition, Missoula Museum of Art, MT, 1985; *Crafts '84,* Bellevue Art Museum, WA, 1984; *Americans in Glass: Evolution and Revolution,* Morris Museum of Arts and Sciences, Morristown, NJ, 1982; *Americans Working in Glass,* Butler Institute of Art, Youngstown, OH, 1982

Collections: American Craft Museum, NYC; Corning Museum of Glass, NY; Safeco, Seattle, WA; Museum of Arts and Crafts, Hamburg, W. Germany; Museum of Decorative Arts, Paris, France; Victoria and Albert Museum, London, England

Related Professional Experience: visiting artist, Pilchuck School, Stanwood, WA, 1979–present

Eleanor Moty
Madison, Wisconsin

Born: Glen Ellyn, Illinois, 1945

Education: B.F.A., U. of Illinois, Champaign-Urbana, 1968; M.F.A., Tyler School of Art, Temple U., Philadelphia, PA, 1971

Award/Honor: NEA Fellowship, 1975

Exhibitions: *Contemporary Metals USA,* Downey Museum, CA, 1985; *Jewelry USA,* American Craft Museum, NYC, and tour, 1984–86; *Modern Jewelry: 1964–1984,* Montreal Museum of Decorative Arts, Canada, and tour, 1984–87; solo exhibition, Birmingham Art Museum, AL, 1981; *Twelve Master Craftsmen,* Museum of Fine Arts, Boston, MA, 1977; *American Crafts: An Aesthetic View,* Museum of Contemporary Art, Chicago, IL, 1976; *Young Americans,* Museum of Contemporary Crafts, NYC, 1969

Collections: Birmingham Art Museum, AL; Minnesota Museum of Art, St. Paul

Related Professional Experience: faculty, Moore College of Art, Philadelphia, PA, 1970–72; U. of Wisconsin, Madison, 1972–present

Edward Moulthrop
Atlanta, Georgia

Born: Cleveland, Ohio, 1916

Education: B.Arch., Case Western Reserve U., M.F.A., Princeton U., NJ, 1941

Awards/Honors: American Institute of Architects award, 1978, 1980; GA Governor's award in the arts, 1981

Exhibitions: *Beyond Tradition: 25th Anniversary Exhibition,* Museum of Contemporary Crafts, NYC, 1981; *Art for Use,* Olympic Winter Games, Lake Placid, NY, and Museum of Contemporary Crafts, NYC, 1980; *The Art of the Turned Bowl,* Renwick Gallery, Smithsonian Institution, Washington, DC, 1978; *Crafts, Art, and Religion,* Smithsonian Institution, Washington, DC, and Vatican Museum, Italy, 1978; *Artists in Georgia,* High Museum of Art, Atlanta, GA, 1974, 1972, 1971; *Craftsmen USA 1966,* Museum of Contemporary Crafts, NYC, 1966

Collections: Coca-Cola, Atlanta, GA; High Museum of Art, Atlanta, GA; International Paper, NYC; Metropolitan Museum of Art, NYC; Museum of Fine Arts, Boston, MA; Museum of Modern Art, NYC; Mint Museum of Art, Charlotte, NC

Louis Mueller
New York, New York

Born: Paterson, New Jersey, 1943

Education: B.F.A., Rochester Institute of Technology, NY, 1969; M.F.A., Rhode Island School of Design, Providence, 1971

Awards/Honors: Ford Foundation grant, 1978; Mellon travel study grant, 1983; NY Foundation for the Arts Fellowship, 1985

Exhibitions: *Contemporary Arts: An Expanding View,* Monmouth Museum of Art, Lincroft, NJ, 1986; *Design in the Service of Tea,* Cooper-Hewitt Museum, NYC, 1984; *Modern Jewelry: 1964–1984,* Montreal Museum of Decorative Arts, Canada, and tour, 1984–87; *Bay Area Sculpture,* M. H. DeYoung Memorial Museum, San Francisco, CA, 1976; *Goldsmith '75,* Renwick Gallery, Smithsonian Institution, Washington, DC, 1975; *Young Americans,* Museum of Contemporary Crafts, NYC, 1969

Collections: General Foods, Rye, NY; Montreal Museum of Decorative Arts, Canada

Related Professional Experience: faculty, Rhode Island School of Design, Providence, 1977–present

Jay Musler
San Francisco, California

Born: Sacramento, California, 1949

Education: California College of Arts and Crafts, Oakland, 1968–71

Award/Honor: NEA Fellowship, 1982

Exhibitions: *New Masks for Modern Living,* Phoenix Art Museum, AZ, 1985; *World Glass Now,* Hokkaido Museum of Modern Art, Sapporo, Japan, 1985, 1982; *Americans in Glass,* Leigh Yawkey Woodson Art Museum, Wausau, WI, 1984; *New American Glass and New American Quilts,* Southern Ohio Museum and Cultural Center, Portsmouth, OH, 1984; *Sculptural Glass,* Tucson Museum of Art, AZ, 1983; *Emerging Artists in Glass,* California Crafts Museum, Palo Alto, 1981; *New Glass: A Worldwide Survey,* Corning Museum of Glass, NY, 1979

Collections: Corning Museum of Glass, NY; Detroit Institute of Arts, MI; Wheaton Museum of Glass, Millville, NJ; Hokkaido Museum of Modern Art, Sapporo, Japan; Kitano Museum, Tokyo, Japan; Museum of Decorative Arts, Lausanne, Switzerland

Joel Philip Myers
Bloomington, Illinois

Born: Paterson, New Jersey, 1934

Education: certificate, Parsons School of Design, NYC, 1954; B.F.A., M.F.A., New York State College of Ceramics at Alfred U., NY, 1963, 1968

Awards/Honors: NEA Fellowship, 1976, 1984; Fellow, American Craft Council, 1980

Exhibitions: *International Exposition of Glass,* Museum of Fine Arts, Rouen, France, 1985; *Americans in Glass,* Leigh Yawkey Woodson Art Museum, Wausau, WI, 1984; *World Glass Now,* Hokkaido Museum of Modern Art, Sapporo, Japan, 1982; *New Glass: A Worldwide Survey,* Corning Museum of Glass, NY, 1979; *Modern Glass from America, Europe and Japan,* Museum of Applied Arts, Frankfurt, W. Germany, and tour, 1976; *Objects: USA,* Johnson Collection of Contemporary Crafts, national and international tour, 1969–72

Collections: American Craft Museum, NYC; Art Institute of Chicago, IL; Corning Museum of Glass, NY; Detroit Institute of Arts, MI; Metropolitan Museum of Art, NYC; Hokkaido Museum of Modern Art, Sapporo, Japan; Museum of Applied Arts, Frankfurt, W. Germany

Related Professional Experience: director of design, Blenko Glass Co., Milton, WV, 1963–70; faculty, Illinois State U., Normal, 1970–present

Risë Rice Nagin
Pittsburgh, Pennsylvania

Born: Norwalk, Connecticut, 1950

Education: B.F.A., Carnegie-Mellon U., Pittsburgh, PA, 1972

Exhibitions: *Contemporary Arts: An Expanding View,* Monmouth Museum of Art, Lincroft, NJ, 1986; *The Creative Spirit: A Celebration of Contemporary American Craft,* Maier Museum of Art, Lynchburg, VA, 1985; *Contemporary Artifacts,* Museum of American Jewish

History, Philadelphia, PA, 1983; *Celebration: Women in the Arts,* William Penn Museum, Harrisburg, PA, 1983, 1982; *Made in Pennsylvania,* Southern Alleghenies Museum of Art, Loretto, PA, 1983; *Crafts 15,* Museum of Art, Pennsylvania State U., State College, 1981; *Lake Superior Biennial National Craft Exhibition,* Tweed Museum of Art, Duluth, MN, 1981; *American Crafts '77,* Philadelphia Museum of Art, PA, 1977; *Young Americans: Fiber/Wood/Plastic/Leather,* Museum of Contemporary Crafts, NYC, 1977

Ron Nagle
San Francisco, California

Born: San Francisco, California, 1939

Education: B.F.A., San Francisco State College, CA, 1961

Awards/Honors: NEA Fellowship, 1974, 1979; Mellon grant, 1981, 1983

Exhibitions: *Who's Afraid of American Pottery?,* Museum of Contemporary Art, Hertogenbosch, Netherlands, 1983; *Twenty American Artists: Sculpture 1982,* San Francisco Museum of Modern Art, CA, 1982; *Currents 4: Ron Nagle,* St. Louis Art Museum, MO, 1979; *Coffee, Tea & Other Cups,* Museum of Contemporary Crafts, NYC, 1971; *Objects: USA,* Johnson Collection of Contemporary Crafts, national and international tour, 1969–72

Collections: American Craft Museum, NYC; Everson Museum of Art, Syracuse, NY; Oakland Museum, CA; Philadelphia Museum of Art, PA; St. Louis Art Museum, MO; San Francisco Museum of Modern Art, CA; Stedelijk Museum, Amsterdam, Netherlands

Related Professional Experience: faculty, Mills College, Oakland, CA, 1978–present

Otto Natzler (worked collaboratively with Getrud Natzler, 1935–71)
Los Angeles, California

Born: Vienna, Austria, 1908

Education: National Training Center for the Textile Industry, Vienna, Austria, 1927

Awards/Honors: Life Fellow, International Institute of Arts and Letters, Zurich, Switzerland, 1960

Exhibitions: solo exhibition, Craft and Folk Art Museum, Los Angeles, CA, 1977; *Form and Fire,* retrospective exhibition of Otto and Gertrud Natzler, Renwick Gallery, Smithsonian Institution, Washington, DC, 1973; retrospective exhibition, collaborative work, M. H. DeYoung Memorial Museum, San Francisco, CA, 1971; first retrospective exhibition, collaborative work, Los Angeles County Museum of Art, CA, 1966; solo exhibitions, collaborative work, Art Institute of Chicago, IL, 1963; Museum of Contemporary Crafts, NYC, 1963; Cincinnati Art Museum, OH, 1960; Bezalel National Museum, Jerusalem, Israel, 1959; Museum of Applied Arts, Zurich, Switzerland, 1959; Museum of Modern Art, Haifa, Israel, 1959; Stedelijk Museum, Amsterdam, Netherlands, 1959–60; Joslyn Art Museum, Omaha, NE, 1955; Los Angeles County Museum of Art, 1944; World Exposition, Paris, France, 1937

Publications: monographs to accompany exhibitions: Craft and Folk Art Museum, Los Angeles, CA, 1977; *Form and Fire,* Smithsonian Institution, Washington, DC, 1973; M. H. DeYoung Memorial Museum, San Francisco, CA, 1971; *Natzler Ceramics,* Los Angeles County Museum of Art, 1966

Collections: American Craft Museum, NYC; Art Institute of Chicago, IL; Cranbrook Academy of Art Museum, Bloomfield Hills, MI; Everson Museum of Art, Syracuse, NY; Los Angeles County Museum of Art, CA; Museum of Modern Art, NYC; National Museum of American History, Smithsonian Institution, Washington, DC; Nelson-Atkins Museum of Art, Kansas City, MO; Oakland Museum, CA; Phoenix Art Museum, AZ; International Ceramic Museum, Faenza, Italy; Museum Bellerive, Zurich, Switzerland

Ruth Nivola
East Hampton, New York

Born: Munich, W. Germany, 1917

Education: schooled in Germany, Switzerland, and Art Institute, Monza, Italy

Exhibitions: *Good As Gold: Alternative Materials in American Jewelry,* SITES tour, 1981–84; *Ruth Nivola—Jewelry in Thread,* Museum of Contemporary Crafts, NYC, 1977

Collection: American Craft Museum, NYC

Richard Notkin
Myrtle Point, Oregon

Born: Chicago, Illinois, 1948

Education: B.F.A., Kansas City Art Institute, MO, 1970; M.F.A., U. of California, Davis, 1973

Awards/Honors: Western States Arts Foundation Fellowship, 1976; NEA Fellowship, 1979, 1981; OR Arts Commission Fellowship, 1985

Exhibitions: *Echoes: Historical References in Contemporary Ceramics,* Nelson-Atkins Museum of Art, Kansas City, MO, 1983; *American Porcelain: New Expressions in an Ancient Art,* Renwick Gallery, Smithsonian Institution, Washington, DC, and SITES tour, 1980–84; *Contemporary Ceramics: A Response to Wedgwood,* Museum of Philadelphia Civic Center, PA, 1980; *Another Side to Art: A History of Northwest Ceramics,* Seattle Art Museum, WA, 1979; *West Coast Ceramics,* Stedelijk Museum, Amsterdam, Netherlands, 1979; *Clay,* Whitney Museum of American Art, NYC, 1974

Collections: Everson Museum of Art, Syracuse, NY; Nelson-Atkins Museum of Art, Kansas City, MO; National Collection of Fine Arts, Smithsonian Institution, Washington, DC; Victoria and Albert Museum, London, England

Related Professional Experience: artist-in-residence, Kohler Co., WI, 1976, 1978

Walter Nottingham
River Falls, Wisconsin

Born: Great Falls, Montana, 1930

Education: B.S., M.S., St. Cloud State U., MN, 1959, 1960; M.F.A., Cranbrook Academy of Art, Bloomfield Hills, MI, 1968

Award/Honor: NEA Fellowship, 1974

Exhibitions: *Fiber R/Evolution,* Milwaukee Art Museum, WI, 1986; *Old Traditions—New Directions,* Textile Museum, Washington, DC, 1981; *Fiber as Art,* Metropolitan Museum of Manila, Philippines, 1980; *American Crafts: An Aesthetic View,* Museum of Contemporary Art, Chicago, IL, 1976; *Walter Nottingham: A Retrospective,* Minnesota Museum of Art, Minneapolis, 1974; *Sculpture in Fiber,* Museum of Contemporary Crafts, NYC, 1972; *Objects: USA,* Johnson Collection of Contemporary Crafts, national and international tour, 1969–72; *Wall Hangings,* Museum of Modern Art, NYC, 1968

Collections: Johnson Wax, Racine, WI; Minnesota Museum of Art, St. Paul; M.S.I. building, St. Paul, MN; Prudential Insurance, Minneapolis, MN; U.S. embassy, Tokyo, Japan

Related Professional Experience: faculty, U. of Wisconsin, River Falls, 1962–present

Nance O'Banion
Oakland, California

Born: Oakland, California, 1949

Education: B.A., M.A., U. of California, Berkeley, 1971, 1973

Awards/Honors: NEA artist-in-residence grant, 1979; NEA Fellowship, 1982

Exhibitions: *Architecture: Fiber Art 1985,* Museum of Decorative Arts, Paris, France, 1985; *New Directions in the New Decorative,* U. of Missouri Art Museum, St. Louis, 1984; *On and Off the Wall: Shaped and Colored,* Oakland Museum, CA, 1983; *Paper,* Museum of Decorative Arts, Lausanne, Switzerland, 1983; *Paper: A New Artistic Language,* Museum Bellerive, Zurich, Switzerland, 1983; *Making Paper,* American Craft Museum, NYC, 1982; *The Art Fabric: Mainstream,* American Federation of Arts national tour, 1981–83; *Paper,* Crocker Art Museum, Sacramento, CA, 1981

Collections: American Craft Museum, NYC; Oakland Museum, CA; Seattle Art Museum, WA; Bellerive Museum, Zurich, Switzerland

Related Professional Experience: faculty, California College of Arts and Crafts, Oakland, CA, 1974–84

Jokan Ohama
Bridgehampton, New York

Born: Kyoto, Japan, 1942

Michael Olszewski
Philadelphia, Pennsylvania

Born: Baltimore, Maryland, 1950

Education: B.F.A., Maryland Institute, College of Art, Baltimore, 1972; M.F.A., Cranbrook Academy of Art, Bloomfield Hills, MI, 1977

Awards/Honors: NEA Fellowship, 1979; PA Council on the Arts Fellowship, 1982, 1985

Exhibitions: *Return of the Figure: A Pennsylvania Perspective,* Southern Alleghenies Museum of Art, Loretto, PA, 1985; *Art Materialized: Selections from the Fabric Workshop,* Independent Curators tour, 1982–84; *Hand Bound Books,* Museum of Applied Arts, Vienna, Austria, 1980

Related Professional Experience: faculty, Moore College of Art, Philadelphia, PA, 1977–present; artist-in-residence, Fabric Workshop, Philadelphia, PA, 1978; Strem, Poland, 1980

Pavel Opočenský
Brooklyn, New York

Born: Karlovy Vary, Czechoslovakia, 1954

Education: School for Jewelry Design, Jablonec, Czechoslovakia, 1971–72; School for Jewelry Design, Turnov, Czechoslovakia, 1973–74

Award/Honor: NY Foundation for the Arts Fellowship, 1986

Exhibitions: *Contemporary Arts: An Expanding View,* Monmouth Museum of Art, Lincroft, NJ, 1986; *Art Quest '85,* Art Museum, California State U., Long Beach, 1985; *Contemporary Jewelry Redefined: Alternative Materials,* Pittsburgh Center for the Arts, PA, 1985; *Jewelry for Head and Hair,* Jewelry Museum, Pforzheim, W. Germany, 1985; *Doubleform,* Ivory Museum, Erbach, W. Germany, 1983

Jere Osgood
Wilton, New Hampshire

Born: Staten Island, New York, 1936

Education: B.F.A., School for American Craftsmen, Rochester Institute of Technology, NY, 1960

Award/Honor: NEA grant, 1980

Exhibitions: *Wood Forms,* Brockton Art Museum, MA, 1981; *New Handmade Furniture: American Furniture Makers Working in Hardwood,* Museum of Contemporary Crafts, 1979; *Works by Master Craftsmen,* Museum of Fine Arts, Boston, MA, 1977; *Bed and Board,* DeCordova Museum, Lincoln, MA, 1975; *Objects: USA,* Johnson Collection of Contemporary Crafts, national and international tour, 1969–72; *Young Americans,* Museum of Contemporary Crafts, 1962, 1958

Collections: American Craft Museum, NYC; Museum of Fine Arts, Boston, MA

Related Professional Experience: faculty, Program in Artisanry, Boston U., MA, 1975–85; studio craftsman, 1985–present

Albert Paley
Rochester, New York

Born: Philadelphia, Pennsylvania, 1944

Education: B.F.A., M.F.A., Tyler School of Art, Temple U., Philadelphia, PA, 1966, 1969

Awards/Honors: NEA Master Craftsman Apprentice grant, 1975, 1976, 1979; NEA Fellowship, 1976, 1984

Exhibitions: *Contemporary Arts: An Expanding View,* Monmouth Museum of Art, Lincroft, NJ, 1986; *Ornamentalism: The New Decorativeness in Architecture and Design,* Hudson River Museum, Yonkers, NY, 1983; *Towards a New Iron Age,* Victoria and Albert Museum, London, England and tour, 1983; *The Metalwork of Albert Paley,* John Michael Kohler Arts Center, Sheboygan, WI, and Hunter Museum of Art, Chattanooga, TN, 1980; *Young Americans: Metal,* Museum of Contemporary Crafts, NYC, 1980; *Contemporary Works by Master Craftsmen,* Museum of Fine Arts, Boston, MA, 1977

Publications: *The Metalwork of Albert Paley,* monograph to accompany exhibition, John Michael Kohler Arts Center, Sheboygan, WI, 1980

Collections: Cooper-Hewitt Museum, NYC; Hunter Museum of Art, Chattanooga, TN; Metropolitan Museum of Art, NYC; National Museum of American Art, Smithsonian Institution, Washington, DC; Philadelphia Museum of Art, PA

Related Professional Experience: faculty, School for American Craftsmen, Rochester Institute of Technology, NY, 1972–84; architectural commissions in forged metal throughout the country, 1974–present

Stephen M. Paulsen
Goleta, California

Born: Palo Alto, California, 1947

Education: U. of California, Santa Barbara, 1965–71

Exhibitions: *Pattern: An Exhibition of the Decorated Surface,* American Craft Museum, NYC, and tour, 1982; *The Turned Object,* Greenville County Museum of Art, SC, 1982; *Toys, Amusements and Fancies,* California Crafts Museum, Palo Alto, 1980

Related Professional Experience: partner, Paulsen and Gruenberg Woodworks, 1976–79; owner, Paulsen Fine Art Woodworks, 1980–present

Michael Pavlik
Shelburne Falls, Massachusetts

Born: Prague, Czechoslovakia, 1941

Education: M.A., College of Arts and Crafts, Prague, Czechoslovakia, 1963

Exhibition: *World Glass Now,* Hokkaido Museum of Modern Art, Sapporo, Japan, 1985, 1982

Collections: Cooper-Hewitt Museum, NYC; Corning Museum of Glass, NY; Whitney Museum of American Art, NYC; Hokkaido Museum of Modern Art, Sapporo, Japan; Museum of Arts and Crafts, Hamburg, W. Germany

Related Professional Experience: faculty and artist-in-residence, Hartwick College, Oneonta, NY, 1974–1985

Ronald Hayes Pearson
Deer Isle, Maine

Born: New York, New York, 1924

Education: U. of Wisconsin, Madison, 1943; School for American Craftsmen, Alfred U., NY, 1948

Awards/Honors: Tiffany grant, 1969; NEA Fellowship, 1973, 1978; Fellow, American Craft Council, 1976

Exhibitions: *Art for Use,* Olympic Winter Games, Lake Placid, NY, and American Craft Museum, NYC, 1980; *Silver and Gold,* Renwick Gallery, Smithsonian Institution, Washington, DC, 1978; *Goldsmith '70,* Minnesota Museum of Art, St. Paul, 1970; *Objects: USA,* Johnson Collection of Contemporary Crafts, national and international tour, 1969–72; solo exhibition, Museum of Contemporary Crafts, NYC, 1963; *Good Design,* annual exhibition, Museum of Modern Art, NYC, 1950–54

Collections: American Craft Museum, NYC; Museum of Modern Art, NYC; Smithsonian Institution, Washington, DC

Related Professional Experience: design consultant and designer of jewelry and flatware, 1954–present; founding member, Society of North American Goldsmiths, 1969

Mark Peiser
Penland, North Carolina

Born: Chicago, Illinois, 1938

Education: Purdue U., W. Lafayette, IN, 1957; B.S., Illinois Institute of Technology, Chicago, IL, 1961

Awards/Honors: Tiffany grant, 1972; NEA Fellowship, 1974

Exhibitions: *Hot Stuff,* St. Louis Art Museum, MO, 1984; *American Glass Art: Evolution and Revolution,* Morris Museum of Arts and Sciences, Morristown, NJ, 1982; *New Glass: A Worldwide Survey,* Corning Museum of Glass, NY, 1979; *American Glass Now,* Toledo Museum of Art, OH, 1972; *Vignettes of Unusual Works of Glass,* Mint Museum of Art, Charlotte, NC, 1971; *Objects: USA,* Johnson Collection of Contemporary Crafts, national and international tour, 1969–72

Collections: American Craft Museum, NYC; Art Institute of Chicago, IL; Corning Museum of Glass, NY; High Museum of Art, Atlanta, GA; Mint Museum of Art, Charlotte, NC; National Museum of American History, Smithsonian Institution, Washington, DC; People's Republic of China

Michael Pierschalla
Cambridge, Massachusetts

Born: Mt. Clemens, Michigan, 1955

Education: School for American Craftsmen, Rochester Institute of Technology, NY, 1978–81; Appalachian Center for Crafts, Smithville, TN, 1981–83

Award/Honor: NEA grant, 1981

Exhibition: *Material Evidence: New Color Techniques in Handmade Furniture,* Renwick Gallery, Smithsonian Institution, Washington, DC, and tour, 1985

Collection: Hunter Museum of Art, Chattanooga, TN

Related Professional Experience: artist-in-residence, Artpark, Lewiston, NY, 1984; faculty, Appalachian Center for Crafts, Smithville, TN, summer 1985; Program in Artisanry, Swain School of Design, New Bedford, MA, spring 1986

Gene Pijanowski
Ann Arbor, Michigan

Born: Detroit, Michigan, 1938

Education: B.F.A., M.A., Wayne State U., Detroit, MI, 1964, 1967; M.F.A., Cranbrook Academy of Art, Bloomfield Hills, MI, 1969

Awards/Honors: NEA Master Craftsman apprentice grant, 1975; Japan/United States Friendship Commission grant, 1978; NEA Fellowship, 1978; Fulbright Fellowship, 1985

Exhibitions: *American Jewelry Now,* American Craft Museum USIA Asian tour, 1985; *Contemporary Metals USA,* Downey Museum of Art, CA, 1985; *Contemporary Jewellery: The Americas, Australia, Europe and Japan,* National Museum of Modern Art, Kyoto and Tokyo, 1984; *Good As Gold: Alternative Materials in American Jewelry,* SITES tour, 1981–84; *Forms in Metal: 275 Years of Metalsmithing in America,* Museum of Contemporary Crafts, NYC, and tour, 1975–76

Collections: Museum of Applied Arts, Vienna, Austria; National Museum of Modern Art, Tokyo, Japan; Worshipful Company of Goldsmiths, London, England

Related Professional Experience: faculty, Purdue U., Lafayette, IN, 1973–81; U. of Michigan, Ann Arbor, 1981–85

Hiroko Sato Pijanowski
Ann Arbor, Michigan

Born: Tokyo, Japan, 1942

Education: B.A., Rikkyo U., Tokyo, Japan, 1964; M.F.A., Cranbrook Academy of Art, Bloomfield Hills, MI, 1968

Awards/Honors: NEA Master Craftsman apprentice grant, 1975; NEA Fellowship, 1978; Japan Foundation Fellowship, 1982

Exhibitions: *American Jewelry Now,* American Craft Museum USIA Asian tour, 1985; *Contemporary Metals USA,* Downey Museum of Art, CA, 1985; *Contemporary Jewellery: The Americas, Australia, Europe and Japan,* National Museum of Modern Art, Kyoto and Tokyo, Japan, 1984; *Good As Gold: Alternative Materials in American Jewelry,* SITES tour, 1981–84; *Clay, Fiber, Metal by Women Artists,* Bronx Museum, NYC, 1978; *Forms in Metal: 275 Years of Metalsmithing in America,* Museum of Contemporary Crafts, NYC, and tour, 1975–76

Collections: Museum of Applied Arts, Vienna, Austria; National Museum of Modern Art, Kyoto, Japan

Related Professional Experience: faculty, U. of Michigan, Ann Arbor, 1978–present

Kenneth Price
South Dartmouth, Massachusetts

Born: Los Angeles, California, 1935

Education: B.F.A., U. of Southern California, Los Angeles, 1956; M.F.A., New York State College of Ceramics at Alfred U., NY, 1959

Exhibitions: *An International Survey of Recent Painting and Sculpture,* Museum of Modern Art, NYC, 1984; *Biennial Exhibition,* Whitney Museum of American Art, 1981, 1979, 1970; *Happy's Curios,* Los Angeles County Museum of Art, CA, 1978; *A Century of Ceramics in the United States: 1878–1978,* Everson Museum of Art, Syracuse, NY, and tour, 1979; *200 Years of American Sculpture,* Whitney Museum of American Art, NYC, 1976; *Sculpture: American Directions, 1945–1975,* National Collection of Fine Arts,

Smithsonian Institution, Washington, DC, 1975; *Contemporary Ceramic Art: Canada, U.S.A., Mexico, Japan,* National Museum of Modern Art, Kyoto and Tokyo, Japan, 1971; solo exhibition, Whitney Museum of American Art, NYC, 1969; *Abstract Expressionist Ceramics,* U. of California, Irvine, 1967; *New American Sculpture,* Pasadena Art Museum, CA, 1964

Collections: Art Institute of Chicago, IL; Hirshhorn Museum and Sculpture Garden, Smithsonian Institution, Washington, DC; Los Angeles County Museum of Art, CA; Museum of Modern Art, NYC; San Francisco Museum of Modern Art, CA; Whitney Museum of American Art, NYC; Victoria and Albert Museum, London, England

Neil Prince (works collaboratively with Fran Kraynek-Prince)
Encinitas, California

Born: New York, New York, 1940

Education: B.C.E., M.C.E., Ph.D., New York U., NYC, 1962, 1963, 1967

Exhibitions: *Fiber Individualists,* Charles A. Wustum Museum of Fine Arts, Racine, WI, 1986; *American Crafts in Iceland,* National Art Museum, Reykjavik, Iceland, 1983

Collections: Arizona State U. Art Museum, Tempe; Fine Arts Museum of the South, Mobile, AL; Sheldon Art Museum, Lincoln, NE

Janet Prip
Cranston, Rhode Island

Born: Hornell, New York, 1950

Education: Moore College of Art, Philadelphia, PA, 1968–70; B.A., Rhode Island School of Design, Providence, 1974

Exhibitions: *Container, Bowls, Boxes,* Western Carolina U., Cullowhee, NC, 1984; *Production: Art/Craft/Design,* Philadelphia College of Art, PA, 1982

Related Professional Experience: partner in Trillium, limited production jewelry business, Providence, RI, 1974–78; P's & Q's, production jewelry business, 1979–81; freelance designer for jewelry industry, 1982–present

John Prip
Rehoboth, Massachusetts

Born: New York, New York, 1922

Education: diploma, Copenhagen Technical School, Denmark, 1942

Award/Honor: Fellow, American Craft Council, 1977

Exhibitions: group exhibition, Philadelphia Museum of Art, PA, 1977; *Goldsmiths & Objectmakers,* Museum Bellerive, Zurich, Switzerland, 1971; solo exhibition, Museum of Contemporary Crafts, NYC, 1971; *Objects: USA,* Johnson Collection of Contemporary Crafts, national and international tour, 1969–72; *A Craftsman's Role in Modern Industry: John Prip at Reed & Barton,* Museum of Contemporary Crafts, NYC, 1962; *American Designers,* Museum of Modern Art, NYC, 1954

Collections: American Craft Museum, NYC; Museum of Modern Art, NYC; Smithsonian Institution, Washington, DC

Related Professional Experience: artist-in-residence and design consultant, Reed & Barton Silversmithing, Taunton, MA, 1957–60, 1960–70; faculty, Rhode Island School of Design, Providence, 1963–present

Robin Quigley
Providence, Rhode Island

Born: New York, New York, 1947

Education: B.F.A., Tyler School of Art, Temple U., Philadelphia, PA, 1974; M.F.A., Rhode Island School of Design, Providence, 1976

Award/Honor: NEA Fellowship, 1979

Exhibitions: *Contemporary Arts: An Expanding View,* Monmouth Museum of Art, Lincroft, NJ, 1986; *American Jewelry Now,* American Craft Museum USIA Asian tour, 1985; *International Jewelry Invitational,* Culture House, Stockholm, Sweden, 1985; *New Visions/Traditional Materials: Contemporary American Jewelry,* Museum of Art, Carnegie Institute, Pittsburgh, PA, 1985; *Jewelry USA,* American Craft Museum, NYC, and tour, 1984–86; *Pattern: An Exhibi-*

tion of the Decorated Surface, American Craft Museum, NYC, 1982; Good As Gold: Alternative Materials in American Jewelry, SITES tour, 1981–84; Young Americans: Fiber/Wood/Plastic/Leather, Museum of Contemporary Crafts, NYC, 1977

Related Professional Experience: faculty, Philadelphia College of Art, PA, 1976–78; partner, P's & Q's, production jewelry business, Providence, RI, 1979–81; faculty, Rhode Island School of Design, Providence, 1981–present

Gretchen Raber
Alexandria, Virginia

Born: San Diego, California, 1943

Education: B.S., State U. of New York, College at New Paltz, NY, 1965; M.F.A., American U., Washington, DC, 1970

Award/Honor: Tiffany grant, 1967

Exhibitions: two-person exhibition, Jewelry Museum, Pforzheim, W. Germany, 1985; Contemporary Jewellery: The Americas, Australia, Europe and Japan, National Museum of Modern Art, Kyoto and Tokyo, Japan, 1984; Jewelry USA, American Craft Museum, NYC, and tour, 1984–86; Pattern: An Exhibition of the Decorated Surface, American Craft Museum, NYC, 1982; Good As Gold: Alternative Materials in American Jewelry, SITES tour, 1981–84

Collection: National Museum of Modern Art, Kyoto, Japan

Related Professional Experience: faculty, Catholic U. of America, Washington, DC, 1975–present

Elsa Rady
Venice, California

Born: New York, New York, 1943

Education: Chouinard Art Institute, Los Angeles, CA, 1966

Awards/Honors: NEA Fellowship, 1981; CA Arts Council grant, 1983

Exhibitions: American Potters Today, Victoria and Albert Museum, London, England, 1985; Ceramics: An American Survey, Ceramics Museum, Barcelona, Spain, 1985; Echoes: Historical Reference in Contemporary Ceramics, Nelson-Atkins Museum of Art, Kansas City, MO, 1983; American Ceramics, Phoenix Art Museum, AZ, 1980; American Porcelain: New Expressions in an Ancient Art, Renwick Gallery, Smithsonian Institution, Washington, DC, and SITES tour, 1980–84; For the Tabletop, American Craft Museum, NYC, 1980; Young Americans, Museum of Contemporary Crafts, NYC, 1969; Design XI–X, Pasadena Art Museum, CA, 1971, 1968; Craftsmen USA, Los Angeles County Museum of Art, CA, 1966

Collections: Museum of Fine Arts, Boston, MA; Cooper-Hewitt Museum, NYC; Everson Museum of Art, Syracuse, NY; Smithsonian Institution, Washington, DC; Victoria and Albert Museum, London, England

Debra Rapoport
New York, New York

Born: New York, New York, 1945

Education: B.F.A., Carnegie-Mellon U., Pittsburgh, PA, 1967; M.A., U. of Californias Berkeley, 1969

Award/Honor: NEA grant, 1976

Exhibitions: Contemporary Arts: An Expanding View, Monmouth Museum of Art, Lincroft, NJ, 1986; Jewelry USA, American Craft Museum, NYC, and tour, 1984–86; Paper—A New Artistic Language, Museum of Decorative Arts, Lausanne, Switzerland, 1983; Good As Gold: Alternative Materials in American Jewelry, SITES tour, 1981–84; Costume Statements, Museum of Contemporary Crafts, NYC, 1971

Collections: Metropolitan Museum of Art, NYC; Polylok, NYC; Cantonal Museum of Fine Arts, Lausanne, Switzerland

Related Professional Experience: faculty, U. of California, Davis, 1970–78

Vernon Reed
Austin, Texas

Born: Pine Bluff, Arkansas, 1948

Education: B.A., U. of Texas, Austin, 1971

Exhibitions: Computer Art Show #2, McAllen International Museum, McAllen, TX, 1985; Contemporary Jewellery: The Americas, Australia, Europe and Japan,

Museum of Modern Art, Kyoto and Tokyo, Japan, 1984; Contemporary Texas Crafts, Museum of the Southwest, Midland, TX, 1984; Jewelry USA, American Craft Museum, NYC, and tour, 1984–86; Pattern: An Exhibition of the Decorated Surface, American Craft Museum, NYC, 1982; Texas Sculpture, Laguna Gloria Art Museum, Austin, TX, 1978

Donald Reitz
Marshall, Wisconsin

Born: Sunbury, Pennsylvania, 1929

Education: B.S., Kutztown State College, PA, 1957; M.F.A., New York State College of Ceramics at Alfred U., NY, 1962

Awards/Honors: American Ceramic Society art award, 1975; Fellow, National Council on Education for the Ceramic Arts, 1976; Fellow, American Craft Council, 1977; NEA Fellowship, 1977

Exhibitions: International Ceramic Invitational, North Central Washington Museum, Wenatachee, 1984; two-person exhibition, Wright Museum, Beloit, WI, 1984; Contemporary Ceramics: A Response to Wedgwood, Museum of Philadelphia Civic Center, PA, 1980; A Century of Ceramics in the United States: 1878–1978, Everson Museum of Art, Syracuse, NY and tour, 1979; group exhibition, Victoria and Albert Museum, London, England, 1978; Salt Glaze Ceramics, Museum of Contemporary Crafts, NYC, 1972

Collections: American Craft Museum, NYC; Art Institute of Chicago, IL; High Museum of Art, Atlanta, GA; Milwaukee Art Museum, WI; Renwick Gallery, Smithsonian Institution, Washington, DC

Related Professional Experience: faculty, U. of Wisconsin, Madison, 1962–present

Suzan Rezac
New York, New York

Born: Vrchlaby, Czechoslovakia, 1958

Education: B.F.A., M.F.A., Rhode Island School of Design, Providence, 1981, 1983

Award/Honor: NEA Fellowship, 1984

Exhibitions: Contemporary Arts: An Expanding View, Monmouth Museum of Art, Lincroft, NJ, 1986; Forty-four Alumni/ae, Museum of Rhode Island School of Design, Providence, 1985; Jewelry International, American Craft Museum, NYC, 1984; Modern Jewelry: 1964–1984, Montreal Museum of Decorative Arts, Canada, and tour, 1984–87; solo exhibition, Museum of Clockmaking and Enameling, Geneva, Switzerland, 1984; International Jewelry Art, Isetan Art Museum, Tokyo, Japan, 1983

Faith Ringgold
New York, New York

Born: New York, New York, 1930

Education: B.S., M.A., City College of New York, NYC, 1955, 1959; Ph.D., City U. of New York, NYC, 1977

Awards/Honors: NEA grant, 1978; honorary Ph.D., Moore College of Art, Philadelphia, PA, 1986

Exhibitions: Faith Ringgold: Painting, Sculpture & Performance, College of Wooster Art Museum, OH, 1985; Biennial Exhibition, Whitney Museum of American Art, NYC, 1985; Faith Ringgold: Twenty Years of Painting, Sculpture & Performance (1963–1984), Studio Museum, NYC, 1984; Faith Ringgold: Soft Sculpture, Museum of African and African-American Art, Buffalo, NY, 1980; Jubilee, Museum of Fine Arts, Boston, MA, 1975; Faith Ringgold: Ten-Year Retrospective, Voorhees Gallery, Rutgers U., New Brunswick, NJ, 1973; American Women Artists, Museum of Art, Hamburg, W. Germany, 1972; Memorial Exhibit for Martin Luther King, Jr., Museum of Modern Art, NYC, 1968

Collections: Brooklyn Childrens' Museum, NYC; Chase Manhattan Bank, NYC; Newark Museum, NJ; Phillip Morris, NYC; Womens' House of Detention, NYC

Related Professional Experience: faculty, U. of California, San Diego, 1984–present; developed International Dolls Collection, 1979; author of numerous writings on black women artists

Amy Roberts
Seattle, Washington

Born: Newark, Ohio, 1956

Education: Cleveland Institute of Art, OH, 1976

Exhibitions: New American Glass, Culture House, Stockholm, Sweden, 1985; Americans in Glass, Leigh Yawkey Woodson Art Museum, Wausau, WI, 1984; Art and/or Craft, Arts Museum, Kanazawa, Japan, 1982; Northwest Crafts, Museum of History and Industry, Seattle, WA, 1982; New Glass, Bellevue Art Museum, WA, and Whatcom Museum of History and Art, Bellingham, WA, 1981; Containers, Fort Wayne Museum of Art, IN, 1980

Collections: American Glass Museum, Millville, NJ; City Light Collection, Seattle, WA; Seattle First National Bank, WA

Related Professional Experience: faculty, Pilchuck School, Stanwood, WA, 1985

Mary Roehm
Ellicottville, New York

Born: Endicott, New York, 1951

Education: B.F.A., Daemen College, Buffalo, NY, 1973; M.F.A., School for American Craftsmen, Rochester Institute of Technology, NY, 1979

Exhibitions: Architectural Clay/Clay in Architecture, Jane Hartsook Gallery, Greenwich House Pottery, NYC, 1986; two-person exhibition, Hudson River Museum, Yonkers, NY, 1984; For the Tabletop, American Craft Museum, NYC, 1980

Related Professional Experience: visual art consultant and crafts coordinator, Artpark, Lewiston, NY, 1979–85

John Roloff
Oakland, California

Born: Portland, Oregon, 1947

Education: B.A., U. of California, Davis, 1970; M.A., California State U., Humboldt, 1973

Awards/Honors: NEA Fellowship, 1977; NEA Visual Arts award, 1980; Guggenheim Fellowship, 1983

Exhibitions: Contemporary American Ceramics: Twenty Artists, Newport Harbor Art Museum, CA, 1985; From the Sunny Side: Six East Bay Artists, Oakland Museum, CA, 1982; Mountain Kiln/Black Orchid—Installation, International Sculpture Conference, Oakland, CA, 1982; Northern California Clay Routes: Sculpture Now, San Francisco Museum of Modern Art, CA, 1979; Biennial Exhibition, Whitney Museum of American Art, NYC, 1975; Coffee, Tea & Other Cups, Museum of Contemporary Crafts, NYC, 1970

Collections: Oakland Museum, CA; San Francisco Museum of Modern Art, CA; University Art Museum, U. of California, Berkeley

Related Professional Experience: faculty, San Francisco Art Institute, CA, 1978–present; Mills College, Oakland, CA, 1980–present

Ivy Ross
New York, New York

Born: New York, New York, 1955

Education: Syracuse U., NY, 1975; B.F.A., Fashion Institute of Technology, New York, NY, 1977

Award/Honor: NEA Fellowship, 1983

Exhibitions: New Images/New York, Museum of Applied Arts, Oslo, Norway, 1986; Materials, International Jewelry Exhibition, Munich, W. Germany, 1984; Jewelry USA, American Craft Museum, NYC, and tour, 1984–86; International Jewelry Art Exhibition, Isetan Art Museum, Tokyo, Japan, 1983; two-person exhibition, Craft and Folk Art Museum, Los Angeles, CA, 1983; Pattern: An Exhibition of the Decorated Surface, American Craft Museum, NYC, 1982; Good As Gold: Alternative Materials in American Jewelry, SITES tour, 1981–84

Collections: Cooper-Hewitt Museum, NYC; Renwick Gallery, Smithsonian Institution, Washington, DC; Museum of Applied Arts, Oslo, Norway; Museum of Applied Arts, Trondheim, Norway; Jewelry Museum, Pforzheim, W. Germany

Ed Rossbach
Berkeley, California

Born: Chicago, Illinois, 1914

Education: B.A., U. of Washington, Seattle, 1940; M.A., Columbia U., NYC, 1941; M.F.A., Cranbrook Academy of Art, Bloomfield Hills, MI, 1947

Award/Honor: Fellow, American Craft Council, 1975

Exhibitions: *The Art Fabric: Mainstream,* American Federation of Arts national tour, 1981–83; *Fiber Works: The Americas and Japan,* National Museum of Modern Art, Kyoto and Tokyo, Japan, 1977; *The Dyer's Art: Ikat, Batik, Plangi,* Museum of Contemporary Crafts, NYC, and tour, 1976–78; *The New Classicism,* Museum of Modern Art, NYC, 1977; *The Object as Poet,* Renwick Gallery, Smithsonian Institution, Washington, DC, and tour, 1976; *Objects: USA,* Johnson Collection of Contemporary Crafts, national and international tour, 1969–72; *Wallhangings,* Museum of Modern Art, NYC, 1969

Publications: *Baskets as a Textile Art,* (1973), *The New Basketry,* (1976), *The Art of Paisley,* (1980)—all published by Van Nostrand Reinhold, NYC; *The Nature of Basketry,* Schiffer Publishing, Exton, PA, 1986

Collections: American Craft Museum, NYC; Brooklyn Museum, NYC; Museum of Modern Art, NYC; Renwick Gallery, Smithsonian Institution, Washington, DC; Stedelijk Museum, Amsterdam, Netherlands

Mitch Ryerson
Cambridge, Massachusetts

Born: Boston, Massachusetts, 1955

Education: B.A., Program in Artisanry, Boston U., MA, 1982

Exhibitions: *Material Evidence: New Color Techniques in Handmade Furniture,* Workbench Gallery, NYC, and Renwick Gallery, Smithsonian Institution, Washington, DC, 1984; *New Furniture,* Victoria and Albert Museum, London, England, 1984.

Arturo Alonzo Sandoval
Lexington, Kentucky

Born: Espanola, New Mexico, 1942

Education: B.A., M.A., California State College, Los Angeles, 1964, 1969; M.F.A., Cranbrook Academy of Art, Bloomfield Hills, MI, 1971

Award/Honor: NEA Fellowship, 1973

Exhibitions: *Woven Works: Tradition and Innovation,* Tweed Museum of Art, U. of Minnesota, Duluth, 1984; *The Art Fabric: Mainstream,* American Federation of Arts national tour, 1981–83; *New Acquisitions: Design Collection,* Museum of Modern Art, NYC, 1979; *International Biennial of Tapestry,* Cantonal Museum of Fine Arts, Lausanne, Switzerland, 1977; *Sky Grids and Other Concepts,* Ella Sharp Museum, Jackson, MI, 1977; *Fur and Feathers,* Museum of Contemporary Crafts, NYC, 1971

Collection: Museum of Modern Art, NYC

Related Professional Experience: faculty, U. of Kentucky, Lexington, 1974–present

Jane Sauer
St. Louis, Missouri

Born: St. Louis, Missouri, 1937

Education: B.F.A., Washington U., St. Louis, MO, 1960

Award/Honor: NEA Fellowship, 1984

Exhibitions: *The New Basket: A Vessel for the Future,* New York State Museum, Albany, and tour, 1984; *American Crafts in Iceland,* National Art Museum, Reykjavik, Iceland, 1983; *4th International Exhibition of Miniature Textiles,* British Crafts Centre, London, England, and international tour, 1980–83

Collections: Prudential Insurance, Dallas, TX; Museum of Applied Arts, Trondheim, Norway

Gayle Saunders
High Falls, New York

Born: Brooklyn, New York, 1951

Education: B.F.A., Tyler School of Art, Temple U., Philadelphia, PA, 1974

Awards/Honors: NEA Fellowship, 1977; NY Foundation for the Arts Fellowship, 1986

Exhibitions: *New Visions/Traditional Materials: Contemporary American Jewelry,* Carnegie Institute, Pittsburgh, PA, 1985; *Contemporary Jewelry: The Americas, Australia, Europe and Japan,* National Museum of Modern Art, Kyoto and Tokyo, Japan, 1984; *Jewelry USA,* American Craft Museum, NYC, and tour, 1984–86; *International Jewelry Art,* Isetan Art Museum, Tokyo, Japan, 1983; *Jewelry International 1900–1980,* House of Artists, Vienna, Austria, 1980; *The Goldsmith,* Renwick Gallery, Smithsonian Institu-

tion, Washington, DC, and tour, 1974; *Touch of Gold,* Philadelphia Museum of Art, PA, 1974

Related Professional Experience: faculty, Parsons School of Design/New School, NYC, 1980–present

Adrian Saxe
Los Angeles, California

Born: Glendale, California, 1943

Education: B.F.A., California Institute of the Arts, Valencia, CA, 1974

Exhibitions: *Twentieth-Century American Ceramics,* Ceramics Museum, Barcelona, Spain, 1985; *Echoes: Historical Reference in Contemporary Ceramics,* Nelson-Atkins Museum of Art, Kansas City, MO, 1983; *The Animal Image: Contemporary Objects and the Beast,* Renwick Gallery, Smithsonian Institution, Washington, DC, 1981; *American Porcelain: New Expressions in an Ancient Art,* Renwick Gallery, Smithsonian Institution, Washington, DC, and SITES tour, 1980–84; *A Century of Ceramics in the United States: 1878–1978,* Everson Museum of Art, Syracuse, NY, and tour, 1979

Collections: Everson Museum of Art, Syracuse, NY; Los Angeles County Museum of Art, CA; National Museum of American Art, Smithsonian Institution, Washington, DC; Nelson-Atkins Museum of Art, Kansas City, MO; Museum of Decorative Arts, Paris, France

Related Professional Experience: faculty, U. of California, Los Angeles, 1973–present

Mary Ann Scherr
New York, New York

Born: Akron, Ohio, 1931

Education: Cleveland Art Institute, Kent State U., Akron U., OH, 1945–50; equivalent M.F.A. professional degree, Kent State U., OH, 1966

Awards/Honors: Fellow, American Craft Council, 1983; honorary Ph.D., Defiance College, OH, 1986

Exhibitions: *Good As Gold: Alternative Materials in American Jewelry,* SITES tour, 1981–84; *Art For Use,* Olympic Winter Games, Lake Placid, NY, and American Craft Museum, NYC, 1980; *Society of North American Goldsmiths,* European tour, 1979; *Craft, Art and Religion,* Vatican Museum, Italy, 1978; *Three Goldsmiths, American,* Goldsmiths' Hall, London, England, 1978; *The Goldsmith,* Phoenix Art Museum, AZ, 1976; *Mary Ann Scherr Retrospective,* Akron Art Institute, OH, 1971; *Objects: USA,* Johnson Collection of Contemporary Crafts, national and international tour, 1969–72

Collections: American Craft Museum, NYC; Metropolitan Museum of Art, NYC; National Museum of American Art, Smithsonian Institution, Washington, DC; Worshipful Company of Goldsmiths, London, England; Vatican Museum, Italy

Related Professional Experience: faculty, Kent State U., OH, 1966–75; faculty, Parsons School of Design/New School, NYC, 1978–present; chairman, Clay/Glass/Metal/Textile dept., 1980–present

Marjorie Schick
Pittsburg, Kansas

Born: Taylorville, Illinois, 1941

Education: B.S., U. of Wisconsin, Madison, 1963; M.F.A., Indiana U., Bloomington, 1966

Award/Honor: NEA Regional Fellowship, 1985

Exhibitions: *Contemporary Arts: An Expanding View,* Monmouth Museum of Art, Lincroft, NJ, 1986; *Contemporary Jewellery: The Americas, Australia, Europe and Japan,* National Museum of Modern Art, Kyoto and Tokyo, Japan, 1984; *Jewelry USA,* American Craft Museum, NYC, and tour, 1984–86; *Good As Gold: Alternative Materials in American Jewelry,* SITES tour, 1981–84; *Face Coverings,* Museum of Contemporary Crafts, NYC, 1971

Collections: Cleveland County Museum, Cleveland, England; Municipal Museum of Modern Art, Apeldoorn, Netherlands; Museum of Applied Arts, Trondheim, Norway; National Museum of Modern Art, Kyoto, Japan

Related Professional Experience: faculty, Pittsburg State U., KS, 1967–present

Cynthia Schira
Lawrence, Kansas

Born: Pittsfield, Massachusetts, 1934

Education: B.F.A, Rhode Island School of Design, Providence, 1956; M.F.A., U. of Kansas, Lawrence, 1967

Awards/Honors: Tiffany grant, 1966; NEA Fellowship, 1974, 1983

Exhibitions: *Jacquard Textiles,* Museum of Rhode Island School of Design, Providence, and Cooper-Hewitt Museum, NYC, 1982; *The Art Fabric: Mainstream,* American Federation of Arts national tour, 1981–83; *Old Traditions—New Directions,* Textile Museum, Washington, DC, 1981; solo exhibition, Museum Bellerive, Zurich, Switzerland, 1979; *The Dyer's Art: Ikat, Batik, Plangi,* Museum of Contemporary Crafts, NYC, and tour, 1976–78; *Forms in Fibers,* Art Institute of Chicago, IL, 1970; *Objects: USA,* Johnson Collection of Contemporary Crafts, national and international tour, 1969–72

Collections: Art Institute of Chicago, IL; Metropolitan Museum of Art, NYC; Renwick Gallery, Smithsonian Institution, Washington, DC; Museum Bellerive, Zurich, Switzerland

Related Professional Experience: faculty, U. of Kansas, Lawrence, 1976–present

James Schriber
New Milford, Connecticut

Born: Dayton, Ohio, 1952

Education: certificate of mastery, Program in Artisanry, Boston U., MA, 1979

Exhibition: *Material Evidence: New Color Techniques in Handmade Furniture,* Renwick Gallery, Smithsonian Institute, Washington, DC, 1985

Related Professional Experience: faculty, Brookfield Craft Center, CT, 1980–85

June Schwarcz
Sausalito, California

Born: Denver, Colorado, 1918

Education: U. of Colorado, Boulder, 1938; U. of Chicago, 1939; Pratt Institute, NYC, 1941

Exhibitions: *California Crafts XIV: Living Treasures of California,* Crocker Art Museum, Sacramento, CA, 1985; *The Goldsmith,* Renwick Gallery, Smithsonian Institution, Washington, DC, 1974; solo exhibition, Jewelry Museum, Pforzheim, W. Germany, 1972; solo exhibition, Museum Bellerive, Zurich, Switzerland, 1971; *Objects: USA,* Johnson Collection of Contemporary Crafts, national and international tour, 1969–72; solo exhibition, Museum of Contemporary Crafts, NYC, 1966; *Craftsmanship in a Changing World,* inaugural exhibition, Museum of Contemporary Crafts, NYC, 1956

Collections: American Craft Museum, NYC; Everson Museum of Art, Syracuse, NY; Minnesota Museum of Art, Minneapolis, MN; Oakland Museum, CA; Renwick Gallery, Smithsonian Institution, Washington, DC; Museum of Applied Arts, Zurich, Switzerland

Warren Seelig
Elkins Park, Pennsylvania

Born: Abington, Pennsylvania, 1946

Education: B.A., Kutztown State College, PA, 1968; B.S., Philadelphia College of Textiles and Science, 1972; M.F.A., Cranbrook Academy of Art, Bloomfield Hills, MI, 1974

Awards/Honors: NEA Fellowship, 1976, 1984; PA Council on the Arts Fellowship, 1983

Exhibitions: *Contemporary Arts: An Expanding View,* Monmouth Museum of Art, Lincroft, NJ, 1986; *Fiber R/Evolution,* University Art Museum, U. of Wisconsin, Milwaukee, 1986; *Cloth Forms,* Dayton Art Institute, OH, 1982; *The Art Fabric: Mainstream,* American Federation of Arts national tour, 1981–83; *Old Traditions—New Directions,* Textile Museum, Washington, DC, 1981; *Third International Textile Triennial,* Central Museum of Textiles, Lodz, Poland, 1978; *Fiberworks,* Cleveland Museum of Art, OH, 1977; *Textiles: Past and Prologue,* Greenville County Museum of Art, SC, 1976

Related Professional Experience: faculty, Colorado State U., Fort Collins, 1974–78; faculty, Fiber/Textiles, Philadelphia College of Art, PA, 1979–present

Paul Seide
Kew Gardens, New York

Born: New York, New York, 1949

Education: certificate, Egani Neon Glassblowing School, NYC, 1971; B.S., U. of Wisconsin, Madison, 1974

Exhibitions: *Illumination: The Quality of Light,* Pittsburgh Center for the Arts, PA, 1985; *Americans in Glass,* Leigh Yawkey Woodson Art Museum, Wausau, WI, 1984, 1982, 1978; *Sculptural Glass,* Tucson Museum of Art, AZ, 1983; *American Glass Art: Evolution and Revolution,* Morris Museum of Arts and Sciences, Morristown, NJ, 1982; *World Glass Now,* Hokkaido Museum of Modern Art, Sapporo, Japan, 1982; *Contemporary Glass: Australia, Canada, U.S.A. and Japan,* National Museum of Modern Art, Kyoto and Tokyo, Japan, 1981; *Glass Routes,* DeCordova Museum, Lincoln, MA, 1981; *New Glass: A Worldwide Survey,* Corning Museum of Glass, NY, 1979; *Great Paperweight Exhibition,* Corning Museum of Glass, NY, 1978

Collections: Corning Museum of Glass, NY; Chrysler Museum of Art, Norfolk, VA; Fine Arts Museum of the South, Mobile, AL; Wheaton Museum of Glass, Millville, NJ; Museum of Decorative Arts, Lausanne, Switzerland; National Museum of Modern Art, Kyoto, Japan

Kay Sekimachi
Berkeley, California

Born: San Francisco, California, 1926

Education: California College of Arts and Crafts, Oakland, 1946–49; Haystack Mountain School of Crafts, Liberty, ME, 1956

Awards/Honors: NEA Fellowship, 1974; Fellow, American Craft Council, 1985

Exhibitions: *Parallel Views: Kay Sekimachi and Nancy Selvin,* California Craft Museum, Palo Alto, CA, 1982; *The Art Fabric: Mainstream,* American Federation of Arts national tour, 1981–83; *Fiber Works: The Americas and Japan,* National Museum of Modern Art, Kyoto and Tokyo, Japan, 1977; *Objects: USA,* Johnson Collection of Contemporary Crafts, national and international tour, 1969–72; *Wall Hangings,* Museum of Modern Art, NYC, 1968; *Modern American Wall Hangings,* Victoria and Albert Museum, London, England, 1962

Collections: American Craft Museum, NYC; Oakland Museum, CA; Smithsonian Institution, Washington, DC; National Museum of Modern Art, Kyoto, Japan; Royal Scottish Museum, Edinburgh, Scotland

Related Professional Experience: faculty, Adult Division, San Francisco Community College, CA, 1965–present

Sylvia Seventy
Healdsburg, California

Born: Alhambra, California, 1947

Education: B.A., California State U., Northridge, 1973; M.F.A., Lone Mountain College, San Francisco, CA, 1978

Exhibitions: *Fiber Art '85,* Museum of Decorative Arts, Paris, France, 1985; *Papier-matière,* Saguenay Museum, Chicoutimi, Canada, 1984; *Making Paper,* American Craft Museum, NYC, 1982; solo exhibition, Redding Museum and Art Center, CA, 1982; *The Art Fabric: Mainstream,* American Federation of Arts national tour, 1981–83; 4th International Exhibition of Miniature Textiles, British Crafts Centre, London, England, 1980

Collections: American Craft Museum, NYC; Champion International Paper, Stamford, CT; Union Oil, Santa Rosa, CA

Related Professional Experience: gallery director, Fiberworks, Center for the Textile Arts, JFK U., Berkeley, CA, 1982–86; faculty, 1982–present

David Shaner
Bigfork, Montana

Born: Pottstown, Pennsylvania, 1934

Education: B.S., Pennsylvania State U., Kutztown, 1956; M.F.A., New York State College of Ceramics at Alfred U., NY, 1959

Awards/Honors: Tiffany grant, 1963; NEA Fellowship, 1976, 1978

Exhibitions: *Northwest Crafts,* Museum of Science and Industry, Seattle, WA, 1982; *Contemporary Ceramics: A Response to Wedgwood,* Museum of Philadelphia Civic Center, PA, 1980; *A Century of Ceramics in the United States: 1878–1978,* Everson Museum of Art, Syracuse, NY, and tour, 1979; *Ceramic National,* Everson Museum of Art, Syracuse, NY, 1966; *Designer-Craftsmen U.S.A.,* Museum of Contemporary Crafts, NYC, 1960

Collections: American Craft Museum, NYC; Everson Museum of Art, Syracuse, NY; Missoula Museum of the Arts, MT; National Collection of Fine Arts, Smithsonian Institution, Washington, DC; Royal Ontario Museum, Toronto, Canada

Related Professional Experience: resident potter and director, Archie Bray Foundation, Helena, MT, 1963–70; independent studio potter, 1970–present

Susan Shapiro (works collaboratively with Andrew Magdanz)
Cambridge, Massachusetts

Born: New York, New York, 1953

Education: B.F.A., California College of Arts and Crafts, Oakland, 1978

Award/Honor: NEA grant, 1979

Exhibitions: *Americans in Glass,* Leigh Yawkey Woodson Art Museum, Wausau, WI, 1984; *Contemporary American Glass,* Corning Museum exhibition at U.S. embassy, Prague, Czechoslovakia, 1984, 1983, 1982; *Glass Routes,* DeCordova Museum, Lincoln, MA, 1981; two-person exhibition, Craft and Folk Art Museum, Los Angeles, CA, 1981; *Contemporary Glass,* Indiana U. Art Museum, Bloomington, 1980

Collection: Roanoke Museum of Fine Arts, VA

Related Professional Experience: studio artist/designer, Avon Place Glass, Cambridge, MA, 1979–present

Richard Shaw
Fairfax, California

Born: Hollywood, California, 1941

Education: B.F.A., San Francisco Art Institute, CA, 1965; M.F.A., U. of California, Davis, 1968

Awards/Honors: NEA grant, 1970; NEA project grant, 1973

Exhibitions: *More Than Meets the Eye: The Art of Trompe l'Oeil,* Columbus Museum of Art, OH, 1985–86; *Directions in Contemporary American Ceramics,* Museum of Fine Arts, Boston, MA, 1984; *American Still Life, 1945–83,* Contemporary Arts Museum, Houston, TX, 1983; *Ceramic Sculpture: Six Artists,* Whitney Museum of American Art, NYC, and San Francisco Museum of Modern Art, CA, 1981–82; *American Porcelain: New Expressions in an Ancient Art,* Renwick Gallery, Smithsonian Institution, Washington, DC, and SITES tour, 1980–84; *A Century of Ceramics in the United States: 1878–1978,* Everson Museum of Art, Syracuse, NY, and tour, 1979; *West Coast Ceramics,* Stedelijk Museum, Amsterdam, Netherlands, 1979; solo exhibition, San Francisco Museum of Modern Art, CA, 1973

Collections: American Craft Museum, NYC; Renwick Gallery, Smithsonian Institution, Washington, DC; Oakland Museum, CA; San Francisco Museum of Modern Art, CA; Whitney Museum of American Art, NYC; National Museum of Modern Art, Tokyo, Japan; Stedelijk Museum, Amsterdam, Netherlands

Related Professional Experience: faculty, San Francisco Art Institute, CA, 1966–present

Carol Shaw-Sutton
Fullerton, California

Born: Los Angeles, California, 1948

Education: B.A., M.A., San Diego State U., CA, 1971, 1976

Award/Honor: NEA Fellowship, 1981

Exhibitions: *The Other Gods,* Everson Museum of Art, Syracuse, NY, 1986; *International Biennial of Tapestry,* Cantonal Museum of Fine Arts, Lausanne, Switzerland, 1985; *The Presence of Light,* Meadows Museum, Dallas, TX, 1984; *The American Landscape,* Cooper-Hewitt Museum, NYC, 1982; *Beyond Tradition: 25th Anniversary Exhibition,* American Craft Museum, NYC, 1981; *Made in L.A.,* Craft and Folk Art Museum, Los Angeles, CA, 1981; *Landscape: New Views,* Herbert F. Johnson Museum of Art, Cornell U., Ithaca, NY, 1978; *Young Americans: Fiber/Wood/*

Plastic/Leather, Museum of Contemporary Crafts, NYC, 1977

Collections: Bank of Denver, CO; Chubb Insurance Group, NYC; Greenville County Museum of Art, SC; Oakland Museum, CA; Saks Fifth Avenue, NYC

Related Professional Experience: faculty, Long Beach State U., CA, 1985–86

Peter Shire
Los Angeles, California

Born: Los Angeles, California, 1947

Education: B.F.A., Chouinard Art Institute, Los Angeles, CA, 1970

Exhibitions: *Art and/or Craft,* Arts Museum, Kanazawa, Japan, and international tour, 1983–85; *On and Off the Wall: Shaped and Colored,* Oakland Museum, CA, 1983; three-person exhibition, Museum of Modern Art, Lodz, Poland, and Museum of Modern Art, Paris, France, 1982; *Made in L.A.,* Craft and Folk Art Museum, Los Angeles, CA, 1981; *Clay III,* Riverside Art Center and Museum, CA, 1978

Collections: Everson Museum of Art, Syracuse, NY; Oakland Museum, CA; Seattle Art Museum, WA; Victoria and Albert Museum, London, England

Related Professional Experience: design team of 23rd Olympiad, Los Angeles, CA, 1984

Helen Shirk
San Diego, California

Born: Buffalo, New York, 1942

Education: B.S., Skidmore College, Saratoga Springs, NY, 1963; Academy of Applied Arts, Copenhagen, Denmark, 1963–64; M.F.A., Indiana U., Bloomington, IN, 1969

Awards/Honors: Fulbright grant, 1963; NEA Fellowship, 1978

Exhibitions: *Contemporary Arts: An Expanding View,* Monmouth Museum of Arts, Lincroft, NJ, 1986; *Contemporary Jewellery: The Americas, Australia, Europe and Japan,* National Museum of Modern Art, Kyoto and Tokyo, Japan, 1984; *Jewelry USA,* American Craft Museum, NYC, and tour, 1984–86; *Modern Jewelry: 1964–1984,* Montreal Museum of Decorative Arts, Canada, and tour, 1984–87; *Tendencies '82,* Jewelry Museum, Pforzheim, W. Germany, 1982; *Good As Gold: Alternative Materials in American Jewelry,* SITES tour, 1981–84; *Forms in Metal: 275 Years of Metalsmithing in America,* American Craft Museum, NYC, and tour, 1975–76

Collections: Minnesota Museum of Art, St. Paul, MN; Texas Tech U., Lubbock; U. of Texas, El Paso; National Museum of Modern Art, Kyoto, Japan; Jewelry Museum, Pforzheim, W. Germany

Related Professional Experience: faculty, San Diego State U., CA, 1975–present; Camberwell School of Arts and Crafts, London, England, 1983

Alan Siegel
New York, New York

Born: New York, New York, 1938

Education: B.A., Brandeis U., Waltham, MA, 1960

Exhibitions: *Contemporary Wood Sculpture,* Crocker Art Museum, Sacramento, CA, 1984; *Invitational Wood and Fiber,* Columbus Museum of Arts and Sciences, GA, 1983; *Art for Use,* Olympic Winter Games, Lake Placid, NY, and American Craft Museum, NYC, 1980; *Whimsy,* Taft Museum, Cincinnati, OH, 1978; *Paint on Wood: Decorated American Furniture since the 17th Century,* Renwick Gallery, Smithsonian Institution, Washington, DC, 1977; *Hue and Far Cry of Color,* Fort Wayne Museum, NJ, 1976; group exhibition, Whitney Museum of American Art, NYC, 1973, 1970; *Lyrical Abstraction,* Aldrich Museum, Ridgefield, CT, 1970

Patrick Siler
Pullman, Washington

Born: Spokane, Washington, 1939

Education: B.A., Washington State U., Pullman, 1961; M.A., U. of California, Berkeley, 1963

Exhibitions: *Architectural Ceramics: Eight Concepts,* American Craft Museum, NYC, and Washington U., St. Louis, MO, 1985; *Works in Clay,* Missoula Museum of the Arts, MT, 1977; *Coffee, Tea & Other Cups,* Museum of Contemporary Crafts, NYC, 1970; *Ob-*

jects: USA, Johnson Collection of Contemporary Crafts, national and international tour, 1969–72

Collection: American Craft Museum, NYC

Related Professional Experience: faculty, Washington State U., Pullman, 1973–present

Glen Simpson
Fairbanks, Alaska

Born: Atlin, Canada, 1941

Education: B.F.A., M.F.A., School for American Craftsmen, Rochester Institute of Technology, NY, 1968, 1969

Exhibitions: *Silversmith by Trade,* U. of Alaska Museum, Fairbanks, 1983; *Remains To Be Seen,* John Michael Kohler Arts Center, Sheboygan, WI, 1983; *American Crafts: A Pacific Heritage,* California State Fairgrounds, Sacramento, 1982; solo exhibition, Alaska State Museum, Juneau, 1981; *Wood, Ivory and Bone,* Alaska State Museum, Juneau, 1980; solo exhibition, Anchorage Historical and Fine Arts Museum, AK, 1977; *Design One,* Anchorage Historical and Fine Arts Museum, AK, 1972; *Art Alaska,* Alaska State Museum, Juneau, and tour, 1971–72

Collections: Alaska State Museum, Juneau; Anchorage Museum of History and Art, AK; U. of Alaska Museum, Fairbanks

Related Professional Experience: faculty, U. of Alaska, Fairbanks, 1969–present

Tommy Simpson
Washington, Connecticut

Born: Elgin, Illinois, 1939

Education: B.S., Northern Illinois U., DeKalb, 1962; M.F.A., Cranbrook Academy of Art, Bloomfield Hills, MI, 1964

Award/Honor: NEA grant, 1978

Exhibitions: solo exhibition, Mattatuck Museum, Waterbury, CT, 1985; *300 Years of American Painted Furniture,* Renwick Gallery, Smithsonian Institution, Washington, DC, 1979; solo exhibition, Parrish Museum, Southhampton, NY, 1970; *Objects: USA,* Johnson Collection of Contemporary Crafts, national and international tour, 1969–72; solo exhibition, Art Institute of Chicago, IL, 1969; *Fantasy Furniture,* Museum of Contemporary Crafts, NYC, 1966

Publications: *Fantasy Furniture,* Van Nostrand Reinhold, NYC, 1968

Collection: American Craft Museum, NYC

Karyl Sisson
Los Angeles, California

Born: Brooklyn, New York, 1948

Education: B.S., New York U., NYC, 1969; M.F.A., U. of California, Los Angeles, 1985

Exhibitions: *Fiber R/Evolution,* University Art Museum, U. of Wisconsin, Milwaukee, 1986; *Fiber Structure National,* Downey Museum of Art, CA, 1985, 1984; *All California Arts and Crafts,* Laguna Beach Museum of Art, CA, 1984, 1976; *Crafts 16,* Museum of Art, Pennsylvania State U., University Park, 1982; *Needle Expressions '82,* Tennessee State Museum, Nashville, 1982

Related Professional Experience: freelance graphic artist, Los Angeles, CA, 1973–83

Gail Fredell Smith
Berkeley, California

Born: San Francisco, California, 1951

Education: B.A., U. of California, Berkeley, 1974; M.F.A., Rochester Institute of Technology, NY, 1980

Exhibitions: *New Furnishings,* Triton Museum of Art, Santa Clara, CA, 1985; *Nine East Bay Furniture Makers,* Berkeley Art Center, CA, 1983

Related Professional Experience: president, Summerwood Designs, architectural design and general contracting firm, Oakland, CA, 1974–78; faculty, California College of Arts and Crafts, Oakland, 1981–present; artist-in-residence, Artpark, Lewiston, NY, 1984; faculty, Penland School of Crafts, NC, 1986

Sherri Smith
Ann Arbor, Michigan

Born: Evanston, Illinois, 1943

Education: B.A., Stanford U., CA, 1965; M.F.A., Cranbrook Academy of Art, Bloomfield Hills, MI, 1967

Exhibitions: *The Flexible Medium: Art Fabric from the Museum Collection,* Renwick Gallery, Smithsonian Institution, Washington, DC, 1984; *Pattern: An Exhibition of the Decorated Surface,* American Craft Museum, NYC, 1982; *The Art Fabric: Mainstream,* American Federation of Arts national tour, 1981–83; *Fiberworks,* Cleveland Museum of Art, OH, 1977; *International Biennial of Tapestry,* Cantonal Museum of Fine Arts, Lausanne, Switzerland, 1977, 1975, 1973, 1971; *Young Americans,* Museum of Contemporary Crafts, NYC, 1969; *Wall Hangings,* Museum of Modern Art, NYC, 1968

Collections: Art Institute of Chicago, IL; AT&T, San Francisco, CA; Borg-Warner, Chicago, IL; General Motors, NYC; IBM, Poughkeepsie, NY; Indianapolis Art Museum, IN

Related Professional Experience: faculty, U. of Michigan, Ann Arbor, 1974–present

Stephen Smyers
Benicia, California

Born: Oakland, California, 1948

Education: B.A., California State U., Chico, 1971

Exhibitions: *American Craft Traditions,* San Francisco International Airport, CA, 1984; *American Glass Now,* Yamaha Corporation, Tokyo, Japan, and tour, 1984, 1982, 1981; *California Crafts XIII,* Crocker Art Museum, Sacramento, CA, 1983

Related Professional Experience: founding partner, Northern Star Glass, 1971–79; owner, Smyers Glass studio, 1979–present

Paul Soldner
Aspen, Colorado, and Claremont, California

Born: Summerfield, Illinois, 1921

Education: B.A., Bluffton College, OH, 1946; M.A., U. of Colorado, Boulder, 1954; M.F.A., Otis Art Institute, Los Angeles, CA, 1956

Awards/Honors: Tiffany grant, 1966, 1972; NEA Fellowship, 1976; Fellow, American Craft Council, 1977

Exhibitions: *Raku and Smoke,* Newport Art Museum, RI, and American Craft Museum, NYC, 1984; *Ceramic Echoes: Historical References in Contemporary Ceramic Art,* Nelson-Atkins Museum of Art, Kansas City, MO, 1983; *A Century of Ceramics in the United States: 1878–1978,* Everson Museum of Art, Syracuse, NY, and tour, 1979; solo exhibition, Renwick Gallery, Smithsonian Institution, Washington, DC, 1978; *Objects: USA,* Johnson Collection of Contemporary Crafts, national and international tour, 1969–72

Publications: *Kilns and Their Construction,* American Craft Council, NYC, 1965

Collections: Everson Museum of Art, Syracuse, NY; High Museum of Art, Atlanta, GA; Los Angeles County Museum of Art, CA; Oakland Museum, CA; Smithsonian Institution, Washington, DC; National Museum of Modern Art, Kyoto, Japan; Victoria and Albert Museum, London, England

Related Professional Experience: faculty, Scripps College and Claremont Graduate School, 1969–present; curator, annual national Scripps College Ceramics Invitational, Claremont, CA, 1970–present; president, Soldner Pottery Equipment, Inc., Silt, CO

Rosanne Somerson
Boston, Massachusetts

Born: Philadelphia, Pennsylvania, 1954

Education: B.F.A., Rhode Island School of Design, Providence, 1976

Award/Honor: NEA Fellowship, 1984

Exhibitions: *National Furniture Invitational,* Tupelo Municipal Art Museum, MS, 1985; *The Tradition of the New,* Brockton Art Museum, MA, 1984; *Ornamentalism: The New Decorativeness in Architecture and Design,* Hudson River Museum, Yonkers, NY, 1983; *Woodforms,* Brockton Art Museum, MA, 1981; *Containers,* Danforth Museum, Framingham, MA, 1979

Collections: Brockton Art Museum, MA; Museum of Fine Arts, Boston, MA

Related Professional Experience: staff, *Fine Woodworking,* Newtown, CT, 1976–81; teaching fellow, Harvard U., Cambridge, MA, 1977–78; self-employed furniture designer/builder, 1978–present; part-time faculty, Rhode Island School of Design, Providence, 1985–present

Robert Sperry
Seattle, Washington

Born: Bushnell, Illinois, 1927

Education: B.F.A., School of the Art Institute of Chicago, IL, 1953; M.F.A., U. of Washington, Seattle, 1955

Awards/Honors: Tiffany grant, 1957; NEA Fellowship, 1984

Exhibitions: *Robert Sperry: A Retrospective,* Bellevue Art Museum, WA, and tour, 1985; *Regional Crafts: An Historical View,* and *Regional Crafts: A Contemporary View,* Bellevue Art Museum, WA, 1983; *Another Side of Art: Ceramics in the Pacific Northwest,* Seattle Art Museum, WA, 1979; *Objects: USA,* Johnson Collection of Contemporary Crafts, national and international tour, 1969–72; *American Studio Pottery,* Victoria and Albert Museum, London, England, 1968

Publications: *Robert Sperry: A Retrospective,* monograph to accompany exhibition, Bellevue Art Museum, WA, 1985

Collections: American Craft Museum, NYC; Bellevue Art Museum, WA; Everson Museum of Art, Syracuse, NY; National Museum of American History, Smithsonian Institution, Washington, DC; Seattle Art Museum, WA

Related Professional Experience: faculty, U. of Washington, Seattle, 1955–82

Rudolf Staffel
Philadelphia, Pennsylvania

Born: San Antonio, Texas, 1911

Education: School of the Art Institute of Chicago, IL, 1931

Awards/Honors: NEA Fellowship, 1977; Fellow, American Craft Council, 1978; PA Governor's award/ Hazlett Memorial Award, 1982

Exhibitions: *Contemporary Arts: An Expanding View,* Monmouth Museum of Art, Lincroft, NJ, 1986; *Directions in Contemporary American Ceramics,* Museum of Fine Arts, Boston, MA, 1984; *Hazlett Memorial Award Exhibition,* Alleghenies Museum of Art, Loretto, PA, and tour, 1982; *American Porcelain: New Expressions in an Ancient Art,* Renwick Gallery, Smithsonian Institution, Washington, DC, and SITES tour, 1980–84; *A Century of Ceramics in the United States: 1878–1978,* Everson Museum of Art, Syracuse, NY, and tour, 1979; *Philadelphia: Three Centuries of American Art 1776–1976,* Philadelphia Museum of Art, PA, 1976; *International Ceramics,* Victoria and Albert Museum, London, England, 1972; solo exhibition, Museum of Contemporary Crafts, NYC, 1967

Collections: American Craft Museum, NYC; Everson Museum of Art, Syracuse, NY; Museum of Fine Arts, Boston, MA; National Museum of History and Technology, Smithsonian Institution, Washington, DC; Philadelphia Museum of Art, PA; Montreal Museum of Decorative Arts, Canada

Related Professional Experience: faculty, Tyler School of Art, Temple U., Philadelphia, PA, 1940–79

Therman Statom
Los Angeles, California

Born: Winterhaven, Florida, 1953

Education: B.F.A., Rhode Island School of Design, Providence, 1974

Awards/Honors: NEA Fellowship, 1980, 1982

Exhibitions: *Americans in Glass,* Leigh Yawkey Woodson Art Museum, Wausau, WI, 1984; *Therman Statom: Fragile Frontiers,* John Michael Kohler Arts Center, Sheboygan, WI, 1984–85; *Sculptural Glass,* Tuscon Museum of Art, AZ, 1983; group exhibition, Montclair Art Museum, NJ, 1982; *International Directions in Glass Art,* Art Gallery of Western Australia, Perth, and tour, 1982–83; *Four Leaders in Glass,* Craft and Folk Art Museum, Los Angeles, CA, 1980; *Young Americans: Clay/Glass,* Museum of Contemporary Crafts, NYC, 1978

Related Professional Experience: faculty, U. of California, Los Angeles, 1983–85

Joan Sterrenburg
Nashville, Indiana

Born: Chicago, Illinois, 1941

Education: B.A., U. of Wisconsin, Madison, 1963; M.A., Stanford U., CA, 1964; M.A., U. of California, Berkeley, 1970

Awards/Honors: NEA Fellowship, 1979; Ford Foundation grant, 1978

Exhibitions: *Papier-matière,* Saguenay Museum, Chicoutimi, Canada, 1984; *Making Paper,* American Craft Museum, NYC, 1982; *Clay, Fiber, Metal by Women Artists,* Bronx Museum, NYC, 1978; *Printed, Painted and Dyed: The New Fabric Surface,* Renwick Gallery, Smithsonian Institution, Washington, DC, 1978; *Third International Exhibition of Miniature Textiles,* British Crafts Centre, London, England, 1978; *The Dyer's Art: Ikat, Batik, Plangi,* Museum of Contemporary Crafts, NYC, and tour, 1976–78

Collections: AT&T, Atlanta, GA; Evansville Museum of Arts and Sciences, IN; IBM, Des Moines, IA, Lexington, KY, and Topeka, KS; St. Louis Art Museum, MO; U. of Notre Dame Art Museum, IN

Related Professional Experience: faculty, Indiana U., Bloomington, 1970–present

Lizbeth Stewart
Philadelphia, Pennsylvania

Born: Philadelphia, Pennsylvania, 1948

Education: B.F.A., Moore College of Art, Philadelphia, PA, 1971

Awards/Honors: NEA Fellowship, 1976; PA State Council on the Arts Fellowship, 1982

Exhibitions: solo exhibition, Pennsylvania Academy of the Fine Arts, Philadelphia, PA, 1984; *Soup Soup Beautiful Soup,* Campbell Museum, Camden, NJ, 1983; *The Animal Image: Contemporary Objects and the Beast,* Renwick Gallery, Smithsonian Institution, Washington, DC, 1981; *The Clay Figure,* American Craft Museum, NYC, 1981; *American Porcelain: New Expressions in an Ancient Art,* Renwick Gallery, Smithsonian Institution, Washington, DC and SITES tour, 1980–84; *Contemporary Ceramics: A Response to Wedgwood,* Museum of Philadelphia Civic Center, PA, 1980; *Young Americans: Clay/Glass,* Museum of Contemporary Crafts, NYC, 1978; *Philadelphia: Three Centuries of American Art,* Philadelphia Museum of Art, PA, 1976; *Clay,* Whitney Museum of American Art, NYC, 1974

Collection: Campbell Museum, Camden, NJ; Hirshhorn Museum and Sculpture Garden, Smithsonian Institution, Washington, DC

Susan Stinsmuehlen
Austin, Texas

Born: Baltimore, Maryland, 1948

Education: Hood College, Fredrick, MD; Indiana U., Bloomington; U. of Texas, Austin, 1966–72

Award/Honor: NEA Fellowship, 1982

Exhibitions: *Americans in Glass,* Leigh Yawkey Woodson Art Museum, Wausau, WI, 1984, 1981; *Ornamentalism: The New Decorativeness in Architecture and Design,* Hudson River Museum, Yonkers, NY, 1983; *Sculptural Glass,* Tucson Museum of Art, AZ, 1983; *International Directions in Glass Art,* Art Gallery of Western Australia, Perth, and tour, 1982–83; *New Works Series,* Laguna Gloria Art Museum, Austin, TX, 1982; *Texas Crafts: New Expressions,* Dallas Museum of Art, TX, 1981

Collections: Corning Museum of Glass, NY; Leigh Yawkey Woodson Art Museum, Wausau, WI

Related Professional Experience: architectural glass installations throughout Texas, 1979–present; president, Glass Art Society, 1984–86

Bob Stocksdale
Berkeley, California

Born: Warren, Indiana, 1913

Education: self-taught

Award/Honor: Fellow, American Craft Council, 1978

Exhibitions: *California Crafts XIV: Living Treasures of California,* Crocker Art Museum, Sacramento, CA,

1985; *The Art of Woodturning,* American Craft Museum, NYC, 1983; solo exhibition, Oakland Museum, CA, 1981; *American Crafts, 1977,* Philadelphia Museum of Art, PA, 1977; solo exhibition, Renwick Gallery, Smithsonian Institution, Washington, DC, 1973; *Bob Stocksdale—Wood Turnings,* Museum of Contemporary Crafts, NYC, 1969; *California Design, VIII–XI,* Pasadena Art Museum, CA, 1964–68; *Good Design,* Museum of Modern Art, NYC, 1960; *Triennial,* Milan, Italy, 1960; *Craftsmanship in a Changing World,* Museum of Contemporary Crafts, NYC, 1965

Collections: American Craft Museum, NYC; Museum of Fine Arts, Boston, MA; Oakland Museum, CA; Philadelphia Museum of Art, PA; Royal Scottish Museum, Edinburgh

Del Stubbs
Chico, California

Born: Red Bluff, California, 1952

Exhibition: *The Art of Woodturning,* American Craft Museum, NYC, 1983

Related Professional Experience: lectures and demonstrations at woodturning conferences, Australia, Canada, Ireland, United States, 1980–86

Pamela Studstill
Pipe Creek, Texas

Born: San Antonio, Texas, 1954

Education: B.F.A., U. of Texas, San Antonio, 1978

Award/Honor: NEA Fellowship, 1982

Exhibitions: *Contemporary Arts: An Expanding View,* Monmouth Museum of Art, Lincroft, NJ, 1986; *Fabrications,* Missoula Museum of the Arts, MT, 1985; *Contemporary American Quilts,* Chateau D'Annecy, France, 1984; *Pattern: An Exhibition of the Decorated Surface,* American Craft Museum, NYC, 1982

Collections: Bank of San Antonio, TX; First National Bank of Boston, MA; IBM, Atlanta, GA

Toshiko Takaezu
Quakertown, New Jersey

Born: Pepeekeo, Hawaii, 1922

Education: Honolulu Academy of Arts, HI; U. of Hawaii, Honolulu; Cranbrook Academy of Art, Bloomfield Hills, MI, 1951–53

Awards/Honors: Tiffany grant, 1964; Fellow, American Craft Council, 1975; NEA Fellowship, 1980; Dickinson College arts award, Carlisle, PA, 1983

Exhibitions: solo exhibition, Florida Junior College, Jacksonville, 1985; two-person exhibition, Community Gallery of Lancaster, PA, 1984; solo exhibition, Dickinson College, Carlisle, PA, 1983; two-person exhibitions, Cleveland Institute of Art, OH, 1979; New Jersey State Museum, Trenton, 1979; *Objects: USA,* Johnson Collection of Contemporary Crafts, national and international tour, 1969–72; solo exhibitions, Museum of Contemporary Crafts, NYC, 1962; Cleveland Institute of Art, OH, 1960

Collections: American Craft Museum, NYC; Cleveland Museum of Art, OH; Everson Museum of Art, Syracuse, NY; Honolulu Academy of Arts, HI; Museum of Fine Arts, Boston, MA; New Jersey State Museum, Trenton; Philadelphia Museum of Art, PA; Smithsonian Institution, Washington, DC; National Museum, Bangkok, Thailand

Related Professional Experience: faculty, Princeton U., NJ, 1966–present

Lenore Tawney
New York, New York

Born: Lorain, Ohio, 1925

Education: U. of Illinois, Champaign-Urbana, 1943–45; Institute of Design, Chicago, IL, 1946–48

Awards/Honors: Fellow, American Craft Council, 1975; NEA grant, 1979

Exhibitions: *Contemporary Arts: An Expanding View,* Monmouth Museum of Art, Lincroft, NJ, 1986; *International Biennial of Tapestry,* Cantonal Museum of Fine Arts, Lausanne, Switzerland, 1983, 1975; *Old Traditions—New Directions,* Textile Museum, Washington, DC, 1981; solo exhibition, Tacoma Art Museum, WA, 1981; *100 Years, 100 Artists,* Art Institute of Chicago, IL, 1979; solo exhibition, New Jersey State Museum, Trenton, 1979; *Objects: USA,* Johnson Collection of Contemporary Crafts, national and international tour,

1969–72; *Wall Hangings,* Museum of Modern Art, NYC, 1969; solo exhibition, Art Institute of Chicago, IL, and tour, 1962

Collections: American Craft Museum, NYC; Art Institute of Chicago, IL; Brooklyn Museum, NYC; Cooper-Hewitt Museum, NYC; Metropolitan Museum of Art, NYC; Museum of Modern Art, NYC; Newark Museum, NJ; Pennsylvania Academy of the Fine Arts, PA; Museum of Applied Arts, Zurich, Switzerland

Related Professional Experience: commission, General Services Administration, Washington, DC, 1977

Byron Temple
Lambertville, New Jersey

Born: Centerville, Indiana, 1933

Education: Ball State U., Muncie, IN; Brooklyn Museum Art School, NYC; apprentice at Leach Pottery, St. Ives, England, 1959

Awards/Honors: NEA grant, 1974; NJ Crafts Fellowship, 1984

Exhibitions: solo exhibitions, Grove Gallery, U. of California, San Diego, 1986; Harrison Museum of Art, Logan, UT, 1985; New Jersey State Museum, Trenton, 1985

Collections: American Craft Museum, NYC; Cooper-Hewitt Museum, NYC; New Jersey State Museum, Trenton

Related Professional Experience: independent studio potter, 1963–present

Billie Jean Theide
Champaign, Illinois

Born: Des Moines, Iowa, 1956

Education: B.F.A., Drake U., Des Moines, IA, 1978; M.F.A., Indiana U., Bloomington, IN, 1982

Awards/Honors: Ford Foundation Fellowship, 1979; Ford Foundation grant, 1980; NEA Fellowship, 1985

Exhibitions: *American Jewelry Now,* American Craft Museum USIA Asian tour, 1985; *Jewelry USA,* American Craft Museum, NYC, and tour, 1984–86; *New Works,* Yamanashi Prefectural Museum of Art, Kofu, Japan, 1984; *California Crafts XIII,* Crocker Art Museum, Sacramento, CA, 1983

Related Professional Experience: faculty, U. of Illinois, Champaign-Urbana, 1985–present

Rachelle Thiewes
El Paso, Texas

Born: Owatonna, Minnesota, 1952

Education: B.A., Southern Illinois U., Carbondale, 1974; M.F.A., Kent State U., OH, 1976

Exhibitions: *Metalsmiths Making Sculpture,* Mitchell Museum, Mt. Vernon, IL, 1986; *Contemporary Metals USA,* Downey Museum of Art, CA, 1985; *Jewelry USA,* American Craft Museum, NYC, 1984–86; *Pattern: An Exhibition of the Decorated Surface,* American Craft Museum, NYC, 1982; *Young Americans: Metal,* Museum of Contemporary Crafts, NYC, 1980; *Designer Craftsman,* Museum of Art, El Paso, TX, 1977; *The Metalsmith,* Phoenix Art Museum, AZ, 1977

Collections: Evansville Art Museum, IN; U. of Texas, El Paso

Related Professional Experience: faculty, U. of Texas, El Paso, 1976–present

Jack Thompson (a.k.a. Jugo de Vegetales)
Chalfont, Pennsylvania

Born: Los Angeles, California, 1946

Education: B.A., California State U., Northridge, CA, 1970; M.F.A., Tyler School of Art, Temple U., Philadelphia, PA, 1973

Awards/Honors: PA Council on the Arts Fellowship, 1981, 1983

Exhibitions: *The Male Animal,* Delaware Art Museum, Wilmington, 1985; *Contemporary Artifacts,* Museum of American Jewish History, Philadelphia, PA, 1983; *Contemporary Soup Tureens,* Campbell Museum, Camden, NJ, 1983; *Feast Your Eyes,* Philadelphia Museum of Art, PA, 1982; *The Animal Image: Contemporary Objects and the Beast,* Renwick Gallery, Smithsonian Institution, Washington, DC, 1981; *Contemporary Ceramics: A Response to Wedgwood,* Museum of Philadelphia Civic Center, PA, 1980; *Ceramic Conjunction,* Long Beach Museum of Art, CA, 1977

Linda Threadgill
East Troy, Wisconsin

Born: Corpus Christi, Texas, 1947

Education: B.F.A., U. of Georgia, Athens, 1970; M.F.A., Tyler School of Art, Temple U., Philadelphia, PA, 1978

Awards/Honors: NEA Fellowship, 1984; FL Fine Arts Council Fellowship, 1979

Exhibitions: *Jewelry USA,* American Craft Museum, NYC, and tour, 1984–86; solo exhibition, Wustum Museum of Fine Arts, Racine, WI, 1984; *Wisconsin Impressions,* Milwaukee Museum of Art, WI, 1984, 1982; *Fabergé and Contemporary Metalwork,* Huntsville Museum of Art, AL, 1976; *Precious Metals—The American Tradition in Gold and Silver,* Lowe Museum of Art, Miami, FL, 1976; solo exhibition, Pensacola Museum of Art, FL, 1976

Collections: American Craft Council, NYC; Northeast WI Arts Council, Green Bay

Related Professional Experience: faculty, U. of Wisconsin, Whitewater, 1979–present

David Tisdale
New York, New York

Born: San Diego, California, 1956

Education: B.S., U. of California, Davis, 1978; M.A., San Diego State U., CA, 1981

Exhibitions: *Contemporary Arts: An Expanding View,* Monmouth Museum of Art, Lincroft, NJ, 1986; *American Jewelry Now,* American Craft Museum USIA Asian tour, 1985; *Contemporary Metals USA,* Downey Museum of Art, CA, 1985; *Jewelry USA,* American Craft Museum, NYC, and tour, 1984–86; *Modern Jewelry: 1964–1984,* Montreal Museum of Decorative Arts, Canada, and tour, 1984–87; *Art to Wear: New Handmade Clothing,* American Craft Museum, NYC, and tour, 1983–84; *The Belt Show,* Craft and Folk Art Museum, Los Angeles, CA, 1982; *Good As Gold: Alternative Materials in American Jewelry,* SITES tour, 1981–84

Collection: Museum of Applied Arts, Trondheim, Norway

Related Professional Experience: faculty, Parsons School of Design/New School, NYC, 1982–present; New York U., NYC, 1984–present; artist-in-residence, Artpark, Lewiston, NY, 1985

Karla Trinkley
Boyertown, Pennsylvania

Born: Yardley, Pennsylvania, 1956

Education: B.F.A., Tyler School of Art, Temple U., Philadelphia, PA, 1979; M.F.A., Rhode Island School of Design, Providence, 1981

Award/Honor: PA Council on the Arts Fellowship, 1984

Exhibitions: *World Glass Now,* Hokkaido Museum of Modern Art, Sapporo, Japan, 1985; *International Directions in Glass Art,* Art Gallery of Western Australia, Perth, and tour, 1982–83; *Contemporary Glass: Australia, Canada, U.S.A. and Japan,* National Museum of Modern Art, Kyoto and Tokyo, Japan, 1981; *Glass Routes,* DeCordova Museum, Lincoln, MA, 1981; *New Glass: A Worldwide Survey,* Corning Museum of Glass, NY, 1979

Collections: Corning Museum of Glass, NY; Chase Manhattan Bank, NYC; Philadelphia Museum of Art, PA; Victoria Museum of Art, Australia

Bob Trotman
Casar, North Carolina

Born: Winston-Salem, North Carolina, 1947

Education: B.A., Washington and Lee U., Lexington, VA, 1969

Awards/Honors: NEA Fellowship, 1984; NC Artists' Fellowship, 1984

Exhibitions: *Portraits of the South—North Carolina,* Palazzo Venezia, Rome, Italy, 1984; *American Crafts in Iceland,* National Art Museum, Reykjavik, Iceland, 1983; *Pattern: An Exhibition of the Decorated Surface,* American Craft Museum, NYC, 1982; two-person exhibition, Greenville Museum of Art, SC, 1982

Collections: Mint Museum, Charlotte, NC; R. J. Reynolds Industries, Winston-Salem, NC; Vice-President's Residence, Washington, DC

Lynn Turner
Berkeley, California

Born: Leavenworth, Kansas, 1943

Education: B.A., Whitman College, Walla Walla, WA, 1965; M.F.A., Mills College, Oakland, CA, 1970

Award/Honor: NEA grant, 1980

Exhibitions: *Design in the Service of Tea,* Cooper-Hewitt Museum, NYC, 1984; *Pacific Currents,* San Jose Museum of Art, CA, 1982; *Westwood Clay National,* Downey Museum of Art, CA, 1981; *American Porcelain: New Expressions in an Ancient Art,* Renwick Gallery, Smithsonian Institution, Washington, DC, and SITES tour, 1980–84; *For the Tabletop,* American Craft Museum, NYC, 1980; *California Ceramics and Glass,* Oakland Museum, CA, 1974

Collection: National Collection of Fine Arts, Smithsonian Institution, Washington, DC

Robert Turner
Alfred, New York

Born: Port Washington, New York, 1913

Education: B.A., Swarthmore College, PA, 1936; Pennsylvania Academy of the Fine Arts, Philadelphia, 1936–41; M.F.A., New York State College of Ceramics at Alfred U., NY, 1949

Awards/Honors: Fellow, American Craft Council, 1977; Honorary Member, National Council on Education for the Ceramic Arts, 1978

Exhibitions: *Contemporary Arts: An Expanding View,* Monmouth Museum of Art, Lincroft, NJ, 1986; *International Ceramics,* Taipei Fine Arts Museum, Taiwan, 1985; *Robert Turner: A Potter's Retrospective,* Milwaukee Art Museum, WI, and tour, 1985; *Directions in Contemporary Ceramics,* Museum of Fine Arts, Boston, MA, 1984; *Echoes: Historical Reference in Contemporary Ceramics,* Nelson-Atkins Museum of Art, Kansas City, MO, 1983; *American Porcelain: New Expressions in an Ancient Art,* Renwick Gallery, Smithsonian Institution, Washington, DC and SITES tour, 1980–84; *A Century of Ceramics in the United States: 1878–1978,* Everson Museum of Art, Syracuse, NY, and tour, 1979; *Objects: USA,* Johnson Collection of Contemporary Crafts, national and international tour, 1969–72

Publications: *A World of Physics and Feeling,* monograph to accompany exhibition, Milwaukee Art Museum, WI, 1985

Collections: American Craft Museum, NYC; Everson Museum of Art, Syracuse, NY; Museum of Fine Arts, Boston, MA; Nelson-Atkins Museum of Art, Kansas City, MO; Philadelphia Museum of Art, PA; St. Louis Art Museum, MO; Smithsonian Institution, DC; National Museum of Korea, Seoul

Related Professional Experience: faculty, New York State College of Ceramics at Alfred U., NY, 1958–79

William Underhill
Alfred, New York

Born: Berkeley, California, 1933

Education: B.A., M.A., U. of California, Berkeley, 1960, 1961

Award/Honor: Tiffany grant, 1964

Exhibitions: *Contemporary Arts: An Expanding View,* Monmouth Museum of Art, Lincroft, NJ, 1986; *Selections from the Permanent Collection,* Museum of Contemporary Crafts, NYC, 1983; *American Craftsmen,* USIA tour, 1972; *Objects: USA,* Johnson Collection of Contemporary Crafts, national and international tour, 1969–72; group exhibition, Albright-Knox Art Gallery, Buffalo, NY, 1965; *Creative Casting,* Museum of Contemporary Crafts, NYC, 1963; *Young Americans 1962,* Museum of Contemporary Crafts, NYC, 1962; group exhibition, Oakland Museum, CA, 1961

Collections: American Craft Museum, NYC; City of San Francisco, CA; Oakland Museum, CA

Related Professional Experience: faculty, New York State College of Ceramics at Alfred U., NY, 1969–present

Peter VandenBerge
Sacramento, California

Born: The Hague, Netherlands, 1935

Education: B.A., California State U., Sacramento, 1959; M.A., U. of California, Davis, 1963

Award/Honor: NEA Fellowship, 1981

Exhibitions: *Northern California Art of the 60s,* De Saisset Museum, Santa Clara, CA, 1982; *The Clay Figure,* Museum of Contemporary Crafts, NYC, 1981; *A Century of Ceramics in the United States: 1878–1978,* Everson Museum of Art, Syracuse, NY, and tour, 1979; *Northern California Clay Routes: Sculpture Now,* San Francisco Museum of Modern Art, CA, 1979; *Clay,* Whitney Museum of American Art, NYC, 1974; *International Ceramics,* Victoria and Albert Museum, London, England, 1972; *Objects: USA,* Johnson Collection of Contemporary Crafts, national and international tour, 1969–72

Related Professional Experience: faculty, California State U., Sacramento, 1973–present

Peter Voulkos
Berkeley, California

Born: Bozeman, Montana, 1924

Education: B.S., Montana State College, Bozeman, 1950; M.F.A., California College of Arts and Crafts, Oakland, CA, 1952

Awards/Honors: Ford Foundation grant, 1959; NEA Fellowship, 1976; honorary Ph.D., Montana State U., Bozeman, 1968; California College of Arts and Crafts, 1972; Otis Art Institute of Parsons School of Design, Los Angeles, CA, 1980; San Francisco Art Institute, CA, 1982; Guggenheim Fellowship, 1984

Exhibitions: *California Crafts XIV: Living Treasures of California,* Crocker Art Museum, Sacramento, CA, 1985; *American Sculpture: Three Decades,* Seattle Art Museum, WA, 1984; *Ceramic Sculpture: Six Artists,* Whitney Museum of American Art, NYC, and San Francisco Museum of Modern Art, CA, 1981; *Peter Voulkos: A Retrospective,* San Francisco Museum of Modern Art, CA, and tour 1978-79; *Objects: USA,* Johnson Collection of Contemporary Crafts, national and international tour, 1969-72; solo exhibition, Museum of Modern Art, NYC, 1960; solo exhibition, Pasadena Art Museum, CA, 1959

Publications: monograph to accompany exhibition, San Francisco Museum of Modern Art, CA, 1978; *Peter Voulkos: A Dialogue with Clay,* by Rose Slivka, New York Graphic Society, Boston, MA, 1978

Collections: American Craft Museum, NYC; Everson Museum of Art, Syracuse, NY; Museum of Modern Art, NYC; Oakland Museum, CA; Pasadena Art Museum, CA; San Francisco Museum of Modern Art, CA; Smithsonian Institution, Washington, DC

Related Professional Experience: faculty, Otis Art Institute, Los Angeles, 1954-58; U. of California, Berkeley, 1959-85

F. L. Wall
Arlington, Virginia

Born: Dover, Delaware, 1947

Education: B.A., U. of Delaware, Newark, 1970; Corcoran School of Art, Washington, DC, 1980–81

Exhibition: *The Art of Woodturning,* American Craft Museum, NYC, 1983

Related Professional Experience: furniture maker/designer, Arlington, VA, 1973–present; faculty, Corcoran School of Art, Washington, DC, 1981–85

Patti Warashina
Seattle, Washington

Born: Spokane, Washington, 1940

Education: B.F.A, M.F.A., U. of Washington, Seattle, 1962, 1964

Awards/Honors: Seattle Arts Commission award, 1985; NEA Fellowship, 1975

Exhibitions: solo exhibition, Tucson Art Museum, AZ, 1982; *The Animal Image: Contemporary Objects and the Beast,* Renwick Gallery, Smithsonian Institution, Washington, DC, 1981; *The Clay Figure,* Museum of Contemporary Ceramics, NYC, 1981; *Contemporary Ceramics: A Response to Wedgwood,* Museum of Philadelphia Civic Center, PA, 1980; *Clay,* Whitney Museum of American Art, NYC, 1974; *International Ceramics,* Victoria and Albert Museum, London, England, 1972; *Clayworks: 20 Americans,* Museum of Contemporary Crafts, NYC, 1971; *Contemporary Ceramic Art: Canada, U.S.A., Mexico, Japan,* National Museum of Modern Art, Kyoto and Tokyo, Japan, 1971; *Objects: USA,* Johnson Collection of Contemporary Crafts, national and international tour, 1969–72

Collections: Detroit Institute of Arts, MI; Everson Museum of Art, Syracuse, NY; Nelson-Atkins Museum of Art, Kansas City, MO; Washington State Arts Collection, Seattle

Related Professional Experience: faculty, U. of Washington, Seattle, 1970–present

Steven I. Weinberg
Providence, Rhode Island

Born: Brooklyn, New York, 1954

Education: B.F.A., New York State College of Ceramics at Alfred U., NY, 1976; M.F.A., Rhode Island School of Design, Providence, 1979

Awards/Honors: NEA Fellowship, 1980, 1984

Exhibitions: *World Glass Now,* Hokkaido Museum of Modern Art, Sapporo, Japan, 1985, 1982; *Americans in Glass,* Leigh Yawkey Woodson Art Museum, Wausau, WI, 1984, 1981, 1978; *American Glass Art: Evolution and Revolution,* Morris Museum of Arts and Sciences, Morristown, NJ, 1982; *Contemporary Glass: Australia, Canada, U.S.A. and Japan,* National Museum of Modern Art, Kyoto and Tokyo, Japan, 1981; *Glass Routes,* DeCordova Museum, Lincoln, MA, 1981; *New Glass: A Worldwide Survey,* Corning Museum of Glass, NY, 1979; *Young Americans: Clay/Glass,* Museum of Contemporary Crafts, NYC, 1978

Collections: Corning Museum of Glass, NY; Leigh Yawkey Woodson Art Museum, Wausau, WI; Metropolitan Museum of Art, NYC; Smithsonian Institution, Washington, DC; Hokkaido Museum of Modern Art, Sapporo, Japan; Museum of Art, Dusseldorf, W. Germany; National Museum of Modern Art, Kyoto, Japan

Howard Werner
Mount Tremper, New York

Born: Deal, New Jersey, 1951

Education: B.F.A., Rochester Institute of Technology, NY, 1976

Exhibitions: *New Handmade Furniture: American Furniture Makers Working in Hardwood,* Museum of Contemporary Crafts, NYC, 1979; *Young Americans: Fiber/Wood/Plastic/Leather,* Museum of Contemporary Crafts, NYC, 1977

Collection: Rochester Institute of Technology, NY

Related Professional Experience: artist-in-residence, Artpark, Lewiston, NY, 1975, 1976; Peters Valley, Layton, NJ, 1977

Katherine Westphal
Berkeley, California

Born: Los Angeles, California, 1919

Education: B.A., M.A., U. of California, Berkeley, 1941, 1943

Awards/Honors: NEA grant, 1977; Fellow, American Craft Council, 1979

Exhibitions: *Art to Wear,* American Craft Museum USIA Asian tour, 1984–85; *Art to Wear: New Handmade Clothing,* American Craft Museum, NYC, and tour, 1983–84; *Paper to Wear,* San Francisco Museum of Craft and Folk Art, CA, 1983; *Good As Gold: Alternative Materials in American Jewelry,* SITES tour, 1981–84; *New Basketwork,* Museum of Decorative Arts, Lausanne, Switzerland, 1981; *Art for Use,* Olympic Winter Games, Lake Placid, NY, and American Craft Museum, NYC, 1980; *Objects: USA,* Johnson Collection of Contemporary Crafts, national and international tour, 1969–72; solo exhibition, Museum of Contemporary Crafts, NYC, 1968

Collections: American Craft Museum, NYC; Renwick Gallery, Smithsonian Institution, Washington, DC; Museum of Applied Arts, Trondheim, Norway

Related Professional Experience: faculty, U. of California, Davis, 1966–79; professor emeritus, 1979–present

Dick Wickman
Madison, Wisconsin

Born: Ashland, Wisconsin, 1947

Education: B.F.A., Layton School of Art, Milwaukee, WI, 1969

Exhibitions: *Wisconsin Wood,* Wustum Museum, Racine, WI, 1983; *The Decorative Arts,* Madison Art Center, WI, 1982

Collection: Coca-Cola, Atlanta, GA

Related Professional Experience: artist-in-residence, Pulpit Rock Artists' Community, Woodstock, CT, 1969–73

Anne Wilson
Chicago, Illinois

Born: Detroit, Michigan, 1949

Education: B.F.A., Cranbrook Academy of Art, Bloomfield Hills, MI, 1972; M.F.A., California College of Arts and Crafts, Oakland, 1976

Awards/Honors: NEA grant, 1978; NEA Fellowship, 1982; IL Arts Council grant, 1983, 1984

Exhibitions: *Fiber R/Evolution,* University Art Museum, U. of Wisconsin, Milwaukee, 1986; *Collection Artists Select,* State of Illinois Center Gallery, Chicago, 1985; *Vivid Form: New Inventions,* Kemper Gallery, Kansas City Art Institute, MO, 1985

Collections: Art Institute of Chicago, IL; Illinois Collection, State of Illinois Center, Chicago; Smith, Hinchman, and Grylls architects, Detroit, MI

Related Professional Experience: faculty, School of the Art Institute of Chicago, IL, 1979-present

Paula Colton Winokur
Horsham, Pennsylvania

Born: Philadelphia, Pennsylvania, 1935

Education: B.F.A., B.S., Tyler School of Art, Temple U., Philadelphia, PA, 1958

Awards/Honors: NEA Fellowship, 1976; Fellow, National Council on Education for the Ceramic Arts, 1983; PA Council for the Arts Fellowship, 1986

Exhibitions: *Contemporary Arts: An Expanding View,* Monmouth Museum of Art, Lincroft, NJ, 1986; *The Creative Spirit: A Celebration of Contemporary Craft,* Maier Museum of Art, Lynchburg, VA, 1985; *Soup Soup Beautiful Soup,* Campbell Museum, Camden, NJ, 1983; *American Porcelain: New Expressions in an Ancient Art,* Renwick Gallery, Smithsonian Institution, Washington, DC, and SITES tour, 1980–84; *Homage to Josiah Wedgwood,* Museum of Philadelphia Civic Center, PA, and tour, 1980–82; *Philadelphia: 300 Years of American Art,* Philadelphia Museum of Art, PA, 1976; *Baroque '74,* Museum of Contemporary Crafts, NYC, 1974; *Young Americans,* Museum of Contemporary Crafts, NYC, 1962, 1958

Collections: Delaware Art Museum, Wilmington; Philadelphia Museum of Art, PA; Utah Museum of Art, Salt Lake City; Witte Museum, San Antonio, TX

Related Professional Experience: faculty, Beaver College, Glenside, PA, 1973–present

J. Fred Woell
Deer Isle, Maine

Born: Evergreen Park, Illinois, 1934

Education: B.A., B.F.A., U. of Illinois, Champaign-Urbana, 1956, 1960; M.S., M.F.A., U. of Wisconsin, Madison, 1961, 1962; M.F.A., Cranbrook Academy of Art, Bloomfield Hills, MI, 1969

Awards/Honors: NEA Fellowship, 1976; NEA grant 1976

Exhibitions: *Good As Gold: Alternative Materials in American Jewelry,* SITES tour, 1981–84; *Viewpoint '80: Art in Craft Media,* Museum of Texas Tech U., Lubbock, TX, 1980; *Goldsmiths,* Phoenix Art Museum, AZ, 1977; *Jewelry '77—Tendencies,* Jewelry Museum, Pforzheim, W. Germany, 1977; *American Metalsmiths,* DeCordova Museum, Lincoln, MA, 1974; *Objects: USA,* Johnson Collection of Contemporary Crafts, national and international tour, 1969–72; solo exhibition, Museum of Contemporary Crafts, NYC, 1967; *Young Americans 1962,* Museum of Contemporary Crafts, NYC, 1962

Related Professional Experience: faculty, Program in Artisanry, Boston U., MA, and Swain School of Design, New Bedford, MA, 1976–present

Beatrice Wood
Ojai, California

Born: San Francisco, California, 1893

Education: U. of Southern California, Los Angeles, 1938; studies with Gertrud and Otto Natzler, 1940

Exhibitions: *American Potters Today,* Victoria and Albert Museum, London, England, 1986; *California Crafts XIV: Living Treasures of California,* Crocker Art Museum, Sacramento, CA, 1985; *The Vessel as Metaphor,* Los Angeles County Museum of Art, CA, 1985; *Beatrice Wood Retrospective,* California State U., Fullerton, CA, 1983; *The Spirit of Dada 1915–1925,* Museum of Contemporary Art, Caracas, Venezuela, 1980; *A Century of Ceramics in the United States: 1878–1978,* Everson Museum of Art, Syracuse, NY, and tour, 1979; *Beatrice Wood: Ceramics and Drawings,* Everson Museum of Art, Syracuse, NY, 1978; *Life with Dada: Beatrice Wood Drawings,* Philadelphia Museum of Art, PA, 1978; *Avant-Garde: Painting and Sculpture in America 1910–1925,* Delaware Art Museum, Wilmington, 1975; *Beatrice Wood: A Retrospective,* Phoenix Art Museum and Tucson Art Center, AZ, 1973; *Beatrice Wood,* California Palace of the Legion of Honor, San Francisco, and Santa Barbara Museum of Art, CA, 1964–65; *Ceramics: Beatrice Wood,* Pasadena Art Museum, CA, 1959; *Contemporary American Industrial Art,* Metropolitan Museum of Art, NYC, 1940

Publications: *Beatrice Wood: A Retrospective,* monograph to accompany exhibition, Phoenix Museum of Art, AZ, 1973; *Beatrice Wood Retrospective,* monograph to accompany exhibition, California State U., Fullerton, 1983; *I Shock Myself,* autobiography, Dillingham Press, Ojai, CA, 1985

Collections: American Craft Museum, NYC; Everson Museum of Art, Syracuse, NY; Los Angeles County Museum of Art, CA; Metropolitan Museum of Art, NYC; Museum of Modern Art, NYC; Philadelphia Museum of Art, PA; Victoria and Albert Museum, London, England

Betty Woodman
New York, New York

Born: Norwalk, Connecticut, 1930

Education: New York State College of Ceramics at Alfred U., NY, 1948–50

Award/Honor: Fulbright Hayes scholarship, 1966; NEA Fellowship, 1980

Exhibitions: *Architectural Ceramics: Eight Concepts,* American Craft Museum, NYC, and Washington U., St. Louis, MO, 1985; *High Styles: Twentieth-Century American Design,* Whitney Museum of American Art, NYC, 1985; solo exhibition, Aspen Museum, CO, 1984; *Ornamentalism: The New Decorativeness in Architecture and Design,* Hudson River Museum, Yonkers, NY, 1983; *American Porcelain: New Expressions in an Ancient Art,* Renwick Gallery, Smithsonian Institution, Washington, DC, and SITES tour, 1980–84; *For the Tabletop,* American Craft Museum, NYC, 1980; *A Century of Ceramics in the United States: 1878–1978,* Everson Museum of Art, Syracuse, NY, and tour, 1979

Collections: Museum of Fine Arts, Boston, MA; Cleveland Museum of Art, OH; Denver Art Museum, CO; Metropolitan Museum of Art, NYC; Museum of Art, Carnegie Institute, Pittsburgh, PA; Philadelphia Museum of Art, PA; St. Louis Art Museum, MO; Museum of Contemporary Art, Hertogenbosch, Netherlands; Victoria and Albert Museum, London, England

Related Professional Experience: faculty, U. of Colorado, Boulder, 1976–present

Fumio Yoshimura
New York, New York

Born: Kamakura, Japan, 1926

Education: M.F.A., Tokyo U. of Art, Japan, 1949

Exhibitions: *Contemporary American Wood Sculpture,* Crocker Art Museum, Sacramento, CA, 1984; solo exhibition, Mitchell Museum, Mt. Vernon, IL, 1984; *Materials and Illusion/Unlikely Materials,* Taft Museum, Cincinnati, OH, 1983; *Wood and Fiber,* Columbia Museum of Art, SC, 1982; *Contemporary American Realism Since 1960,* Pennsylvania Academy of the Fine Arts, Philadelphia and international tour, 1981–83; *Katachi—Form and Spirit in Japanese Art,* Albuquerque Museum of Art, History and Science, NM, 1980; *The Object as Poet,* Renwick Gallery, Smithsonian Institution, Washington, DC, and tour, 1976; *Tokyo Biennial,* Tokyo Museum of Art, Japan, 1974; solo exhibition, Pennsylvania Academy of the Fine Arts, Philadelphia, PA, 1970; *Made with Paper,* Museum of Contemporary Crafts, NYC, 1967

Collections: Albuquerque Museum of Art, NM; Delaware Art Museum, Wilmington; Mississippi Museum of Art, Jackson; Philadelphia Museum of Art, PA; Taft Museum, Cincinnati, OH

Related Professional Experience: faculty, Dartmouth College, Hanover, NH, 1981–present

Ann Young
Phoenix, Arizona

Born: Bryn Mawr, Pennsylvania, 1949

Education: B.F.A., Virginia Commonwealth U., Richmond, 1976; M.F.A., Rhode Island School of Design, Providence, 1978

Award/Honor: AZ Commission on the Arts Artist Fellowship, 1982

Exhibitions: *New Masks for Modern Living,* Phoenix Art Museum, AZ, 1985; *Jewelry USA,* American Craft Museum, NYC, and tour, 1984–86; *For the Tabletop,* American Craft Museum, NYC, 1980; *Young Americans: Metal,* Museum of Contemporary Crafts, NYC, 1980; solo exhibition, Virginia Museum of Fine Arts, Richmond, 1977

Claire Zeisler
Chicago, Illinois

Born: Cincinnati, Ohio, 1903

Education: Institute of Design, Illinois Institute of Technology, Chicago, mid-1940s

Award/Honor: honorary Ph.D., Moore College of Art, Philadelphia, PA, 1981

Exhibitions: solo exhibition, Whitney Museum of American Art, NYC, 1985; *The Art Fabric: Mainstream,* American Federation of Arts national tour, 1981–83; *Claire Zeisler—A Retrospective,* Art Institute of Chicago, IL, 1979; *Fiber Works: The Americas and Japan,* National Museum of Modern Art, Kyoto and Tokyo, Japan, 1977; *American Crafts: An Aesthetic View,* Museum of Contemporary Art, Chicago, IL, 1976; *Textile Objects,* Museum of Applied Arts, Berlin, W. Germany, and tour, 1975–76; *International Biennial of Tapestry,* Cantonal Museum of Fine Arts, Lausanne, Switzerland, 1973, 1971; *Objects: USA,* Johnson Collection of Contemporary Crafts, national and international tour, 1969–72; *Woven Forms,* Museum of Contemporary Crafts, NYC, 1963

Publications: monograph to accompany exhibition, Art Institute of Chicago, IL, 1979

Collections: American Craft Museum, NYC; Art Institute of Chicago, IL; Museum of Contemporary Art, Chicago, IL; Museum Bellerive, Zurich, Switzerland; Museum of Decorative Arts, Nantes, France; National Museum of Modern Art, Kyoto, Japan; Stedelijk Museum, Amsterdam, Netherlands

Arnold Zimmerman
New York, New York

Born: Poughkeepsie, New York, 1954

Education: B.F.A., Kansas City Art Institute, Kansas City, MO, 1977; M.F.A., New York State College of Ceramics at Alfred U., NY, 1979

Awards/Honors: CT Commission on the Arts grant, 1981; NEA Fellowship, 1982

Exhibitions: *Contemporary Arts: An Expanding View,* Monmouth Museum of Art, Lincroft, NJ, 1986; *RISD Clay Invitational,* Museum of Rhode Island School of Design, Providence, 1984; *Young Americans: Clay/Glass,* Museum of Contemporary Crafts, NYC, 1978

Collections: Everson Museum of Art, Syracuse, NY; Montreal Museum of Decorative Arts, Canada

Related Professional Experience: artist-in-residence, Archie Bray Foundation, Helena, MT, 1977; Omaha Brickworks, NE, 1983

Edward Zucca
Woodstock, Connecticut

Born: Philadelphia, Pennsylvania, 1946

Education: B.F.A., Philadelphia College of Art, PA, 1968

Awards/Honors: CT Commission on the Arts grant, 1979; NEA Fellowship, 1981; NEA grant, Federal Courthouse restoration, 1984

Exhibitions: *Artiture: Furniture of the 80s,* Pittsburgh Center for the Arts, RA, and tour, 1984–85; *Ornamentalism: The New Decorativeness in Architecture and Design,* Hudson River Museum, Yonkers, NY, 1983; *Woodforms,* Brockton Art Museum, MA, 1981; *New Handmade Furniture: American Furniture Makers Working in Hardwood,* Museum of Contemporary Crafts, NYC, 1979; *Bed and Board,* DeCordova Museum, Lincoln, MA, 1975; *Young Americans,* Museum of Contemporary Crafts, NYC, 1969

Collections: Best Products, Richmond, VA; Brockton Art Museum, MA; Seattle Art Museum, WA; *US News & World Report,* Washington, DC

Mary Ann Toots Zynsky
New York, New York

Born: Boston, Massachusetts, 1951

Education: B.F.A., Rhode Island School of Design, Providence, 1973

Awards/Honors: NY State Council on the Arts grant, 1981; NEA Fellowship, 1982

Exhibitions: *Architecture and Design,* Museum of Modern Art, NYC, 1986; *Contemporary Art Exhibit,* Museum of Art, Rouen, France, 1985; *World Glass Now,* Hokkaido Museum of Modern Art, Sapporo, Japan, 1985; *Pilchuck Glass,* Cheney Cowles Museum, Spokane, WA, 1984; *Sculptural Glass,* Tucson Museum of Art, AZ, 1983

Collections: Corning Museum of Glass, NY; Leigh Yawkey Woodson Art Museum, Wausau, WI; Museum of Modern Art, NYC; National Museum of American History, Smithsonian Institution, Washington, DC; Museum Bellerive, Zurich, Switzerland

BIBLIOGRAPHY

Abstract Expressionist Ceramics. Irvine: University of California Art Gallery, 1966.

Albers, Anni. *On Weaving.* Middletown, CT: Wesleyan University Press, 1965.

American Glass Now. Toledo, OH: Toledo Museum of Art, 1972.

Anderson, Ross, and Barbara Perry. *The Diversions of Keramos: American Clay Sculpture 1925–1950.* Syracuse, NY: Everson Museum of Art, 1983.

Andersen, Timothy J., Eudorah M. Moore, and Robert M. Winter, eds. *California Design 1910.* Pasadena: California Design Publications, 1974.

Arts & Crafts in Detroit 1906–1976: The Movement, the Society, the School. Detroit: Detroit Institute of Arts, 1976.

Bernstein, Mel. "The University Impact on Ceramics: Charles Fergus Binns at Alfred University," *NCECA Journal,* 5 (1984): 38–43.

Bing, Samuel. *Artistic America, Tiffany Glass and Art Nouveau.* Cambridge: MIT Press, 1970.

Boris, Eileen. *Art and Labor: Ruskin, Morris and the Craftsman Ideal in America.* Philadelphia: Temple University Press, 1986.

California Innovations. Fullerton: California State University Art Gallery, 1981.

Clark, Garth. *Ceramic Art: Comment and Review 1882–1977: An Anthology of Writings on Modern Ceramic Art.* New York: E. P. Dutton, 1978.

_____. *A Century of Ceramics in the United States 1878–1978: A Study of Its Development.* New York: E. P. Dutton in association with Everson Museum of Art, 1979.

_____. *American Potters: The Work of Twenty Modern Masters.* New York: Watson-Guptill Publications, 1981.

Clark, Robert Judson, ed. *The Arts and Crafts Movement in America 1876–1916.* Princeton: Princeton University Press, 1972.

Conn, Richard. *Native American Art in the Denver Art Museum.* Denver: Denver Art Museum, 1979.

Constantine, Mildred and Jack Lenor Larsen. *Beyond Craft: The Art Fabric.* New York: Van Nostrand Reinhold Company, 1973.

_____. *The Art Fabric: Mainstream.* New York: Van Nostrand Reinhold Company, 1981.

Darling, Sharon S. *Chicago Ceramics & Glass: An Illustrated History from 1871 to 1933.* Chicago: Chicago Historical Society, 1979.

_____. *Chicago Furniture: Art, Craft & Industry, 1833–1983.* Chicago: Chicago Historical Society in association with W. W. Norton & Company, 1984.

Davies, Karen. *At Home in Manhattan.* New Haven: Yale University Art Gallery, 1983.

Design in America: The Cranbrook Vision 1925–1950. New York: Harry N. Abrams in association with Detroit Institute of Arts and Metropolitan Museum of Art, 1983.

Designer Craftsmen U.S.A. 1953. Brooklyn: Brooklyn Museum, 1953.

Dewhurst, C. Kurt, Betty MacDowell, and Marsha MacDowell. *Artists in Aprons: Folk Art by American Women.* New York: E. P. Dutton in association with Museum of American Folk Art, 1979.

Dorothy Liebes: Retrospective Exhibition. New York: Museum of Contemporary Crafts [American Craft Museum], 1970.

Duberman, Martin. *Black Mountain College: An Exploration in Community.* New York: E. P. Dutton, 1972.

Eaton, Allen H. *Handicrafts of the Southern Highlands.* New York: Russell Sage Foundation, 1937.

_____. *Handicrafts of New England.* New York: Harper & Brothers, 1949.

Emery, Oliva and Tim Andersen. *Craftsman Lifestyle: The Gentle Revolution.* Pasadena: California Design Publications, 1978.

Fairbanks, Jonathan L. and Elizabeth Bidwell Bates. *American Furniture, 1620 to the Present.* New York: Richard Marek Publishers, 1981.

50 Years Bauhaus. London: Royal Academy of Arts, 1968.

The First World Congress of Craftsmen. New York: American Craftsmen's Council, 1965.

Fischer, Hal. "The Art of Peter Voulkos," *Artforum* 17 (November 1978): 41–47.

Graburn, Nelson H. H., ed. *Ethnic and Tourist Arts: Cultural Expressions from the Fourth World.* Berkeley and Los Angeles: University of California Press, 1976.

Grimes, Mary K. *The Impact of Art Deco.* Indianapolis: Indianapolis Museum of Art, 1976.

Hampson, Ferdinand, ed. *Glass: State of the Art 1984.* Lathrup Village, Mich.: Habatat Galleries, 1984.

Harrington, LaMar. *Ceramics in the Pacific Northwest: A History.* Seattle: University of Washington Press, 1979.

Hayden, Dolores. *Seven American Utopias: The Architecture of Communitarian Socialism, 1790–1975*. Cambridge: MIT Press, 1981.

High Styles: Twentieth-Century American Design. New York: Summit Books in association with Whitney Museum of American Art, 1985.

Horn, Richard. *Fifties Style: Then and Now.* New York: Beech Tree Books, 1985.

Lambourne, Lionel. *Utopian Craftsmen: The Arts and Crafts Movement from the Cotswolds to Chicago*. New York: Van Nostrand Reinhold Company, 1980.

Littleton, Harvey. *Glassblowing: A Search for Form.* New York: Van Nostrand Reinhold Company, 1971.

Lucie-Smith, Edward. *The Story of Craft: The Craftsman's Role in Society.* Ithaca, NY: Cornell University Press, 1981.

_____. *A History of Industrial Design,* New York: Van Nostrand Reinhold Company, 1983.

Ludwig, Coy L. *The Arts & Crafts Movement in New York State 1890s–1920s*. Hamilton: Gallery Association of New York State, 1983.

Marshall, Richard and Suzanne Foley. *Ceramic Sculpture: Six Artists*. Seattle: University of Washington Press in association with Whitney Museum of American Art, 1981.

New Glass: A Worldwide Survey. Corning, NY: Corning Museum of Glass, 1979.

Nordness, Lee. *Objects: USA*. New York: Viking Press, 1970.

Pierce, H. Winthrop. *History of the School of the Museum of Fine Arts, Boston, 1876–1930*. Boston: T. O. Metcalf, 1930.

Pulos, Arthur J. *American Design Ethic: A History of Industrial Design to 1940*. Cambridge: MIT Press, 1983.

Randall, Ted. "The University Impact on Ceramics: A Personal Perspective of the Last Five Decades," *NCECA Journal* 5 (1984): 44–49.

Rich, Jane Kinsley, ed. *A Lasting Spring: Jessie Catherine Kinsley, Daughter of the Oneida Community.* Syracuse, NY: Syracuse University Press, 1983.

Rossbach, Ed. "Fiber in the Forties," *American Craft* 42 (October/November 1982): 15–19.

Schrader, Robert Fay. *The Indian Arts & Crafts Board: An Aspect of New Deal Indian Policy.* Albuquerque: University of New Mexico Press, 1983.

Schweiger, Werner J. *Wiener Werkstaette: Design in Vienna 1903–1932*. London: Thames and Hudson, 1984.

Selz, Peter. *Funk*. Berkeley, University of California Art Museum, 1967.

Slivka, Rose. *Peter Voulkos: A Dialogue in Clay.* Boston: New York Graphic Society, 1978.

Smith, Mary Ann. *Gustav Stickley: The Craftsman.* Syracuse, NY: Syracuse University Press, 1983.

Stone, Michael. *Contemporary American Woodworkers*. Layton, UT: Peregrine Smith, 1986.

Teague, Walter Dorwin. *Design this Day: The Technique of Order in the Machine Age*. New York: Harcourt, Brace and Company, 1940.

"Twenty-Five Years of Craft Horizons," *Craft Horizons* 26 (June 1966): 69–71.

Weidner, Ruth Irwin, comp. *American Ceramics before 1930: A Bibliography.* Westport, CT: Greenwood Press, 1982.

Weimann, Jeanne Madeline. *The Fair Women: The Story of the Woman's Building, World's Columbian Exposition, Chicago 1893*. Chicago: Academy Chicago, 1981.

Wildenhain, Marguerite. *Pottery: Form and Expression*. Palo Alto, CA: Pacific Books, reprint, 1973.

Wingler, Hans M. *The Bauhaus: Weimar, Dessau, Berlin, Chicago*. Cambridge: MIT Press, 1969.

Wixom, Nancy Coe. *Cleveland Institute of Art: The First Hundred Years 1882–1982*. Cleveland: Cleveland Institute of Art, 1983.

The Woven and Graphic Art of Anni Albers. Washington, DC: Smithsonian Press, 1985.

SUGGESTED FOR FURTHER READING

Compiled by Joanne Polster

GENERAL

The Craftsman in America. Washington, DC: National Geographic Society, 1975.

Diamonstein, Barbaralee. *Handmade in America: Conversations with Fourteen Craftsmasters.* New York: Harry N. Abrams, 1983.

Garner, Philippe, ed. *The Encyclopedia of the Decorative Arts 1880–1940*. New York: Van Nostrand Reinhold Company, 1978.

Garner, Philippe. *Contemporary Decorative Arts from 1940 to the Present*. New York: Facts on File, 1980.

Gombrich, E. H. *The Sense of Order: A Study in the Psychology of Decorative Art*. Ithaca, NY: Cornell University Press, 1979.

Hall, Julie. *Tradition and Change: The New American Craftsman*. New York: E. P. Dutton, 1977.

Hedges, Elaine and Ingrid Wendt. *In Her Own Image: Women Working in the Arts*. New York: Feminist Press/McGraw-Hill Book Company, 1980.

In Praise of Hands: Contemporary Crafts of the World. Greenwich, CT.: New York Graphic Society in association with World Crafts Council, 1974.

Lucie-Smith, Edward. *The World of the Makers: Today's Craftsmen and Craftswomen.* New York: Paddington Press, 1975.

Miller, Lynn F. and Sally S. Swenson. *Lives and Works: Talks with Women Artists.* Metuchen, N.J.: Scarecrow Press, 1981.

Munroe, Eleanor. *Originals: American Women Artists.* New York: Simon & Schuster, 1979.

Pearson, Katherine. *American Crafts.* New York: Stewart Tabori & Chang, 1982.

Pye, David. *The Nature of Design.* London: Studio Vista/Van Nostrand Reinhold Company, 1964.

_____. *The Nature and Art of Workmanship.* Cambridge: Oxford University Press, 1968.

Selz, Peter. *Art in Our Times: A Pictorial History 1890–1980.* New York: Harry N. Abrams, 1981.

Slivka, Rose, ed. *The Crafts of the Modern World.* New York: Horizon Press in collaboration with World Crafts Council, 1968.

Yanagi, Soetsu. *The Unknown Craftsman: A Japanese Insight into Beauty.* New York: Kodansha International, 1972.

BOOKBINDING

Smith, Philip. *New Directions in Bookbinding.* New York: Van Nostrand Reinhold Company, 1974.

CLAY

Axel, Jan and Karen McCready. *Porcelain: Traditions and New Visions.* New York: Watson-Guptill Publications, 1981.

Birks, Tony. *Art of the Modern Potter.* New York: Van Nostrand Reinhold Company, 1976.

_____. *Hans Coper.* London: William Collins Sons & Company, 1983.

Cameron, Elizabeth and Philippa Lewis. *Potters on Pottery.* New York: St. Martin's Press, 1976.

Cooper, Emmanuel. *A History of World Pottery.* New York: Larousse & Company, 1981.

Herman, Lloyd E. *American Porcelain: New Expressions in an Ancient Art.* Forest Grove, OR: Timber Press, 1980.

Houston, John, ed. *Lucie Rie.* London: Crafts Council, 1981.

Lane, Peter. *Studio Porcelain.* Radnor, PA: Chilton Book Company, 1980.

Leach, Bernard. *The Potter's Challenge.* New York: E. P. Dutton, 1975.

Nordness, Lee. *Jack Earl: The Genesis and Triumphant Survival of an Underground Ohio Artist.* Racine, WI: Perimeter Press, 1985.

Peterson, Susan. *Shoji Hamada: His Way and Work.* New York: Kodansha International, 1974.

_____. *The Living Tradition of Maria Martinez.* New York: Kodansha International, 1977.

_____. *Lucy M. Lewis, American Indian Potter.* New York: Kodansha International, 1984.

Préaud, Tamara and Serge Gauthier. *Ceramics of the Twentieth Century.* New York: Rizzoli, 1982.

Rawson, Phillip. *Ceramics.* Reprint. Philadelphia: University of Pennsylvania Press, 1984.

Rhodes, Daniel. *Pottery Form.* Radnor, PA: Chilton Book Company, 1976.

Storr-Britz, Hildegard. *Contemporary International Ceramics.* Cologne: DuMont Buchverlag, 1980.

Wechsler, Susan. *Low-Fire Ceramics: A New Direction in American Clay.* New York: Watson-Guptill Publications, 1981.

FIBER

Magdalena Abakanowicz. New York: Abbeville Press in association with Museum of Contemporary Art, Chicago, 1982

Chase, Pattie. *The Contemporary Quilt: New American Quilts and Fabric Art.* New York: E. P. Dutton, 1978.

Fiberarts Design Book. New York: Hastings House, 1980.

Fiberarts Design Book II. Asheville, NC: Lark Communications, 1983.

Kuenzi, André. *La Nouvelle Tapisserie.* Lausanne: Bibliothèque des Arts, 1981.

Larsen, Jack Lenor. *The Dyers' Art: Ikat, Plangi, Batik.* New York: Van Nostrand Reinhold Company, 1976.

Lévi-Strauss, Monique. *Sheila Hicks.* New York: Van Nostrand Reinhold Company, 1976.

The New American Quilt. Asheville, NC: Lark Communications, 1981.

Rossbach, Ed. *Baskets as Textile Art.* New York: Van Nostrand Reinhold Company, 1973.

_____. *New Basketry.* New York: Van Nostrand Reinhold Company, 1976.

Soft Art (in German). Berne: Benteli Verlag, 1980.

Verlet, Pierre et al. *The Book of Tapestry.* Paris: Vendome Press, 1977. Distributed by Viking Press. Includes a 73-page section on contemporary fiber art.

GLASS

Beard, Geoffrey. *International Modern Glass.* London: Barrie & Jenkins, 1976.

Grover, Ray & Lee. *Contemporary Art Glass.* New York: Crown Publishers, 1975.

Ricke, Helmut. *New Glass in Germany.* Düsseldorf: Kunst & Handwerk/Verlagsanstalt Handwerk, 1983.

Stennet-Willson, Ronald. *Modern Glass.* New York: Van Nostrand Reinhold Company, 1976.

STAINED GLASS

Lee, Lawrence. *The Appreciation of the Arts: Stained Glass.* London: Oxford University Press, 1977.

Lee, Lawrence et al. *Stained Glass.* New York: Crown Publishers, 1976.

Ludwig Schaffrath: Stained Glass and Mosaic. Krefeld: Scherpe Verlag, n.d. Distributed by C&R Loo, Emeryville, CA.

Sowers, Robert. *Language of Stained Glass.* Forest Grove, OR: Timber Press, 1981.

METAL

Cartlidge, Barbara. *Twentieth-Century Jewelry.* New York: Harry N. Abrams, 1985.

Dormer, Peter and Ralph Turner. *The New Jewelry, Trends and Traditions.* London: Thames & Hudson, 1985.

Jewelry and Metal Objects from the Society of North American Goldsmiths. Pforzheim: Schmuckmuseum, 1979.

Schollmayer, Karl. *Neuer Schmuck.* Tübingen: Verlag Ernst Wasmuth, 1969.

Ward, Anne et al. *Rings through the Ages.* New York: Rizzoli, 1981.

WOOD

Domergue, Denise. *Artists Design Furniture.* New York: Harry N. Abrams, n.d.

Garner, Philippe. *Twentieth-Century Furniture.* New York: Van Nostrand Reinhold Company, 1980.

Jacobson, Edward. *The Art of Turned-Wood Bowls: A Gallery of Contemporary Masters—and More.* New York: E. P. Dutton, 1985.

Jones, Michael Owen. *The Handmade Object and Its Maker.* Berkeley and Los Angeles: University of California Press, 1975.

Krenov, James. *A Cabinetmaker's Notebook.* New York: Van Nostrand Reinhold Company, 1976.

_____. *Worker in Wood.* New York: Van Nostrand Reinhold Company, 1981.

Maloof, Sam. *Sam Maloof Woodworker.* New York: Kodansha International, 1983.

Nakashima, George. *The Soul of a Tree: A Woodworker's Reflections.* New York: Kodansha International, 1981.

CURRENT PERIODICALS

Explanation of entries: Date given is the founding date of the periodical.
Ind = Indexed in
AI = *Art Index*
ArtBib = *Art Bibliographies Modern*
RG = *Readers' Guide to Periodical Literature*
RILA = *International Repertory of the Literature of Art*

GENERAL

American Craft. American Craft Council, 401 Park Avenue South, New York, NY 10016. 1941, bimonthly. Ind: AI, ArtBib, RG.

American Indian Art. 7314 East Osborn Drive, Scottsdale, AZ 85251. 1975, quarterly. Ind: AI, ArtBib.

Archives of American Art Journal. AA-PG 331, 8th and F Streets NW, Washington, DC 20560. 1960, quarterly. Ind: AI.

Art & Artists. Foundation for the Community of Artists, 280 Broadway, New York, NY 10007. 1971, bimonthly. Ind: AI.

Art in America. Brant Art Publications, 980 Madison Avenue, New York, NY 10021. 1913, eleven issues yearly. Ind: AI, RG, RILA.

Artnews. 5 West 37th Street, New York, NY 10018. Eleven issues yearly. Ind: AI, ArtBib, RG.

Black Art. 137-55 Southgate Street, Jamaica, New York 11413. 1976. Ind: AI, ArtBib.

Clarion. Museum of American Folk Art, 49 West 53rd Street, New York, NY 10019. 1977, three issues yearly. Ind: AI, ArtBib, RILA.

Craft International. World Crafts Foundation, 247 Centre Street, New York, NY 10013. 1980, quarterly. Ind: AI.

Crafts. Crafts Council, 8 Waterloo Place, London SW1Y 4AT, England. 1973, bimonthly. Ind: AI, ArtBib.

Design Quarterly. Walker Art Center, Minneapolils, MN 55403. Available from MIT Press, 28 Carleton Street, Cambridge, MA 02142. 1946, quarterly. Ind: AI, ArtBib.

Industrial Design. 330 West 42nd Street, New York, NY 10036. Bimonthly. Ind: AI.

New Art Examiner. New Art Association, 300 West Grand Street, Chicago, IL 60610. 1973, ten issues yearly. Ind: AI, ArtBib, RILA.

Smithsonian. Smithsonian Associates, 900 Jefferson Drive, Washington, D.C. 20560. 1970, monthly. Ind: RG.

Winterthur Portfolio. Henry Francis DuPont Winterthur Museum, Wilmington, DE 19735. Available from University of Chicago Press, Journals Division, P.O. Box 37005, Chicago, IL 60637. Three issues yearly. Ind: AI.

Woman's Art Journal. Woman's Art, 7008 Sherwood Drive, Knoxville, TN 37919. Biannually. Ind: AI, ArtBib, RILA.

Women Artists News. Midmarch Associates, P.O. Box 3304, Grand Central Station, New York, NY 10163. 1975, quarterly. Ind: AI, ArtBib, RILA.

CLAY

American Ceramics. 15 West 44th Street, New York, NY 10036. 1982, quarterly. Ind: AI.

Ceramics Monthly. Professional Publications, P.O. Box 12448, Columbus, OH 43212. 1953, ten issues yearly. Ind: AI, ArtBib, RILA.

Journal of Ceramic History. City Museum and Art Gallery, Broad Street, Hanley, Stoke-on-Trent, Staffs., England. 1968. Ind: –.

NCECA Journal. National Council on Education for the Ceramic Arts, P.O. Box 1677, Bandon, OR 97411. 1969, annually. Ind: –.

Studio Potter. P.O. Box 65, Goffstown, NH 03045. 1972, biannually. Ind: AI.

FIBER

American Fabrics and Fashions. Doric Publishing Company, 343 Lexington Avenue, New York, NY 10016. 1946, quarterly. Ind: AI.

American Indian Basketry. P.O. Box 66124, Portland, OR 97266. 1979, quarterly. Ind: –.

Fiberarts. Lark Communications, 50 College Street, Asheville, NC 28801. 1976, bimonthly. Ind: AI.

Shuttle Spindle & Dyepot. Handweavers Guild of America, 65 LaSalle Road, West Hartford, CT 06107. 1969, quarterly. Ind: AI.

Surface Design Journal. Surface Design Association, 311 East Washington Street, Fayetteville, TN 37344. 1976, quarterly. Ind: –.

Textile/Art. 3 rue Félix-Faure, 75015 Paris, France. 1976, quarterly. Ind: –.

Textile History. Pasold Research Fund, Becketts House, Edington, Nr Westbury, Wilts, England. 1970, annually. Ind: AI.

Textile Museum Journal. Textile Museum, 2320 S Street NW, Washington, D.C. 20008. 1970, annually. Ind: AI.

GLASS

Glass Art Society Journal. Glass Art Society, P.O. Box 1364, Corning, NY 14830. 1976, annually. Ind: –.

Journal of Glass Studies. Corning Museum of Glass, Corning, NY 14831. 1959, annually. Ind: AI.

Neues Glas/New Glass. Verlagsanstalt Handwerk GmbH, Auf'm Tetelberg 7, Postfach 8120, 4000 Dusseldorf, Fed. Republic of Germany. 1980, quarterly. Ind: AI.

New Work. New York Experimental Glass Workshop, 142 Mulberry Street, New York, NY 10013. 1980, quarterly.

Stained Glass. Stained Glass Association of America, 1125 Wilmington Avenue, St. Louis, MO 63111. 1906, quarterly. Ind: AI.

METAL AND JEWELRY

Anvil's Ring. Artist-Blacksmiths' Association of North America (ABANA), c/o Ruth Cook, P.O. Box 303, Cedarburg, WI 53012. 1973, quarterly. Ind: –.

Metalsmith. Society of North American Goldsmiths (SNAG), 6707 North Santa Monica Boulevard, Milwaukee, WI 53217. 1975, quarterly. Ind: AI.

Ornament. P.O. Box 35029, Los Angeles, CA 90035-0029. 1974, quarterly. Ind: AI.

PAPER AND BOOK ARTS

Fine Print. P.O. Box 3394, San Francisco, CA 94119. 1975, quarterly. Ind: AI.

Guild of Book Workers Journal. Guild of Book Workers, 521 Fifth Avenue, New York, NY 10175. 1962, biannually. Ind. –.

WOOD

Fine Woodworking. Taunton Press, P.O. Box 355, Newton, CT 06470. 1975, bimonthly. Ind: AI.

Furniture History. Furniture History Society, c/o Department of Furniture and Woodwork, Victoria and Albert Museum, London SW 7, England. 1965, annually. Ind: AI, ArtBib.

Photo credits, Craft Today: Historical Roots and Contemporary Perspectives

Windsor side chair
American, circa 1820–1840
Maple, pine, ash
36 x 15⅝"
Courtesy, The Brooklyn Museum, Brooklyn, NY
Dick S. Ramsay Fund
(59.188.3), p. 16

Shaker side chair
American, New England, circa 1880
Beech with woven tape seat and back
33¾ x 18¼ x 21¼"
Courtesy, The Brooklyn Museum, Brooklyn, NY
Anonymous Gift
(66.111.1), p. 17

Star of Bethlehem quilt with 20 stars
American, circa 1840–1850
87 x 91"
Courtesy, The Metropolitan Museum of Art,
  New York, NY
Gift of Mr. and Mrs. Samuel Schwartz, 1973
(1973.64), p. 19

Navajo blanket
American, Germantown type, circa 1880–1890
Courtesy, Southwest Museum, Los Angeles, CA
Photo: 19,809, p. 20

Woven textile
Peruvian, Pre-Inca period: Highlands region,
  Tiahuanaco II Culture
Tapestry woven in colored wools on cotton warp
Fragment, 27½ x 22¾"
Courtesy, The Metropolitan Museum of Art,
  New York, NY
Gift of George D. Pratt, 1930
(30.16.8), p. 21

Textile (detail)
English, 19th century
Designed by William Morris (1834–1896)
Courtesy, The Cooper-Hewitt Museum, The
  Smithsonian Institution's National Museum
  of Design, New York, NY
Gift of Cowtan & Tout, Inc.
(1935-23-26), p. 22

Earthenware pitcher with landscape decoration
American, 1889–1890
Rookwood Pottery, Cincinnati, OH
Decorated by Clara Chipman Newton
6½ x 3¾ x 2⅛"
Courtesy, The Brooklyn Museum, Brooklyn, NY
Gift of J. Ethel Brown
(56.32), p. 23

*Earthenware umbrella stand with stork
  decoration*
American, circa 1890
J.B. Owens Pottery Company, Zanesville, OH
Decorated by Albert Haubrich
22⁵⁄₁₆ x 11¼" diam.
Courtesy, The Metropolitan Museum of Art,
  New York, NY
Gift of Ronald S. Kane, 1969
(69.53), p. 24

Vase (called *The Peacock Vase*)
American, circa 1896
Tiffany and Company, New York, NY
Favrile glass
14⅛" h.
Courtesy, The Metropolitan Museum of Art,
  New York, NY
Gift of H.O. Havemeyer, 1896
(96.17.10), p. 25

George Ohr
Bowls
American, circa 1900
Glazed clay
Left: 4¼" h.; right: 3¾" h.
Courtesy, The Museum of Modern Art,
  New York, NY
Mrs. John D. Rockefeller 3rd Purchase Fund,
  p. 26

Mission rocking chair
American, circa 1910
Stickley Brothers Quaint Furniture Company,
  Grand Rapids, MI
Oak with upholstered seat
31⅞ x 28¼ x 29¼"
Courtesy, The Brooklyn Museum, Brooklyn, NY
Gift of H. Taplitz and E. Cohen
(82.242), p. 28

Lady's desk and chair
French, Paris, 20th century
Designed by Jacques-Emile Ruhlmann
  (1879–1933)
Macassar ebony
Desk: 44¼ x 23½ x 14⅞"
Chair: 31½ x 17½ x 20"
Courtesy, The Metropolitan Museum of Art,
  New York, NY
Purchase, Edward C. Moore, Jr. Gift
(23.174 and 25.231.3), p. 30

Cranbrook Academy of Art Museum,
  1938–1942
Eliel Saarinen, architect
Courtesy, Cranbrook Archives, Bloomfield Hills,
  MI, p. 31

Anni Albers
Tikal
American, 1958
Pictorial weaving of cotton, plain weave, and leno
35½ x 29½"
American Craft Museum, New York, NY
Gift of Johnson Wax Company, 1979
(79.7.1), p. 32

Dorothy Liebes
Automotive upholstery fabric (detail)
American, 1957
Power loomed, cotton, Du Pont nylon, metallic
Designed for Chrysler Corporation, Plymouth
  Fury 1957
Manufactured by Collins & Alkman Corporation
American Craft Museum Archives,
  New York, NY
Photo: Ferdinand Boesch, p. 34

Dorothy Liebes in her New York studio
American Craft Museum Archives, New York,
  NY, p. 34

Peter Voulkos
Throwing series at Teachers College, Columbia
  University, New York, NY, 1956
American Craft Museum Archives, New York, NY
Donated by Don Cyr and Columbia University
Photo: Ryusei Arita, p. 35

Peter Voulkos
Slab ceramic construction
American, 1956
39 x 17 x 11"
American Craft Museum, New York, NY
Gift of Mr. and Mrs. Adam Gostomski, 1962
(62.1), p. 35

Robert Arneson
Typewriter
American, 1966
Glazed clay
6 x 11½ x 12½"
Courtesy, Allan Stone Gallery, New York, NY
Photo: TK Rose, p. 36

Harvey K. Littleton
Cross Vase
American, 1964
Blue/green clear glass from #475 marbles
12 x 8½ x 3½"
Courtesy, The High Museum of Art, Atlanta, GA
Purchased with funds from the Decorative Arts
  Acquisition Trust
(1984.33)
Photo: John Littleton, p. 38

Harvey K. Littleton at work in his studio
American Craft Museum Archives, New York,
  NY, p. 38

Wendell Castle
Ghost Clock
American, 1985
Bleached mahogany
87½ x 24½ x 15"
Courtesy, Alexander F. Milliken, Inc.,
  New York, NY
Photo: Bruce Miller, p. 39

Scott Burton
Pair of Rock Chairs
American, 1980–1981
Gneiss
Left: 49⅜ x 36 x 47"; right: 44 x 46 x 74"
Courtesy, The Museum of Modern Art,
  New York, NY
Acquired through the Philip Johnson, Mrs.
  Joseph Pulitzer, Jr., and Robert Rosenblum
  Funds, p. 40

The following organizations and galleries assisted with this project

Alaska State Council on the Arts, Anchorage, Alaska
Brookfield Craft Center: Gallery, Brookfield, Connecticut
Contemporary Crafts Association, Portland, Oregon
Indiana Artist-Craftsman Inc., Indianapolis, Indiana
Kentucky Art & Craft Foundation, Louisville, Kentucky
King County Arts Commission, Seattle, Washington
Maine Crafts Association, Deer Isle, Maine
New York Experimental Glass Workshop Gallery, New York, New York
Oregon School of Arts and Crafts, Portland, Oregon
Pacific Basin School of Textile Arts, Berkeley, California
Southeastern Center for Contemporary Art, Winston-Salem, North Carolina
Southern Arts Federation, Atlanta, Georgia
Southern Highland Handicraft Guild, Asheville, North Carolina
United States Department of the Interior, Indian Arts and Crafts Board, Washington, DC

The Allrich Gallery, San Francisco, California
Alternative Work Site, The Bemis Project/Artist Colony, Omaha, Nebraska
Jayne H. Baum Gallery, New York, New York
Grace Borgenicht Gallery, New York, New York
Rena Bransten Gallery, San Francisco, California
Braunstein Gallery, San Francisco, California
C D S Gallery, New York, New York
Garth Clark Gallery, New York, New York, and Los Angeles, California
Convergence, New York, New York
Charles Cowles Gallery, New York, New York
Craft Alliance Gallery, Saint Louis, Missouri
Susan Cummins Gallery, Mill Valley, California
Helen Drutt Gallery, Philadelphia, Pennsylvania
The Elements, New York, New York
Exhibit A Inc., Chicago, Illinois
Linda Farris Gallery, Seattle, Washington
Fendrick Gallery, Washington, DC
Foster/White Gallery, Seattle, Washington
Nina Freudenheim Gallery, Buffalo, New York
Allan Frumkin Gallery, New York, New York
Fuller Goldeen Gallery, San Francisco, California
Galerie 99, Bay Harbor Islands, Florida
The Gallery at Workbench, New York, New York
Habatat Galleries, Miami, Florida, and Lathrup Village, Michigan
Hadler Rodriguez Galleries, Portsmouth, Texas, and New York, New York
Hand and the Spirit Crafts Gallery, Scottsville, Arizona
O.K. Harris Works of Art, New York, New York
Heller Gallery, New York, New York
Gallery Fair, Mendocino, California
Gallery Henoch, New York, New York
Nancy Hoffman Gallery, New York, New York
Rhona Hoffman Gallery, Chicago, Illinois
Hokin/Kaufman Gallery, Chicago, Illinois
Holsten Galleries, Stockbridge, Massachusetts
Jordan-Volpe Gallery, New York, New York
Julie: Artisans' Gallery, New York, New York
Robert L. Kidd Associates/Galleries, Birmingham, Michigan
Kurland/Sommers Gallery, Los Angeles, California
Maurine Littleton Gallery, Washington, DC
Marian Locks Gallery, Philadelphia, Pennsylvania
Mariposa Gallery, Albuquerque, New Mexico
Miller/Brown Gallery, San Francisco, California
Alexander F. Milliken, Inc., New York, New York
Modern Master Tapestries, New York, New York
Gallery Naga, Boston, Massachusetts
New York Experimental Glass Workshop, New York, New York
Netsky Gallery, Coconut Grove, Florida
Northwest Gallery of Fine Woodworking, Seattle, Washington
Objects Gallery, Chicago, Illinois
Marilyn Pearl Gallery, New York, New York

Perimeter Gallery, Chicago, Illinois
Theo Portnoy Gallery, New York, New York
Elaine Potter Gallery, San Francisco, California
Pritam & Eames, East Hampton, New York
Max Protech Gallery, New York, New York
Rosanne Raab Associates, Scarsdale, New York
Betsy Rosenfield Gallery, Chicago, Illinois
Sacred Circle Gallery of American Indian Art, Seattle, Washington
William Sawyer Gallery, San Francisco, California
Saxon/Lee Gallery, Los Angeles, California
Esther Saks Gallery, Chicago, Illinois
Snyderman Gallery, Philadelphia, Pennsylvania
Bernice Steinbaum Gallery, New York, New York
Swan Galleries, Philadelphia, Pennsylvania
Traver Sutton Gallery, Seattle, Washington
Jan Turner Gallery, Los Angeles, California
Twining Gallery, New York, New York
B.Z. Wagman Gallery, St. Louis, Missouri
Dorothy Weiss Gallery, San Francisco, California
Willard Gallery, New York, New York
Yaw Gallery, Birmingham, Michigan
Zolla/Lieberman Gallery, Chicago, Illinois

Index of plates, listed by artist

The American Craft Council

The American Craft Council (ACC) is the foremost advocate of the contemporary craft movement in the United States. It seeks to inspire and support craftspeople, to encourage artistic and technical excellence in the crafts, to develop new markets, to provide educational resources for artists and the general public, and to stimulate popular appreciation for finely handcrafted objects encountered in daily life.

The Council was founded in 1943 by Aileen Osborn Webb, a philanthropist and champion of craft. Mrs. Webb and like-minded associates believed that creativity is inherent in the human spirit and that the urge for self-expression through creation is too powerful to be destroyed by the spread of machine-made goods.

Today five ACC programs carry on Mrs. Webb's vision. The American Craft Museum, with its permanent collection, exhibition program, and accompanying catalogues, showcases the finest work and draws attention to new directions in the field. The richly illustrated magazine, *American Craft,* informs more than 200,000 readers about contemporary craft with profiles of craftspeople, surveys of exhibitions, critical commentary, a national calendar, and news reports. American Craft Enterprises, Inc., ACC's subsidiary, organizes annual national craft fairs in Baltimore, San Francisco, and West Springfield, Massachusetts. The ACC library (with its artists' registry) and the ACC slides and films program collect, produce, and share information on the crafts for the benefit of art professionals and the general public.

The Council, a nonprofit organization with 33,000 members, is open for all people to join.